Legitimate Dangers

D0449651

Editors
Michael Dumanis
Cate Marvin

Legitimate Dangers
American Poets of the New Century

Sarabande Books
LOUISVILLE, KENTUCKY

Copyright © 2006 by Michael Dumanis and Cate Marvin

All rights reserved

No part of this book may be reproduced without written permission of the publisher. Please direct inquiries to:

Managing Editor
Sarabande Books, Inc.
2234 Dundee Road, Suite 200
Louisville, KY 40205

Library of Congress Cataloging-in-Publication Data

Legitimate dangers : American poets of the new century / edited by Michael Dumanis and Cate Marvin.— 1st ed.
         p.   cm.
Includes bibliographical references.
ISBN 1-932511-29-6 (pbk. : acid-free paper)
1. American poetry—21st century. I. Dumanis, Michael, 1976– II. Marvin, Cate, 1969–
PS617.L44 2006
811'.608—dc22   2005014822

13-digit ISBN 978-1-932-51129-1

Cover art: *The Box* by Bo Bartlett, 2002. Oil on linen, 89.25 x 107.5 inches. Provided courtesy of the artist and P.P.O.W. Gallery, NY.

Cover and text design by Charles Casey Martin

Manufactured in Canada
This book is printed on acid-free paper.

THE KENTUCKY ARTS COUNCIL

Sarabande Books is a nonprofit literary organization. The Kentucky Arts Council, a state agency in the Commerce Cabinet, provides operational support funding for Sarabande Books with state tax dollars and federal funding from the National Endowment for the Arts, which believes that a great nation deserves great art.

SECOND PRINTING

for Rodney Jones, who gave us the idea
and for Amber Dermont, who endured

Contents

Mark Bibbins

Sherwin Bitsui

Richard Blanco

Joel Brouwer

Oni Buchanan

Julianne Buchsbaum

Stephen Burt

Terrance Hayes

Steve Healey

Thomas Heise

Brian Henry

Christine Hume

Major Jackson

Lisa Jarnot

Natasha Trethewey

Pimone Triplett

Karen Volkman

G. C. Waldrep

Joe Wenderoth

Greg Williamson

Emily Wilson

Rachel Zucker

Preface by Mark Doty
Group Portrait with Yak

Once when Dean Young was trying to defend some poems to a group of interrogators who weren't enchanted by the work at hand, he said a simple but wonderful thing: "Well, the poet's trying to write a poem that never existed before."

I don't remember the poems in question, and I suspect that Dean himself didn't like them all that much, even though he was their eloquent advocate. He was trying to defend, in the interest of openness, a certain form of postmodern lyricism to readers who didn't want to go there. But what he said seems the wisest reminder for readers of poetry of any stripe. When someone is trying to make something that doesn't exist yet, for which there is no clear template, it's going to look unfamiliar, and it's likely to arrive with struggle, uncertainty, and a quality of raggedness. What makes things feel polished or "finished" is very often their adherence to familiar codes. The new arrives with its edges less charted; it tends less to "click like the lid of a well-made box" than to jangle or vibrate or sigh. Or even to provoke or irritate, as it presents itself with opacity rather than transparency. The new poem seems to say, *You don't know yet what I am.*

Here is a huge trove of work by young poets trying to write a poetry that hasn't already been inscribed. It's probably fair to say that *every* younger poet tries, has always tried, to write a poem that never existed before, trying to push through existing modes toward some individual arrival. But I have the sense that this project is more urgent, for the generation to which Marvin and Dumanis belong. Why should this be the case? Something about the sheer bulk of American poetic production now, the intense self-awareness that the interconnected community of American poetry provokes? Or the need to set oneself apart, in a world that feels increasingly and alarmingly different from the place where we stood not many decades ago? A crisis in the understanding of self and language that has emerged with increasing clarity over the last thirty years?

Dean Young's remark was much in the spirit of a famous comment of Jean Cocteau's to the effect that everything is ugly before it becomes beautiful. I wouldn't say these poems would look shocking to a reader unaccustomed to their mode, but they do proclaim their differences. They are not, by and large, much interested in the representation of experience, in the recollection and recounting of events in the life of the poet. Either they don't share my generation's belief that narration might lead to insight, or else they think we've worn out that idea. Their overwhelming preference is, instead, for performative speech: they are concerned with the creation of a voice, a presence on the page meant to be an experience in itself, not necessarily to refer to one that's already taken place.

Every realistic portrait of a generation resists the temptation to generalize, but based on the poems here it's certainly possible to identify some favorite habits, some characteristics of the collective project before us:

- these poets like rapid shifts, turns of tone, quick movements, and don't want to be pinned down. Their love of speed feels anxious or exuberant or both;
- they prefer comic deflation, an omnipresent irony, a nervous humor, an edgy vaudeville to an assumed sincerity;
- they presume the biographical stuff of selfhood is pretty much uninteresting, and favor instead the representation of temperament / subjectivity / thinking in the moment.

Finally, despite the common ground I'm naming, they are cheerfully eclectic. Diction is borrowed from a range of sources, and formal modes from hither and yon. I am delighted, in the workshops I teach, and in the manuscripts of younger poets I read, that there's a broad sense of the possibilities of reinvention. The world of aesthetic possibilities feels like a large market, open for the shopper. Would you like to make a discontinuous, comical ode today, or a dense and elliptical elegy, or a monologue in the voice of a yak?

A generation of American poets lined up for a photograph, as in one of those old school portraits, eighty-five faces arranged in rows to be looked at, now, and years later, identified, considered, remembered or not. That's the remarkably ambitious thing that Michael Dumanis and Cate Marvin have done, in this capacious group portrait of a book. Like all portraits, it has a point of view; here, out of everyone in a certain age group at a certain level of accomplishment, is the work the editors most admire. Therefore its curators make a sort of representation of themselves, through all these voices. If they and their choices often share generational preoccupations and signature modes of vocalizing, the poems are also thrillingly energetic, funny, passionate, deftly inventive, and bracingly inclusive. It leads me back, unexpectedly, to Pablo Neruda, who would have turned 102 the year of this book's publication, and whose platform for a broadly inclusive, impure poetry seems as fresh and to the point as ever.

This is the poetry we should be after, he wrote, *worn away, as if by acid, by the labor of hands, impregnated with sweat and smoke, smelling of lilies and of urine, splashed by the variety of what we do, legally or illegally. A poetry as impure as old clothes, as a body, with its food stains and its shame, with wrinkles, observations, dreams, wakefulness, prophecies, declarations of love and hate, stupidities, shocks, idylls, political beliefs, negations, doubts, affirmations, taxes....*

Introduction

In her "Aphorisms on Modernism," composed during the First World War, the poet Mina Loy rather extravagantly wrote,

> MODERNISM is a prophet crying in the wilderness that
> Humanity is wasting its time.
> CONSCIOUSNESS originated in the nostalgia of the universe
> for an audience.
> LIVING is projecting reflections of ourselves into the
> consciousness of our fellows.

The present, for the Modernists, was a turbulent period of political instability and rapid technological and social change. Modernism, as all aesthetic movements, was a direct reaction to a specific historical, political, and social time where the modes and literatures of the past no longer suited the aspiring artist eager to reflect upon his or her seemingly unique present historical moment. Writing a few years after Loy, Gertrude Stein, in her manifesto "Composition as Explanation," played down the notion that the twentieth century was all that different in substance from past eras by asserting,

> The only thing that is different from one time to another is what is seen and what is seen depends on how everybody is doing everything. This makes the thing we are looking at very different and this makes what those who describe it make of it, it makes a composition, it confuses, it shows, it is, it looks, it likes it as it is, and this makes what is seen as it is seen. Nothing changes from generation to generation except the thing seen and that makes a composition.

For Stein, the manner in which things were composed, the "how," was constantly in flux. The actual world of joys and tragedies and things endured by a specific life—the "what"—was always more-or-less the same, regardless of which war was being fought, whether ragtime or jazz was the sound of the time, whether the tragically hip wore monocles, indulged in absinthe, and rode in horsedrawn carriages to the opera, or, alternately, drove Tin Lizzies to the nearest speakeasy to dance the Charleston and drink bathtub gin with Flapper Girls.

   In the eight decades separating us from the historical moments in which Loy and Stein were writing, the United States endured another World War, a forty-year Cold War, a Great Depression, and a Great Society, long periods of turbulence, brief periods of seeming stasis, passing caravans of influential literary movements, and mass temporary shifts in dominant aesthetic tastes and sensibilities. However, the human condition, at its essence, has remained essentially unchanged.

The contributors to *Legitimate Dangers: American Poets of the New Century* do not reject the poetry of the past simply because it has preceded them; on the contrary, they display enthusiasm for and oftentimes pay tribute to the best work of their predecessors. Many of the younger poets writing today are as interested as the Modernists were in creating something never-before-seen-in-its-particular-form, a poem that is visionary, outrageous, suspect of itself, uncensored in its sentiments, and sincere in what it's trying to show the reader, a poem complicated and ambivalent in its emotions in the same way all people are more complicated and ambivalent than they initially let on. The poems in this book at times have more in common with the poems of the Modernists than with the personal narratives and lyric meditations on the particulars of daily life that dominated the poetry of the generations immediately preceding this one. The younger poets of today tend not to be as interested in the articulation of micro everyday private trials and tribulations or of specific responses to specific current public events. Rather, they aspire to not only cry out from the wilderness but also be heard by those few others who read poetry that are also, in their own way, mapping and exploring the same wilderness. The common goal is to confront the macro metaphysical concerns of the private self as well as the macro political, historical, and social themes of the culture at large. Theirs is a poetry searching for universal truths, for a rhetoric reflecting the consciousness of our time. The intricate patterning and pyrotechnic complexity of many of these poems is often balanced with direct, clearly stated observations of life in the world as these writers see it:

> These words want to answer your questions.
> These words want to stave off your suffering,
> but cannot. I leave them to you…
>
> ("Wind in a Box," Terrance Hayes)

> And the soul begs always, *Leave me leave me*
> while the body says simply, *Stay.*
>
> ("A Crash of Rhinos," Paisley Rekdal)

> *Everything in the world is a knife,*
> *everything in the world cuts a little from you.*
>
> ("Hotel d'Avignon," G.C. Waldrep)

whatever I say
is a kind of petition, and the darkest
days must I praise.

("Author's Prayer," Ilya Kaminsky)

While this new American poetry has much in keeping with the irreverent candor, sheer inventiveness, and spirit of the Modernists, the poets in this book do not represent, as the Modernists did, a conscious break from the past. They recognize their historical moment is just another in a continuum of not-all-that-dissimilar historical moments. In "The Vampire Finch," Robyn Schiff, writing in tight syllabics evocative of Marianne Moore's poems, transports us at a breakneck speed across geography and time, from the murder of a bird on Galapagos by a parasitic vampire finch to Bram Stoker's *Dracula* narrative to Vermeer's paintings to the murder committed by Leopold and Loeb to the genocide committed by the Nazis. Thus, a poem succeeds in beginning "Roosting in a crater with one / red foot on either side of her stony egg, / the red-footed booby endures the finch / feeding on her tail…" and ends, "…Leopold knew / a good place to hide the body / from his days of bird-watching where the train / cut through the still marsh and 'From the air vents we / could see civilians laughing.'" Such an approach to history echoes the opening of T.S. Eliot's *Four Quartets*: "Time present and time past / are both perhaps present in time future, / And time future contained in time past." Schiff compacts into one moment of time, into the space of a single poem, the history of the modern world.

Likewise, many of the poets in this book, while consciously writing in a particular geographic location from an inherently subjective stance, are also eager to fit the entire world into the small room of the poem. The way John Donne in "Good-Morrow" desired to make "one little room an everywhere" and Frank O'Hara told the city of New York in "Steps," "all I want is a room up there / and you in it," Joshua Beckman places himself at the controls, directing the air traffic of the world so as to bring the distant and familiar closer together:

hooray! For Lagos, Accra, Freetown, Dakar
your son is on the telephone the Germans
landed safely Seattle off to Istanbul
tiny planes please circle oh tiny planes
do please please circle

("Ode to the Air Traffic Controller")

Included in these pages are poets as likely to be preoccupied by the political events of the twenty-first century (see Lisa Jarnot's "The United States of America" or Juliana Spahr's "December 1, 2002") as they are by the political events of the 1940s ("The night floated down like a thousand allies / lashed to black parachutes," writes Kevin Prufer in his poem "On Finding a Swastika Carved on a Tree in the Hills Above Heidelberg") or the events of 1865 (see David Berman's "April 13, 1865"). These poets find apt metaphors in the world of cartoon animation (read both parts of Nick Flynn's "Cartoon Physics"), blaxpoitation films of the Seventies (see Thomas Sayers Ellis' "Slow Fade to Black"), or film noir (see Kevin Young's "Rushes"). Their influences cut across pre-established literary camps: Joshua Beckman and Karen Volkman, considered by some to be avant-garde poets, are writing sonnets. Josh Bell begins a tender love poem with the line, "Come practice your whorish gestures in the graveyard, Ramona." Stephen Burt writes a seemingly traditional free-verse narrative about a family moving to a new neighborhood, but ends each of the thirty lines with the word "place." And in her long, carefully controlled poem "History," written in highly accessible diction, Tracy K. Smith includes the following deliciously over-the-top, experimental, devastating stanza:

> Of course there are victims in this poem:
>
> victim victim victim victim victim
> victim victim victim victim victim
> victim victim victim victim victim
> victim victim victim victim victim
> victim victim victim victim victim
> victim victim victim victim victim
> victim victim victim victim victim
> victim victim victim victim victim
> victim *you are here* victim victim
> victim victim victim victim victim
> victim victim victim victim victim

Most of the writers assembled here choose not to affiliate with a single aesthetic tradition. They draw from a wide range of seemingly opposed poetic practices—Modernism, Formalism, Confessional Poetry, the New York School, the Beats, the Language Poets, the Black Arts Movement, French Surrealism, contemporary Eastern European poetry—and navigate successfully, often in the same poetic work, between the elliptical and the straightforward, the public and the deeply personal, order and disorder, humor and seriousness, sincerity and manner.

In the early stages of editing this book, we came across a letter by Robert Frost where he suggested that "there are no two things as important to us in life and art as being threatened and being saved.... All our ingenuity is lavished on getting into danger legitimately so that we may be genuinely rescued." We wanted to create a representative anthology of writing by emerging poets who seem to us particularly interested in getting themselves into danger. We looked for writers with a singular and unmistakable voice who are steadily amassing a body of work that feels innovative, virtuosic, and entirely their own. We were most interested in visceral, daring poems that challenged the reader's sensibilities, poems that engaged the reader both emotionally and intellectually, poems that were patently *unsafe*, at once artful and authentic, sophisticated in technique and pure in motivation.

In his introduction to Paul Carroll's 1968 *The Young American Poets*, an anthology that likewise showcased the nascent voices and fresh names of an emerging generation—the early poems of 34-year-olds Ted Berrigan and Mark Strand, 27-year-old Robert Hass, the 25-year-olds James Tate and Louise Glück, and 23-year-old Anne Waldman—poet James Dickey wrote,

> Everyone who cares about poetry hopes that each young or new poet to appear on the scene may be the one to bring forth the whole magnificent potential of poetry and lay it on the page, and thus realize the promise that poetry makes in age after age but seldom succeeds in keeping…to bring the reader to the place where the flame breaks forth from the pit and the gods speak from the burning bush, lifting human words…into the realm of salvation, redemption and rebirth.

As teachers of poetry, we believe that our most invested students, and the best aspiring writers of any generation, harbor the same ambition Dickey spoke of. They strive to hone the skill and instinct necessary in order to create, out of the building blocks of language, something so transcendent, fearless, resonant, and honest that you, the reader, don't want the poem you're experiencing to end. That you already know, when you first see and hear the poem, that you'll return, time and again, in search of something pure or beautiful or true to the thoughts, images, and words the poem offers you. As readers eager to be challenged and transformed by the poems of others, we know this doesn't happen very often. But isn't it amazing when it does, when the words of a stranger seduce you so intensely that they simultaneously sear and soothe you, when they become intrinsic to your sense of self and truth and world?

Some years ago, we both attended a lecture by the novelist Alan Gurganus. "All writing is about seduction," he began, then turning to a member of the audience, asked, "Take off your shirt," and, turning to another, said, "Take off your pants." Even Gurganus's approach to talking about writing, his mock-request that students strip for him, felt seductive, bringing to mind Tomas, the doctor-protagonist in Milan Kundera's novel *The Unbeararable Lightness of Being*, who would seduce women merely by saying to them, as a doctor will say to a patient, "Take off your clothes."

The students were excited by Gurganus's pick-up line because what he was doing was audacious and inherently transgressive—especially in a sterile classroom setting: Gurganus was subverting the audience's notions of the relationship between the writer and the reader, and, most significantly, daring to utter a greater fundamental truth that had the power, once you grasped it, to alter your world paradigm or change your life. All human interaction is, in a sense, an attempt by one person to seduce another. Seduction, the voluntary submission to the charm or power of somebody else's words and manner—to have the very way you breathe affected by proximity to someone out of your control—now *that* could be dangerous. To successfully seduce, it is essential to have both style and substance, candor and coyness, genuine feeling and the ability to mask it, an ease of speech, a sense of urgency, patience, restraint, and timing. And it is equally essential, when seducing, to know when to hold back. Seduction—be it romantic, political, intellectual, or otherwise—is dangerous not only to the one being seduced, but to the seducer, who runs the risk of exposure. The rich, mellifluous beginning of Olena Kalytiak Davis's intimate address, "Sweet Reader, Flanneled and Tulled," immediately comes to mind:

> Reader unmov'd and Reader unshaken, Reader unseduc'd
> and unterrified, through the long-loud and sweet-still
> I creep toward you. Toward you, I thistle and I climb.

The eighty-five poets in our book were born no earlier than 1960, had no book published prior to 1995, and had published no more than three books of poems (excluding chapbooks or collaborations) as of mid-2004, when we started making our selections. We felt that writers whose first book was published over ten years ago could not be considered "new" and writers who have published more than three books of poems in the last ten years were already substantially represented and could not be categorized as "emerging." These parameters precluded us from including work by some poets born after 1960 whose work seems very much in dialogue with many of the poems in the book—Sherman Alexie, Denise Duhamel, James Harms, Bob Hicok, Mark Levine, Tim Liu, Campbell McGrath, Jena Osman, Claudia Rankine, Reginald Shepherd, Eleni Sikelianos, and Liz Waldner—but enabled us to focus primarily on a group of writers, most of them still in their thirties, whose first books were published in the twenty-first century, and also to include several poets whose first books have just been published or are on the verge of publication. At the beginning of this project, we decided to not have an open call for submissions because we were astonished to be able to come up, from memory, with over 150 names of newer American poets whose work interested us, and then simply read as much of everything else that we could get our hands on as possible; after consultation with other poets and the careful reading of numerous additional books, literary journals, and anthologies, we expanded our list to over 250 poets. After a series of difficult choices, we whittled down the unwieldy list to eighty-five writers that both of us emphatically agreed on. In our taste as readers, we knew what most seduced us: ambitious, carefully controlled work that exhibited heightened lyric intensity, verbal daring, and wit, and appealed both to our emotions and our intellect.

We also favored poems which maintained a high degree of clarity and control on the line and sentence level, while achieving a greater complexity as a whole and not necessarily shying away from the mysterious, the occasionally hermetic, or the slippery. Neither of us feels that a poem needs to hold the reader's hand or be "about" something, especially about a specific event, thought, or experience. We believe that if you start a poem with a certain aim in mind and do nothing other than satisfy that aim in your poem, you haven't really written a poem. Eliot has remarked (however coyly), "In 'The Waste Land' I wasn't even bothering whether I understood what I was saying"; we believe good poems are felt before they are understood and mistrust the poem which knows all too well what it is saying and where it is headed. We feel that opacity and accessibility are relative terms: what is opaque to one reader may emotionally resonate with another. However, we agree with Gertrude Stein that "sentences must not have bad plumbing—they must not leak." For every poem we selected, we felt that the writer made good conscious choices word-by-word, one line after another, that caused the overall poem to have a powerful unified effect. For example, when Joyelle McSweeney says, mysteriously, "Others were more economical than I. But I / had my red marble" ("Persuasion"), both assertions, taken separately, are clear and accessible. The speaker's possession of a red marble enables her to derive a measure of satisfaction despite her being less economical than others: the stated preference for the marble over economic considerations may also be taken as a stated preference on behalf of the poet for the poem which favors indulgence over deliberate restraint. The juxtaposition of the sentences is unexpected and surely complicates the narrative, but it does not feel arbitrary and anyone can understand the two assertions themselves.

One additional criterion in our selection was the willingness we saw in the poets we chose to take risks, to say what others may consider highly transgressive or unsayable, to defy a reader's expectations, or subvert traditional narratives. We were seduced by poems which wrote against the subject matter in order to achieve a more powerful effect, the way that Dylan Thomas, in "A Refusal to Mourn the Death, by Fire, of a Child in London," defied the conventions of elegy so as to declare, "After the first death, there is no other." In this anthology, such risks were only interesting to us when they paid off, when the dangers were well-handled and legitimate, as in Sabrina Orah Mark's terrifying Holocaust narrative "Hello," where the speaker dares to say, "I fell in love on the night train to Warsaw. Every human situation strikes me as a terrific joke. I am a torn off blouse in that red river. Ha ha holocaust," or in Richard Siken's "A Primer for the Small Weird Loves," where the speaker fearlessly and candidly traces a personal history that connects his sexual orientation with a sequence of violent occurrences. Siken's poem begins,

> The blond boy in the red trunks is holding your head underwater
> because he is trying to kill you,
>   and you deserve it, you do, and you know this,
>   and you are ready to die in this swimming pool
>   because you wanted to touch his hands and lips and this means
>   your life is over anyway.

The risks we were interested in pertained not only to content but also to form: it is risky to write a poem like Burt's "Paysage Moralisé" with thirty lines ending in the same word, it is risky to write a poem like Kevin Young's "Errata," where every line contains a deliberate malaprop, and it is likewise risky to end a poem mid-sentence as Sabrina Orah Mark does in "Hello."

What you have before you, reader, is a guide to some of the best poets of the twenty-first century in the early stages of their careers and to some of the most original, ambitious, dangerous, redemptive, and inspiring poems they have written to date. These poets have made their way to you from all over the world—born everywhere from Libya, Japan, the former Soviet Union, and the Philippines to a Native American reservation in Northeastern Arizona; Fairbanks, Alaska; Gulfport, Mississippi; Rutland, Vermont; and Palm Beach, Florida. Many—such is, for better or worse, the consequence of the professionalization of creative writing in the United States—attended graduate writing programs (the University of Iowa Writers' Workshop continues to attract many young poets, as do Columbia University, the University of Massachusetts, the University of Houston, Indiana University, low-residency writing programs such as Vermont College and Warren Wilson College, and numerous other schools), but none of them write what could be derisively termed bland workshop poetry. Ranging in age from their late twenties to their mid-forties, they have received some of the nation's top honors for writing, including Wallace Stegner Fellowships to Stanford, Fellowships to the Fine Arts Work Center in Provincetown, Guggenheim Fellowships, grants from the National Endowment for the Arts and the Rona Jaffe Foundation, and Whiting Writers' Awards. Many have published widely in the country's most prominent literary journals and some have been selected for inclusion in the annual *Best American Poetry* series. Some have published books through the National Poetry Series and the Yale Series of Younger Poets, others publish with prominent trade or university presses, while others, often by choice, have given their books to independent publishing houses, such as Graywolf, Copper Canyon, Verse Press, Alice James Books, Ahsahta Press, and Flood Editions. Since it is not easy to eke out a living in this country as a poet, it's not surprising that most, though not all, either teach in MFA programs or liberal arts colleges, or are enrolled in PhD programs. On the other hand, some of these poets have successful careers unrelated to the teaching of literature or creative writing—as lawyers, an employee of a quantitative trading firm, a doctor, a concert pianist, and an assistant manager of a Brooks Brothers clothing store. They live all over the country—while many have gravitated toward traditionally writer-friendly cities such as Chicago, San Francisco, Minneapolis, and New York, others live in small towns and urban centers in Alabama, Alaska, Arizona, Georgia, Missouri, Montana, North Carolina, and elsewhere. What they all have in common is a dedication to the written word; a fascination with the beautiful and the ugly, the sacred and the profane, a singular and unmistakable voice; and the potential to fulfill the promise that their predecessors spoke of, to risk doing something dangerous, to rescue us.

We hope this book will serve as a much-needed introduction to these talented new poets. Now, Reader, take off your shirt.

Michael Dumanis and Cate Marvin
Houston, TX, and Staten Island, NY, June 2005

There are no two things as important to us in life and art as being threatened and being saved. What are ideals of form for if we aren't going to be made to fear for them? All our ingenuity is lavished on getting into danger legitimately so that we may be genuinely rescued.

— Robert Frost

Legitimate Dangers

Rick Barot

Rick Barot was born in 1969 in the Philippines, and grew up in the San Francisco Bay Area. He attended Wesleyan University, the University of Iowa Writers' Workshop, and Stanford University, where he held a Wallace Stegner Fellowship and later served as a Jones Lecturer in Poetry. His poems have been honored with a grant from the National Endowment for the Arts, and regularly appear in such journals as *New England Review, The New Republic, Poetry,* and *The Threepenny Review.* Barot's first book is *The Darker Fall* (Sarabande, 2002). Formerly the Jenny McKean Moore Visiting Writer at George Washington University and the Thornton Writer-in-Residence at Lynchburg College, Barot now lives in Tacoma, Washington, and teaches both in the low-residency MFA Program at Warren Wilson College and at Pacific Lutheran University.

Many Are Called

to burn at least one thing they once owned: she tears
the page from his book and sets light to whatever
she said to him there, words to smoke, paper

to black snow. She would like a sleep as big as
a building, whose key she firmly keeps in her hand,
its teeth writing into her palm. *Be as nothing*

in the floods, I read yesterday on the bus home,
which was a way of saying that in the dimmed glass
all of us and none of us could be found. But one

face was like sun reflecting on ice, lit by what
the Walkman poured into it, its champagnes. One
made me think of the mushroom in the woods

like a face pressed to a photocopier's flash,
the face and its goofy pain. Many are called to save
what they can: he rolls up his pants and wades

into the fountain, where the gull has its leg caught
on a wire. The bird flaps away to join the wheeling
others, their strokes on the air like diacritical

marks over the sentences uttered below them.
A friend writes about how cold he had been, nearly
drowned in the spring-melt river when the horse

tipped over. It is months away now, but still
I have him there, in the darkening field, the fireflies
a roused screensaver. Many are called to close

upon themselves like circles: Kafka, waking because
a dog is lying on him. He doesn't open his eyes
but he can feel its weight, its paw smelling

faintly of hay. Or the woman crying in the park,
her shopping cart tumbled, shoes and cans spilled out
like junk from a shark's stomach. Or the man

walking home along the houses and the lawns
of his sadness: *If there must be a god in the house…*
Under the new trees and the new moon of his sadness:

He must dwell quietly. Many are called to form
a deity out of what they know: he quizzes me
on the capital of every African country, he paints

his toenails silver because I ask him. A friend writes
about the church where a fresco will always show
them: cleanly naked at first, then full of the blame

of their own guile, then clothed, worried with age,
the woman in her room setting fire to something
she had, the man in the meadow, wishing his rib back.

Eight Elegies

I.
One kind of rain gets to be
exactly the rain you want, disbursing
lightly in its fall an atmosphere
that you walk into as into
a confetti rain, getting kissed while
umbrellas click like flashbulbs around you.

II.

She said, "I want whatever CD was in
the player, the shirt that was on the hook
in the closet, the earrings he gave me
that I gave back, the ugly
painting I made of him."
Her friend made sure to put back
the yellow police tape he had to take down
when he went for the things.

III.

Once, during a Midwestern blizzard,
I let in two Mormon missionaries
because I didn't want them believing
that the snow, the doors closed against them,
were a form of extra credit. Each one
was an Adam in a blue suit, blond,
clear-faced. Their bodies, because I spent the hour
imagining them, were clean as statues:
above the hipbone, above the knee, a cord
of muscle; each shoulder was soap-smelling.
I made coffee and tried to listen,
my stomach felt raw with meanness.
Later, telling a friend the story, I understood
I had failed at a charity
that went beyond having faith.
We were by the river, the water full of broken
ice-plates. My friend told about
his grandmother scolding him for ironing
a shirt's bottom, the part that would get wrinkled
anyway. The snow, held briefly,
faded into the heat of his hair.

IV.

Wanting death, which of the senses
would the mind kill first?
My sister's lover, tying knot after knot
in practice, would he have heard
the traffic humming in the air,
the steady undercurrent? Would he have felt
the cat's tongue, the sandpaper

dampness against his arm?
Did memory, shaking away bracelets
and scents, leave the room?
And love, piece by piece, light as a nest?

V.
In a poem I keep returning to,
there is so much hunger
that a man gets killed for the few bills
he has in his pockets. In the café,
telling himself to leave something
for the waiter, the murderer has a blizzard
of words in his head: *coffee*
and *toast* muddling into *rum* and *fare*.
What always startles me
is that he should have any words
coming to him at all, the words
composing the day and all that he did in it.
The same way, blocks from home
and not about to turn back, I'm stuck
thinking of *coat*. Or my sister,
in the restaurant kitchen where she works,
thinking into *knife* and *basil*
so clearly that she becomes the knife,
becomes the basil. In a book
of paintings I look at, there's a color
the artist calls *gris clair*,
a color like onionskin floating on water.
In one painting the sky is this color,
with hills below overlapped in vellum shapes.
I think of the painter going home, exhausted
by his own attention: *gray, boulder*,
night and *hydrangea*, each word
completed by his love and by his care.

VI.
I slept there once, his walk-up room
a perfect brick cube.
The wood floors were scratched at
as though an animal had been kept there.
The windows had an airshaft
view, and opened to the noise
of air conditioning and the quarrelling

of taxis. I woke to humidity,
heavy as a blanket on me.
The air smelled of cat litter and diesel.
But walking out of the building,
to every color the day had,
I knew I was in a great city.

VII.
She didn't open the small box,
put it on the floor so that
in a few weeks the things of her room
seemed to pity it: first surrounding it
like figures around a fire,
then covering it altogether, the shopping bags
and the coats, the sweaters, the socks.

VIII.
One kind of rain has you
at the bus-stop at five o'clock,
on the sidewalks a gruel of newspapers.
Walking there from work, I had seen
an old man suddenly stop,
bend to the gutter, and let out
a yellow sleeve of vomit.
The rain wasn't snow
but seemed determined to be.
I wanted the day spooled back,
all the way back, to the dark under
the dresser, the dark inside cabinets,
inside suitcases and bottles,
all the way back, to the night
I argued with a friend's voice on the phone,
went outside to have a cigarette,
and saw the woman made-up
so garishly that there was no question
she meant to have you look
at the orange pile of hair,
the red pumps, the trailing tinsel boa,
her quick soft laugh carrying now
night into night into night.

Reading Plato

I think about the mornings it saved me
to look at the hearts penknifed on the windows
of the bus, or at the initials scratched

into the plastic partition, in front of which
a cabbie went on about bread his father
would make, so hard you broke teeth on it,

or told one more story about the plumbing
in New Delhi buildings, villages to each floor,
his whole childhood in a building, nothing to

love but how much now he missed it, even
the noises and stinks he missed, the avenue
suddenly clear in front of us, the sky ahead

opaquely clean as a bottle's bottom, each heart
and name a kind of ditty of hopefulness
because there was one *you* or another I was

leaving or going to, so many stalls of flowers
and fruit going past, figures earnest with
destination, even the city itself a heart,

so that when sidewalks quaked from trains
underneath, it seemed something to love,
like a harbor boat's call at dawn or the face

reflected on a coffee machine's chrome side,
the pencil's curled shavings a litter
of questions on the floor, the floor's square

of afternoon light another page I couldn't know
myself by, as now, when Socrates describes
the lover's wings spreading through the soul

like flames on a horizon, it isn't so much light
I think about, but the back's skin cracking
to let each wing's nub break through,

the surprise of the first pain and the eventual
lightening, the blood on the feathers drying
as you begin to sense the use for them.

Dan Beachy-Quick

Dan Beachy-Quick was born in 1973 in Chicago, grew up in Colorado, and attended Hamilton College, the University of Denver, and the University of Iowa Writers' Workshop. His poetry has been honored with a Lannan Foundation Residency and has appeared in *Colorado Review, Conduit, Ploughshares, Poetry, Volt,* and elsewhere, and his reviews and criticism commonly appear in such journals as *The Denver Quarterly, Jacket, Rain Taxi,* and *The Southern Review.* His three books of poems are *North True South Bright* (Alice James, 2003), *Spell* (Ahsahta, 2004), and *Mulberry* (Tupelo, 2006). Beachy-Quick lives in Chicago with his wife Kristy and daughter Hana Frances. He is Associate Chair of the MFA Writing Program at the School of the Art Institute of Chicago.

Prologue

Editor,

Here are the lines my mind fathomed.
They are tar-dark. I wrote them on pages
Breathless and blank, as beneath water
Men's minds are blank but for needing
A next breath. Sir, turn
This page and the thick door opens
By growing thinner, ever thinner,
Until the last page turns and is turned
Into air. Don't knock. The ocean knocks
Ceaseless on my little craft, and I am
Asking you, Will my craft hold? I send me
To you on a paper-thin hull. Don't knock.
I'm in there. I breathe on one lung
For both lungs' air; my hand is wet
With knocking my knuckle to wave, and
Though the wave opens, I am never
Let in. I promised you the deep wave
's inner chamber, I'm sorry.
      Do you see, Sir—
How the crest of a book builds at the binding
And finally spills over on to no shore?
Don't knock. I will ask the water to open for you
If you'll stop. Don't knock, don't knock, Sir—
Oh, it is not you. My wife's at my study door

And knows the wood won't open from wanting
Wood to. I must seal this craft's last plank
In place, and voyage it over ocean to you.
"Come in." She's knocking. "Come in."
Her hand's on my wooden shore, door—
I go. Send word, send word. If you don't, I'll know.

Unworn

Count me among those almonds   your eyes
Count me   among those almonds your eyes
Never opened. Your mouth   on the floor-fallen pear
Never opened   your mouth on the floor-fallen pear
Count among those almonds   floor-fallen, your eyes
Your mouth   on the pear never   opened me

Open the water-glass with a shattering   disregard
Open the water-glass   with shattering   Disregard
My nervous   finger.   I make me pick up that shard.
My nervous   finger makes me   pick up that shard
That makes   my finger: *shattering-water*   Pick up
The glass-shard   I open me   with a nervous disregard

What are you to me?   through the window   I see the leaf:
What you are to me   Through the window I see   the leaf-
Bare, budding elm scratch   a nerve against the sky's
Bare budding   Elm, scratch your nerve against the sky—
The sky against the window   scratched   through the elm to me
I are what you see: a nerve bare-budding   your leaf

I never opened my bare nerve   to see the leaf
Scratch a nervous window against the sky
I count me up among those   the almonds
Floor-fallen   You are the elm worn on a finger
Make your mouth disregard   that budding   glass, the pear-shard—
Through what shattering   water your eyes   opened me with me

Psalm (Traherne)

I lived inside myself until I loved
   And then I lived, Lord   then I lived
With thirst   and happiness was thirst

And thirst lived in the center, Lord
   Of every water-drop   as in a seed
A mouth hungers

And then a mouth is filled with grain,
   And then the mouth becomes the field
Of grain   until the field closes Lord, begging

"Devour me again—   with less
   Distraction."   Forgive me the sun
Eclipsed by gold   Forgive me

The gold divorced of coin   forgive
   Me the coin melted to ring   and most, Lord
Forgive my hand that wears the ring:

That hand I use at noon to shield my eye
   From sun.   An infant-eye believes
The star at finger tip is diamond

And doesn't burn and night, Lord
   Night when most I loved
The sky's   burden was light   and joyful

The universe you made   you made
   For me alone   The new moon's tender knife
Has cut the dawn to day   At noon, Lord

I see the world is most like you, shadowless
   And impossible of shadow. To throw
A stone at star draws me near you, Lord

Who am not separate, no   Who am not less
   Than grain devoured, Lord   A tooth can break
A husk   by husk can be broken   both are prayer, Lord

Both are prayer As I, open-eyed am open
   To You   As close-mouthed, I speak you
Best my hymn   Lord, speak you   best my prayer.

Afterword

Editor,

Mappemundi. That word: I meant
To anchor myself in song *with* song.
Adrift, I sang shoals at the margin. No,
I sang depth, I mean. I thought myself
Past the margin, Why do I hear you laugh?
I mean
        I only spoke no Sirens
When the waves calmed me and no
Monsters when the ocean frenzied—
All was on the page I thought upon.
I see, Sir, the whale dives past margin.
I see the world is flat and the map flat
That records it, and both page and world
Speak each other forever. Put a fold
In eternity and it is just as flat and wide.
Take the map of the world and fold it
Into a boat and the boat becomes the world.
If only, Sir, if only the whirlpool sucked
Through the page into no words—
There with the whale the world could end.
Is that what I want? Why I sang?
Even my "No" is breath cupped in the sail.
A red pen is rudder, uncapped, red ink
On horizon is sunrise: delete dawn, Δ shadow,
Δ shadow at noon.
                Here's my submission,
My last request. I've printed my words
On one side of each page. Now turn each
Page over. Spread them out on the floor
Until the floor is blank with no words.
Spill out into hallway on this wave. Walk it.
When the blank page ends in white tile
You won't notice. When you walk out
The glass door the taxi's horn will be the hawk
's cry. Out my front door, the traffic is ocean.
I hate the sunset's every red ribbon
Because, untied, they reveal
A lamp gone out. A day. No oil can be lit
In a pewter midnight that, once burned,
Will never burn again. I see the dark edge

Of day saline beneath water. No anchor
In song. The world is flat if the page is flat.
Delete all. Here's one country: my hand.
It seals the envelope. Here's one country:
My lips, my tongue. They seal the envelope.
Suffer whiteness. My white hand in a white cloud.
My lips white with salt. The white rain—I see it—
Sings white a lullaby to the milky white ocean
And the milky white ocean   calms

It calms as it dives down.

Joshua Beckman

Joshua Beckman was born in 1971 in New Haven, Connecticut, and attended Hampshire College. His poems have appeared in *Gulf Coast*, *Harper's*, *The Massachusetts Review*, *Poetry*, and other journals. His books of poetry are *Things Are Happening* (American Poetry Review, 1998), *Something I Expected To Be Different* (Verse, 2001), and *Your Time Has Come* (Verse, 2004). Beckman and the poet Matthew Rohrer collaborated on the collection *Nice Hat. Thanks.* (Verse, 2002) and released an audio CD of their live collaborations, *Adventures While Preaching the Gospel of Beauty* (Verse, 2003). Beckman is also the translator of Tomaz Salamun's *Poker* (Ugly Duckling Presse, 2003) and Carlos Oquendo de Amat's *Five Meters of Poems* (Ugly Duckling Presse, 2005). He lives in Staten Island, New York, and in Seattle, and is an editor at Wave Books.

["Final poem for the gently sifting public begins on the streets..."]

Final poem for the gently sifting public begins on the streets,
the police turning corners, the people exact in their gaits,
the all-knowing god existent in minds everywhere.
The shower running because I am sitting on the floor with a joint,
in my small book there is a story about this.
The crude protectiveness of one mistaken person seems too much.
The floor is rented.
The shower is rented.
The water is purchased almost unintentionally.
It is not memory that treats you this way,
you should know that by now.
Why is there no music in the house.
Why have you begun to set a record for dreariness,
may I ask you that.
Why can't the chevrolet seem like a swan
when that is what I want.
Surrealism is old, so everyone should get some.
Why did the water disappear before the swan arrived.
Why did the swan disappear before the swan arrived.
Why won't the poem write itself as I drift into the shower,
as I levitate above the yoga mat,
as I perform the perfect pose upon the yoga mat.
I ask little of the passing hand of mental celebrity.

I am not greedy.
I will do what I am told.
I will not attempt to create the eucalyptus tree
or steal the lines of other poets.
Oh Peter, I stole a tree from your poem
and now it is gone, and you at home
and me without your number.
Is it me crashing into the typewriter as waves?
Is it me exploding with letters that mean nothing?
Is it me moving about the city like a police car
not looking for trouble and not finding it?
No, it is the drink.
It is the days.
No, it is the passing.
Bakersfield, California cried out
and I said something like
"I cannot hear you above the crashing defense
of heaven and hell that goes on here."
We were at the center of unimportant things that made noise.
They informed us of nothing.
If we were swept up in the high school students
going to get high, and we went with them to get high,
and they allowed us that when we brought the stuff,
and if they didn't knock us into the river,
and if they didn't secretly hate us,
and if they didn't notice our brains fighting,
and if they were content and did not disown us for this fighting,
and if they secretly had wishes unrelated to us in our presence,
and if we babbled unmindfully and they said
"that dude is fucked up" so we could hear,
and if no one cared how we kept looking at them,
how our thoughts swirled around them,
and if they didn't push us in the river,
but thought that is how you get when you get like this,
we would ask to pass the oxygen,
we would watch them leave,
we would say look out for the police,
they are moving in a grid,
they are carried by something greater than themselves,
they are in control of their cars but their cars are in control,
and this is not a paradox,
they are more afraid of you than you are of them,
they would say, we know, fuck them,
and we would know what they meant,
that they meant no harm.

["I like your handsome drugs. Your pleasant..."]

I like your handsome drugs. Your pleasant
drugs. Your frozen fingernails. Your painted
fingernails. That man screamed out, "The
karate chop of love," before tackling that woman.
The breeze. Your sort of quiet happy voices.
The karate chop of love. Your handsome drugs.
If you, in all your sexiness, could just bring that
over here. A barrel of fried chicken. That girl
named Katie. A birthday party. Yeah. I go
running in, all ready to show everyone the
karate chop of love. And that girl named Katie.
A barrel of chicken. The breeze. This
birthday party is fucked without the karate
chop of love. Your handsome drugs.

["The thirst of the crowd. We laid the surfer down...."]

The thirst of the crowd. We laid the surfer down.
The child and the child. Come look what I have found.
Our country is in disgraceful times and you bring
this around. The thirst of the crowd. Another dead thing
on the ground. A body. The dimness and the broken board.
The display of a body. The child and the child.
Come look what I have found. Lay the surfer down.
Another dead thing on the ground, and you
brought this around. The child and the child.
Come look what I have found. A surfer there upon
the ground. The child and the child. Far away a little
sound. Come look what I have found. The crowd
and the crowd. The surfer lay out on the ground.
In the disgraceful dimness of our country, your body.

["The canals. The liquor coming through…"]

The canals. The liquor coming through
the straw. The canals the land and
the bridge and the landing by the bridge
destroyed. The liquor. The little anger
growing inside the friends. The canal.
The pile of wood up against the bank.
The liquor. The friends. A little
anger growing inside them. The canal.
The jets. The wood in piles along
the bank. The dead. The jets. Liquor
through a straw. Speaking. A little anger
grows inside them. The jets. The dead.
The bank. The sky. The friends. The jets.
The dead. A little anger grows inside them.

Ode to the Air Traffic Controller

Melbourne, Perth, Darwin, Townsville,
Belém, Durban, Lima, Xai-Xai planes
with wingspans big as high schools
eight hundred nine hundred tons a piece
gone like pollen, cumulus cirrus
altostratus nimbostratus people getting skinny
just trying to lose weight and the sky
the biggest thing anyone ever thought of
Acceptance, Vancouver, Tehran, Maui
school children balloons light blue nothing
one goes away not forever, in fact
most people, at least if you are flying
Delta, come down in Salt Lake City
Fairbanks, Kobe, Auckland, Anchorage
from Cleveland a hundred Hawaii-bound Germans
are coming in low, not to say too low
just low pull up Amsterdam pull up Miami
historically a very high-strung bunch
smokers eaters tiny planes must circle
we have bigger problems on our hands
New York, Tokyo, Hong Kong, Paris
the boy who has been ignoring dinner

throws thirteen paper planes out the window
does it look like this? Tashkent, Nome, Rio,
Hobart, yes yes it looks just like that
now do your homework Capetown Capetown
lots of rain good on one good on two
go three go four go five go six
Mau, Brak, Zella, Ghat, an African parade
good on two good on three
please speak English please speak English
good on five good on six gentlemen:
the world will let us down many times
but it will never run out of coffee
hooray! for Lagos, Accra, Freetown, Dakar
your son is on the telephone the Germans
landed safely Seattle off to Istanbul
tiny planes please circle oh tiny planes
do please please circle

Josh Bell

Josh Bell was born in 1971 in Terre Haute, Indiana. He attended Indiana State University, Southern Illinois University at Carbondale, and the University of Iowa Writers' Workshop, where he was later awarded a postgraduate Paul Engle Fellowship. His poems have appeared in such magazines as *Boston Review, Gulf Coast, Hotel Amerika, jubilat, Verse,* and *Volt.* Bell's first book is *No Planets Strike* (Zoo Press, 2005). He was the 2003-2004 Diane Middlebrook Fellow at the Wisconsin Institute for Creative Writing and is currently pursuing his PhD at the University of Cincinnati.

Poem to Line My Casket with, Ramona

Come practice your whorish gestures in the graveyard, Ramona.
Come sharpen your teeth on the tombstones.
Cough up the roots if you know what's good for you.
When coyotes are teaching their young to howl,
ghoulies rehearse the Courtship of Wrist-bones.
When you hear clawing at the square of Styrofoam
serving as a window in the caretaker's shack,
then you must count each step going up to the mausoleum,
and my ghost will appear in the churchyard.
He'll kiss the back of your knee in the moonlight.
These are not promises, but eerie enough, regardless.
You must count out loud, Ramona, the steps,
because this is the time to watch what eats you.
I used to love the way the wind whistled through your teeth
when you drove the back roads, above your legal limit.
I used to have these poses. They turned into habits.
I used to love the folks that loved me.
And they've been sad ones, my years since being dead.
And they've been coming, the folks who claim to love me.
And I hardly recognize myself. There aren't mirrors, as such.
The drum section rattles it out, down by the high school.
I hear them, or is it the caretaker drunk in his wheelbarrow?
You used to play the wheelbarrow, I recall.
You used to wash your underwear in the sink.
Above ground, the wind whistles through the tombstones.
Below ground, the wind sleeps and has colors.
Below ground, colors are how I dream of making my comeback.

There's a difference between *a* white dress and *the* white dress.
You used to strip off *the* white dress in a highly professional manner.
You used to dangle the remote, and I'd come get it.
You used to skip church. You used to skip dinner parties.
Now you've been seen hoisting condoms from the pharmacy.
There are twelve condoms to a pack. A pack of lovers mills outside your door.
A pack of the dead are heading toward the showers.
A pack of dead lovers is referred to as "a creep" of dead lovers.
More than one dead lover is weeping. But oh, how it was me who loved you then.
You with your cracked lips, with your love and your other defilements kept
    alive in a bucket.
When I first died, I stole a lock of your hair while you slept.
Now I dip it in ink when the mood strikes,
and the times you visit and kneel so pretty on the grass above me,
that's not scratching you hear. It's writing.

Zombie Sunday (Had We but World Enough and Time)

Gentle handed holy father, or whomever,
how I love curling up on the moldy couch
in the vacant lot, across from the skating rink,
where I pretend to hold your hand, in the rain,
and we are queer for each other, are we not?
You've dropped, like a lady's handkerchief, your several hints:
the Bible, for example, which was a gift,
and where you wrote on the inside cover—
like a green schoolgirl—your first name with my last.
Also the flowers, who offer their meager,
vegetable kindness when you are lonely for my voice.
Yet this is no time for the trademark
coyness, when matter is decaying,
when the stars, don't think I haven't noticed,
are stuck in clots and barely sparking,
like bad plugs, and the celestial spheres
have ground to a missionary halt.
GHHF, or whomever, you are old enough
to be my mother, or whatever,
and all the old girlfriends are jealous.
You have drowned one world already,
so confident, so tall, yet when lightning flashes,
I have to think, it is your knees that crack.

Baby, what are you waiting for?
I see how you look at me, across rooms,
like I'm just the kind of firmament
you could really cast some light onto,
and with those knees, like two greased moons
in glass sacks, if you fell to them,
and asked, how could I say no?
The very rivers would double back
to their invisible mothers and the mountains
would cross their legs and squirm.
So loosen the bald hinges of the universe
and step down through the canopy.
Come over here and tell me who you like.
Come sit in the back row during Algebra class
and let's see the skin that time forgot,
let's do the math, let's knock the handle
off the moon, let's review the tape,
let's practice your lines, and lord when you left me
I turned in my library card, I shaved
my head and wept for days, the sun
pulsing like a tumor in a bank of cloud
above the pawnshop, inoperable and shy.
Who but me will take you in?
You, who could clean us from the very streets—
between your holy thumb and forefinger—
like so much scum on floss? You have
stricken me, thusly, there-over, from the records
even once. But now I'm going to have
to have those inimitable favors of yours,
a peek across the sizable dowry of time,
and as sordid and easy as you were
in the days of old, with your debutante
sea-splitting and the profligate haunting
of the hedge, if you do come again,
come eagerly, like it was your first time,
and please have the nerve to wear
something abominable and white.

Meditation on *The Consolation of Philosophy*

And on that final night I tore eye-holes
in a black pillowcase, slipped it over my head,
made love to myself in the mirror,

and couldn't bring myself to finish.
I've begun telling the truth and now
I need objective help. Certain things
I need to do can't be accomplished
without a circumspect accomplice.
A girlfriend. Back in the good old days
those condemned to death hustled up
cash to tip their executioner; a sharper
blade, a meditated stroke, etc., but the last
woman I bade wear a black pillowcase
while she made love to me didn't (make
love, wear the hood) even though
I put ten dollars on the night stand
before services rendered. My surrender,
of sorts, to the animal largesse lurking
behind the puzzled genius of the hood,
and who'll complain if the blade's on its fifth
neck of the day, or your executioner
shows up drunk? You? "Off with your...
arm. Damn. Here we go." Look, I'm not
really into that kinky stuff, but a body
requires service. Take Boethius, whom
I haven't read. He wrote his uplifting
Consolation of Philosophy in prison,
then they cinched a wet leather helmet
on his head, and tossed him to the sun.
I bet when the leather dried, shrank,
cut in, I bet it gave, a bit, as the convict's
blood got it wet; enough for false hope,
a peek at slack-jawed Romans standing
around with clean hands. Boethius
got lucky. I mean, he never had a chance
to take it all back, to plead for exile
and promise to burn his manuscripts.
What would the sun say to that? It wouldn't
be good. You can't reason with a star,
friend, or the people you put in your will
or your bed. That's why we give advanced
directives to those who handle our bodies
during the few hopeful seconds they have
call to handle them—sex, hospitalization,
death in beds, closets, coffins, coffee tins
(like your Uncle Mike)—it doesn't matter:
Someone has to promise that they'll pull

the plug or man the screws, and then
follow through, no matter how badly,
when the time comes, we want them not to.

Sleeping with Artemis

I hadn't been that ashamed since
the Spartiate festival of the Hyacinthids,
and it was harder than we thought, sleeping
with Artemis. We brought sandwiches;
she brought arrows and stuck them
fletching up in the sand. We were vastly
unequipped. I looked to the heavens,
like you will, and asked for guidance
and a shield. To no avail. Furthermore,

the wine didn't help like we thought.
She drank it down, cursed our mothers,
and only got reckless, really, popped
the blister on her heel, drew the bow,
and, with both eyes shut, skewered
Crissippus. We scattered like snacks.
I believe it happened in that clearing
by the stream, where much transpired
as of late: two dead last April—the girl

who smoked flowers—that quiet kid who
turned into bark. We should have known
better, with the storied plants along the bank
and the instructive constellations in the sky.
Then she swept up out of the hedge like
a jack-knifed lion, a moon on each shoulder,
but you read the report. Indeed, sir,
we felt hairless, the offspring of mice,
when she quoted Hemingway, then turned
the forest to her wishes: leaves dropped

like bombs: branches shook: and where
the hounds came from, no one can tell.
From time to time, picking us apart now
from the stream, knee-deep and eyeing
the rushes for movement, she'd glance down

to her shirt, but it was always someone
else's blood. I remember her teeth
weren't as straight as you'd think.
But something about her was perfect.

David Berman

David Berman was born in 1967 in Williamsburg, Virginia. He graduated from the Greenhill School in Addison, Texas, the University of Virginia, and the University of Massachusetts MFA Program. His band, the Silver Jews, has released five albums from Drag City Records: *The Natural Bridge, Starlite Walker, American Water, Bright Flight,* and *Tanglewood Numbers.* Berman's poems have appeared in such journals as *The Baffler, The Believer, Fence,* and *Open City.* His first book is *Actual Air* (Open City Books, 1999). Berman resides in Nashville, Tennessee.

Democratic Vistas

The narrator was shot by the sniper he was describing
and I quickly picked up his pen.

What luck, I thought, to be sitting up here in the narrator's
tower where the parking lots look like chalkboards and the characters
scurry around or fall down and die as I design it.

Then I started to read the novel I'd inherited, and didn't like
what I discovered.

Most of the characters were relentlessly evil, taken right off the bad
streets of the Bible.

The narrator would interrupt the story at all the wrong times, like a
third wheel on a date, and deliver shaky opinions like "People who
wear turtlenecks must have really fucked-up necks."

He would get lost in pointless investigations, i.e., was Pac-Man an
animal, so that when we returned to the characters many pages
later, their hair had grown past the shoulder and their fingernails
were inches long.

In support of the novel, I must say it was designed well. The scenes
were like rowhouses. They had common sidewalls, through which one
could hear the faint voices and footsteps of what was to come.

I've lived those long driving scenes. Everyone knows how hard it is,
after you've been on the road all day, to stop driving. You go to sleep
and the road runs under the bed like a filmstrip.

I also liked the sheriff's anxious dream sequence, where he keeps
putting a two-inch-high man in jail, and the tiny man keeps walking
out, in between the bars.

After a sleepless night he's awoken by the phone. There's a sniper in
the University tower. The sheriff stands before the bathroom mirror.
Drops of Visine are careening down his face.

They are cold and clear
and I can count them through my rifle scope.

April 13, 1865

At first the sound had no meaning.
The shot came from the balcony,
as if the play had sprung an annex,
and I, John Sleeper Clarke,
pictured stars through oak scaffolds
as the news traveled over
the chairscape like a stain.

In that dark room lit by gas jets
the Welshman to my left conceded
the armrest we'd been fighting over
and doctors and half doctors
flowed into the scarlet aisles
to help.

I did not take to the image
of a bay mare waiting in the alley
or a manhunt through Maryland.

I remember standing up,
as the others did,

and how the assassin was in midair
when the stagehands wheeled out clouds.

Community College in the Rain

Announcement: All pupils named Doug.
Please come to the lounge on Concourse K.

Please join us for coffee and remarks.

Dougs: We cannot come. We are injured by golf cleats.

Announcement: Today we will discuss the energy in a wing
and something about first basemen.

Ribs will be served in the cafeteria.

Pep Club: We will rally against golf cleats today.
The rally will be held behind the gymnasium.

There is a Model T in the parking lot with its lights on.

Dougs: We are dying in the nurse's office.
When she passes before the window, she looks like a bride.

Karen (whispers): We are ranking the great shipwrecks.

Announcement: In the classroom filled with dishwater light,

Share your thoughts on public sculpture.

All: O Dougs, where are you?

Dougs: In the wild hotels of the sea.

From His Bed in the Capital City

The Highway Commissioner dreams of us.
We are driving by Christmas tree farms
wearing wedding rings with on/off switches,
composing essays on leg room in our heads.

We know there is policy like ice sculpture,
policy that invisibly dictates the shape

of the freeway forests and the design
of the tollbooths that passing children
send their minds into.

Photography's remainder is sound and momentum,
which we were looking to pare off the edges
of the past anyway, so snapshots of Mom
with a kitchen table hill of cocaine
or the dog frozen in the attitude
of eating raw hamburger
get filed under "Misc. Americana,"
though only partially contained there,
as beads of sap we are always leaking
from the columns of the bar graph.

The voices of the bumperstickers tangle in our heads
like cafeteria noise and we can't help but be aware
that by making this trip, by driving home for Christmas,
we are assuming some classic role.
It is the role he casts us in: "holiday travelers."

He dreams us safely into our driveways
and leaves us at the flickering doors.

Erica Bernheim

Erica Bernheim was born in 1974 in New Jersey, and grew up in Ohio and Italy. She holds a BA from Miami University of Ohio and an MFA from the University of Iowa Writers' Workshop. Her poems have appeared in *26, The Black Warrior Review, Bridge, The Canary, Gulf Coast, Volt,* and other journals. Currently, she teaches literature and creative writing in the Chicago area, and is a PhD candidate in Literature and Creative Writing at the University of Illinois at Chicago.

I Love How Your Eyes Close Every Time You Kiss Me

a line from a song by Bobby Vinton

You are alone and you are easy. You see
the history of your life and lineage in your
mitochondrial genes, cells, confirming what
we suspected: bottleneck, enlargement, plague,
vulcanologists from everywhere, studying the
site, thinking aren't you a cute disease. The
music is so loud you blink every time there is
a drum. Yes, best we heirloom quietly, for we
are powerful weak. Overcoat, spread your wings.
Almost a legend, knots laced with passed-over
glass, daddies in pastel suits next to the only
surviving witness from a life best spent in big years,
dreaming of sliding on your belly. Tough night,
wet ink, loose seams. There is plenty of time for
nothing and you should volunteer for it. Time allotted
is never enough. Roll over and tell me you're a
sofa, backboned by an old quilt, tied to the notion
of design, of pattern, of words so staccato they bang
like rats atop the roofs of government embassies,
that is, without regard for what those below will
try to assume you are: harmless and preoccupied,
known through your gestures to be true.
The ropey cuisine of another planet awaits you
tonight, something freeze-dried and wet
just for you, and molded into whatever you
want: lids and caps, some beans or rice, coelacanth,

but the remains will leave their fossils
on your plate. Memory is like this, patterns
already laid out across neurons and blisters,
each occasion which follows will fit
into that shape, even sans arms or eyelashes,
rendered sharp-tongued with bad desire.

Like a Face

Any tale of spontaneous human combustion
must take place in the South. History's wagon carries
me in its horrible mouth of an entryway. An arrow
relies on less, taste this, rising from the swollen
finger raised to measure air's currents.
The girl allergic to water battles for aquagenics.
Sweat, blood, saliva and tears blister her skin.
She bends her head for the most dangerous of kisses.
She drinks whole milk and is allergic to her
own body. She will dream of swimming and touching
snow. Her lips feel as close and sharp as razors, the light
explodes, and you surrender your addiction to No-Doz.
Something in breath dies slowly, a fern, a stilted horseman,
a moon seen in daytime, or this harvest gone rotten badly.
How long will you stay in this mess, waiting to learn
when to duck, when it's safe to run: a plate of eyelashes,
a walk on water, nothing more. Loving days.
A maze with no entrance, and we strain to see
it anyhow. I find myself on the wrong side of your
affections, afflictions, you say, and suddenly these are
sidelines. I tell stories so often, I don't remember the event,
signs written in languages I never learned to read.
What I told you made no difference, lighthouse, philosopher,
my sleep. Oh, but it trickles down the side of
a bed I never meant to lie in. Say something
about the state of dedication. What I wish for you
is nothing but fraud and petulance, camphor in
your proceedings, a brick in your mailbox, a wicked
bitter woman stealing your truck. I hope you can
believe this is not about you. You wake up
to find you've been tying your shoes with a dead man's
hand. You try to build a fire beneath a chimney
with no flue.

Anne Boleyn

*"The people will have no difficulty in finding a nickname for
me. I shall be Queen Anne Lackhead."*
—Anne Boleyn, upon learning of her impending execution

Who would have guessed
it was you and brother George
who invented the French Kiss
across someone else's deathbed,
perhaps, but this is how
we grow up: six-fingered and
a birthmark on the neck can
mean a witch, but one who holds
out, doesn't give so easily,
until realizing three years later
no one is indispensable, not
even the head of a kingdom
who will be ruled by uneven bodies.
What is wrong with a voice
that only wants opera? Work.
Pleasure in work. You
were not fair. Skin changes color
to show emotion. Yours
remained sallow. Your final threat,
Anne, the seven-year drought,
did they know then? Each
number like a calculator's,
formed from the pieces that made
each previous now unnecessary.
If the word "picnic" had existed,
would you have chosen this life?
Another king died from peaches
and new cider; there were poisons
that asked for months to impregnate
clothing, letters, and cooks were meant
to sample everything or be themselves
boiled. The luxury of privacy.
The taste of your future. Every birth
becomes a death sentence. You may
bring food to an execution, but
you must pin up your hair so as not to
interfere with the blade. Death, quickly.

Pavese Said Death
Will Come Bearing Your Eyes

It is late at night
and you are making
soup for other people.
There are wool sweaters
in piles around your
ankles and your nose
seems full of blood.
A little boy brought
a newspaper for you
today; it was bright
and cold. You were
thick and unlovely until
your body hit the
water. Now. When cops
lie, you call it the
blue wall. You will
develop a great true
love for the metronomes,
placing them on the
shelves of your closets,
keeping track of your
frequently silent comings.
Automatic, quiet, more
of everything. When the
season begins, these
girls you know will all
buy Bibles, creatures of
habit. You are not
ready for a reunion,
whatever it is. Who-
ever made this room
knew his flashes of
brilliance wouldn't last
much longer, so he
painted in huge colors
and couldn't bring himself
to buy a watch, your
father's dead, and it
is late. Even
dishonest people become

involved in terribly
disappointing ventures,
and you say this is one,
this is for your grace.

Mark Bibbins

Mark Bibbins was born in 1968 in Albany, New York, received his MFA from The New School, and has lived in New York City since 1991. A founding editor of the journal *LIT*, he has taught at SUNY-Purchase, and now teaches in The New School's MFA program. Individual poems have appeared in *Boston Review*, *Colorado Review*, *The Paris Review*, *Poetry*, *The Yale Review* and elsewhere, including the anthologies *The Best American Poetry 2004* and *Great American Prose Poems*. Bibbins received a Lambda Literary Award for his collection of poems *Sky Lounge* (Graywolf, 2003), and was awarded a 2005 Poetry Fellowship from the New York Foundation for the Arts.

Just Yesterday

Before prayer in the schools we had the Crusades
and we cleaned out the stockpot once a year.

Virtually everything we ate induced narcosis,
a condition we often confused with god.

Some told of a river that ran outside the city walls
and of how it moved to avoid their touch,

a giant serpent twisting forever away. If it wasn't the devil
it was the work of the devil, like everything else we wanted.

Remorse held us together until we died young
and most of us never realized we were mammals—

indeed we were suspicious of birds but rats, well, rats
we found charming, with their eyes so full

of sympathy, their need for warmth like our own. We also
wanted love to suffice. Flies that collected on the lesions

of the dying: angels one and all: no one could be too careful.
It seemed a flood was forever rinsing ideas from my tongue

so I said nothing or spoke louder, I was always drowning.
I couldn't have changed anything.

All right there was the alchemist
and I loved him but I could not save him.

Once I dreamt of electricity. Was this the river,
the one that altered its course like a wounded thing?

We had no trees, only sticks.
Huge gears turned in the sky.

All but Lost

My love lives down by the butchery,
at night he keeps coins on his eyes.

When we were still called children
I clothed myself in hides and relished

the generators that shook the ground.
Tesla didn't like jewelry, couldn't bear

to touch human hair and claimed
to have destroyed his sexuality

at the age of forty but of course everyone
was doing that then.

I sang Piaf songs
till they burned my tongue—precocious is

as precocious does—the French
all but lost to me now. Fate

presented itself as a ghost I could smell
under the floorboards as I listened

to mice gnawing on books I had
already memorized. When the doctor put

leeches on my torso he made no effort
to hide his arousal or the anisette

on his breath. He said I would
not die yet. He said the martyr's

a murderer locked in a room
till the saint slips him the key.

Groupie

All the money I lied about, the makeshift
stomach pump—forget everything

and the way to where it happened. The guitar
god wants me/has me/ditches me/calls me

from the road and can I wire some money, he's
gotten into a situation: a barren tour-bus fridge

so can I meet him in Trenton and bring a bag.
The next nude reveals herself

and she's thin in the way the age demands—
not conventionally pretty, not conventionally shaved,

but a rail to rail against if there's time and there is.
I'm at work on a new line of lipsticks—Foie Gras,

Primordial Soup, Contusion—everyone who tries them
gets beautiful.

The girls and I wanted to be famous,
instead we love an astronaut who blows

sunshine up our asses from halfway to its source. Fuck him.
Our supply lines have snapped—no more K, no more X,

no more. I take comfort in gossip, the usual
gossip, but different: this one stitched a quilt of moths,

another painted all his rooms gold. We, the girls and I,
we pull the wings off swan boats, follow our favorite

to the stars and the capsule in which we keep
recipes we've saved for our successors so they do not starve.

Slutty

We couldn't get near the bathroom
                    with all the models

holding back their hair
over the porcelain bowls.

The chef barely knew how to fling
parsley, so in the end   no one mourned

the hors d'oeuvres' demise.
The champagne was another story.

                A great mystery
to me as well you should be,

your legs seemed longer when
you cartwheeled under the streetlights:

Straddle me and I'll give you
all the gossip, all the sugar.

        —What would one do
with *all* the sugar anyway?

Caress can still be the right word,
the streets   dark and aflash

with rain   sliding through the city
on its way. A third party wants

in, that warmth. You love
the noise stars make when they fall.

In the morning   we are knocked around
by the wind   of approaching trains.

You play the drawn-on eyebrow,
        you play the figure-me-out—

        I'd like something too
                to tear at me.

Sherwin Bitsui

Sherwin Bitsui was born in 1975 in Fort Defiance, Arizona, and grew up in White Cone, on Northeastern Arizona's Navajo Reservation. He received his AFA in Creative Writing from the Institute of American Indian Arts in Santa Fe, New Mexico, and, in 2005, a BA in Creative Writing from the University of Arizona. His poems have appeared in *American Poet*, *The Iowa Review*, and elsewhere, and have been recognized with a Truman Capote Fellowship, a Witter Bynner Foundation Individual Poetry Award, and an Academy of American Poets Student Poetry Award. Bitsui now lives in Tucson, where he teaches for Arts Reach, a writing program for Native American students. His first book is *Shapeshift* (University of Arizona Press, 2003).

The Northern Sun

I find it necessary to breathe the morning air, to smell the potatoes frying, and watch the ceiling smoke into soft, white abalone dreadlocks, when I wake up abandoned, inscribed with *never open, look into, or stash in the backseat of your car.* I wear a mask made from the map of Asia.

Search for me in a ravine, on a cliff's edge reaching for the sun. Find me on the hood of a car racing through stars, on the velvet nose of a horse seeking its dead master waiting with saddle and bridle.

It is necessary to see the reflection of birds on the temporary ponds of melting snow. Grandfather, you named each mesa: sister, brother, friend, and I steered onto the pavement not knowing that inside our houses, the rain would clear and our fragrance would leap from our pores and into the canyons to be covered by crumbling black rocks.

Sometimes the mud on my boot breaks over fresh carpet, the payroll forgets our names, while the insects on our lips find our hidden names inscribed on their wings, and we roll through thorns to find the patterns of our loneliness scribbled on our bodies like images of dragons tattooed on rocks in a Route 66 mineral shop.

After this, you will reach to scratch your back and feel nothing but a black hole, spiraling like the agitator in an empty washing machine. You will bend backward with your mouth pressed to the linoleum, whispering, *sister, I need a sister,* but you will not be able to reach her. You will be ten inches away, and never have you knelt low enough to hear the undercurrent of a breeze lost to twilight summers.

The cigarette ignites the bedsheets, and I write my last sentence. Lamp shades cover me; my eyelashes wriggle in my pants pockets. *Your vocabulary is like the breakfast menu of a science convention.* Bricks ripple underfoot, the moon reveals her daughter for the first time in twenty eight days, born with fists instead of hands.

A writer breaks every pen he can steal from the henhouse; disappointed, he returns to the hospital and informs the nurses that he should be pulled from the flames immediately. He sweats, points at his right foot, and says that he regrets flying back to earth obscenely underdressed to witness what he calls a malnourished theater eating its legs for dinner.

Is this what I deserve: a white anthropologist sitting beside me at a winter ceremony? *Listen. Your people speak like weeping Mongolians.* Perhaps it is because we have been staring at airplanes too long, I tell him, that our throats have turned into hollowed-out spider legs extending over the rough wings of a salivating moth, who rejected its cocoon as a child, saying how ugly it made him feel to be in a bed that resembled an anchor rusting in the shadow of a feeble cloud.

This time we feel the padlocks snap. Prison inmates untie their imaginations, which can sometimes be seen in the high desert of Arizona, lukewarm magma flowing through the sky at a ninety-degree angle. The last time I saw the sun reflected red, I was pulling a screaming baby from her clutching, drunk mother on Highway 77 at noon. As the mother bounced off the pavement, I shut the baby's eyes and kicked the dead driver's foot from the gas pedal. The rear tires spun backward.

The beer in my refrigerator still smells like bread in the morning. My mother's goose bumps continue to make me shiver when she tells me to scratch her back. The IHS doctors gave her some lotion, but it doesn't help, so we scratch and scratch and scratch....

I just wanted a decent cup of coffee and a cheaper view of the Washington Monument, which loomed like a bright sun stream in a forest where the dark holds you like the wind holds you in a desert canyon. The cabdriver asked if I was American Indian. I said, *No, I'm of the Bitter Water People.*

The glittering world, this place that we fly into where traffic lights play tag with our eyes when we lie back singeing our faces with the light of passing freight trains. What's there but rum and Coke? Bottle walls standing knee-deep in confusion and rat traps disguised as dreamcatchers?

Five years ago, my language hit me like saw-toothed birds reaching to pull my tongue from my mouth. I didn't know what to expect when my grandmother poured gasoline on the leaves and then fired it, saying, *This is the last time I'll ever harvest.* It was the way the sunset caught her cracked lips, the way her lips folded inward, which made me realize that there were still stories within her that needed to be told, stories of when we still wove daylight onto our bones and did not live like we do now, as night people.

Somewhere in here, our minds glow like fog lights, a Coke can bleeds sugar, and the eyes of a turtle ooze from a high school water fountain. Somewhere in Chinle, Arizona, a blender is surrounded and pelted with gravel and cement stones by children whose parents drift through cheap wine bottles like steam rising from the necks of hemorrhaging antelopes.

Frogs smell rainstorm against a shield of ocher clouds. Two A.M., the first flakes of ash surround a family of beetles dining in the cracks of the *hooghan*'s fading walls, the flashlight of a policeman siphons dark waters from the spit can of an old medicine man singing the last four songs of his life. Inward, I can feel the gravel in my veins soften.

Apparition

1.
I haven't _____
since smoke dried to salt in the lakebed,
    since crude oil dripped from his parting slogan,
       the milk's sky behind it,
          birds chirping from its wig.

Strange, how they burrowed into the side of this rock.
    Strange…to think,
        they "belonged"
and stepped through the flowering of a future apparent in the rearview mirror,
visible from its orbit
    around a cluster of knives in the galaxy closest to the argument.

Perhaps it was September
that did this to him,
    his hostility struck the match on handblown glass,
not him,
    he had nothing to do with their pulse,
    when rocks swarmed over

and blew as leaves along the knife's edge
into summer,
    without even a harvest between their lies
        they ignited a fire—

        it reached sunlight in a matter of seconds.

2.
It is quite possible
    it was the other guy
        clammed inside my fist
who torched the phone book
and watched blood seep from the light socket.

Two days into leaving,
    the river's outer frond flushes worms imagined in the fire
onto the embankment of rust,
    mud deep when imagination became an asterisk in the mind.

In this hue—
    earth swept to the center of the eye,
        pulses outward from the last acre
held to the match's blue flame.

Mention _____,
    and a thickening lump in the ozone layer
    will appear as a house with its lights turned off—
        radio waves tangled like antlers inside its oven,
because *somewhere*
    in the hallway nearest thirst,
        the water coursing through our clans
    begins to evaporate
        as it slides down our backseats—
its wilderness boiled out of our bodies.

Chrysalis

It wasn't the leaves that descended upon you
or the horse that knelt on the river's edge,
pushing his nose through mist,
    a root that wanted to peel itself into a flower.

It was ash,
dry as the skeletons of drained soup cans
on the river front
where a man's coarse throat bleeds
because the language is a dying thing,
covered in blankets,
      beaten with forks and spoons.

These baskets have become graves,
      a shot glass of tears tucked between the legs of a veteran,
a wristwatch pulled tightly around his tongue
so that he may savor this hour
when death drags its tail across the necks of hunted children,
who are shivering again under the sun's sharp chin,
half awake in a boat on a shore of gray gulls,
pressing grapes into their eyes,
drinking the wine that leaks from their shadows.

Cities break into sand before the approaching shovel;
their windows glisten in the soft light of the Milky Way
as I remember it.
      How young I was to read the passages of the Bible,
my wings caked in earth,
mud forming in my footsteps,
water seeping from my lips when he came to drink.
He came to drink and would not stop.
He was a bee pollinating the milky surface of the moon reflected in the rearview
      mirror.

The deer blinked and all was well again,
calm as the breeze blowing through prison gates.
I shave the edges of my mustache and imagine cutting the policeman's arm from
his flashlight.
But still it did not stop the lions from sniffing the snouts of dying bulls,
or the red squaw from selling her jewelry in aisles of restaurants serving leaves
      and grass.

And no, there is no one here.
This casket: the seed of a blood clot.

Bread dipped in gunpowder is to be fed to the first graders in that moment
when their hair is cut
      and a ruler is snapped,
and their whispers metamorphose into a new chrysalis of thought.
A new wing emerging from the lips of these Indians,

who are no longer passing thoughts in the paragraphs of an oil-soaked
      dictionary
but hooves carved into talons,
hilltops from which light is transformed into the laughter of crickets.

I want to remain here
where he doesn't drink my lips
or remove the cocoons my eyes have become.

Rattles erupt on the north horizon.
The harvester unties her shoelaces.
I see the sun, eclipse it with my outstretched palm,
and dig away my reddening skin.
      "It wasn't like this before," I tell myself.
When I am thrown into a fluorescent room where the sink hunches
like an eagle claw,
it stops,
pulls the wind to a breathing space the size of a mouse's lung,
and I am drowning in the air around my feet again.

Antelope are gnawing into the walls of the city.
And *those* Indians are braiding yucca roots into the skin of their scalps again.

I want to fall beside them,
count their fingers:
      five hundred and five rows of spilled blood marking the trail home.
The trail will not be followed again,
because there in the ears of the Indians
are echoes of the hissing belt
and the laughter of thieves
measuring the length of the treaty
with the teeth of the jury that is seduced by the glimmers of gold.

It is ash, all of it!
Fruit flies buried in the skin of onions,
canyons seeking the river that has left them orphaned,
cars cruising their velvet wheels over teeth and beaks,
eyeless dogs barking in hailstorms,
and owls, two of them coming from the east,
carrying the night between them: a wet blanket designed by a woman who
      dreams of lightning,
saying that we have finally become mountains
rising above a valley of weeping dishrags that cling to the ground below,
raising fences and crosses and houses.

And no, this is not about sadness:
the gasp of a mute who buries his legs in the arroyo bottom
when the first drops of rain pepper his forehead,
who earlier that morning brought a leaf into the front yard,
saying that we may grow from this,
we may inch into the next world
and rummage for nectar in the thinning bones of shadowless thieves.

This plate before me is made from broken tusk; this fork, the fingers of a rat,
and we eat leather in caves behind the train tracks.
These caves where our hair breaks into ash when washed
are a place of birth;
the first cry echoing from the amphitheater
was a song sung in thinning air.

This is not about the rejection of our skin;
the mud dries as it is poured into our ears.
But the linguist still runs his hands up the length of our tongues,
perplexed that we even have a tongue   at all.

Richard Blanco

Richard Blanco was born in 1968 in Madrid. In his words, he was "made in Cuba, assembled in Spain, and imported to the United States"—his pregnant mother and the rest of his family came to Madrid as Cuban exiles, then left Spain when he was forty-five days old, eventually settling in Miami. Blanco holds a BS in Civil Engineering and an MFA in Creative Writing from Florida International University. He has worked as a furniture designer, graphic designer, and professional engineer, and has taught creative writing and Latino literature at Central Connecticut State University, American University, and Georgetown University. His poems have appeared in such journals as *The Nation*, *Ploughshares*, and *TriQuarterly*, and in such anthologies as *The Best American Poetry 2000* and *Great American Prose Poems*. Blanco's two books of poems are *City of a Hundred Fires* (University of Pittsburgh Press, 1998) and *Directions to the Beach of the Dead* (University of Arizona Press, 2005). At present, he lives in Miami.

Elegant Endings

A foggy night, a long silver train, someone's hand
pressed on the glass, crystallized breaths eclipsing
a face in a window slowly moving past someone left
with smoke clinging around their feet—that ending.
Or the one with the glass shells of runway lights—
cobalt, carmine, and jade dotting a stretch of tarmac
below a plane lifting someone into the hull of night.
Or maybe, the grand good-bye kiss in Paris black
and white at the beginning or end of some war—
another great ending—elegant, noble, final. But
we're not a movie. I'm still driving without a script
around your house, spying through the windshield
into the tempera light of your bedroom window
insisting that you are there, just as I remember you:
reading Cisneros' poems under your halogen lamp,
feeling as alone as Cuba, or playing Mercedes Sosa
on the balcony, while you finish a portrait or blend
the right shade of green for a canvas of palm trees.
Maybe you're drawing the ancient Taíno symbols
you taught me: *Guabanex* and *Ayá* which means
I trust in God, I fear no one—but tonight I am afraid
and driving around you again, around the silences
we've slammed behind doors or never answered,
and all the apologies brought with roses and notes.

Around and around the scent of wet coral across
your shoulders, the specks of paint on your hands,
the memory of breaths thickening your lean torso.
Around and around your window one more night
to catch that one last glimpse of your silhouette
that will let me drive away, vanish beyond the lights
at the end of your street, for good—that ending.

We're Not Going to Malta...

because the winds are too strong, our Captain announces, his voice like an
oracle coming through the loudspeakers of every lounge and hall, as if the
ship itself were speaking. We're not going to Malta—*an enchanting island
country fifty miles from Sicily*, according to the brochure of the tour we're
not taking. But what if we did go to Malta? What if, as we're *escorted on
foot through the walled "Silent City" of Mdina*, the walls begin speaking to
me; and after we *stop a few minutes to admire the impressive architecture*,
I feel Malta could be *the* place for me. What if, as we *stroll the bastions and
admire the panoramic harbor and stunning countryside*, I dream of buying
a little Maltese farm and raising Maltese horses in the green Maltese hills.
What if after we *see the cathedral in Mosta saved by a miracle*, I believe
that Malta itself is a miracle. What if, before I'm *transported back to the
pier*, I am struck with Malta fever and determine I am *very* Maltese indeed,
that I must return to Malta, learn to speak Maltese with an English (or
Spanish) accent, work as a Maltese professor of English at the University
of Malta and teach a course on *The Maltese Falcon*. Or what if when we
stop at a factory to shop for famous Malteseware, I discover that making
Maltese crosses is my true passion. Yes, I'd get a Maltese cat and a Maltese
dog, make Maltese friends, drink Malted milk, join the Knights of Malta,
and be happy for the rest of my *Maltesian* life. But we're not going to
Malta. Malta is drifting past us, or we are drifting past it—an amorphous
hump of green and brown bobbing in the portholes with the horizon as the
ship heave-ho's over whitecaps, wisping into rainbows for a moment, then
dissolving back into the sea.

Perfect City Code

for M.C.

1.0   Streets shall be designed *Euro–Style* with 300-ft right-of-ways,
        benches, and flowered traffic circles, to provide a distinct sense of
        beauty, regardless of cost.

1.1   There shall be a canopy of trees and these shall be your favorite: *Giant Royal Palms*, 25-ft high, whereas their fronds shall meet in cathedral-like arches with a continuous breeze that shall slip in our sleeves and flutter against our bodies so as to produce angel-like sensations of eternity.

1.2   There shall be bushes, and these shall also be your favorite: *Tea Roses* @ 2-ft o.c., to provide enough blooms for casual picking; whereas said blooms shall spy on us from crystal glasses set next to the stove, over coffee-table books, or in front of mirrors.

1.3   Sidewalks shall be crack-proof and 15-ft wide for continuous, side-by-side conversations; they shall be painted either a) *Sunflower-Brown,* b) *Mango Blush,* or c) *Rosemont Henna*; whereas such colors shall evoke, respectively: the color of your eyelashes, of your palms, the shadows on your skin.

1.4   There shall be an average of 1 (one) Parisian-style café per city block, where I shall meet your eyes, dark as espresso, above the rim of your demitasse, and hold your hand like a music box underneath the table; where we shall exercise all those romantic, cliché gestures we were always too smart for.

1.5   There shall also be 1 (one) open-air market per city block to facilitate the purchasing of tulips, mints, baci, and other typical items to lavish on our lives; whereas every night I shall watch you through a glass of brandy as you dice fresh cilantro and dill, and disappear into the scent steaming around you.

1.6   Utility poles and structures that obstruct our view shall not be permitted. At all times we shall have one of the following vistas: birds messaging across the sky, a profile of mountains asleep on their backs, or a needle-point of stars.

1.7   There shall be an *Arts District* and we shall float through gallery rooms on Saturday afternoons perplexed by the pain or conflict we can't feel in a line or a splatter of color (works that glorify or romanticize tragedy shall not be allowed).

1.8   There shall also be a *Historic District* to provide residents with a distinct sense of another time. And we shall live there, in a loft with oak floors and a rose-marble mantle where our photos will gather, and our years together will compete with the age of the brick walls and cobblestones below our vine-threaded balcony.

NOTE: In said city, there shall be a central square with a water fountain where we shall sit every evening by the pageantry of cherubs, where we shall listen to the trickle of their coral mouths, where I shall trust the unspoken, where you shall never again tell me there's nothing here for you, nothing to keep you, nothing to change your mind.

How It Begins | How It Ends

somehow, somewhere
wind pares a mountainside
shaves underneath a cliff's chin or
steals a dune from the desert
somewhere a parched field
is raped by greedy gusts
or a ripe stone is ground
and powdered into a soul
everywhere something dead
burns alive into a ghost
of carbon-gray ash
a metamorphosis of the solid
into an almost invisible earth

the clever dust slips in
through a cracked window
underneath the front door
and comes to rest on a tabletop
across the top edge of a frame
over an array of aging photos
on blocks of consumed books
a relentless disintegration
gingerly settles out of beams
of morning light, a daily gift
collecting in the corners of the room
in my eyes, on my hair, over my skin
I inhale, exhale, move on

Joel Brouwer

Joel Brouwer was born in 1968 in Grand Rapids, Michigan, and holds degrees from Sarah Lawrence College and Syracuse University. His poems have appeared in *AGNI, Chelsea, Crazyhorse, The Paris Review, Ploughshares, Poetry,* and other magazines. He has held fellowships from the NEA, the Wisconsin Institute for Creative Writing, and the Mrs. Giles Whiting Foundation. Brouwer is the author of two books of poems, *Exactly What Happened* (Purdue University Press, 1999) and *Centuries* (Four Way Books, 2003). He teaches creative writing at the University of Alabama.

Aesthetics

Your brother has leukemia? Carve ivory. The elections were rigged? Write a villanelle. A girl shivers in streetlight, takes off her mittens, pulls a silver yo-yo from her pocket. Dogs bark behind a fence. Use oil on wood. Concentrate on pacing when choreographing your divorce; you will have to move through it forever. Two men in green fatigues tie a woman flat to a metal table. One has a rubber hose, the other a pliers. A third man arrives with sandwiches and a thermos. A body has soft and hard parts, like a piano. Music comes from where they meet.

Divorce

Got your letter. And the crate of dead crows. Are you trying to tell me something? Thought you might want to know—I'm taking a class on how to be a man. This week we learned that if you want to be one, you can't be celery, a hotel room, or the Big Dipper. I raised my hand: *How about a crow?* The professor said, *Good, good! How* about *a crow?* We're graded on participation. Yes, you can keep the clock. Will you please send my hands and feet? They're in the nightstand, where you used to keep your fingers.

Hamartia Symbolized by the Stray

who cried at their tent flap. Dakota dawn.
Frost steamed in the stubble. Crazy Horse swung

his long chalk leg over a mountain, as if
he could ride it to safety. The dog stayed
and stayed. They told each other it was love.
Let's review their errors so far. Crazy Horse
never claimed he could save anyone, least
of all himself. The hound loved leftover
beans and hashbrowns, not them. And they loved not
each other but figures of each other set
down each freezing evening in small notebooks,
his blue and hers red, while the flashlight lashed
to the tent's crown with twine swung above them,
a metronome slowing down the tempo.
And burrowing down into the sleeping bags
they'd zipped into a single downy pouch.
And the sprays of hard white stars which bit down
on the charred November sky so soon to
snow while the stray searched the packed earth beneath
the picnic table once more before sleep.
And chocolate shakes from General Custard.
Bright green cress torn dripping from icy streams.
That no one in the world knew where they were.
Hen-of-the-woods hissing in the skillet.
The valiant rustbucket they rode in on
and trusted they'd ride back out. All of these
and more but not, it would eventuate,
each other, an error which would soon initiate
their slow etiolation, foreshadowed here
by wet green wood that would not catch, ink blanched
in rain, and gray leaves snapping underfoot
like glass eyes. Blind Crazy Horse's errant
arrow made a bridge and the stray lay down and
died on it. They covered it with a jacket
and told each other at least it didn't suffer.
But the arrow groped on toward its mark.

"Kelly, Ringling Bros. Oldest Elephant, Goes On Rampage"

—The New York Times, February 3, 1992

Her reasons for snapping seem clear: barbed tip
of the whipcord, squirming toddler cargo
glopping Sno-Cone on her back, cramped freight cars,

stale hay, the vet's incessant vitamin shots...
Or maybe it was boredom. Think of all the circles
she wore into the earth. Twenty-seven years of plod,
orbiting the ringmaster's megaphoned jokes
while squads of ballerinas dug their heels
into her spine. Perhaps it wasn't pain
but repetition: the routine—balance beachball
on trunk-tip, wag ears—as sure and dull
as gravity. The question then is not why

but why today? Why this exact instant to rage
through the bleachers, tossing clowns like peanut husks,
sending dozens of kids to nightmare clinics?
What spark or fulcrum, what sudden volition
rose like a bubble through her four tamed tons
and burst in her meaty head?

After all, means of escape are always
at hand. Nothing remarkable
about shotgun triggers or train tickets,
the hard part is when to use them.
You yourself, right now, with a few
well-placed blows, could knock your world down
to the pile of boards it started as,
pick up a hammer and begin again from scratch:
move to Phoenix, raise cattle, change your name.
The brittle unbearable rests in your palm.
Will you close your fist or won't you, and why?
They shot her forty times before she died.

The Spots

Appeared to her in Massachusetts. Purple and green.
And immediately

vertigo rushed up like an angry dog
to a fence. She went white, fell down the well

of herself and wept.
Late at night, in the motels, when she'd fallen

asleep, I cried too. I whispered curses to the awkward stacks
of white towels. Hating anything out of balance. Hating

her, her new failure. In the mornings
my checkbook voice returned, low and soft. For an angry dog

whose yard you wish to cross.
We both hated my balance, hated her imbalance, needed each.

Sudafed acupuncture ear candle.
Yoga chewing gum Zoloft Chinese tea.

She was afraid of going blind. She constantly described
colors and shapes, as if I had gone blind.

They turned orange. They floated. They darted.
We went arm in arm without passion, like elderly French.

Internist neurologist ophthalmologist.
Otolaryngologist neurologist psychiatrist.

She would not allow the warm towel over her face in the MRI.
The nurses seethed. She set her jaw and vanished

into the gleaming white tube. The machine banged like hammers
on a sunken ship's hull. She listened to Beethoven through headphones.

The magnetism passed through her mind in waves,
like wind through chestnut trees, touching

everything and changing nothing. Her courage! If courage
is what stones have. My God, how I loved her. Badly.

The spots were like metaphors. They told us something
by showing us something else. And so I believed they were metaphors.

They were not.

Oni Buchanan

Oni Buchanan was born in 1975 in Hershey, Pennsylvania. She holds Bachelor's degrees in English and Music from the University of Virginia, an MFA from the University of Iowa Writers' Workshop, and an MM in Piano Performance from the New England Conservatory of Music. Her poems have appeared in *American Letters & Commentary*, *Colorado Review*, *Conduit*, *Fence*, *Verse*, and elsewhere, including *The Best American Poetry 2004*. Buchanan is also the recipient of numerous music awards, and performs solo piano recitals in concert series across the country. Her first CD, *Solo Piano*, was released in 2004, and her second CD is scheduled for release in 2006. Buchanan's first book of poems is *What Animal* (University of Georgia Press, 2003). She lives in Boston with fellow poet Jon Woodward, and is on the piano faculty at the New School of Music.

The Only Yak in Batesville, Virginia

At first I spent hours gazing at the black and white horse
in the farthest pasture. He was so far away,
so tiny between the fence slats, and even then I knew
all he cared about was his mane and that his tail
was properly braided. He never so much as galloped
in my direction. Even the flies that edged
his beautiful eyes never flew into my wool
or landed on my nose. The love affair

was over before it began. I started to dream
of a dry cistern in the middle of the forest
and dry leaves where the other yaks could play
until leaves stuck out of their hair and they looked
like shrubs. In my dream they lived
in the cistern and each morning looked out
with periscopes before scrambling up the concrete walls
to search in the forest for sprouting trees.

In winter I realized that for the other yaks
it was fall all year round, and that it had to be fall,
because otherwise they couldn't roll in the leaves
to look like shrubs, and there had to be a cistern,
because otherwise they couldn't huddle in the pitch black,
and I knew then that I had forgotten

what a yak looks like, though I am a yak,
and I knew then that I had been away for a long time.

The Girls

As our reward, she cut for the girls the nervous ribbon.
The figurines nearby filled with food the girls didn't want.
And the tire in the stream and the shoe hidden
inside the tire and the sludge hidden inside the shoe.
To make a home for the girls in the fern-forest where the brambles arched.
And stickers of the animals.

She read to the girls and the girls behind the outhouse
burying our talents. Slits
in the ground, the vent
closing up Venetian. Valved.
The crayoned Valentines filed in the slot machine.
Behind the warping
and the poison red berries from the hedge.
And the girl-song written by the girls.

She was handing out the flashlights and the batteries, then the stranger
loves the girls more.
The air so stiff, stream-clogged.
He gives the girls the guns to choose, which girl of
which of you, the girls with the guns against each the other's girl-heart.
I was standing by her first, then the stranger
loves my sister more. My sister with the gun against my heart.
Only the birds eat these berries, not the girls.
Only the birds with their mouths smeared red, with their bird-mouths puckere
The birds fill their mouths.

The Term

My clock is fast. I don't know how fast. I wanted
to be with him on the glacier, just the two of us
freezing and turning away from each other in our ice bed
while the floe droned south, inexorable. My swelling cycle

with the moon, my gibbous. It's not
a flattering light. Somebody would have been

better off without, and I'm certain it's me, but we've
already pushed off with a paddle toward the main-ice, all the colors

kept under. Six feet deep. I stepped over it
the first time, sheer luck—make room for me. A door
to the rubble. So as not to interrupt the dark pulse, *no
difference, no difference.* So as not to disrupt the blossoming

litter, their tiny digits. Sometimes the rootless chasm-bridges—
top-shards snatched by the antarctic winds, gambled, cast
like pick-up sticks—can't be distinguished
from the surface, cannot hold the weight.

Even the delicate-pawed cadaver dogs…they
have learned from someone other than me
not to flinch. Not to drop the mementos down the ice-maw.
A trail in the ice scrub leading. His scribble:

Momentous: the bulbous hatched today, a halo of babies.
I saw a map of me, the ground not to scale. Light strapped on the head
where the third eye would open. Just that they be
synchronized, his breath recorded in ice, his voice a pigment

in the tendrils of ice algae. I didn't write the obituary
and by then I'd forgotten. Blown-glass birds on the windowsill
sending rainbows in scattered patterns around the makeshift
kitchen, our hut for observation. Other women

grown for concubines. He could freeze it off,
or freeze it off. No magnifying glass to see the babies closer.
The babies spilling from the tapered end of the tear, I'd thought
a rupture from the swell, I'd thought it would

burst me please. If only the old others were here, if
the others. The dogsleds padlocked to the chain
nailed with a stake into the ice. For shame, he would say.
And I *am.* On all fours, I'm all for it.

Room 40

When it's time to move, he takes me for a walk.

Sometimes we go into the other room and sometimes into the kitchen.

When we pass by the mirror, he points in at the collar—polished, so the metal spa
She's always there, very quiet.

Sometimes I look at her but only when he points. I must,

except when the eyes weigh down so the lashes touch and the body
folds itself fan-wise .

       creased out of napkins like in the red booth when my father took us
       and taught us the words in French, when it was the tree with the
       blossoms like pink-fringed feather and the paintbrush

He jerks on the chain as a reminder. He used to make up stories for her.

Before the fits. Before the sobbing that took up the space

so he couldn't breathe in his favorite chair, the green one. Cried her

swollen body still. And the trembling still.

             My beautiful quiet girl.

Once I said his name like a question, and he walked away
into the other room and shut the door.

There are two
rooms. The room where I'm kept in the evening, to be quiet

while he works, tapping and tapping on the keys and laughing
out loud and telling stories when the phone rings and he answers it

because it's someone from the outside. The outside, always
swelling and fumbling and searching, when we are so safe here, warm, and the wind
   blinds down.

Then, the room where I'm kept
in the morning. Where the pillows are and the heater billowing and fogging.

And the desk I looked in once, an accident, and the pictures
of strangers like me there, forty or fifty, cut out of magazines
and pictures of strangers like him, cut out of magazines.

At first, he played
the songs for me and I would sing and wear the outfits.

And spin to his knees from the far corner, and how I would hold him then, how I
   would hold him—

Some days he takes me in the elevator

                    and the 3 in a circle with the light behind it

to the room with machines to build the strength back up. The doorman

keeps the big room empty for us. He bows to me in his uniform.
He sees her. She has a wide satin ribbon tied around her throat.

My beautiful girl, your throat

like a Parmigianino

            (like in the afternoon when he came to me, when with his cuffs
            unbuttoned I kneeled to his wrists and the cathedral bells through
            the window a scarf that wrapped us together and the day a blue
            square that led to the piers splintered with boats, light-strung and
            wreaths on the masts

Home
is the button with the number 7. My favorite number is 73,

and my favorite animal is the dolphin. And the green planets
I cut out of paper and lined with wires in orbit. He does not

hear me when I speak. I said to him, Green is my favorite color too.

Transporter

Oh raw, raw—
They send me out on an errand for the words.
They send me out to switch the samples and the charts.
You, who are marked for this coincidence.

And if I stopped moving like sometimes the sky tells me.
And if I stopped moving like sometimes the weight of the walk, like all the
   separate materials
in their separate jars, primary and ignorant.

The winged girls appeared then by the Susquehanna selling electronic wares and
    digital wares.
In their silver head wraps, and with wrists braceleted with thin silver hoops, they
    lined
the black plastic pieces on an observation podium for the onlooker to consider.

And will we go swimming then when the waters are warm. And will we swim
before they detonate the three-mile island. The glow-ring with its
circumference expanding in shock concentrics

and the populace running, clogged
against the bodies of the populace running.

The carillonneur tugs the ropes for the separate bells in order.
Somewhere the sandwiches are wrapped in plastic and tucked neatly under the boat sea
Somewhere the canned pear-halves, the smog-sided buildings
hunched in the urine and the vomit.

And in the warm waters, and will
the waters be warm?
Water, i.e., a metal spigot sticking from the earth like a lance reamed through.

The money was to see the angel joints move on their own silvery hinges.
The exchange of tiny discs of ice.

It's not natural but it's natural for long enough. I trust that you will wake me in time.
I have to get home, you see. I have to fix the engine.
The light is glowing at least I can say the light is glowing.
Thin as a wire, then who comes dancing with the shears—the reeds

grown out of the whisper to whisper it again in the wind.
The basilica filled with light, light pouring through the stained-glass station windows.
One of us will open up the earth for the other of us
and then seal it behind.

Julianne Buchsbaum

Julianne Buchsbaum was born in 1970 in Los Angeles, and spent her childhood in various places, including New York City, Dallas, Iowa City, and Pittsburgh. Buchsbaum attended Beloit College, the University of Iowa Writers' Workshop, and the University of Pittsburgh, and now lives in Missouri, where she is a PhD student in English and Creative Writing at the University of Missouri-Columbia. The recipient of the 1999 Randall Jarrell Poetry Prize and of a Paul Engle Fellowship in Poetry from the James Michener Foundation, Buchsbaum has published poems in Conduit, The Denver Quarterly, The Gettysburg Review, Gulf Coast, Southwest Review, and elsewhere. She is the author of two books of poems: Slowly, Slowly, Horses (Ausable, 2001) and A Little Night Comes (Del Sol Press, 2005).

Thrillsville

When the mind begins to see the lies it loves
with eyes that could have looked elsewhere,
old pain repullulates. Errors of architecture,

errors of eros, the train ride out is not
the train ride in. Is this the kind of life
you left us for? No one has a face in the dark.

Needles keep pulling away from their source
in the spruce, manganese, more ascetic angles,
without danger to the traveler who goes back home

and finds a dog digging a hole in the yard,
cells multiplying in the veins of the sick.
Even now, when the city is dark, I get lost

without you—you who would ride your horse
hard against a famished glamour, would deceive
yourself with oracles, with flawed mechanics,

though the weatherman predicts rain in April,
tractors lurk like malignant growths in the fields
of soybeans outside of town and the town itself

is a necropolis of wrought-iron gates. This is how
your heart is—needles behind, needles before.
No one gets to keep the face they came here with.

The Power Plant

Under the copper-clad latticework of the power plant,
you were a mix of vandal and sylph and I waited
in the parking lot for hours. It was easy to vilify,

not easy to fix. In a world the color of lampposts,
it was hard to take to wife and hard to be taken
to wife, season of bureaucracy, season of gleam.

Imagine what we fled into, what the fire became:
bright red flags warning of high-voltage lines run
underground. I imagined what we would become

in the house we sat alone in. Darkness was scattered
everywhere like the hairs of a cat and I told you
a tale of nettles, of the sandman palming off his nada,

caressing your will with null. The hazards were buried
under the corruptions of autumn. Lamps were lit
underground, you said *Hush now,* like a mother, *here*

you are safe. You told me a tale, it was hard to be taken.
The sky was ash and smoke, a man made of sand.
Buried leaves became a bureaucracy, a fairyland in flames.

I was taught, in the parking lot of the power plant,
we're safe here. In the lynch force of its latticework,
you were a cross between mob and aristocrat.

In Squire Park with M., Esquire

Summer finally lies facedown
in the red leaves of the equinox.

Beneath a nail-colored sky a shell-
shocked girl taunts me like a planet

with an iron core. She's always
changing her face, breathless

as a god-besotted pamphleteer
making her bed in some other,

less plastic world. We will never
know the implications of rhetoric

in this place of rife ephemera.
For days I dream we are

a euphoria of fused parts, love's
Trojan horse welcomed recklessly

into a recluse heart, beating,
then not beating, the river coursing

southward out of sight. The wind
carries no part of the park to me,

no weeds white as cartilage studded
with bells of dew. Vetch underfoot,

feverfew, a sense of either/or
in the trove of shadows. Her look

of lassitude is not a mask.
She is mine. I must not touch her.

Phantoms of Utopia

Out in the streets, the phantoms of utopia
are darkening, tangling their hair

in waveforms, turning bitter.
The fog they feared has become colossal.

They've been doing the same thing for years now
and no new data. Still the pig iron

and smelted steel drift in on a barge
from Guatemala. Still the cars

carry their smells onto highways.
Those cars are not like ships on the sea.

The radars are there, invisible schemes
and frequencies, without odor or color or need.

Through exotic reticulations of trees
they send their strange intelligence.

Out in streets full of barbiturates,
the phantoms of utopia are seeking the historical

in florid landscapes, splayed flowers,
fondly arranged limbs. All day

they appear to be cultivating their thoughts
and the delicate, plantlike extensions

of their thoughts. *Goodbye fine rain falling,
goodbye idea of the good.* Outside,

daylight is blue against spruce trees
and a dead girl lives again in your memory,

sunlight a broth breaking over her mouth,
a breath, why DNA, why anything?

At dusk, the phantoms of utopia
close the doors to their houses

as if increments of evil were veiled
in the fog that haunts them. The reproach

in their eyes makes you shy. Minus
an inner sanctum, they are like you.

Slowly, Slowly, Horses

Night designs a darkness of horseweed.
Without this fear
in me I would not know where to be.
The field is steeped
in darkness where the horses died.
I would not know
how to be silent. Something cold grooms
what's left of their hides,
the tussocked weeds, and it is not, no,
it is never the wind.
If it were the wind, I would hear it the way

a drowning man
tastes water, the way a horse remembers
grass, the cramp of colic.
Night is nothing but night before red
spiders foam
from its mouth, before horses paw
the dirt at dawn.
Give them room to breathe, I say.

I rode bareback once in a brown lake;
they couldn't see us
from the house, couldn't save us if
we went down.
Mountains loomed around and *no one,*
I promised myself,
no one ever again. My mouth made
the slack shape
water makes when something falls into it.

Night is such a furled feminine thing
around the muscles
of horses, the nettles in their fetlocks,
it is nothing
but the night before and the night after,
only starrier,
uglier. I try to shake them from it, take
their pain away,
they're dirty, I think, *I'll make them clean.*
It goes cold
again as horsetails lash the air; shadows
hemorrhage
in the heart of the field, flooding it, and I flee.
All night long
I see the violent iron frowns of horseshoes.
Someday this pasture
will be pavement. See the barbed wire?
See the weeds?
Once I had a breath I did not breathe.

Stephen Burt

Stephen Burt was born in 1971 in Baltimore, and grew up in and around Washington, D.C. He received his BA from Harvard University, did graduate work at Oxford University, and received his PhD from Yale University. Burt's poems have appeared in *Barrow Street, The Bloomsbury Review, Boston Review, The Paris Review, Yale Review,* and elsewhere, and he regularly publishes his book reviews and critical studies, as well as articles on obscure pop groups, comic books, and women's basketball, in a wide range of publications, including *The Believer, The Boston Globe, The Nation, London Review of Books, The New York Times Book Review,* and *Times Literary Supplement.* Burt edited the book *Randall Jarrell on W.H. Auden* (Columbia University Press, 2005), and is himself the author of the critical study *Randall Jarrell and His Age* (Columbia, 2002). His two books of poetry are *Popular Music* (Center for Literary Publishing, 1999) and *Parallel Play* (Graywolf, 2006). He lives in St. Paul, Minnesota, where he is an Associate Professor of English at Macalester College.

Ocean State

for Forrest Gander & C.D. Wright

If the car has stalled by the mall in the shape of a star
it must be for a reason
                look around: courage
the sea is in sight
             it has no name

Your water tower hangs in exclamation
swelling
             over Warwick, R.I.
holding its shape as if never giving out
holding   as if giving nothing away
too slick for a roost
           its claim *Come and choose wrong*

           what distinguishes what humans built
from what is human   it stands unmoved in rain

Ford Escorts mill outside the glass arcade
Accords   hold to obstreperous queues
sad puppy   what are you waiting for

old quarries hope
                    shapeless as diaries
unform'd   ovariform   or multiform

the gradualism of water has left them their salt

ramage   ransack   leave no thing behind

Persephone (Unplugged)

I wake in the dark. My face is a stunned
Cathode-ray tube, a pomegranate
Unharmed. If I were a girl, I would be a girl.
I hate my career, I want to go home
To Avonlea. I am a tortoise shell,
A bell on an alarm clock, a Les Paul.
There are rarely men in my dreams.

The fear in your eyes is no less real
For having bounded up from *Ariel*
Than the disappointed stars on the movie channel.
If I were only a girl, I could give you a hand.

Each afternoon the off-white trumpet-flowers
I just miss touching on my way home from work
Crumple like pillowcases, like antique gloves.
It must be the dew that lifts them
Before first light: clarinet, English horn,
Querulous soprano saxophone.
They are the hills in "Sheep in Fog,"
Tight-lipped in their straight lines.

There are rarely men in my dreams.
One time I became the famous skyscraper
Whose windows littered Boston during storms,
A sparkling skirt spiraling through updrafts.

I wake in the dark. The battle of frogs and mice
Continues under my floorboards.
Somebody from Reuters is there with a big flashlight
And a microphone on her collar. Can't you leave?
Can you take me with you to Avalon?
Can you make a prediction for 1995?

If I were a girl, I could follow you, I say.
The woman from Reuters motions me to hush,
A decisive skirmish is taking place.
The bullfrogs are winning.
All the mice are wearing my pink nightgown.

Paysage Moralisé

Mom and Dad must have believed they had found a safe place:
The ten- and twelve-year-olds they could place
In the neighborhood schools, the teens who would take their place
In a few years, and the young adults who would replace
Themselves if all went well could each find a place
In this frivolous landscape, which nonetheless offered no place
Without its form of scrutiny. Sneakers displaced
The gravel and kicked open a secret place
Under the storm drain, its covers yanked back into place
Above the echoing concrete; a tourney took place
Around the one basketball hoop. It was no place
To write home about, but it wasn't your place
To complain: you nearly lost your place
In the slow novel of your own life (date and place
Of publication unknown) in which you place
As a supporting character. Mark your place
With a match, shut the book, and attend: "I've been running in place,"
Said Ellen, meaning only that her displays
Of mental acuity seemed to have taken place
Not as stunts, nor as ends in themselves, only as place—
Holders for later goals she could never quite place
In her own field of view, but sped toward, hoping to place
In the annals of distance running, as if to plac-
Ate the team on which the whole town plays.
You, on the other hand, have kept your place
In the bleachers complac-
Ently... Look: they sprint toward Kate's new place,
As sunlight keeps them, in its sewn-up lace,
Content with a kiss, a trophy for second place,
And everything you would want, had you once stood in their place.

Morningside Park

Without fear or fault, the green
Expanse of it drops off at acute
Angles, sudden and inconveniently,
Till laden branches bless the rest of the boulevard.
Here you too may mail a letter abroad
Or unfold laundry,
Perform essential services, clip shade
In transient humidity.
                            Bedazzled,
Like a friend you've missed for years, except
That he doesn't know who you are, or want to,
This puffy guy jogs up
Then down, then up the stairs.
I want to cry
At all costs: look, quick wind, I'm one of you!
But each afternoon
The sun strikes, as in bowling,
And all is cleared away, although the wind
Competes: it cleans its area, then punches
Out as night comes on
And drops off the residues, rainily, later, in Queens,
Among the distant congregations. Somebody
Trots a cat on a leash; the smaller
Mutts look up a bit, unnerved,
And prance up, almost bounce, on their back legs,
Having their very
Own vertiginous day.

Nothing I do can satisfy those I care for.
Appropriate flowers grow harder and harder to find.

Dan Chiasson

Dan Chiasson was born in 1971 in Burlington, Vermont. He attended Amherst College and Harvard University, where he received his PhD. The former Director of the Poetry Center at SUNY-Stony Brook, Chiasson now teaches at both Wellesley and Amherst Colleges. He has received a Pushcart Prize, a Whiting Writers' Award, and a Whiting Award in the Humanities, and published poems in The New Yorker, The Paris Review, Poetry, The Threepenny Review, and elsewhere. He is author of two books of poetry, The Afterlife of Objects (University of Chicago Press, 2002) and Natural History (Knopf, 2005). He lives in Sherborn, Massachusetts, with his wife, Annie Adams, and their son, Louis.

My Ravine

How will you know what my poem is like
      until you've gone down my ravine and seen

the box springs, mattresses, bookcases, and desks
      the neighboring women's college dumps each year,

somebody's hairdryer, someone's Herodotus
      a poem's dream landscape, one-half Latinate and

one-half shit, the neighboring women's college's shit?
      Wheelbarrow upon wheelbarrow a humpbacked

custodian hauls old dormitory furniture down
      and launches it watching it roll into the pile.

You won't know how my poem decides what's in,
      what's out, what decorum means and doesn't mean,

until you follow him home after work and see him
      going wild all night imagining those girls' old beds.

You won't know what I'm trying for until you hear
      how every fall in my backyard a swarm of deer

materializes, scavenging where the raspberries touched
      the radishes, now ploughed under, itching the lawn

for dandelions, stare at each other and wander
        bewildered down my ravine and turn into skeletons.

Vermont

I was the west
once. I was paradise.

My beauty ruined me: the old
excuse. Perhaps

if I was rich, remote
or fine—but paradise

is always just
too close, too coarse.

Men made me;
though in memory they seem
more steel than

flesh, more copper
than intelligence or whim, ambition, will—

what makes men, anyway? Always
groaning on the far end

of some lever, sharpening some blade.

If I were farther, Jupiter
or Babylon, the ocean
bottom, I

might have been a story. Stories never ruined anybody.

But paradise is always only
close enough, just

west, the next, the next, the sun
halved every evening on the same line of

the poem, the poem itself

a minute in the history of minutes. Then
decorative and north,
unstoried, white. And after that, pure

thoroughfare. My signs are written twice.

Song for a Play

The grief of little boys will make
them monsters, O,
but winter isn't here, hello.

The grief of little girls will make
them sad and sexy.
They'll dress themselves to be

undressed. They'll have an accident, no no.
The mad mothers, hello.
They all name cats after their long

dead brothers, but that isn't winter.
Winter has a long beard
and a hundred petty quarrels.

The suave fathers are leaving, O. They're leaving
but they wave. They wave
but let their watches stop. They like

the drama of the last tick as the spring
goes slack. Time
is their mausoleum.

The sad old men. When
the world forgets them
they read paperbacks and straighten up.

The ladies with the catheters and
bath benches are here
but winter, O, not winter, no.

But then the snow falls down
the yellow bus stops short
and skids, a tin accordion

there's one voyeur for every
widow's window
and it's winter, O, it's here, hello.

Stealing from Your Mother

I.
Knowing her schedule you're half
way there. Watch the house dim and become

a museum; then

the familiar door, familiar
corridor, familiar
drawer. You know

the heirlooms from the junk.

You saw her cooing attachments form
over the years; now

you know where her best stuff is.

Her ring. Her wedding china.
The cameo of her grandmother.

Those are *pearls* that were
her pearls, and she

is somewhere else now, Florida
or on an errand; you know
several escapes.

There in her closet, under
columns

of forgotten dresses, the sheer

dry-cleaner's plastic like a second skin—

Reward. Now it never wasn't yours.

II.
The poem takes on a conscience. You wish
for your old self, unscrupulous,

pissed. You aren't exceptional.
Your wife wears pearls. Your real house

is a trick of light; the old one, gone,
is real enough to burn. Lacking

conviction, you will spend forever
sentencing yourself. You know

what you did. You know you know
what you did. No one is hearing your ornate confession.

The Elephant

How to explain my heroic courtesy? I feel
        that my body was inflated by a mischievous boy.

I was the size of a falcon, the size of a lion,
        once I was not the elephant I find I am.

My pelt sags, and my master scolds me for a botched
        trick. I practiced it all night in my tent, so I was

somewhat sleepy. People connect me with sadness
        and, often, rationality. Randall Jarrell compared me

to Wallace Stevens, the American poet. I can see it
        in the lumbering tercets, but to my mind

I am more like Eliot, a man of Europe, a man
        of cultivation. Anyone so ceremonious suffers

breakdowns. I do not like the spectacular experiments
        with balance, the high-wire act and cones.

We elephants are images of humility, as when we
        undertake our melancholy migrations to die.

Did you know, though, that elephants were taught
        to write the Greek alphabet with their hooves?

Worn out by suffering, we lie on our great backs,
        tossing grass up to heaven—as a distraction, not a prayer.

That's not humility you see, on our long final journeys:
        it's procrastination. It hurts my heavy body to lie down.

Carrie
St. George Comer

Carrie St. George Comer was born in 1971 in Eufaula, Alabama. She received her BA from Kenyon College and her MFA from the University of Massachusetts at Amherst. Her poems have appeared in *The American Poetry Review, Black Warrior Review, Conduit, Fence, The Iowa Review,* and other journals. Her first collection is *The Unrequited* (Sarabande, 2003). Comer lives in Miami Beach, Florida, with her husband, Benjamin Alsup, and teaches English at the University of Miami.

Long Goodbye

See the body. It is small and thin.
How the bones show through the skin.
See the flecks of polish on the nails,
the nail polish called glitter moth.
Touch the head. Listen for chimes.
Allow your hand through the hair,
the pale hair spread in the mad science light
of mid-morning rain. Press your lips to the feet.
The glitter from the party stuck to the toes
sticks to your lips. Your lips glimmer
like moths by the orange bulb, like rain
on a queue of white shoes in the grass,
like a starry two A.M. and the hole made
by a wild night, through which boys
in white nightshirts step calmly, and descend.
See the body. Still beneath the sheet.
The rain in the window falling sideways
like moths moving westward.
In the room with high ceilings,
in the room with one lamp on,
in the room where you first touched me, see the body.
In the room where paintings lean against the walls.
In the room where you stroke you bare chest,
where you comb and comb your gold hair.
In the room, in the room, in the room where we first
made it, where you pressed your lips to it,
wrapped your big fingers round it,

slid your bold hand right through it. See the body.
Small and thin. Tired and worn. The head bells,
the circles, the room without windows. The room
with the radio on; talk of visitation, talk of fata morgana,
installments of light, boxes of air and darkness,
in the room with no light in it. In the room where we first touched it.
In the room where we were born, where we will die.
See the body. The rageless body. Tell me, what do *you* do with yours?
In the room with one lamp on, what do *you* do, and how?
You have seen it, you have touched it, so was it good?
And did you feel the need to cry when it was done?
There there, they are bringing it out now.
They carry it through the tin corridor of voices
and through the back door. Wrapped in gossamer,
wrapped in cerecloth, in wire, in rosevine,
in silk thread from the shoe factory, in webbing, in chains,
in rope. See the body wrapped in thread from the shoe factory.
Thread made of stolen horses. Thread made of dogs.
Threads of rain.
The body wrapped and left in the driveway.
The body rolling into the street.
Polish on the nails peeking out of the shroud, glitter on the feet.
Wave farewell to the body. Sing to the body as it rolls down the hill,
into the grove and toward the river. Throw marigolds and sing.
Throw doveblooms and sing. Throw a white rose and sing.
Sing low, sing high, sing never come back here again.

Shelburne Falls

A hand in a crevice, the tongue at rest in the mouth,
and also,
the pressure of one body against another: summer, waxed and honeyed.

Rain on the motorbike, rain on the helmet.
Worms on hooks drift beneath the river's surface.

***

On the bridge of flowers,
a bushel of sweet pea, half-open yellow pods; the tropicanas bleed and fade.

Say it, you were alone. You were alone.

On Nightbeat,
a woman's face split like a potato by a bullet, her eye on a spring,
she'd meant to lodge it in her brain, of course.

That's you on the bridge of flowers, watching a dime drop into the water.
That's you in the restaurant, nursing a clam plate.

Say it, this life we share, it will not do.

This dusty house.
These lackluster friends.
These children, and all their friends.

***

Here comes my brother, in his woe suit,
      his woe shoes,
      his woe hat.

Last time we saw him he waved from a ledge of blue light,
his belongings in a paper sack:

goodbye, goodbye.
Now he's here again, in his woe car,
      with his woe dog,
      how he yowls outside the door.

And all my cousins, in a local motel, watching strippers

play with fruit;
the room with pictures of horses on the walls, the ones with white blazes.

***

From here, I watch young boys leap from the rocks.

And there you are, hurling yourself into the air and mooning us.
And then the girl,

who chickened and slipped.
Her ear leaked as they pulled her pale body from the water.

Say it, you were alone. *I was alone.*

And the girl fell from the rocks,
and then what? *Her head struck,*
her ear leaked. I was painting my toes and imagining the deaths

of loved ones. She interrupted me.

Whether the bullet rents the face or buries itself in the skull,
if it blows through the heart,

still, the world, it grows less and less familiar.

***

One town over, a man sketches before dawn,
wingéd humans, only he's serious. His wife carves an ear out of clay.

Two towns over, a one-legged teen poses naked for a magazine.

Listen, seeds shaking in a paper ball,
the banana vendor's whistling.

***

Someday I'll hear it,
the footsteps of my children as they stop to watch the video,
me when I lived with my brand-new cat eyes:

she was plump and fell with a noise
blood leaked from her ear and a large man pulled her from the water

***

Summer: a body rebuilt. Then another.

We arrived in sunlight and drove off in sunlight,

sunlight through rain. Summer: nude and barely breathing,
the sky turning pink and a hush in the willow tops,

love by the humming light,
                          field stars.

That's you knee-deep in river water, thin as a crane.
That's you working the lure from a fish throat.

We're snaking back around now.

We're cheering as the bull enters the woman,
as half-light falls on the roses.
This world

peculiar and at the same time, filled with horses,
large photographs of horses,

their heads on fire.

Arbor

Do you remember the love?
Do you remember the passion that took place there?

No.

Do you remember the white fence? The vine of white blossoms?

Not really.

Do you recall the white mug that rested on the wrought-iron table or the
white gloves that lifted the mug to the thin lips?

No. I don't remember any of that. I wasn't there.

Oh, you were there alright. You couldn't get enough of those long gloves,
those polished shoes, those flowers like stars that came through the trellis
slats like grapes. White grapes. And white like a veil of wind. Do you
remember? We rocked each other in bed at night when noises covered the
old room like a hailstorm, like a wind in the frozen branches. It was Easter.
There were hats everywhere. Hats trimmed with shells and magnolias and
birds made with real feathers. Lilies wrapped around hats like stars.
Remember the girl with grasshoppers in her hair?

No. What color were they?

White. Remember our camel journey? Remember the runaway camel?
Remember the rings in his nose? His ankle bracelets? The great chains of
jasmine he wore to ride through town? Remember the great chains of
jasmine? Remember the abuse we took from the coffee lady? The curtains
hanging everywhere? The mirrored pants? Do you remember those sickly

sweet balls of dough dipped in syrup? The little moon stuck to her white dress? Not crescent, fully waxed, and red, like a spot of blood. I felt sick over everything I had ever done. Remember that?

Not sure.

Remember the murdered pigs and the women who dismembered them?

God, no.

Remember the guesthouses that were really brothels? That man that kept stroking your hair? The girls with numbers pinned to their dresses? The monkeys that ruled the town? The rooms were like enormous showers with barred windows. Remember the funerals that kept us up at night?

What funerals? And what moon?

Remember the time we blew each other under the stars? You know. I blew your schmetterling. You blew my papillon. Remember?

No.

Yes you do, you rode into town for daffodils because I said we must sound like tree frogs bathing in the throat of a daffodil. And as I lay there waiting in the grass, someone was throwing banana peels out of the neighbor's attic window. And I slept in the lingering scent of banana and daffodil. White banana. White daffodil. White grapes hanging in the air like little babies filled with light. And you don't remember?

No, I don't remember.

Do you remember anything, anything at all?

Nope.

Nothing at all?

No, nothing at all.

Well I could never forget. Someone was crying in the juniper bushes because we'd decided to grow old together. And someone was turning the garage into a planetarium. A milk truck stopped at every doorstep and the clinking bottles chased an egret into the clouds. Remember? A red sun rose and burned everything.

Olena Kalytiak Davis

Olena Kalytiak Davis was born in 1963 in Detroit, Michigan. She is a graduate of Wayne State University, the University of Michigan Law School, and the Vermont College MFA Program. Her poems have appeared in numerous journals and anthologies, including four volumes of The Best American Poetry. The recipient of a Guggenheim Fellowship, a Rona Jaffe Foundation Writer's Grant, a Pushcart Prize, several grants from the Alaska and Juneau Arts Councils, and numerous other honors and awards, she is the author of two collections of poetry, And Her Soul Out Of Nothing (University of Wisconsin Press, 1997) and shattered sonnets love cards and other off and back handed importunites (Tin House/Bloomsbury, 2003). She lives and writes and raises her two children in Anchorage, Alaska.

Sweet Reader, Flanneled and Tulled

Reader unmov'd and Reader unshaken, Reader unseduc'd
and unterrified, through the long-loud and sweet-still
I creep toward you. Toward you, I thistle and I climb.

I crawl, Reader, servile and cervine, through this blank
season, counting—I sleep and I sleep. I sleep,
Reader, toward you, loud as a cloud and deaf, Reader, deaf

as a leaf. Reader: *Why don't you turn
pale?* and, *Why don't you tremble?* Jaded, staid
Reader, You—who can read this and not even

flinch. Bare-faced, flint-hearted, recoilless
Reader, dare you—Rare Reader, listen
and be convinced: Soon, Reader,

soon you will leave me, for an italian mistress:
for her dark hair, and her moon-lit
teeth. For her leopardi and her cavalcanti,

for her lips and clavicles; for what you want
to eat, eat, eat. Art-lover, rector, docent!
Do I smile? I, too, once had a brash artless

feeder: his eye set firm on my slackening
sky. He was true! He was thief! In the celestial sense
he provided some, some, some

(much-needed) relief. Reader much-slept with, and Reader I will die
without touching, You, Reader, You: mr. small-
weed, mr. broad-cloth, mr. long-dark-day. And the italian mis-

fortune you will heave me for, for
her dark hair and her moonlit-teeth. You will love her well in-
to three-or-four cities, and then, you will slowly

sink. Reader, I will never forgive you, but not, poor
cock-sure Reader, not, for what you think. O, Reader
Sweet! And Reader Strange! Reader Deaf and Reader

Dear, I understand youyourself may be hard-
pressed to bare this small and un-necessary burden
having only just recently gotten over the clean clean heart-

break of spring. And I, Reader, I am but the daughter
of a tinker. I am not above the use of bucktail spinners,
white grubs, minnow tails. Reader, worms

and sinkers. Thisandthese curtail me
to be brief: Reader, our sex gone
to wildweather. YesReaderYes—that feels much-much

better (And my new Reader will come to me empty-
handed, with a countenance that roses, lavenders, and cakes.
And my new Reader will be only mildly disappointed.

My new Reader can wait, can wait, can wait.) Light-
minded, snow-blind, nervous, Reader, Reader, troubled, Reader,
what'd ye lack? Importunate, unfortunate, Reader:

You are cold. You are sick. You are silly.
Forgive me, kind Reader, forgive me, I had not intended to step this
      quickly this far
back. Reader, we had a quiet wedding: he&I, theparson

&theclerk. Would I could, stead-fast, gracilefacile Reader! Last,
good Reader, tarry with me, jessa-mine Reader. Dar-
(jee)ling, bide! Bide, Reader, tired, and stay, stay, stray Reader,

true. *R.: I had been secretly hoping this would turn into a love poem.* Disconsolate. Illiterate. Reader,
I have cleared this space for you, for you, for you.

Thirty Years Rising

I needed to point to the buildings, as if they all stood
for something, as if Detroit could rise again
into its own skyline, filled in
as it always is inside me:
each cracked sidewalk, each
of the uniformed girls, braided
and quiet as weeds, each bicycled boy, each man
with a car and a wife, the ones I slept with
and arranged, neatly, like a newly laid
subdivision.

But I was driving with my brother
who doesn't like to think
of the thirty years rising
inside us, the leavened truth. He's arrived
at the heavy black X of destination
on the inside of his forehead
and he doesn't want to see me
looking like this: open-palmed
and childishly dressed, with hipbones
instead of children, aching
to put my sneakered feet on his new leather
dash.

He doesn't want to hear me
say something fucked-up, something like:
It's in my bones. My sternum
runs like Woodward Avenue,
it's pinnated, parked on, full
of dirt, holding women in wigs and cigarettes, bars
lit from the outside in, it's overflowing
with pooltables and ashtrays. My ribs
are holding up factories and breweries, two-bedroom
houses and multi-storied lives, this strip,
this city, these sidestreets,
a bony feather.

He's lived here all his life.
But I gave up these streets
for so many others. I hopped
turnstiles to ride the Metro,
memorized EL tracks and Muni stations
until I had a huge worn subway
map on the inside of my head, but couldn't get off at any stop,
couldn't begin to live in any city, and couldn't sleep
with anybody but myself. I gave up
this body for so many others. I've been both
an exaggeration of myself and someone
who looks just like me but sounds different.
But now I'm back
to visit both, and I need to point
to my first hotel room;
to the mortuary above which
my tall half-chinese half-german
punkrockboyfriend fingered me
like a book in his little bed;
and to the hospital where our bonemother
died so late or so early that
we were both sound asleep.

I didn't say it,
but: My sternum is breaking
with this, it's sinking
like Woodward as Detroit rises around
my brother's turn, rises and falls.
Falls not at all like this light summer rain
but hard, like someone else's memory,
insistent, unwanted, but suddenly,
and again, being claimed.

All the Natural Movements of the Soul

the swan dive
the back flip
the jack knife

the way it wants to lean over things—

I was bent over my poems
like some crazy mother. Dinner was burning

on the floor. Yes, the distinct smell
of piss. Not much washing
but the spinning, the rinsing,
the sad steam of those who launder hung
in the air; there were slots for quarters,
they were the sockets of my eyes.

I don't want to blame anyone, but somehow:

the situation is always grave.

Then one afternoon, everything goes into remission.

Then there are whole days when nothing happens,
when I start asking simple questions like:

in what do you believe?

The way the soul wants
to lean over things,
the way the soul wants to leave

the way it wants to write
another lunch poem
it wants to protect itself
it wants to become famous
at the same time.

There were whole day-long days,
summer days like grace notes:

the trill of being high on a porch
that wrapped itself around the stars.

We sat around trying to name
the things that do not exist.
We sat there wanting to touch
everything again and again, only this time
we would be blindfolded, our arms ribboned
behind our backs, using only our tongues.

I thought, please don't grow
familiar. I think I said it out loud:
Please don't let me love you
that horrible way.

The situation is grave:

the way we lean over each other, the way years
later we emerge: hunchbacked, hooded,
with full grown tender things called souls.

The Unbosoming

I have been a day boarder, Lord. I have preferred the table to the Bed.
I have proffered, Lord, and I have profited, Lord, but little, but not. I was Bored,
Lord, I was heavy, Lord. Heavy bored. Hopeless, Lord, hideous, Lord. Sexless.
I was in love, Lord, but not with You. The nine malic moulds, Lord.
The butcher, the baker, the under-taker. Lord, I was taken under. I Repeat
Myself, Lord. I re-peat myself as the way back, the way back to Myself,
Lord. I have trembled, Lord. His face, Lord, and Yours. I am unlovely, Lord, I Nam
Not precious, Lord. Spy better, Love, and You will see: Inamnothing. I have Seen
How lovely, Lord, how lovely You are, Lord, but I refused to kneel. I Refuse
To knell Your loveliness. I refuse to kiss. And I refuse to tell. I am unwilling, Love.
I am unwell. Unkempt. My hideous loins, Love. My body, which is all Wrack
And screw, Love. All slack and crewel. At Your beck and call, Love, at His Beck
And call. Crestfallen, Love. Of the fallen breast. Un-clean of eye. Loose of Thigh.
Ridiculous, Love. Most serious, Love. Unshod. Unshriven. In vain and in Rain,

Love. I Live and I Wire. I Wive, Lord, but I Fathom Not.

If You Are Asked

Tell them

Your view has always been mullioned. Admit
Your own visions have always struck you
As useless, the way a photograph of spring can mean nothing
In spring. Refer to the books that have left you thumbmarked, open:
Or if you cannot remember their authors, simply show them
The thumbmarks, the indentations, that is, that are

Your temples. Mention you suspect the rest
Is merely ablation. Do not confuse them by speaking of the spite
Weeded out from the spikenard, of what the rosemallow does
Before it blooms. The saltmarshes, melting. The wired horizon.
Perhaps you should warn them:

This may not be for the faint of heart.

If you speak of the cloud
Of your unknowing, the longboat
Of your unknowing, the easychair
Of your unknowing, to them it will sound
Redundant.

Pace yourself.
Keep it short.

You do not want to risk disappearing in the middle
Of a sentence. Do not talk

Swedenborg, not even out in the garden,
Not even when you know what you are talking about: the burden
Made of burdock, the nettlesome heart. Why mention
The plow, the harrow, the tending to the empty? Remember,

To them you look just like a thirty-three(nine)-year-old woman.
You are a thirty-three(nine)-year-old woman, with or without

Your strange husbandry: the quiet apiary
Out back, the seed packets of fallow.
Do not get in that
Car. Admit that your life is still
Still and folded.

Show them the contact
Sheet. Do not

Mislead them by telling them your father died
Without troubling you. By not mentioning he never really wanted to be
That lucky. His rough-hewn hands.

You have already told them about your rose-strewn mother.

About the thin girl who lives across the street:
Tell them, you suspect some people actually inhabit
Their bodies. You, however, have suffered in a different

Way.

Do not call it suffering.

When asked about youth admit yours too was wasted.
When asked about beauty admit that you have been asking, too.
When asked about truth simply nod, yes.

You have already told them about your rose-strewn mother.

Try not to repeat yourself. When they ask you
About your influences

Be truthful, begin by mentioning
The weather: point to the lowlying clouds, or, if necessary,
The empty sky.

Then, but not angrily, quote them some Hopkins or just try to
Use the verbs: selves, faiths in a sentence

Out on a street that follows itself, a longing, in your pocket

A fraying photograph of spring and a list of words
You have always dreamt of.

You always knew you could not keep god's attention.

And it doesn't work, bulletproofing the heart.
The phenomenology of the soul, you have turned
And returned to it: the tending and the attending, the paying

With only your attention. Now, thin as a cloud,
You have carefully begun scraping out the inscape.
Tell them you fully intend to pitch it slowly
From without and within with pitch.

You have always wanted to be plainspoken.
You would have preferred to be misunderstood, tell them,

Like this.

Mónica de la Torre

Mónica de la Torre was born in 1969 in Mexico City and came to the U.S. in 1993 on Fulbright scholarship, in order to pursue an MFA at Columbia University. Her poems, reviews, and translations appear in *American Poetry Review, ARTnews, BOMB, Boston Review, Cabinet, Chain, Fence,* and elsewhere. De la Torre has translated the *Selected Poems of Gerardo Deniz* (Lost Roads, 1999), co-authored *Appendices, Illustrations & Notes* with artist Terence Gower (Smart Art Press, 2000), and co-edited, with Michael Wiegers, the anthology *Reversible Monuments: Contemporary Mexican Poetry* (Copper Canyon, 2002). *Acúfenos,* a collection of her poems in Spanish, is forthcoming from Editorial Ditoria in Mexico City. De la Torre is a PhD student at Columbia and Poetry Editor of *The Brooklyn Rail*. She lives in Brooklyn.

How to Look at Mexican Highways

1. You are not going anywhere.
    1.1. No one is waiting for you.
    1.2. In case someone is waiting for you, you can always explain the delay later.
    1.3. Blame it on the traffic, no one else knows that you chose to walk.

2. Don't look at the pavement, look at the things that you don't see when you're indoors.
    2.1. Water towers.
    2.2. Cables.
        2.2.1. Cables bringing other people's voices and faces onto TV monitors.
        2.2.2. Cables bringing electricity to light bulbs and refrigerators.
    2.3. Laundry on clotheslines.
    2.4. Empty cans of food.
        2.4.1. With flowers growing out of them.
        2.4.2. With cactuses growing out of them.

3. Feel the waves surrounding you.
    3.1. Waves bringing other people's voices to the speaker of your sound system.
    3.2. Waves of street sounds.

4. Measure how fast you can run up and down staircases; compare that to the speed the cars driving by.

5. When you tire, stand in the middle of the overpass.
    5.1. Look down.
    5.2. Try to look ahead, attempt to delineate the city's skyline.

5.2.1. If there's too much pollution, look down again.
5.2.2. Hold on tighter to the rail.
5.2.3. Stay there a bit longer; remember no one is waiting for you.
5.2.4. You're not going anywhere.

6. Through the rails you will see stories unfolding on the street.
  6.1. Pay attention.
  6.2. You are not them.
  6.3. They are not them.
    6.3.1. They are one plus one plus one, indefinitely.

7. You're surrounded by monads going somewhere.

8. There is a purpose to their movement.

9. Desire is a federacy.

Driven by a Strange Desire

I. Before Breakfast

When the sun turns gray and I become tired
of looking at your many colored shoes

I will give you balloons for all the holes
we speak too much to fill. Who believes

in air, nowadays? Or do you prefer tea
with the dried fruit I will have to throw out

the window of your room? Because I want
this to stop I want this to stop I want this

II. Toward the Moors in Spain

To kill the dragons is a different thing
in my family there are only lizards.

In Sevilla—never famous for its lamps—
a dissected crocodile hangs from a roof.

The reptile, the Crown's Byzantine gift. Its teeth
suspended in the air of the cathedral.

I stole a pair of shoes; but didn't run away
from the orchard where water had women's scent.

Thirst is not fear, thirst is not green, but has wings
like dragons, or airplanes. As oranges

in Sevilla, driven by a strange desire
to stay where they are. Floating. Suspended.

III. Toward Virgo

The Milky Way is not only expanding;
the Bang is not only a Bang. It is drifting

and being pulled away from, let's say, something.
Because dark matter is ninety nine of what

there is and visible matter is so small
it clusters together and forms a Great Wall.

China and Spain and my eyes reading the paper.
We are still together, are we not, wondering if.

Golfers in the Family

for Carolee Schneemann

A Brit exclaims "O to build character in a playground riddled with hazards!
O gusts of wind, bumpy treeless fairways, deep bunkers, knee-high rough!"

Golf should be played by the seashore was the dictum Scots received from
Nature. They have been much relieved to find this in accord with their
Calvinist beliefs. Man is meant to suffer; never more than when he goes out
to enjoy himself.

Despite his preference for courses designed to penalize players who stray
from the path from tee to green, an American claims "Games ought not to
be played in moral gymnasiums: give me vistas, decorative ponds, token
fairway bunkers!" (Far more than anybody else, Americans have found
hanging watercolors of golf courses in the bathrooms of their homes in
good taste. The choice of Wal-Mart's interior decorators to have them
enliven restrooms must also have been informed by this longing for pastoral
environments.)

As in other developing countries, in Chinese boomtowns the real business deals are done while playing golf. (Some test potential partners by playing with them first.) If in China the way of doing business is lubricated by guanxi, in Mexico, for instance, it's lubricated by the drinks the caddy helpfully provides. (By the way, certain circumstances allow for betting to be considered business.)

Whatever one's nationality is one mustn't forget the ancient maxim: *Forget length when you're in a bunker from hell; make sure you get out of it before you get ambitious.*

Wives and daughters of golfers around the globe identify with their being excluded from the game; they either don't understand the language of golf or they speak it with far too much trepidation. They like that their men are out facing hazards, the familiarity between tea and tee, and the fraternal spirit of the handicap system.

(Another aside: It is not infrequent for some women to picture men naked when they feel harassed by them. In their minds, men almost immediately lose their threatening power. Some men feel naked at the golf course, their weaknesses far from concealed. Golf outfits spell overcompensation.)

Those who nervously flick remote controls tend to oversee the intended poetry of this far from telegenic game. Any player would sustain that more than any other sport, the aim of the game—to complete the course in the fewest possible strokes—looks infinitely easier than it is.

Like courses themselves, the history of the game has been non-linear. Main controversies have involved, unsurprisingly, the introduction of techno-logical advances into the game. Rubber-core balls were considered nearly prosthetic when they first appeared in 1898. Those who excelled at playing with the Indian gutta-percha balls stuck to them, assuming that the fashioning of their shots required far more artistry and improvisation. The gutty had in turn replaced the 400-year-old feather ball, which got soggy when wet and was stuffed with top-hatfuls of boiled feathers. (Bear in mind that while I write this someone is firing innumerable shots not far from here.) One can guess why balls needed to be nicked and cut in order not to duck quickly in flight. Indented and dimpled balls were far more resistant than smooth-surfaced ones, which would necessarily dent when banging trees and other hard surfaces.

Speaking of birds, to see is to believe. Not wanting to soil the idea of golf as the game of eternal hope with its promised lands beyond every horizon, we'll leave out the issue about the dead blackbirds, blue jays, coots, geese, grackles, gulls, mallards, robins, starlings, widgeons and other etceteras.

Without enough information to prove that the pesticides used to enhance the greens' greenness provide courses with bountiful doses of neurotoxins and mutagenic substances, why ruin people's chance to experience earthly paradise? Those 546 geese collected in a golf course in Hempstead at least can say they died in heaven. The reader should try to figure out whether snakes and rodents suffer from context disorder when the desert they dwell in is transformed into a tropical environment. *Change or die!*

Let us tread upon a course where the cardinal rule of enlightened (and Spartan, indeed) design is followed: a first class hole must present the player with an alternate route to the green.

Timothy Donnelly

Timothy Donnelly was born in 1969 in Providence, Rhode Island, and attended Johns Hopkins University, Columbia University, and Princeton University. He has been Poetry Editor of *Boston Review* since 1995. His own poems have appeared in *Conduit, Crowd, Denver Quarterly, Fence, jubilat, The Paris Review, Verse,* and elsewhere. His honors include a fellowship from the New York State Writers Institute, *The Paris Review*'s Bernard F. Conners Prize, and Columbia University's David Craig Austin Award. In 2003, he was named an "It Poet" by *Entertainment Weekly*. His first book of poems is *Twenty-seven Props for a Production of* Eine Lebenszeit (Grove Press, 2003). Donnelly teaches in the Writing Division of Columbia University's School of the Arts. He lives in Brooklyn.

Twenty-seven Props for a Production of *Eine Lebenszeit*

Let there be *lamps* of whatever variety
presents itself on the trash heaps. Let chance
determine how many, but take pains
to use only low-watt bulbs, and keep the lion's share
flickering throughout the performance.
In particular, one gooseneck should pulsate religiously
on the leeward corner of an *escritoire*,
which is a writing table, or an unhinged door

suspended on sawhorses. These will be spattered
in a clash of pigments, signifying history.
Dust is general over all the interior.
You are very tired. You are very weary.
On the floor, one *carpet*, its elaborate swirling
recalling the faces of wind on old maps.
And let there be *maps*, at least half reimagining
the world according to a scattered century:

a shambles, patched. Now for the *wall-clock*
which hangs prodigiously over every act. Let's rig it
so the hour revolves in a minute, the minute
in a blur. Grab hold of an enormous *mirror*
and mount it divinely—that is, too high to bear human reflection.
And what do you call it when you can't endure

the scraping of the blades of all creation?
There'll be a *bucket* of *that*, another for the *suet*,

a third marked SESAME but filled with *sand*.
Place this last a judicious distance
from the bamboo *cage* in which one *ostrich*, plucked,
stands Tantalus-style, its beak eternally
approaching the rim of the third of the buckets.
Does the bird want seed, or is it onto the trick
and terrified, frantic to bury its head in the sand?
Will it never end? But look who I'm asking!

Take your worry to the *sofa*, lie there.
There's a pillar of *books* and a French *periodical*
on either side. Before you know it,
it's always midnight. Now the *owl* of Minerva
takes its flight down the nickel wire.
Now a *dampness* pumps from the tightened fist
of a cold *contraption*, a sort of inverse
radiator, you can't control it, and it isn't pretty.

Tell me you love me. There's a severed *hand*,
or is it a fruit peel? Tell me you love me
and I make it mild. Take your panic to the *sleigh-bed*,
slump there. There's a snatch of *heather*
and a cracked *decanter* on the starboard side.
Before you know it, it's always never.
You know I hate it when you whimper, don't you?
Now shut them big ambiguous eyes.

Now shut that cavernous cartoon mouth—
and here's the *sock* to fill it, periwinkle!
You know I hate it when we don't coordinate.
Now what's that rapping at the shattered *window*?
It's the only egress, I neglected to mention.
But here's a *rope* with knots to help you shimmy down—
a dozen square knots, the last a hangman's.
Now take your heaving to the *curtains*, part.

They're dove gray, dolly, and fall like art.

Three Panels Depending on the Heart

1. Known Minutiae

Because I could forever, my theatrical body
doubled over the bathtub estranged, a volcano;
might continue clenched in this arrangement

of numb white tile, white fixture, unfeelingly
learning, a bent apprentice to the pitch
of the wave of what mourning tows me along.

Because it is wrong, to know I should stop
but not stop, meaning: not push the urge
or act to conclusion, make good of my face and have faith

in her heaven. And because I am crude,
wanting anyone   you   to proctor this drama
however impure, I unlock the loud door.

I have known only minutes, known minutiae
of sorrow but not the sad hour, what such should amount to:
that crushed lids burnish a hazel eye green;

that the body, in shock, throws interior out
to consider itself in new aspects of grief
too sudden to count. I have failed part to part

with the heat of a novice. So father, be father.
Do difficult math in this doorway of air,
unhold to prepare me. Do not repeat how full is my

heart. Tell me   how   much must it part with.

2. Willful to Sicken

Among mourners, she is stillest, a stone pillar
against the cruel fact of August, the slumped
animal heat of a summer worn out welcome,

out poppies, out purpose. In the window up front,
a saint floats solemnly, tongued by the flame
that will make him a martyr; nine cherubim poke

through the wreath of his smoke, at ease as he is
easeful at heart, burning. Whatever happens
happens, almost invariably. Even I know this.

And if I am meant, I am meant to keep calm, watch
everything unfold, cold as apostles—days,
nights, down in the shadows, devoted, fretless; an echo

banging on the eggshell vault—but why am I
almost always the opposite, swine from the bible
set loose and diabolical, a herd of my own?

I have felt what I feel form a swarm of contagion
reddening to pass through the pores of my face
and willful to sicken, to work itself into another—

I am not what I would be but know how I am,
willing her to pivot, to confront me
sloppy when taken to the trough of such leaf-green

grief that I can't resist. And when she turns
in the pew before mine, face pressed smooth
as the linen that proves her, I rise choked

through an incensed air, proud of my heart
because of what wrecked it, and prouder to infect
the one left living that would wreck it more.

3. The Truer

I will not give in. I will grow more strange.
I will wrap myself around your ghost till the ghost
itself wants letting go, till it shimmers free.

—And what an empty struggle. It'll only show
it wasn't you I held this way; there will be deceiving.
I've found my strengths since last we spoke,

and they're all tenacity; I've hitched to the house
as I would before, stood in the shade of your
stolid tree and wrapped myself around that, too.

I am not adapting. In a book of primates,
I'm the one macaque left clinging fast
as the others flee, all eyes and drastic

limbs and will, though the last acacia
falls to drought. When arboreal things
take leave of trees, or the ghosts of trees,

they slump in threnody. My hands are yours
that block it out, and we will never know it.
Though tussocked grasses bend and fade

in the risen wind, though the risen wind
rides its own solution. Though the planets fizzle,
I will not give in. Though deserts shudder,

supervene, I will grow more strange, and you will
watch that weathering. Crude in the heart
you once held delicate, creased in the face

you once turned from, frantic to practice
returning. Weakened, surely. But the stronger for it.
And the truer. You will not mistake me.

The New Intelligence

After knowledge extinguished the last of the beautiful
fires our worship had failed to prolong, we walked
back home through pedestrian daylight, to a residence

humbler than the one left behind. A door without mystery,
a room without theme. For the hour that we spend
complacent at the window overlooking the garden,

we observe an arrangement in rust and gray-green,
a vagueness at the center whose slow, persistent
movements some sentence might explain if we had time

or strength for sentences. To admit that what falls
falls solitarily, lost in the permanent dusk of the particular.
That the mind that fear and disenchantment fatten

comes to boss the world around it, ugly as the damp-
fingered guest who rearranges the cheeses the minute the host
turns to fix her a cocktail. A disease of the will, the way

the false birch branches arch and interlace from which
hands dangle the last leaf-parchments and a very large array
of primitive bird-shapes. Their pasted feathers shake

in the aftermath of the nothing we will ever be content
to leave the way we found it. I love that about you.
I love that when I call you on the long drab days practicality

keeps one of us away from the other that I am calling
a person so beautiful to me that she has seen my awkwardness
on the actual sidewalk but she still answers anyway.

I say that when I fell you fell beside me and the concrete
refused to apologize. That a sparrow sat for a spell
on the windowsill today to communicate the new intelligence.

That the goal of objectivity depends upon one's faith
in the accuracy of one's perceptions, which is to say
a confidence in the purity of the perceiving instrument.

I won't be dying after all, not now, but will go on living dizzily
hereafter in reality, half-deaf to reality, in the room
perfumed by the fire that our inextinguishable will begins.

Birdsong from Inside the Egg

As meteors pierce the sky's tin vault,
so molecules sail through the many

pores of my own enclosure, what trash what
treasure, piss and brilliance, a fleet of

snippets shed from the vast exterior's
chaos haystack, flop and fodder, there

is no NO, not here, not yet. I have been
forever, I am not yet born. Into the one

tremendous whistling laze of this, my
pulsed amalgam, I admit the all, a just lie

back and snap! arrangement, confetti
hoof and concertina, what blind mouth's

breath what pleasant nesting. I am
a composition, the one life's work I have

been forever, the loom and the wool and the mat
for dreaming. The song that's tensed

in past as happened "just like that" is
too much once, and lying back to bask in basking's

tongues of flash, I can't believe it.
One's quarantine's a peace pinched-in

with heavenly visits. A heavenly visit
has no close. Take the most exquisite

moment in the gallop, where all four
hooves now tread the air, and stretch it

taut indefinitely, shot through as it is
with hops and dung and does and loves,

and you have an inkling. An inkling sparks
half the congregation when you rub it right,

half the congregation when you rub it wrong.
I am song forever. I will not have sung.

Ben Doyle

Ben Doyle was born in 1973 in Warsaw, New York, and grew up in and around Cuba, New York. He completed his undergraduate education at SUNY-Oswego and West Virginia University, and received his MFA from the University of Iowa Writers' Workshop. His poems have appeared in *Boston Review, Colorado Review, Fence, The New Republic, Tin House,* and elsewhere. The Editor of Kuhl House Books, Doyle is also bassist and singer for the rock and roll band, Braille Drivers, and producer of the recently formed girl-group, The Diets. His first collection of poems, *Radio, Radio* (Louisiana State University Press, 2001), won The Academy of American Poets' Walt Whitman Award. Doyle is currently an Assistant Professor of English at Denison University in Granville, Ohio.

The War Is Over

Not an acquiescence of surrender,
the bra hung from the flagpole.

The bra is black & there is no wind for once.
For once there is no wind & a spark that is a bird
brings a straw to an empty C-cup. A spark

that is a spark. That is the sun on the steel pole.
That is the oldest thing & then is gone, like the war,

whose trench is gone, because it is full of
red iron-clot soil, because there are lawnchairs
reclined on top of it (empty, but warm, still warm,

sweat-wet & stretched-out) & a white plastic table
with a pitcher of dark iced tea upon it.

The ice is half melted. Clear water waits near the brim.
The wasp waving in it annoys a piece of dust so minute
it might not be there. In its head is only enough space

for a split second of a song it heard the third of July, a trombone belch
muted with a pink plunger-head. The war was over again,
the parade began hitchless, history was history, a refugee

pinned a Purple Heart on a brave bomb & a drop of brown
blood rolled down its chest like a tumbling tumbleweed

as the saints came marching in in white fur hats, in white plastic
shoes, in tuxedoes matching the color-scheme of decrepit glory,
glockenspieled, anacondad in sousaphones, a trombone

with a wasp on its brass bell resting its wings.
It is pausing on my reflection, midtone, in the center of my stain.

Then there is the snapshot of the sky departing generously,
perhaps forever. Appropriately dark, we finally see the "grand finale"
& realize it is only the preceding parts pushed closely together

& we think we are all a bit relieved,
although we are afraid to admit even this.

Our Man

We knew we had our man when his limp switched.
And when the glove fit. And by his unusual hat size.
We knew we had our man when the ballistic tests
returned from headquarters. When the other glove fit.
We knew we had our man by the scratches around his eyes.
When the van of nuns gave their eyewitness testimony,
that's when we knew we had our man. We knew we
had our man by his guilty plea, & by his high-pitched
voice (which matched the tapes)—just like a woman's.
When we dialed up his web page. We knew we had our
man when we located the security footage, & voilà: our man.
Let the record show that we knew we had our man by the
blood dousing the scene, by the semen deposits, the prints.
We knew we had our man when we pried his trunk open
and found the grocery bags stuffed with horsehair beards,
bleach, dye, tan-in-a-bottle, the ransom note, the suicide
note, the travelers' checks, the unmarked bills, the bodies,
the bunk passport; the certificates of authenticity. Maps of steam
tunnels that span the city's subterrain. We knew when his alibi
didn't stack up—she had never seen him; his parents
(weeping their loss in their bests) never had known him a day.
When the other glove fit. We knew we had our man when

the contract shrink pronounced him saner than anyone
in the pine-polished courtroom, & when we showed
an epic of motive, but without a crime or victim
our man stumbled home sovereign, encumbered only by a row
of famished reporters, cars & buses feeling themselves
through the streets, corpuscular, a slight headwind.

Forensics

1
What was happening in the kitchen awfully.
How many chambers in the grinning gun.
When we surveyed the pink dot on the lanai's rail.
Where is the case with the conic sections in.
Why was it all congealing the autos spilled over.
Who really is Peter the Voyeur the getaway driver.
When it was happening were they aghast or what.
What is ball lightning anyway, hell's hail. Who are walking
nearer our inauspicious congregation. Why always this
the girders of the place look chewed
by moths in cloth & clumsy. Where the enormous intellect
that sputters out answers like a ground-meat grinder.
How is it going. When was the story named "Mysteries Explained"
                    starting:

> *Lemme tell you somethin'! Do you know what you gotta go through if*
> *you're a witness? You gotta put on a shirt & tie, drag myself downtown*
> *& hang around till the case comes up, which you never know when. And*
> *by the time it does, you forget what you was gonna say, & the other*
> *lawyer makes a monkey out of you! And it all goes on your record!*

2
What we need is a crane & to chain chains
around this blood-soaked ＿＿＿＿＿＿. The kitchen
workers hang from the vents with duct tape.
We need the ＿＿＿＿＿＿ put on a slide, there were
signs of struggle. There is always some precedent:
You have heard, I think, about H.,
whoever he was, & how he met his death because his
father had too much suspicion...this you will not believe,
and I can hardly prove it, but I am that same H....
You would not have known me, not in any part,

for I was simply one great wound... Can you compare
your loss with my disaster—an enormous clear glass slide,
a landing pad for the _____. Cracked clear through,
splintered, blooddust clinging to tiny & numerous shards

3
Try to create an own legend
to gloss the map that extends
strangely understep. The grass
is browning swinging on the
roof of.   The ceiling.
The pavement hard & heading
between bent buildings.
An ice atom atoms are even
in the tugging air. Northward
toward the axis pin. I am
a sling dusting for whorls.
Hundreds. Hair in a hanged man's
mouth a vernacular of fiber
a punctuation of blood, roots.
The map has no legend is only
a square of white fur. Outside
the square: the wall,
the wall, the cold wet red wall

4
Flowers. Dew hardens on & on &. How many first frosts
on us. Underfoot a rug of brittle plantbones.
At ten, I saw a man in a whitecoat pinch
a red rubber ball with steel tongs & dip it in a bowl
of steam. He hurled the ball wallward & it
shattered like glass. Was glass. Red glass, slowly melting
soft in the science center. We went to the aluminum
cone to watch the girls touch it. Eleven, their hair floats
like big wings up & everywhere. The electric surge
in the heart if I touched it—giggling, the girls are giggling.
Someone's intestine in a silver saucepan. Eager I look for
traceable blade ruts & fold it into a plastic bag.
Evidence hardens in or around us. Twelve,
a room an open wound, frothed with clues.

Thomas Sayers Ellis

Thomas Sayers Ellis was born in 1963 and grew up in Washington, D.C. A cofounder of The Dark Room Collective, an influential African American writers' group and reading series, he holds an MFA from Brown University. Ellis's poems have appeared in The American Poetry Review, AGNI, Boston Review, Grand Street, Ploughshares, Tin House, and elsewhere, including two volumes of The Best American Poetry. He has received a Pushcart Prize and fellowships from the Ohio Arts Council and The Fine Arts Work Center in Provincetown. Ellis's first collection, The Good Junk (1996), was published in the first annual Graywolf Take Three series. He is also the author of The Genuine Negro Hero (Kent State University Press, 2001) and The Maverick Room (Graywolf 2005), as well as the coeditor of On the Verge: Emerging Poets and Artists (New Cambridge Press, 1994). Ellis teaches at Case Western Reserve University and in the low-residency MFA program at Lesley University, serves as a contributing editor for Callaloo, and is currently compiling and editing Quotes Community: Notes for Black Poets. He lives in Cleveland, Ohio.

Sticks

My father was an enormous man
Who believed kindness and lack of size
Were nothing more than sissified
Signs of weakness. Narrow-minded,

His eyes were the worst kind
Of jury—deliberate, distant, hard.
No one could outshout him
Or make bigger fists. The few

Who tried got taken for bad,
Beat down, their bodies slammed.
I wanted to be just like him:
Big man, man of the house, king.

A plagiarist, hitting the things he hit,
I learned to use my hands watching him
Use his, pretending to slap mother
When he slapped mother.

He was sick. A diabetic slept
Like a silent vowel inside his well-built,
Muscular, dark body. Hard as all that
With similar weaknesses

—I discovered writing,
How words are parts of speech
With beats and breaths of their own.
Interjections like flams. Wham! Bam!

An heir to the rhythm
And tension beneath the beatings,
My first attempts were filled with noise,
Wild solos, violent uncontrollable blows.

The page tightened like a drum
Resisting the clockwise twisting
Of a handheld chrome key,
The noisy banging and tuning of growth.

Atomic Bride

for Andre Foxxe

A good show
Starts in the
Dressing room

And works its way
To the stage.
Close the door,

Andre's cross-
dressing, what
A drag. All

The world loves
A bride, something
About those gowns.

A good wedding
Starts in the
Department store

And works its way
Into the photo album.
Close the door,

Andre's tying
The knot, what
A drag. Isn't he

Lovely? All
The world loves
A bachelor, some-

thing about glamour
& glitz, white
Shirts, lawsuits.

A good dog
Starts in the yard
And works its way

Into da house.
Close your eyes.
Andre's wide open,

One freak of the week
Per night, what
A drag. Isn't

He lovely? All
The world loves
A nuclear family,

Something about
A suburban home,
Chaos in order.

A good bride starts
In the laboratory
And works his way

To the church.
Close the door,
Andre's thinking

Things over, what
A drag. Isn't
He lovely? All

The world loves
A divorce, something
About broken vows.

A good war starts
In the courtroom
And works its way

To the album cover.
Close the door,
Andre's swearing in,

What a drag.
Isn't he lovely? All
The world loves

A star witness,
Something about
Cross-examination.

A good drug starts
In Washington
And works its way

To the dance floor.
Close the door,
Andre's strung out,

What a drag,
Isn't he lovely? All
The world loves

Rhythm guitar,
Something about
Those warm chords.

A good skeleton
Starts in the closet
And works its way

To the top of the charts.
Start the organ.
Andre's on his way

Down the aisle,
Alone, what an encore. All
The world loves

An explosive ending.
Go ahead, Andre,
Toss the bouquet.

Slow Fade to Black

for Thomas Cripps

and in memory of The Lincoln, The Republic
& The Booker T. Theaters,
formerly of U Street, N.W.

Like a clothesline of whites
Colored hands couldn't reach,
a thousand souls crossed
promised air and the screen glowed
like something we were supposed
to respect & fear. Daylight
& Sunday were outside,
waiting to segregate darkness
with prejudices of their own.
A silhouette behind a flashlight
led us down an aisle
into The Shadow World,
rows & rows of runaways
awaiting emancipation.
Theater, belly, cave,
ate what got in.
We half dreamt weightlessness,
salvation, freedom, escape.
A resurrection of arms,
we wished were wings,
reached in & out of greasy buckets
picking something the precise
color & weight of cotton.
Just above heads,

Pam Grier & Richard Roundtree
dodged bullets
and survived falls from as high
as heaven—miracles
not worth building
dreams on. And like an ampersand
between eyes & ears,
the soundtrack strung
together images
the way popcorn butter & soda syrup
held us to earth.

Zapruder

Day off in dark suit and hat,
looking through the viewfinder
of a new eight millimeter Bell & Howell camera,
paying no mind the open windows, the seizure.
Just how more than half the targets on the grassy knoll
are potential customers, models, women,
how accident and aim could fit them all,
including the car, into frame. It was the sixties,
so before the volume of the motorcade
turned north up Houston then down on Elm,
they passed the camera between them like a joint,
a silent investment. His secretary stood next to him,
confident that their film would change lives,
that what the women wore to greet the president
would influence their sewing machines and needles.
Clicking the power on added something
above and below human to autumn. Now comes history,
that moment when everything begins to wave:
arms, flags, lens, minutes, seconds, silence,
dressmaker, souvenir, evidence.

Andrew Feld

Andrew Feld was born in 1961 in Cambridge, Massachusetts. He received his BA from the University of Massachusetts and his MFA from the University of Houston, where he was awarded a James Michener Fellowship. His other honors include a Wallace Stegner Fellowship from Stanford University, the "Discovery"/The Nation Award, two Pushcart Prizes, and a poem in The Best American Poetry 2005. His work has appeared in AGNI, New England Review, Poetry, The Virginia Quarterly Review, and elsewhere. His first book, Citizen: Poems (HarperCollins, 2004), was a National Poetry Series Selection. Feld is Associate Professor and Writer-in-Residence at Carthage College. He lives in Racine, Wisconsin, with his wife, the poet Pimone Triplett, and their baby, Lukas.

On Fire

Having been taught by fools, how else could I have ended up
but as I am? a man who panics at the sound of his own voice,
a blusterer, afraid that within the five-pointed maple leaf there lies
another name he never knew; ready, always, to be found wrong.

Listen: in my tenth year they put me in a room where one plane
watched another plane fly over a city. It was morning in both
places. In black & white at first the explosion looked like water
rising. Captured, they say, on film, as in: pulled out of time

so we can rewind it and watch it happen again, as in a memory,
as in: this is a memory we all have, these are our family pictures.
There was that kind of shame. As if the fire really had been stolen.
And sitting on the floor there was one boy who even earlier

that year came home to find his mother hanging from a rope
in the kitchen. What didn't he know that he needed this film
to teach him? Already what he knew was enough to terrify
the teachers, so that they couldn't look at him. But they also

couldn't not look at him. As if he was an obscene pleasure.
And he was beautiful. Complete. But what he carried in him
seeped out as hate for anyone of the same sex as his mother.
It was that simple: even a fourth-grade mind could understand.

So the girls stayed away. And from the other side of the common
room, where the books full of numbers being added, subtracted
and divided were kept, our new teacher watched, helpless, knowing
he also needed this knowledge, but she couldn't give it to him.

Which might be why she let me touch her. Because she couldn't
get near him and my head against the antique white lace of her
dress was a good enough *almost*. Her hair was light brown, if I
remember correctly. *Innocent* is supposed to mean *free from hurt*

but it can also mean you don't know what you're doing. As when
I felt that touching her wasn't enough and I wanted to press closer,
until someone felt pain, or until I passed through her dress and found
myself inside her. It didn't matter if she was an adult and I was ten:

what I wanted wasn't sex. Or not what I have learned to think *sex*
is. Her dress was made of a material called *vintage*, which meant
that although it had managed to avoid all the minor catastrophes
of red wine stain and hook snag, along with the major disasters

of history, no one had treated the cloth with chemicals, to make it
flame retardant. And on the whole length of the hand-sewn inner seam
that started at her wrist and ran all the way down to her ankle,
no one had remembered to place even one small label warning:

if you touch the sleeve of this garment to the still-hot coils
of an electric stove, it will explode. Which is what happened.
There's the kind of scream you hear in movies. What I heard
twenty-seven years ago didn't sound anything like that. It was

sharper and can't be recorded. No matter how many times
you rewind the film. You keep going back and each time
there's a little less there. Until the memory has become
the event. And how you feel about the memory. The materials

have burnt away. There was so much fabric and all of it on fire.
Her hair too, which was long, as I remember. She came running
from the faculty kitchen, as if she could escape what she was
turning into. But all she did was excite and encourage the flames.

The Boxers

Here, in the middle of all this Houston heat, the two
sixteen-year-old feather-weights step-by-stepping around
a center which should be large enough to hold them both

are working out, with painful, close attention, a number
of terrible ideas. The heat in here is an idea: it has a purpose
and a taste: it tastes like mile after mile of train passing

by the chicken-wired windows, the endless linked cars
full of what you don't know. The idea is that suffering
teaches you to suffer well, as though the end result

of dehydration isn't the skin & kidneys closing up
until what the body holds turns toxic, but the appearance
of something new willed into the blood, made of pain,

which you can then direct at the only person in the building
as beautiful as you are. Although of course there's nothing
sexual about this, the brief embrace of two boys, wet

with the same water you'd find at the bottom of any ocean.
And from the benches their plain-faced girlfriends watch, deep
in their impenetrable adolescence. As if all this was on TV,

as normal as the newsman saying *a train carrying industrial
waste has derailed and is burning outside the city*, and the simple
precautions: *Stay indoors. Close your windows. Don't breathe.*

But these two boys are in it, the sweat washing down
their stomachs and backs rinsing the black air off their skin,
turning the absurd abstractions of last night's news

into visible concentric rings around the waistbands
of their nylon Everlast shorts, as if all this was designed
to be a further test of their endurance, or show us

how even while you sleep your body can be making
serious mistakes, taking in lungful after lungful
of other people's errors. The soaked fabric sticks

to their thighs so closely you can see the hairs
underneath and the moving weave of muscle and almost
the tight string stitched through the overlapping plates

of stomach muscle and cinched tight between them,
drawing them closer until the old men outside the ring
begin to shout they didn't come here to see lovers

and another man comes in to pull them apart.

Intermission

As always, the music was divided
halves: first three new pieces
debuts, and then the Brahms
was advertised as. In the fifteen
as jarring notes resolved into
I watched a woman walk
by her local celebrity. To be
breasts, two loaves of blue-white
a green gown, with a stone
the angle of everyone's attention
the bad press of her break-up
of carpet in front of her. It was
weren't her. There were estates
and an island, injuries measured in
banks use, and an element someone
all of. Fire, or air. Of course
they wanted was the silver
veins. I mean her story was
and public, like good gossip.
scaffolding, she glided through
small blue pool over the emerald
spilling its light the infant's
carried away between
old name on the papers
To make a diamond like this,
the courthouse steps, *you*
pounds of dirty money
legs. But the diamond
passing through and her
grown up in was like a baptism
I hope. It's easy to hate the
the name she renounced means
means a stag trying to out-run
Of course I might have been
she was and the stone spilling

into two unequal
making their dissonant
symphony the evening
minutes between,
familiar tones of talk,
across the lobby, spot-lit
blunt: I stared at her
skin pushed up by
in the cleft. I followed
and there she was,
unrolling a few steps
a good story, if you
on three continents
the long numbers
wanted to own
I'm exaggerating. All
she kept liquid inside her
personal, like history,
A ship set free from its
the room, carrying a
carpet, liquid and
fist-sized brilliant she
her breasts when she put her
and the decision was final.
she told the press on
take two hundred and fifty
and squeeze it between your
was so clean light blinked
return to the name she had
in its waters. Or so
indecently rich. And
blood-sport, which
an arrow in its neck.
misinformed about who
its eaux-de-vie inside

the square neckline of her green gown, glass, not a
brilliant example of the damages she was entitled to.
But the line of fire flicking from facet to facet inside
the pear-shaped pendant seemed real, a gem-cutter's
art turning our common glances into an ecstatic light
counter-pointing itself, our looking made visible as
sparks on her skin. The suits and dresses crowded
around the bar stared star-struck at the stone in her
cleavage as she walked by, lifting their glasses up as
the current which carried her toward the now-open
double-doors rose over their waists and the recessed
ceiling lights blinked in three sets of three, to signal
that the music would continue with, or without us.

Monica Ferrell

Monica Ferrell was born in 1975 in New Delhi, India, and grew up in northern New Jersey. She attended Harvard University, Columbia University's MFA program, and Stanford University, where she was a Wallace Stegner Fellow. Ferrell's poems have appeared in *Boston Review*, *Fence*, *New England Review*, *The New York Review of Books*, *Tin House*, and elsewhere. She is the author of a novel, *The Grace Notes* (Dial Press, 2006). The recipient of a "Discovery"/*The Nation* Award, a Van Lier Fellowship from the Asian American Writers' Workshop, and many other fellowships and grants, Ferrell has taught at California College of the Arts and Rutgers University, and is now an Assistant Professor in the Creative Writing Program at SUNY-Purchase. She lives in Brooklyn.

Myths of the Disappearance

I rise like a red balloon, untethered and vacant.

The essence of my dolor has become rarefied,
Holy; like a fragrance, bodiless, without referent.
It is a pale shadow on the sun, a wasp's wing, accidental
Splash of poison on the white rose's thorn—
I twist it in my fingers and faint. *Shall I tell you?*

There was one bad fairy at my birth, there came one curse,
One blister, one drop of mercury in the moult of me
And everything was ruined after.

               Still it is
No good; the words drift from me like ashes.
I am so old now, I have left half my life
In caves hollowed out in rock by the seashore:
I prayed in each one, and could not find my way back,
Or lied when the password was asked, or turned my back,
Making gestures of despondency at the roiling surf.

      In a mirror I shot all my hateful selves, the yesterdays.

Geburt des Monicakinds

I woke. A tiny knot of skin on a silver table
Set in the birth-theater, blinking in the glare
Of electric lights and a strange arranged

Passel of faces: huge as gods in their council.
I was the actor who forgets his lines and enters
On stage suddenly wanting to say, *I am.*

I was almost all eye: they weighed me down,
Two lump-big brown-sugar bags in a face
Which did not yet know struggle, burden;

How the look of newborns unnerves. Then
They wrapped me in pale yellow like a new sun
Still too small to throw up into the sky.

          It was midnight when they injected me
With a plague; tamed, faded as imperialism, pox
Had once put its palm-leaf hand over a quarter of Earth

Saying, *these.* Now it was contracted to a drop:
And in the morning I knew both death and life.
Lapped in my nimbus of old gold light, my

Huge lashes drooped over my deepened eyes, like
Ostrich-feather shades over twin crown princes: wet heads
Sleek and doomed as the black soul of an open poppy.

Stories from the Tower

I. Dolorous Garde

Nights in the castle we dream of hounds
we once ran, all those unused names.
Another word departing the room.
Our hands becoming abstract.
Blurred memory of purpose recedes,
recedes again, something outside the frame,
beyond where the tapestry unravels.
Mouth of the drawbridge filling with leaves.
When we came we passed the Hanged Men:

how do you forget such branches?
Such birds. Kay says he remembers fruit
but I don't believe him. I don't remember
graves. I had my lady's favour
but I burnt it at the grate. They will not keep that.

II. Women Singing

Echoes of iron die away, dissolve
into that other darkness. This metal ring
we once called shield is less than useless
now, it is the emblem of what once was
bearing my former name on its brow.
All that has faded to the place of sound,
white field outside my vision. Whenever
I turn around it is not there, a dog's tail,
wordless shadow snuffing out speech.
Days burnished, colored with the curse of rust,
and nights of shooting silver, we wake to see
a ghost slipping out of the room. And want to follow it.
Down below the women are gutting fish, singing.
Picture the red entrails, what fate tangled itself there.

III. Sleeping Beauty

Now I have been asleep a long time.
I am grown opal, unbreakable: a white blade
stretched along the bed. Out my tower window
all the animals are arranged
like frozen jewels in the snow: the horses
dozing, their lumps of maple sugar
spitted with cold. And the birds, nodding
on the line, full of fairy slumber. In life
they will not know such peace again,
such absolute rest. They are swallowed whole:
feathers tucked in stillness, hearts like a coal
become unburnable in this world.

I am suspended
in my error's ether: what business did I have
trying to spin my own thread?
This is what is meant by *fate*.

IV. Sleeping Beauty

At night: the snow. Always this unvarying
deepening. No sound, no wind, no life:
I am not yet dead. Nor sleeping.
Ask for a sign you will not get one.
Ask for time the bottom drops out
and steadily unravels, an uncontrollable
white thread unspinning the winding-sheet.
In my cedar chest the folded gowns
turn over and sigh to each other,
lost in dreams of breezes belonging to spring evenings.
Once I could move where now it is all mind,
all solitude. Nights like this it seems impossible *he* could make
a difference. Even the steps have surrendered to be stone:
There is a kind of vacancy too immense to ever melt.

V. Prisoner of the Golden Cage

Now, in this blue room, we will give ourself
up, let the long siege go, like a fist
opening to find the crushed bug flown.
Come cousin, it is the hour of surrender:
let us not say it is not so. Snow
is falling on the mosque, is falling
on the gold dome. I remember
lessons we received at the hands of the Master
who pinned butterflies to the enormous page
and turned it. Once there *was* something here,
but that was a long time ago, another world.
Please don't be angry: the sea is singing
me to sleep, the water pouring its green
poison into my ear: *earth ends, earth ends.*

Miranda Field

Miranda Field was born in 1962 in a North London suburb, and came to the United States in 1981. She attended Carleton College, The New School, and the Vermont College MFA Program. Her work has appeared in *AGNI, BOMB, Boston Review, Colorado Review, Denver Quarterly, Fence, Ploughshares, TriQuarterly,* and elsewhere. Field's first book, *Swallow* (Houghton Mifflin, 2002), won the Katherine Bakeless Nason Literary Publication Prize. Currently, she teaches in the Creative Writing Program at The New School, and lives in New York City with her husband, the poet Tom Thompson, and their two sons.

Childhood's House

Dogs guard each approach:
one to the widow's walk's every vantage point.
One humor for every aspect
of the wind: ill-tempered, selfless, obedient, obstinate.
Then the four daughters of the house
start to stir, then wander, then the dogs begin
slackening to fattened hogs.
And lie there sighing and melting
in the rich ground under our apple trees.
I'm the daughter who hits the dogs with sticks
for asking for too much too often.
But my hunger equals theirs: recidivist
scroungers, with what license should I shame them?
They have such finite lives. Sevens and sevens...
One of them as I speak, all humility, feeds a lilac bush her flesh.
Flowers of May. My birthday flowers.
My voice is a short leash. It hurts her to listen,
since she can't answer. But the others, when I don't call them in
they wander. Out of the pen of slavish
adoration into wilderness.

Miraculous Image

When an effigy cries,
        the wood she's carved from rots.
Tears, tight-reined, migrainous
        implosions. Two trenches
of decay down the cheeks,
        the dress wearing itself
away, the heart's embroidered
        harness. And inside,
never intended to be seen,
        naked, breathing,
wormholes, striations of the grain.
        What holds the parts in place:
glue of knackered hooves.
        Such havoc the pierced hands
wrestle—the soft blue mantle of Heaven
        melts about the body,
the body shriven, its gilt
        stars of scabbed paint
flaking off. Leaven.
        How our undressings lift us…
A sacred thing undone grows brave,
        a convict with nothing
in the world to lose—
        the baby sheds his baby fat,
his gold hair calms, mouse-brown.
        Epiphanies glance off him then,
a human thing, and hungry.

Scold's Mask

Before the tongue wags,
caliper the tongue. The tongue delivers lashes.
Buckle the mask to tourniquet the tongue.
The mule-snout of the scold's mask
blunts the pointed finial tongue, the hasp-tongue
back to loaf-shape, to shovel-shape,
to food, to tool, to good machine, to tabernacle
of intentional action. Not toy
that wills itself to whirring in the toy-box.

The atmosphere the tongue lies bedded in—
the tongue's environs—
makes an ideology of its lewd motions.
A mildew in the market.
A pathogen in the aspic.
Cut off the flow that feeds the tongue,
or twist or tie it tightly.
Or stuff the hole it cobras from with gauze.
Tonight, the tongue is a particularly muscular vine.
Tonight it redoubles its efforts to ascend
Heavenward. The husband-tongue, the "love-muscle" tongue.
What miracles of synchronized swimming,
what exquisite tension between buried root and forcefully
arrowing-forth prow.... It's hard to hood this.
One tongue finds another to entwine,
one tongue grows a bindweed round another's stem.
And consider carefully this ramification of the stickiest index:
its extremities are relentlessly expansionist
but slow motion, transfixing with sense
whatever they contact. And of all members mobilized
by voluntary acts, this exceeds by far all others
in numbers and varieties of its intentions.
But if caught in time, it can be constricted in childhood.
It can be ratified, espaliered. It can be trained
to arabesques of sexual servility. And citizenry.
It can be sectioned. And seduced to science.
It can be stilled for years, and stiffened.
But by an insidious magic is rendered stretchy again—
by certain essences, by liquors, yes, by questions.
And when released extends its pliant self.
And waves like a monarch from her cordoned carriage.
And bends back constantly to self-excite.
And lavishes its machinations on the orchid-pulse,
on the honey-pot, the homily, the come-on.
The muscles that move the lips
and mouth of man and the human tongue
are more numerous and subtle than any other animal's.
Whatever the tongue supplies,
its poisons or its balms,
there's an open market for. But an indentured source.

Subway

At first the meaning won't come out from hiding:
a piston-motion, a tongue-flickering, urgent
but contained. What it does is not come. What it does is
hold back and beckon, fire off its small explosion
in your brain: desire to penetrate the bulwark

distance. He *wants* you to see. He takes the weaponry
of looking, bends it back. The boy miles off, safe.
The boy untouchable—on the far platform,
such a fortress built between you, such a crow's-nest
distance, and the smile you can't see says

so far off you don't exist...

But you are here, and his shape pins the air
above the tracks, lit figure in a black space any eye can enter.
Not public, this place he makes, hammering
the locked dark with his fist, in the slip between rush hours.
Private, though you're invited in.

The boy leans forward, propped by nothing,
his prick in his hand lost in the glittering latitudes
of white, identical tiled walls, then seen, then unseen...
Small crux of flesh. Forest of rusted girders. Lost context,
buried city nothing enters without a toll.

And tunnels into it and tunnels out open in the shadows: valves
velvet with soot, the thought opening and shutting:
The train is coming / the train will never come...
The ending of the boy's tension, crescendo, holds back,
keeps refusing to yield, to you, to him, insists

it will stay, insists it will always be
about to end—nagging ghost of the choked-off, the buried—
the way a child stands still and holds her breath
until her lips darken, carotids blue and knotted in the frail neck.
See me? Watch me die. In the dark

he will not come. In the dark his work
has no reward, the cap tipped down, the—he could be anyone,
one tile, one shout inside the city's wash of sound—

lottery of flotsam on the downtown platform.
On the walls, urgent scrawls: *In a cradle of sand,*

an endless storm blows...but words are old, thoughts
oxidize. Exposure to the rush hour burns, the breathed air
burns. There is a war. There always is. And words
go missing from the messages
that line these walls, signs papered over signs...

At (place name erased) *twenty-four-hour workdays*
fill an order for five thousand body bags...
Signs speak quietly. Signs whisper,
and workers work overtime, work nights, nights...
The bones, tendons

in the white wrist pumping, pulling, so much work
to be done to accomplish one small explosion.
The neurons fire, the mind feeds on the spark—meaning: yes—
motion of stitching?—no—engines?—yes—motion of pistons...
Beneath the shut-tight lid, beneath the hood

of any machine, obsessive repetition, invisible hands...
It's quiet, the dark air, secretive.
Inviting, this dark cave, smelling of piss, hidden,
though he insists you see, and you work hard to see,
and you work secretly. Not to be seen seeing, yes. Anyone

can enter it like this: the private sector of this public darkness.

Housefire

The spark struck in secret under the stairs in dust
in the cellar smolders the way a face does, and the life
inside it, after a slap. A mortification, stains

on the floor of a caged thing's cage. In dust
in the cellar where our bicycles lean
broken-antlered in the dark. Among molds

in the cellar where the cat swollen with poison
curls in the damp to extinguish herself. It's dark outside;
inside the dark becomes particles a little like rain

stilled. Behind chicken-wired glass the garden
shakes a few leaves down. Most of winter's work is done,
the pond lidded, the ruts of the bicycles' wheels

cast in iron. The fire begins by itself, a breathing-life-into,
a kindling: cells of our skin, soil from the garden;
tinder for the fire's insistence. The fire has been impatient

to begin all along. The house is its accomplice.
Roots of the black walnut hold tight the foundations,
hence nothing grows here, nothing flourishes.

But flames brush the root hairs, make them stand on end.
Like a story's ending, not quite to wake us is the fire's
intention. To stroke us with its smoke, our sleeping faces.

Nick Flynn

Nick Flynn was born in 1960 in Scituate, Massachusetts. After a stint at the Fine Arts Work Center in Provincetown, he attended graduate school at New York University. His poems, essays, and nonfiction can be found in *The New Yorker, The Paris Review, The New York Times Book Review,* and elsewhere. Flynn's two books of poetry are *Some Ether* (Graywolf, 2000), winner of the PEN/Joyce Osterweil Award, and *Blind Huber* (Graywolf, 2002). His most recent book, *Another Bullshit Night in Suck City* (Norton, 2004), a memoir about his father and homelessness, won the PEN/Martha Albrand Award. Flynn has been awarded fellowships from the Library of Congress, the Amy Lowell Trust, and the Guggenheim Foundation. He teaches at the University of Houston each spring, and spends the rest of the year elsewhere.

Swarm

When you see us swarm—rustle of

wingbeat, collapsed air—your mind
tries to makes us one, a common

intelligence, a single spirit un-
tethered. You imagine us merely
searching out the next

vessel, anything

that could contain us, as if the hive
were just another jar. You try

to hold this ending, this
unspooling, make it either

zero or many, lack

or flurry. *I was born,*
you begin, & already each word
makes you smaller. Look at this field—

Cosmos. Lungwort. Utter each
& break

into a thousand revisions of yourself.

You can't tell your stories fast enough.
The answer is not one, but also

not two.

Hive

What would you do inside me?
You would be utterly

lost, labyrinthine

comb, each corridor identical, a
funhouse, *there*, a bridge, worker

knit to worker, a span
you can't cross. On the other side

the queen, a fortune of honey.

Once we filled an entire house with it,
built the comb between floorboard

& joist, slowly at first, the constant

buzz kept the owners awake, then
louder, until honey began to seep

from the walls, swell
the doorframes. Our gift.

They had to burn the house down
to rid us.

Emptying Town

—*after Provincetown*

Each fall this town empties, leaving me
drained, standing on the dock, waving *bye-
bye*, the white handkerchief
stuck in my throat. You know the way Jesus

rips open his shirt
to show us his heart, all flaming & thorny,
the way he points to it. I'm afraid
the way I miss you

will be this obvious. I have

a friend who everyone warns me
is dangerous, he hides
bloody images of Jesus around my house

for me to find when I come home—Jesus
behind the cupboard door, Jesus tucked

into the mirror. He wants to save me
but we disagree from what. My version of hell
is someone ripping open his
shirt & saying,

look what I did for you.

Cartoon Physics, part 1

Children under, say, *ten*, shouldn't know
that the universe is ever-expanding,
inexorably pushing into the vacuum, galaxies

swallowed by galaxies, whole

solar systems collapsing, all of it
acted out in silence. At ten we are still learning

the rules of cartoon animation,

that if a man draws a door on a rock
only he can pass through it.
Anyone else who tries

will crash into the rock. Ten-year-olds
should stick with burning houses, car wrecks,
ships going down—earthbound, tangible

disasters, arenas

where they can be heroes. You can run
back into a burning house, sinking ships

have lifeboats, the trucks will come
with their ladders, if you jump

you will be saved. A child

places her hand on the roof of a schoolbus,
& drives across a city of sand. She knows

the exact spot it will skid, at which point
the bridge will give, who will swim to safety
& who will be pulled under by sharks. She will learn

that if a man runs off the edge of a cliff
he will not fall

until he notices his mistake.

Cartoon Physics, part 2

Years ago, alone in her room, my mother cut
        a hole in the air

& vanished into it. The report hung &
        deafened, followed closely by an over-

whelming silence, a ringing
        in the ears. Today I take a piece of chalk

& sketch a door in a wall. By the rules
        of cartoon physics only I

can open this door. I want her
        to come with me, like in a dream of being dead,

the mansion filled with cots,
        one for everyone I've ever known. This desire

can be a cage, a dream that spills
        into waking, until I wander this city

as a rose-strewn funeral. Once
        upon a time, *let's say*, my mother stepped

inside herself & no one
        could follow. More than once

I traded on this, until it transmuted into a story,
        the transubstantiation of desire,

I'd recite it as if I'd never told anyone,
        & it felt that way,

because I'd try not to cry yet always
        would, & the listener

would always hold me. Upstairs the water
        channels off you, back

into the earth, or to the river, through pipes
        hidden deep in these walls. I told you the story

of first learning to write my own name, chalk
        scrawl across our garage door,

so that when my mother pulled it down I'd
        appear, like a movie.

Katie Ford

Katie Ford was born in 1975 in Colorado, and grew up in Oregon. She holds degrees from Whitman College, Harvard University, and the University of Iowa Writers' Workshop. Her poems have appeared in numerous journals, including *American Poetry Review, Colorado Review, Partisan Review, Ploughshares,* and *Seneca Review.* Her first book is *Deposition* (Graywolf, 2002). Ford is an Assistant Professor of English at Loyola University in New Orleans, and also regularly teaches for the Iowa Summer Writing Festival. She is the poetry editor of the *New Orleans Review,* lives in the Faubourg Marigny district of New Orleans with her husband, the novelist Josh Emmons, and is at work on her second book.

Flesh

One breath began the world, one can take it back again.

(Ask if I remember when.)

I would have preferred the void. At least there you know there is nothing to find.

Now the sun lowers behind the river, bare
sycamores fill with sundown. Long bones
like iron branching in the stained glass
of the incarnation. There is only so long I can watch
things do down.

(Also ask what happened to my body.)

Some leaves only show after the sun is fully down, the light violet
and blue, a second river, one with no drawbridge to lean over and look.
The brown geese walk on the frozen river, shuddering to dry
their simple bodies.

(Also about my body.)

In the winter the last leaves fall, or remain
clipped to the branch, lobes opening
from the base of each swollen leafstalk. No seed
this time of year, tight and inscripted within,
to tell it what it is.

(Ask me what I believe.)

(What was said about disobedience.)

When I speak I hear a rustling of leaves, of wings and ashes, of someone
straightening something undone. A sweeping up of the left
ungathered, and the bridge is lifted by its inner chains.

If you are speaking I cannot hear you.

Nocturne

I can see the whole city, lights edging the harbor like yellow pins in uneven
cloth beneath the hands of a woman cutting the measured lines of a dress;
when it is done she will put it on to see if it fits.

Blackish harbor, facing east no facing west, lights
meaning anything but *exit*, ships waiting for dawn so they can navigate out,
fog in the cove, cigarette smoke in this

restaurant at the top of the Prudential.
Please do not use your hands to touch my face.
Please let me be decided.

Lights fringe the harbor, she is sewing a dress a centimeter too small,
you tap off ashes, I lean into the winding smoke because it is not myth,
because I can bring even an ending into the body.

The city now unsettled beneath us. My face eye-level in the glass.

Please help me get up from this table.
Please put that thing down.

She turns an edge under. Smoke is taken in, smoke like a text
etched into two tablets of lung. Here, and here: Sinai.

Atoms fill their due portion of each ash.

Please look somewhere else with your eyes.

She undoes the knotted threads where she wants the blue and gray strips closer
to each other, crop of lavender, dust.

Please do not touch my face.

When she is done she takes off her clothes, raises her arms to get into the dress,

Please do not touch my face.

The harbor at its darkest, stillest, like a question in a throat.

The Hands of the Body Without the Body, and Nothing to Hold

How she worked was this: *Give me what I need, I am bending down,*
this is the last thing I'll ask—a fossilized backbone, a clay vase, a cylinder of darker

ground where oil seeped out of a jar. Something—the hollow of her lung?—
with whispering inside it, *bring me something, bring me something.* An ax in her

hand digging into the hillside, poison oak everywhere. Her body everywhere
covered with rash. In her sack of air the whispering warped and tripled

by a thin border: *This is the site. This is the thing. Let, to those who have, more*
    be given.
It's that she wants something solved, ended, even darkly, a crow stopped by glass.

The gash tearing further, tissue exposed. Rocks grind under
the wheel of a truck coming uphill. Even an umbilical cord of exhaust

cannot pull her into the unsought present.
Polluted metaphysic, bolt where the engine gives out.

Night begins, untrustworthy for what it does to the eye, the pupil blown open,
the iris branching its genealogy. Dust climbs,

her skin the color of the hill, hives beneath, red poppies in smog.
She thinks, *the rip in the fabric would prove—the linen preserved would show—*
    the buried

text would give—(and so on). Blackbirds huddle beneath the parked truck
    (*Bring me*
something.), each wing a jag of obsidian sheeting off its rock (*Anything.*).

The broken-up hill bears its spine, its dream of ladders—
(The self wants to find the self elsewhere.). She bears down on its rounded bone.

Why do you seek the living among the dead? She bears down. *What do you seek?*
She bears down. *Why are you afraid?*

My hand is torn open, I have nothing to show. *Why are you afraid?* I am
afraid I might find the entire stone church beneath this hill. Altar, crypt, bodies

curled like leaves in ash. I am scared I will find it all and still it will not move me.

Colosseum

I stared at the ruin, the powder of the dead
now beneath ground, a crowd
assembled and breathing with
indiscernible sadnesses, light
from other light, far off
and without explanation. Somewhere unseen
the ocean deepened then and now
into more ocean, the black fins
of the bony fish obscuring
its bottommost floor, carcasses of mollusks
settling, casting one last blur of sand,
unable to close again. Next to me a woman,
the seventeen pins it took to set
her limb, to keep every part flush with blood.

*

In the book on the ancient mayfly
which lives only four hundred minutes
and is, for this reason, called *ephemeral*,
I couldn't understand why the veins laid across
the transparent sheets of wings, impossibly
fragile, weren't blown through in their half-day
of flight. Or how that design has carried the species
through antiquity with collapsing
horses, hailstorms and diffracted confusions of light.

*

If I remember correctly what's missing
broke off all at once, not into streets
but into rows portioned off for shade as it
fell here, the sun there
where the poled awning ended. Didn't the heat
and dust funnel down
to the condemned as they fought
until the animal took them completely? Didn't at least one stand
perfectly still?

*

I said to myself: Beyond my husband there are strange trees
growing on one of the seven hills.
They look like intricately tended bonsais, but
enormous and with unreachable hollows.
He takes photographs for our black folios,
thin India paper separating one from another.
There is no scientific evidence of consciousness
lasting outside the body. I think when I die
it will be completely.

*

But it didn't break off all at once.
It turns out there is a fault line under Rome
that shook the theater walls
slight quake by quake. When the empire fell,
the arena was left untended
and exotic plants spread a massive overgrowth,
their seeds brought from Asia and Africa, sown accidentally
in the waste of the beasts.
Like our emptying, then aching questions,
the vessel filled with unrecognizable faunas.

*

How great is the darkness in which we grope,
William James said, not speaking of the earth, but the mind
split into its caves and plinth from which to watch
its one great fight.

And then, when it is over,
when those who populate your life return

to their curtained rooms and lie down without you,
you are alone, you are quarry.

*

When the mayflies emerge it is in great numbers
from lakes where they have lived in nymphal skins
through many molts. At the last
a downy skin is shed and what proofed them
is gone. Above water there is
nothing for them to feed on—

they don't even look, except for each other.

They form hurried swarms in that starving, sudden hour
and mate fully. When it is finished it is said
the expiring flies gather beneath boatlights
or lampposts and die under them minutely,
drifting down in a flock called *snowfall*.

*

Nothing wants to break, but this wanted to break,
built for slaughter, open arches to climb through,
lines of glassless squares above, elaborate
pulleys raising the animals on platforms
out of the passaged darkness.

When one is the site of so much pain, one must pray
to be abandoned. When abandonment is that much more—
beauty and terror before every witness
and suddenly you are not there.

Arielle Greenberg

Arielle Greenberg was born in 1972 in Columbus, Ohio, and grew up in Schenectady, New York. She attended Jewish day school; studied literature, performance art, and film studies at SUNY-Purchase; and received her MFA from Syracuse University. Her poems have appeared in *American Letters & Commentary*, *American Poetry Review*, *Black Warrior Review*, *Denver Quarterly*, and elsewhere, including two volumes of *The Best American Poetry*. Greenberg has served as poetry editor of *Salt Hill* and on the editorial board of *How2*, and is now poetry editor for the journal *Black Clock* and a founding editor of *Court Green*. She is the author of two books of poems—*Given* (Verse, 2002) and *My Kafka Century* (Action Books, 2005)—and the coeditor, with poet Rachel Zucker, of a forthcoming anthology of essays by women poets on mentorship. Greenberg has taught at Syracuse and Bentley College, and now teaches at Columbia College Chicago, where she is Assistant Director of the Poetry Program. She lives in Evanston, Illinois, a few blocks from Lake Michigan.

Afterward, There Will Be a Hallway

The sky is violet like no other hypnosis.

Out the night window, the moon is a slip of coin over the skyscraperscape, gold and red grids of night windows.

We (the clown, the doll, the murderer and I) are in love.
With the moon.

She ascends: the sky purples, clouds, she rises, now grinning, becoming a burning door. We love her still.

So that when she begins the medusa eclipse,
we do not look away. We are sweetened.
We are sweetened out of sight.

The apocalypse afterwards is muddy and bound to our apartment.
Someone, one of us, takes advantage and is after. The rest of us collapse
in corners. Am I waiting for the soft thump or for administering it?
In the dark, our bodies are rag. We belong to the group. There is a limp,
and a dizzy.

Afterward, there will be a hallway. I am anxious at both ends.

Berlin Series

for E.

I. Basement

If you don't know boys, you can't follow them. It has always been
this way. When I was smaller, boys were larger. They have circles
for heads, and in the cartoons, everything is backwards and made
from dots. In dreams, boys pray or they make trouble. It has
always been this way. This is a poem about a war.

II. Dizzy

The music of the Ancient Egyptians was something like be-bop,
only more orange. The music of New Jersey is asphalt and brothers.
In the fields there is a horror that takes place. I ran from it,
knowing that the mouth of something which can't speak is not
hardly a mouth at all. Music is in the organs. By this I mean the
heart and also the belly. Is music a criminal? I think that children
know this answer.

III. Push

Vision is a guess made by the power of subtraction.
This is obviously about a person alone.

IV. Casual

And here we again return to music and to felony.
Always where there is a radio there is the desire for company,
and the desire for relaxation, and also the desire, perhaps, for touch.
When I was a child I had many positions, and some of them
involved leaning and some made me expose my body. In this way I
made friends.

V. This

If you live in a city your whole life, you naturally end up wanting
air. It is a natural thing. The children of cities, especially, let's
say, the boys of smaller cities near the places they manufacture

newspaper, want air and they think they want trees. But they don't really want the trees. *Ce n'est pas naturel.* Neither is love.

VI. This

We make marks, and in this way we are like the species of fish who leave their ink when they are frightened. Artists are very much like terror, terrified fish. At least, that's the medical side of it. You could say I got this piece of advice from my brother, but it is not related completely.

VII. Died

We do not trust ourselves. The chain of being is passed from father to son. For me it was passed in a field with a spray can. It is all in toys, the memory, and this shows how I am not ready to give up the toy. This shows how all memory is false. As you can see, this is about a lost dog.

Nostalgia, Cheryl, Is the Best Heroin

The house knows this and the kitchen knows this.

The shingles taste of lovers, and the little bedroom is the girl whose lover has bruised her into what he thinks he knows he wants.

He thinks. He knows. He wants. A dark little house. The afghan of tenderness.

In front of the bruise, the townspeople have gathered for the nod-out into plush plush love, so easy and out. The cabinet wants more. This community of beating. This neighborhood of oblivion. The cabinet has less and wants more.

This is a terrible story, Cheryl. It is an instructional essay for a sweet beating. It is an open letter to linen closets everywhere.

Where does the girl keep her lust for the past hidden,
in case the punishers come?

The house pushes for its needs. He needs.

The dishtowels, Cheryl, they are all so limp, so
exhausted from the avoidance of sex. The oven is
white with love. The couch is falling in under the
weight of personal memory: too tight, too wired.

An electric horse, this little house addiction.

The mouth of the garage is dry and has no bicycles.

The lover is beat and the lover is over.

Bend over, tender dream. And ready for the smack.
The window-frames are abused of their hunger. And
he forgets. And the house keeps on.

Saints

1) Knives of the Saints

I returned your book of poetry to the store.
I returned to the scene of the crime because once I'd had you
the words floated into a ribbon of type.
Because it was where we once slung violent hash.
I returned a favor.
I returned the box to its proper shelf
that made not sense to me smelling of lavender,
and it waited to be made into a miracle.
I came carrying my wings in my teeth.
I came to under the organza influence of your best slap.
I came out. I came around.
I came back like a cat, the kind from hell.
I came to believe I'd been returned.

2) Chives of the Saints

When the waiter said "you're *wel*come"
she was waylaid, completely soup.
Dumplings healed her. Broth sustained.

Between the server and the servee passed
an Olympic torch of familyhood, a fruit crepe
of happiness. She was thankful for being welcomed
into his arms like a brown rice bowl.
She was thankful to be so single, so unbetrothed
to the service she gratefully received.
You are welcome, she thought of herself,
an utter dish festooned with gratuity.

3) Lives of the Saints

Most are quite ordinary.
They speak in English, the tongue of regular paperbacks.
They read for awhile, looking occasionally away.
They get hungry at the usual times slated for hunger.
They do not write the menu in script on a chalkboard held by a ceramic
    pig in a toque.
They simply make humble but delicious
grilled cheese sandwiches, pressing their handprints
into the flaming bread, branding it,
blending ascientifically four kinds of cheese, including a dry jack.
They prefer to drink along a tomato juice.
They like to later drag a bicycle down from its stern hook and squeeze
    the wheels.
They like to spend time in the garage, damply almost dying on purpose.
Then they go back inside the split-level ranch and eat potato chips,
casually licking the bottom of the bag salt from their fingers.

Analogies

Let's play Houston We Have a Problem in which Houston
is to space program as bubble is to astronaut as crown is to queen
as queen is a golden shilling in the shoe of every solider whose
heart she owns in a little daggered box.

Let's play Hunter
Bring Me the Heart of the Fairest Maiden in which
coffin is to promise as dwarf is to washing-day and drudgery
is a bramble of roses and thickets keep out villains from the bedroom.

Let's play Hiding from the Nazis in Our Secret Annex
in which attic is to linen closet as map is to romance as certain death
is to romance as gasoline is to showerhead.

The mutable child is more like us every day:
mute, mutated, mutant. As speech is to therapy.

Let's play Maryann and Mary Jane, Best Friends Forever
and Also Identical Twins, Run an Eternal Day Care
for Orphans and Autistic Babies Which Transcends Our Own Playing
So That Even When We Don't Think We're Playing We Are in which
the babies
are to wheelbarrows as apple tree is to biting red ants as mint bush leaves
are to the secret names of boys as nightgowns are to cartwheels
as fireworks are to piggyback and you go first.

Let's play Veterinarian in which safety pin is to stitches
as Kleenex is to bandage for the amputated limb as you or I
are slightly more crippled for the better, from this game.

Jennifer Grotz

Jennifer Grotz was born in 1971 in Canyon, Texas, and grew up in various small Texas towns. She holds a BA from Tulane University, an MA and MFA from Indiana University, and a PhD from the University of Houston. Her poems and translations have appeared in *The Best American Poetry, Kenyon Review, New England Review, Ploughshares,* and elsewhere, and have been recognized with a James Michener Fellowship and the Texas Institute of Letters' Natalie Ornish Prize. Grotz has served as a Poetry Editor for *BORN, Gulf Coast,* and *Indiana Review.* She is the author of the letterpress chapbook *Not Body* (Urban Editions, 2002) and the full-length collection *Cusp* (Houghton Mifflin, 2003), winner of the Katherine Bakeless Nason Literary Publication Prize. She lives in Houston, Texas, where she coordinates the biennial Krakow Poetry Seminar in Poland, and serves as the assistant director of the Bread Loaf Writers Conference.

The Last Living Castrato

Difficult to believe, a knife ensures the voice,
soprano notes proceed intact while chest hair and beard
accompany the new lower octaves, the voice expanding

beyond sex, limited only by lung. And now whole
operas composed for castrati are abstract and
unperformable, now whole species of off-humans who

were sacrificed for air, for air sinking and rising
in their throats, are extinct, now facsimiles
reproduce for our ears what is digital mastery,

bleeding soprano and countertenor. Except for
the brief miracle of Edison's recording:
the last living castrato's voice brimming through

static and hiss. Technology at its beginning and
old-school opera at its decline, that cusp
between where a voice spanning five octaves sang

to give us proof of the voice, and of how
we doctored it to make it more whole, to widen
emotion's aperture. He held it

in his mouth. Audiences would beg for
the aria to be sung over and over,
interrupting the story, which was only

an excuse for the voice. The voice is *how*,
rising, rising, so as to dive,
and he held it in his mouth releasing

our cruel sacrifice, our gratitude
to hear it fall, driven to where
the voice takes us: silence, applause.

Not Body

When silence is a small quick word
that keeps being said. When lips
open to tongue. Silence punctuates
a spitting, a glowing wick,
wax warping to drape you
like a hood. You grow wild,

become a stubbornness.
Something like a whisper keeps coming forward.
Such a busy flame, leveling everything
to a hardened pool.
I'll keep the vigil.

Let a little light come tell me what.
Let a flicker make me brave.

I've always insisted on you. If I could
be sure. If the night were safe, not slippery
like a flame. If the body were more than a clock.
If the body could be seen through like a window.
If the body lives to be burned.

Then you: unpredictable and loyal. Then you:
snuffed out, or replaced
with the sweet valedictions of smoke.

The Wolf

It was dawn when the wolf turned away from me,
his paw in a steel trap. Though I admire wakers
swimming up to the surface toward sky—the clear,
dry ocean of the mind—I sank back.

His paw bloodied in unretractable teeth,
I was able only to loosen the trap from its chain.
He circled the tree with clatter and limping.
When he fell, exhausted, the trap's jaw opened.

The pack of wolves approached swiftly then,
their silence devastating amid the scuffing leaves.
I knew what would happen, I heard each heavy pant
as the wolves lined up. The sleep was torn, reentered...

When he comes back like an animal, when he runs like one
able to hear far-off cries, then he is most lost to me.

Kiss of Judas

It's not greed I feel in me, the silver in my pocket
slapping my thigh like knives (*I know I am about to die*)
but the knowledge my kiss will betray you, betray me (*I welcome
this kiss, I want it on my lips, I want to hear its click*)
when I cup your chin in my hand, when I stare in your eyes
(*I am frightened by my Father, by my Judas, who comes
sheepishly toward me through the crowd of soldiers*)
I am unsure it could be more full than this moment,
I am so fearful of heaven, the grand cacophony of spears
jabbing skyward around us, torches blazing light in your face,
a redundancy (*I love his dark skin and how his robe swings
heavy, how he has caught me*) They were dirty men to deal with,
they hate you, they are jealous (*why am I only love?*)
Find me your truest of all, I could be years
but not eternity (*please come kiss me*) I am drawn toward
a destruction (*I want to be generous*), and if I cry
I know you forgave me before they counted coins
into my palm (*give myself to this inevitable,
to someone oblivious in his unasking*), before Peter losing
his temper (*I will replace the ear*) Loss is
what is irreplaceable (*rise to this moment and say,*

I let you go and be and may you be pleased) So obvious in words
(*not control of him, not word of him, not hope of him, but
permission*) I will kiss the savior (*every muscle relaxed now*)
but I am not the one who matters (*I am to be erased,
so that I might exist somewhere else, present but*)
you will push me (*like music, no traces of it afterward*)
gently away, seal us apart (*I chose him knowing his love
would be painful, would make my heart heavy and anxious
for this to pass*) and I am not sure how much
longer I will linger (*Both of us shall be wretched*)

Matthea Harvey

Matthea Harvey was born in 1973 in Bad Homburg, Germany, grew up in England and Wisconsin, and attended Harvard University and the University of Iowa Writers' Workshop. Her poems have appeared in *The Best American Poetry 2003*, *Denver Quarterly*, *The New Republic*, *The New Yorker*, *The Paris Review*, and elsewhere. Harvey's two collections are *Pity the Bathtub Its Forced Embrace of the Human Form* (Alice James, 2000) and *Sad Little Breathing Machine* (Graywolf, 2004), a finalist for The Academy of American Poets James Laughlin Award. Currently, she lives in Brooklyn, teaches at Sarah Lawrence College, and serves as the Poetry Editor of *American Letters & Commentary*.

Abandoned Conversation with the Senses

In the back they are collecting
bullets so do you really want to talk

about love? When a bee is on my chin
should I not mind it? Shall I let

the pretty water sink the boat?
Learn something from me for once

will you. A tent inside the barn
may be just what we need.

The bull shakes the snow off its back.
Yes its meat is nice to eat.

No it's not a snowstorm.
All this explaining exhausts me.

I'll be leaving some traps in the forest.
Do come admire the trees.

Our Square of Lawn

From the parrot's perch
the view is always Hello.

We try not to greet one
another. When the boys come

after school I shout
"You are not cameras"

at them & they run away.
Fact will muzzle anything.

I look at myself in
a spoon & I am just

a head. Never learned
how to make ringlets—

was always too literal.
The trees are covered

with tiny dead bouquets.
The ducks have been eating

grass with chemicals on it,
ignoring the signs. At night

from our glass-fronted box
we watch them glow.

It is the closest we come
to dreaming.

Ideas Go Only So Far

Last year I made up a baby. I made her in the shape of a hatbox or a cake.
I could have iced her & no one would have been the wiser. You know how
trained elephants will step onto a little round platform, cramming all four
fat feet together? That's her too, & the fez on the elephant's head. Applause
all around. There was no denying I had made a good baby. I gave her a
sweet face, a pair of pretty eyes, & a secret trait at her christening. I set her
on my desk, face up, & waited. I watched her like a clock. I didn't coo at
her though. She wasn't that kind of baby.

She never got any bigger, but she did learn to roll. Her little flat face went
round & round. On her other side, her not-face rolled round & round too.

She followed me everywhere. When I swam, she floated in the swimming pool, a platter for the sun. When I read, she was my peacefully blinking footstool. She fit so perfectly into the washing machine that perhaps I washed her more than necessary. But it was wonderful to watch her eyes slitted against the suds, a stray red sock swishing about her face like the tongue of some large animal.

When you make up a good baby, other people will want one too. Who's to say that I'm the only one who deserves a dear little machine-washable ever-so-presentable baby. Not me. So I made a batch. But they weren't exactly like her—they were smaller & without any inborn dread. Sometimes I see one rolling past my window at sunset—quite unlike my baby, who like any good idea, eventually ended up dead.

Definition of Weather

(abbr.)	W.
(accus.)	You little wretch.
(anat.)	Organs of indeterminate rumbling.
(attrib. false) Ashbery	My charming weather-wuss, I'll wed you in Anatolia.
(bibl.)	Elijah asked the brothers to stop throwing stones at their sister. They did not stop. The next day an asteroid killed their pet rabbit.
(cinetamog.)	*The Divan's Demise*—real-time footage of raindrops coming through the window & staining a lavender velvet sofa. (129 min.)
(colloq.) "under the weather"	Aren't we all.
(culin.)	Pancake ice.
(demons.)	Zeus, *this* is the unnecessary storm I was talking about.
(ellip.)	Ergo.
(exclam.)	Your oracular bones!
(fem.)	Hurricane Helen
(hist.)	Queen Victoria's coronation: raindrops break & enter into what had been ordained A Fine Day.
(mil.)	Cloud Formations
(ornithol.)	Initially canaries were thought to fall from the clouds after a tropical storm.

(poet.)   Reverse ascension.
(sl.) tornadoes & hurricanes   Cones 'n Canes
(theol.)   Yes.

Pity the Bathtub Its Forced Embrace of the Human Form

1.
Pity the bathtub that belongs to the queen its feet
Are bronze casts of the former queen's feet its sheen
A sign of fretting is that an inferior stone shows through
Where the marble is worn away with industrious
Polishing the tub does not take long it is tiny some say
Because the queen does not want room for splashing
The maid thinks otherwise she knows the king
Does not grip the queen nightly in his arms there are
Others the queen does not have lovers she obeys
Her mother once told her *your ancestry is your only*
Support then is what she gets in the bathtub she floats
Never holds her nose and goes under not because
She might sink but because she knows to keep her ears
Above water she smiles at the circle of courtiers below
Her feet are kicking against walls which cannot give
Satisfaction at best is to manage to stay clean

2.
Pity the bathtub its forced embrace of the whims of
One man loves but is not loved in return by the object
Of his affection there is little to tell of his profession
There is more for it is because he works with glass
That he thinks things are clear (he loves) and adjustable
(she does not love) he knows how to take something
Small and hard and hot and make room for
His breath quickens at night as he dreams of her he wants
To create a present unlike any other and because he cannot
Hold her he designs something that can a bathtub of
Glass shimmers red when it is hot he pours it into the mold
In a rush of passion only as it begins to cool does it reflect
His foolishness enrages him he throws off his clothes meaning
To jump in and lie there but it is still too hot and his feet propel
Him forward he runs from one end to the other then falls

To the floor blisters begin to swell on his soft feet he watches
His pain harden into a pretty pattern on the bottom of the bath

3.
Pity the bathtub its forced embrace of the human
Form may define external appearance but there is room
For improvement within try a soap dish that allows for
Slippage is inevitable as is difference in the size of
The subject may hoard his or her bubbles at different
Ends of the bathtub may grasp the sponge tightly or
Loosely it may be assumed that eventually everyone gets in
The bath has a place in our lives and our place is
Within it we have control of how much hot how much cold
What to pour in how long we want to stay when to
Return is inevitable because we need something
To define ourselves against even if we know that
Whenever we want we can pull the plug and get out
Which is not the case with our own tighter confinement
Inside the body oh pity the bathtub but pity us too

Terrance Hayes

Terrance Hayes was born in 1971 in Columbia, South Carolina. He attended Coker College and the University of Pittsburgh's MFA Program. His poems have appeared in *The Best American Poetry*, *Callaloo*, *jubilat*, *The Kenyon Review*, *Ploughshares*, and elsewhere. He is the recipient of a Whiting Writers Award, the Kate Tufts Discovery Award, a Pushcart Prize, an NEA Fellowship, and other honors. His books of poems are *Muscular Music* (Tia Chucha, 1999), *Hip Logic* (Penguin, 2002), a National Poetry Series selection, and *Wind in a Box* (Penguin, 2006). Hayes has taught in Japan, Ohio, and Louisiana, and is currently an Associate Professor at Carnegie Mellon University in Pittsburgh, where he lives with his wife, the poet Yona Harvey, and their two children.

Wind in a Box

I claim in the last hour of this known hysterical breathing,
that I have nothing to give but a signature of wind,
my typewritten handwriting reconfiguring the past.

To the boy with no news of my bound and bountiful kin,
I offer twelve loaves of bread. Governed by hunger,
he wanted only not to want. What is the future

beyond a premonition? What is the past
beyond desire? To the preacher, I leave a new suit, a tie
made of silk and shoes with unscuffed bottoms.

To the mirror, water; to the water, a book with no pages,
the author's young face printed on the spine.
I wanted children taller than any man on earth.

If everyone was like me, I said to the mirror.
To my lover, I leave enough stories to fill an evening.
Enough sleep to walk from one coast to another

without pause. I held no counsel with god.
I cut open the fruit of a tree without speaking to the tree.
I ate food prepared by strangers. To the black cashier,

I leave nothing. Her story is the one I was given.
To all the carpenters looking at the ceiling, nothing.
Here in the last moments of my illiterate future,

may the people know I did not matter.
Shoeprints at the door. Shoeprints on the old road.
To the boy with two lights going on and off in his stare,

I leave the riddle of the turtle who had shelter,
but no company. To the black girl, grace. To the black girl,
mirrors; a father blessed with the gift of mind-reading,

men who do not wound her, men she does not wound
herself for, and mother love. Unable to shed the old skin
and stand, I stand here in the hour of my hours alive.

These words want to answer your questions.
These words want to stave off your suffering,
but cannot. I leave them to you. Enough sky

and a trail. Wood and enough metal for machines.
Father in Heaven, what am I going to do when I'm dead?
Let my shadow linger against the earth, protect my children.

The Blue Terrance

I come from a long line hollowed out on a dry night,
the first son in a line of someone else's children,
afraid of water, closets, other people's weapons,
hunger and stupidity, afraid of the elderly and the new dead,
bodies tanned by lightening, afraid of dogs without ethos,
each white fang on the long walk home. I believe all the stories
of who I was: a hardback book, a tent behind the house
of a grandmother who was not my grandmother, the smell of beer,
which is a smell like sweat. They say I climbed to the roof
with a box of light bulbs beneath my arm. Before the bricks,
there were trees, before the trees, there were lovers
barely rooted to the field, but let's not talk about them,
it makes me blue. I come from boys throwing rocks
bigger than their fists at the head of the burned girl,
her white legs webbed as lace on a doily. In someone's garage
there was a flashlight on two dogs pinched in heat.
And later, a few of the puppies born dead and too small

to be missed. I come from howls sent up all night and all day,
summers below the hoop and board nailed to a pine tree.
I come from light bulbs glowing with no light and no expressions,
thrown as far as the will allows like a night chore, like a god
changing his mind; from the light broken on the black road
leading to my mother. Tell me what you remember of her
now that her walk is old, now that the bone in her hip strains
to heal its fracture? I come from the hot season
gathering its things and leaving. I come from the dirt road
leading to the paved one. I will not return to the earth
as if I had never been born. I will not wait to become a bird
dark enough to bury itself in midair. I wake up sometimes
in the middle of the country with fur on my neck.
Where did they bury my dog after she hung herself,
and into the roots of what tree are those bones entangled?
I come blessed like a river of black rock, like a long secret,
and the kind of kindness like a door that is closed
but not locked. Yesterday I was nothing but a road
heading four ways. When I threatened to run away
my mother said she would take me whereever I wanted to go.

The Elegant Tongue

It's Yoyo who says Tonguing, a form of kissing
favored among the half-lit young, is mostly overrated
and rarely practiced among married folk like us,
but we give it a try, clumsy as two elephants swapping
gin-tinged saliva Friday night to prove the idea
is always better than the act, and since I am wistful
as the blind old lumberjack who touched the elephant's knee
and fumbling for his ax declared, *This animal is most like a tree*,
I remember my tongue sandpapered against vowels in a mouth
named Yolanda in the dark of a yellow bus long ago,
and I tell Yoyo how that girl may still be somewhere thinking fondly
of our tangle. Forgive me: I believe, as the elephant must,
that everything is punctured by the tusks of Nostalgia.
They use those things to uproot roots, but let's never forget
the old blind warrior who touched the elephant's tusk
and said, *This thing is most like a spear*, and took it as a sign
that Man should spend his life defending his house
and though he probably wasn't wrong, it's the best intentions
that turn need into want, which is another way of saying
the tongue is mostly disgust coated in desire,

or desire coated in disgust depending on the way you look.
My tongue is unusually short, but I'm happy to say
Yoyo prefers my lips. If you are not an elephant more adept
at using your trunk than your tongue, you cannot wrestle,
nor caress, nor blow water into the air while your kiss
is being chewed in a dining room beside a house plant
called *The Mother-in-law's Tongue* because of its sword-shaped
leaves or perhaps because it has no mind for boundaries,
though boundaries too are a matter of the way you look.
The African elephant, for example, can be found in countries
like Angola, Botswana, Cameroon, Ethiopia, Ghana, Kenya,
Mali, Nigeria, Rwanda, Senegal, Somalia, South Africa,
and Zimbabwe, and that must mean a tongue knows
nothing about territory. It's a spit of land, a promontory.
Remember the blind prisoner who touched the elephant's flank
and said, *This creature is most like a wall,* and believed it
meant all the world should be a jail? Some say it's mostly walls
that constitute a marriage, and in many ways that may be true
since Yoyo will not divulge the slip and slither administered once
by a boy plucked from the pews of her serious Pentecostal history,
which I know featured a perspiring, eye-tossing glossolaliac
mouthing nothings only the faithful could decipher so that *Fuck*
might be translated as the sound at the beginning
of *Forgiveness,* and the hands of the white-bloused ladies,
her momma among them, patting the convulser's shoulders
might be said to emulate several vibrating reeds.
I'm talking about the rapture of tongues. The holy rollers
say it's most like a flame in the devil's blackout
because in Acts, tongues of fire are said to alight on the Apostles,
filling them with the Holy Spirit and allowing them to speak
in a language understood by foreigners from several countries.
Darling, kiss me again in the nastiest possible way.
When the blind fondle the elephant's trunk, an organ
of 15,000 miraculous multipurpose muscles, and hiss,
This creature is most like the serpent in Eden,
tell them, If there is goodness in your heart, it will come
to your mouth, and if that doesn't work,
tell them, It's not the forked tongue that does the piercing.

A Postcard from Okemah

Turned from the camera's eye, hovering,
between river & bridge, the hung woman

looks downstream, & snagged in the air
beside her, the body of her young son.

They are tassels on a drawn curtain;
they are the closed eyes of the black boy
who will find them while leading his cow
to the river bank; they are the bells

that will clamor around the animal's neck
when it lowers its head to drink.
The boy dangles in midair
like a hooked fish, his pants hanging

from his ankles like a tailfin.
On the bridge women pose
in aprons & feathered bonnets,
the men wear wide-brimmed hats

with bow ties or dungarees;
there are three small girls leaning
against the railing, & a boy nestled
beneath the wing of his father's arm.

I count sixty-seven citizens & children
staring at what must have been a flash
& huff of smoke. The photographer
must have stood on a boat deck,

though from this angle
he could have been standing on the water
with his arms outstretched.
He must have asked them to smile

at the camera & later, scrawled his copyright
& condolences on the back of the postcards
he made for the murdered man's friends.
"The Negroes got what would have been due

to them under process of the law,"
the sheriff said. His deputy
had been shot when the posse searched
the suspects' cabin for stolen meat.

To protect her son, the mother
claimed she'd fired the gun.

The mob dragged them both
from the jail bound in saddle string.

If you look closely you can see a pattern
of tiny flowers printed on her dress;
you can see an onlooker's hand opened
as if he's just released a dark bouquet.

Now all of Okemah, Oklahoma, is hushed.
Now even the children in attendance are dead.
After that day in 1911, it did not rain again.
To believe in God, this is the reckoning I claim.

It is a Monday morning years too late.
All the rocking chairs & shopping carts,
all the mailboxes & choir pews are empty.
I cannot hear the psalms of salvation

or forgiveness, the gospel of Mercy.
I cannot ask who is left more disfigured:
the ones who are beaten or the ones who beat;
the ones who are hung or the ones who hang.

Talk

like a nigger is what my white friend, M,
asked me, the two of us alone and shirtless
in the locker room, the bones beneath my skin

jutting like the prow of a small boat at sea,
the bones beneath his emitting a heat
that turned his chest red and if you're thinking

my knuckles knocked a few times
against his jaw or my fingers knotted
at his throat, you're wrong because I pretended

I didn't hear him, and when he didn't ask it again,
we slipped into our middle school uniforms
since it was November, the beginning

of basketball season, and jogged out
onto the court to play together
in that vision all Americans wish for

their children, and the point is we slipped
into our uniform harmony, and spit out *Go Team!*,
our hands stacked on and beneath the hands

of our teammates and that was as close
as I have come to passing for one
of the members of The Dream, my white friend

thinking I was so far from that word
that he could say it to me, which I guess
he could since I didn't let him taste the salt

and iron in the blood, I didn't teach him
what it's like to squint through a black eye,
and if I had I wonder if he would have grown

up to be the kind of white man who believes
all blacks are thugs or if he would have learned
to bite his tongue or let his belly be filled

by shame, but more importantly, would I be
the kind of black man who believes silence
is worth more than talk or that it can be

a kind of grace, though I'm not sure
that's the kind of black man I've become,
and in any case, M, wherever you are,

I'd just like to say I heard it, but let it go
because I was afraid to lose our friendship
or afraid we'd lose the game—which we did anyway.

Steve Healey

Steve Healey was born in 1966 in Washington, D.C. He attended the University of Virginia and received his MFA from the University of Massachusetts. Healey's poems have been published in *American Poetry Review, Crowd, Fence, jubilat, Open City, Verse,* and elsewhere. He lives in Minneapolis, where he is pursuing a PhD in English Literature at the University of Minnesota. Healey serves as Associate Editor of the journal *Conduit* and teaches regularly at colleges in the Twin Cities area, as well as several Minnesota correctional facilities. His first book of poems is *Earthling* (Coffee House Press, 2004).

As Western Culture Declined Without Its Knowing

His body is credits rising because
the movie is over. It's a small door open
to the counterfeit light of dead stars

while another vernal equinox, the sequel
to last year's version, comes true,
making day once again equal night.

It's a hand searching for unfamiliar faces
and the syllables they once spoke,

because now he's the only thing
he knows, and there's word this galaxy
is drifting in a different direction

than previously believed. This means
an unknown attracts it, although
it remains intact, iceberg-like,

promoting togetherness, each person
frozen and individually wrapped
inside an enormous shape,

moving simultaneously toward
the same unknown. There's also word

that the Palos Verdes butterfly,
believed to be extinct, has been
"rediscovered" in southern California.

Almost a hundred of them were found
"flitting around a pocket of deerweed"
next to an oil refinery. This is

visibility after a period of hiding,
proof that the audience had not been
there. Now after three million years

someone has found a near-human skull
in an Ethiopian riverbed, and it had
been there all along. After all that time

it's raining on his shoulders, he hears
it falling from three-dimensional clouds,

clouds his lidless eyes will become one day,
freshly dead in his favorite armchair.

Yes, the sky is broke, the sperm count
on the decline, a funeral procession
an endless corridor of vehicles,

headlights carving the right-of-way,
corpse made-up, well-dressed. And yes,

somewhere in this transparent moment
a mouth reveals an aerial view
of the subdivision he grew up in.

A public clock slips forward
so he'll appear to lose an hour
of sleep. A darkness hugs the globe.

So his value depends not on what
he was but how he's remembered,
wrapped in seamless skin.

He's entering a new wilderness.

It's a garden of enormous fruit
against a skyscraper backdrop.

It's the outer space he's been looking for.

Where Spring Is

I could be a hole
if the room's not already full of them.

We all have insides to let go,
and the room's outside. It's dusk.
I slouch and disappear, reading
instructions. White snow all around.

What happens to dusk when you stare
at it? "A fully conscious state,"

this is the song about the space
between branches, "in which normal pain
is not felt." Objects appear smaller

when I miss you, I could swallow
analgesics on a slow rocket,

I could write postcards from the garden:
"It's a Latin garden: *ranuculus,
prunus, ixia, iris.*" Then English

flowers nicely after the Black Death;
the fourth wall is rarely missed.

Thank God these few mistakes
have friends, i.e., pilgrims.

A nation can depend on conditioned air,
and surely it's spring there
not just in name. With all the melting,

streets river. Time again to honor
my favorite avant-garde milliner
who wore an exceedingly normal hat

when, just before spring, she
killed herself by the river.

Just before, I mean, some things
haven't happened before. The animals
coming back to life, for example,

they stagger around the house.

My Wrist Split Open

because I flew through the glass door when
the bad animal scared me, but the doctor
said I could go to the beach because
my cut would like to drink salt. Then

I went in the ocean with my happy boat,
a wave swallowed us and my boat swam away
from my hand. A shiny man told it to come back

but it kept going all the way to Spain
and swam into the hand of someone who looks
like me. They have water everywhere,

they have ice cubes and eyes, and sometimes
it rains on TV. When it doesn't rain
the backyard splits open and I hate something
in there that wants to drink me like juice.

When the clock points out the window
we make the bathtub hold its breath and turn
the knobs. I get inside and it doesn't rain
in China till we let the dirty water go.

When the hiccups come I hold my breath
so little men can run around and fix me
while my heart keeps counting *one potato, two.*

If I breathe too soon my hiccups come back
and kill the little men. Then I have to pee,

I'm sitting in the pew and no one can leave
so my legs try to fly. Before bed I try
to pee but it's never enough. Sleep looks
like the inside of a marble, and sometimes

there's a hole in my bed, and something I hate
in there drinks me and pees in the sheets.

Then the marble rolls down the stairs
and I run up the hill and tell the good birds
not to be afraid. They say the phone is for me

and I climb into the box of my teeth
and say the words that run through wires

into faraway ears. The moon is the color
of a pill that tastes like nothing,
and it climbs into the box.

Thomas Heise

Thomas Heise was born in 1971 in northern Michigan. He grew up in southern Florida, and went on to receive a BA from Florida State University, an MA in Creative Writing from the University of California at Davis, and a PhD in American Literature from New York University. His poetry and essays have appeared in *Gulf Coast, Ploughshares, Verse,* and other journals. In 2004, he received the *Gulf Coast* Prize for Poetry. His first book of poems is *Horror Vacui* (Sarabande, 2006). A former curator of the Reading Between A and B Series in New York's East Village, Heise is now a member of the English Faculty at McGill University in Montreal, Canada, and is working on a second book of poems while completing a critical volume on 20th-century urban American literature and culture.

Corrections

We were mistaken. The Queen never
loved a horse. The whole mystery
will surface when we recover
the missing notebook from
the wreckage. "In summer, she'd
wander the lawn in her white robe,
the light in her hair" is a misquote.
Apologize. Fill in the blank
with your trumpet. On page nine all
the names are untrue. We were
mistaken. The man running from
the crime scene remains unidentified.
My whereabouts: unknown. I am
lost in Newfoundland. We were
mistaken. Erasure on your heart's
fifth amendment should read: *No*

one slept here. Memorialize it—

dream   it   permanent.   Even

the   sparrow   you   lifted   dead

from   the   basket   was   an   error.

My Pietà

He held me bone-tight. He held me backward.
He held me high with the bellows
to smoke the beehive, hanging delicate
as a lung in the branches and bleeding
a half-gallon of honey while he held me. He held me
in the bathtub, scrubbed ashes from my small tongue.
He held me in the pond of his hand,
as if I were a tadpole, and wouldn't let go.
He held me hostage. I would hide
in the dumpster. Under the rain bucket
during thunderstorms. Holding my breath
among the lawn statues of gnomes and giant toadstools
until he found me, held me, walked me home.
When I fell asleep in the attic, he would carry me down
and sing to me. One winter he held a rope, lowered me
by the ankles to the well's bottom.
I ascended upside-down through the dark thermometer
with a blood orange in my teeth. He had a beard
of new snow. I held cold to his pant leg
while our dog leapt and snapped at a sound
in the air only he could hear. When I fell
in love, he reached out to me and held me down
when she slinked away on our dirt road alone,
sheepish, depressed. He held me as the constellations
mingled through the torn curtain.
A beanstalk sprouted through a hole
in our above-ground pool. A band of raccoons
commandeered the upstairs and stared
at us as he held me in his reading chair.
He grew older, he held my ear
to his artificial heart on a daily basis.
He grew sick, he held me like a suckling child.
We grew smaller and smaller and would crawl
after each other through tall grass growing through our carpet.

The walls of the house fell away.
We curled in a bird's nest. I could barely hold
his tiny thumb in my fingers.
We felt a shell growing around us.
The dog was barking.
And then rain, we could hear it tapping,
we held each other, then a blast
of hot light roared through.

Zombie

In your three-piece suit and your tuxedo shoes
you're dressed as if to go, but in your coma
you do not come or go. The wife you left
has come down from the mountain to give
you a matching ring of glass. Your doll-sized
daughter has brought you a kelp flower
that smells of salt to pin to your lapel.
Into your welmish eye, she says,
the world is drearful and you should go now.
But nothing rouses you from the deepwater sleep
in which you melt like an iceberg. On a canopied bier
fit for a sun king, you float and dream of what?
Your kaleidoscope? An octopus? The suitcase,
packed with a warm coat and dried apricots
for your soft teeth, waits at the door.
On the far shore your mother waves for you.
Her little white flag is a seagull's wing.
There you do not go to her. The bridge stops
in midair, the perch of the swan diver.
The canoe decays into a trough of rosemary,
so I'll bury it with roses: *He loves me, he loves
me not, he loves me, he loves me not he loves
me not. Can you hear me?* My ear to your ear
and my dumb voice boomerangs. Your brain
a beehive, its combs dormant from the first
snowfall are full of rings and echoes.
On the floor the cat crouches, lapping
your spilled coins: *clink clink clink.*
The gargoyle climbs down from his gable
to sit in your rubber plant. He sings a lullaby.
Your paper lips sip an air tube, passive
as a bored child. Your daughter has just

pulled off your caterpillar mustache.
Your wife has turned into a sunspot.
Today I have a small blue heart made of velvet.
I listen for the chanticleer to declare
all-clear for you to go. He has gone,
flown kamikaze into yesterday's sun.
Now my kingdom of dirt will not fill
the flowered urn where I will store
and sift your ruins bitter for a golden hair.
Now my arm is growing into an orange branch
as I speak. The moon has risen full
behind my leafy eyes. I want to sleep, but
the owl who is eating my tongue says no.

Brian Henry

Brian Henry was born in 1972 in Columbus, Ohio, and grew up in Richmond, Virginia. He holds a BA from the College of William and Mary, received his MFA from the University of Massachusetts, and was a Fulbright Fellow in Australia. Since 1995, he has co-edited *Verse* magazine. Henry's poems have appeared in numerous journals, including *American Poetry Review*, *Boston Review*, *The Canary*, *New American Writing*, *The Paris Review*, and *Volt*. His debut collection, *Astronaut* (Carnegie Mellon University Press, 2002), first appeared from Arc Publications in 2000 in England, where it was shortlisted for the Forward Prize. Henry has since published two more books of poems—*American Incident* (Salt, 2002) and *Graft* (New Issues, 2003)—edited *On James Tate* (University of Michigan Press, 2004), co-edited *The Verse Book of Interviews* (Wave, 2005), and is presently co-editing (with John Kinsella) an anthology of American poetry for Salt Publishing. Henry's fourth book of poems, *Quarantine*, is forthcoming in 2006 from Ahsahta Press. The winner of the 2003 Poetry Society of America Alice Fay di Castagnola Award, Henry has taught at Plymouth State College and the University of Georgia, and now teaches at the University of Richmond.

The Pyramid

And some admired it for its form.
A handful felt entitled to a piece of it, could not resist the urge.
Not a leaf could touch it, no horse could get a handle on it.
An astrophysicist claimed she could keep time by it.
Pilots swerved and swore by it.
A cloud, cumulus nimbus, covered it for a century or two.
The lives of scorpions remained unaffected by it, as did the lives of most
    Vikings.
No one ever really *saw* it, though a few declared otherwise, most notably
    one Frenchman of minute stature.
Air lifted beneath it, separated the thing from the idea of the thing.
Separated from the idea of itself, it abandoned all hope.
Hope abandoned, it divided again, divided until it became unknown.
Unknowable, all assertions against it became null and void.
Not null and void—not nothing, but not a presence either.
Those in the know called for a forum, to disentangle this absence and
    presence business.
Emergency measures were declared, a transcontinental voyage was ordered.
Those in the know died en route of shock, malaria, or scurvy.
Hence it remains a mystery.

Skin

Never mind the fantasy about the tweezers and the tongue,
the one about the bicycle pump and the twisted rim.
Never mind the angle of penetration, or the number
of blessed repetitions in the series of withdrawals and givings-in.

Never mind the dream about the bean-bag chair and the virgin,
the one about the tree and the bull terrier off its chain.
Never mind the song the words will not attach to,
the visions that arrive with the noises next door,

when a sneeze, or a sob, is mistaken for something else
and someone finds himself clinging to the wall,
perhaps with a glass to his ear, or his glasses on,
hoping something dark and old-fashioned has pulled him

from sleep this close to dawn. Never mind the crack
between the blinds and the sill, where a single moan
will keep him waiting an hour for another, his face pressed
against the pane, one eye open, half-blind but guided.

And never mind the woman in the grass beneath the statue.
Her palms are cupping her head, her skirt an inch off-center,
glasses gleaming as the sun hums on the monument
of the general, the skin of her arms slowly going red.

Rooms

There are rooms that know you, rooms you know
and can name, rooms that rise and stutter
into view if you stare long enough.
Rooms where nothing happened
but in your head, where the world went on
apart from you, you trying to rise to it.
Rooms with walls of white blocks,
one window, the only sound the bang
bang banging of the headboard
against the wall, your bed still.
The room where the bed fell on you,
the room where the hand going down
was not your own, the groping tongue
the proof. The room you talked

your way out of, four men of monosyllables,
thick arms and necks flushed pink,
closing in, emptying the air between.
The room where you were walked in on,
the room where you were the walker,
both times the last time in that room.
The room with no door, a woman
across the threshold, you crawling to her,
over her to the bathroom to press your cheek
against the white, your name
an indictment among stalls.
The room the sun never touched,
the sound of cars dropping you to sleep,
your pupils large and hungry for light.

Submarine

On this side the engine room, on that side the boiler
room. Both, you'll recall, are off-limits to all
but the few with proper clearance. The access.
So our tour will bypass—don't touch that door—
those and bring us, group, to the sleeping place.
As is clear, the quarters are spartan, to keep
the sleepers focused on slumber. Distractionless.
The triple bunks deter—don't sit there, please—
horseplay, fucking, and flatulence while
providing some semblance of private moments.
The walls are thin, the floor is loud. Two cameras
in two corners. A toilet across the hall.
Yes, the men, they share it. And the one shower.
Food is prohibited in every room but
the eating place. The men are there now, eating
in silence and without fluids, to ease
digestion. Twenty minutes. Plus five for post-
prandial stretching. Yes, that, too, is super-
vised. Four cameras. Eighty-eight in all,
if one counts the six behind mirrors,
which I do. How many mirrors? Ten.
No, no one can say which four front no lenses.
I knew once but cannot recall. Which brings us
to the missile room. Beautiful, isn't it? So still.
Not a person here to spoil the air until
we filled the room. By all means, touch the casing.

Read the fine letters and numbers. They are polished
daily, so your smudges won't stay. That smell?
I could say it's the citrus in the solvent
used to wipe the fingerprints away, the acid
needed for the third stage in the process.
But in truth you are smelling fear. They know
we are down here, what we carry, but cannot
say what they know, for to say would
be to acknowledge, and to acknowledge would
be to shake, and to shake would be to pray.
And that being a godless country, they cannot pray.
We? We can pray all we want as we wait.
And here, we wait. With unparalleled efficiency
we wait.

Christine Hume

Christine Hume was born in 1968 in Fairbanks, Alaska, and has lived in fifteen different states and countries. She holds an MFA from Columbia University and a PhD from the University of Denver. Her poems have appeared in *The Best American Poetry 1997* and such journals as *AGNI, Boston Review, Conjunctions, Fence, Harper's, The New Republic, McSweeney's,* and *Volt,* and her reviews and critical essays have appeared in the anthologies *American Women Poets in the 21st Century* and *Poets in the 21st Century: The New Poetics,* as well as in *Augfabe, The Chicago Review, The Constant Critic, Context, Verse,* and elsewhere. Hume is the author of *Musca Domestica* (Beacon, 2000), winner of the Barnard New Women Poets Prize, and of *Alaskaphrenia* (New Issues, 2004), winner of the Green Rose Award. She lives in Ann Arbor, Michigan, and is an Associate Professor at Eastern Michigan University.

Explanation:

Many of the stories circulating about my escapades are not true. I would like to believe myself, but I've never taken to tourist routes—Wild vagaries of common air! Mild wagers of the feint and bent! Forget the serotonin-drenched titillations of blowhards, listen here.

It is NOT TRUE: I have never climbed into the hollower world below, never even attempted it; but I have roared above the summit in a lost world. And I hasten back to that Eden of poisonous snows.

It is NOT TRUE: I am not the only woman to ride sixteen blighted horses, ride a bike eaten out by rust, eat a map riddled with circles and fingerprints, circulate a mean withdraw sickness, and draw kill in a woods with two moons. Absolutely not.

It is TRUE: I am the only trespasser on Mighty Mac's windchill. I saw huge blocks of ice caribou and hoary moose moving toward the ocean. I hid among those shapely half-ideas that throng dim regions beyond daylight. My eyes, being infected with many nameless blues, could see straight through possessive air.

It is NOT TRUE: I did *float* for a story while my back was in a cast from an accident caused by shifting traplines. The heaviness of hydrogen only made me *feel* weightless: exposure emptied me further, but I still had a pulse from underneath. I did locate my prey in a dream, but its hole was already foaming. I did not fly to it.

It is NOT TRUE: I have landed on most of the mountain's glaciers, but I was not transformed. My blood did not turn to gold or anything like propane. My heart was not bitten in half by avarice or parasites. An acoustic lack may have racked my rectum for heaven, but I had adopted an Alaskan ear long before; with it, it's not unusual to hear from inside the hammer: stampeded terrain, yea avalanche.

It is TRUE: I did originate the future. I was up to here in memory; I had had it. The future was better protected than the past. Therefore, I left a group of inconnus in the lurch to become a remora to their forged expectations. All points of view turned up dead on sodden hills.

It is NOT TRUE: I embezzled no indescribable sky event. Perhaps now we can agree with the trouble eustasy caused my ex.

It is NOT TRUE: I did not dash my son's brains against the rocks. The beauty of this place is mad, a drug for driving you blind and diplopic; its amplified contradictions played the music of his messy slip.

It is TRUE: Thereafter, I used my milk to feed a drove of walruses, shattered on the shore like glass. If this sentiment offends, be assured I offer it only half-hearted.

It is NOT TRUE: The hoax was not my idea. I claim many ideas that are not my own, but everyone knows that licking a glacier can change your DNA and reprogram your bones to be bombs. You like to gainsay such things because it pleases your frontier.

Sampler City

The cities came from twelve girls
within one. The sample girls
searched for a bloodeye in the city
weighty with mountain fluenzas.
In the sample city, most expectorants
enchanted them; in the sample city,
feral mistook fevers for cold fear.
An ample girl broke for a fair
to middling. Some girl had not yet
started to fast. No girls reared the cities
or selected randomly. Their secrecy
carries like a red wool coat, and their coughing

transferred to the girl entire.
The know-best girl felt her wholehearted oats
running overloud and melted.
Girls resembled the state hospital,
and a plague slept between them.
A sample girl contracted a young tarnish there;
she lay outside her own drunkenness.
She doesn't want to be known as "hospital girl."
The legality of one large ague
concocted another four or agony.
Girls who had never had additional names
characterized the sample. The modern girls'
mercy was phlegmy or pneumatic, stitched
in lavish symptoms. Through their methods,
a drowsy of watching. Find a few
autonomous girls, the scarcity girls, the type girls
who sneeze at nothing. Contamination hailed
in the cities, and no girls called club today.
Girls are cities of no containment. Their games
congest the sample's chaste purpose;
one girl's flare-ups come-and-get the others.
Every girl was once a catchall but commitless.

Hume's Suicide of the External World

the hanging man wandered out of a moonshine dream

smuggled dope in pelts and gold in a Risk game

   that cheated his confidences by the dozen

time being, Moot's pond compressed the blue

a brand-new pond began to self-destruct

morning jackhammers fed underground ponds

their kinetic fury melted down the public, exposing another

there he found a pass in alien rain and dragged ass

   kicked himself out of himself said the note

weighed one miracle against a fifth

soft spiders criss-crossed the night interference

   liquored the branches

asleep, he fell out of hours on fire

its wings stabbed at him angry

he walked out on the roof reshod in tin cans

   electromagnetic blue lure

outlandish blue of his tongue and palm

threw an ambsace and a score of dreams rolled

if he had an eye for every eye on deck

   I want to shoot a gun
   I want to come down

his speech had left him overly alert

renaming the domain and its potent pheromones

he saved some sounds that had wanted to die in his mouth

and listened at the other end of *deserve*

   headless, out of the state blue

out of its panic grass shook out his hologram

   signed Asphyxia, signed Arctic Cat

his walking stick made stars along the scavenger's path

touching off oil fires in the dice's outcry

their music confused him into affection

for a dynamite belt and Zero pond

   time tranced and put him on ship

a black-voiced bird recognizing his torture

signed his full name on the slanting shore

he weathered genital waves to quit having a curse

   then a blue man crawled out from under a horse

whose rusted bit hushed his greedy depictions

his haunches were meat, signed Nitid Piss

and no dragoman staggered out of Candyland looking for him

he had never mouthed something so dead sweet

   signed Sugar Melted on a Sidewalk

the chalk outline of him thieved the looks off a bottle

another coast unhung the spectral blue

   to drink sea water, coat your mouth with bird fat
   to look down from the sky, use ataxia

wrote his note on the wrapping of the rope

vendetta-tethered, his telepathy crested

he left a note in a mailbox abducted by mudflats

   the consequence continually shifts

once the map locked, he tripped out of a torn place

   his head full of broken asphalt

during a mistake he walked out of my forehead

making my own mind very hard for me

dragging its chain of islands insane islands insane

Comprehension Questions

What kind of phantom is the ship?

Where does the girl hide her great distances?

Accordingly, what is the rate to multiply by to find the intense sensitivity of minor characters?

How do the men abandon ship?

Why do they trouble the forest with their strange butterflies and huge suns full of complete daylight?

What role does the dog play in developing catastrophe?

If the setting permitted biological time, would red shift through the captain's mirage?

What dark authority lurks among the unpruned spruce?

Whose foreshadowing crawls out and what sets it off?

Do you believe the wave is not a girl in furs?

Is this a comedy or a tragedy of secret motions?

Why should a zephyr so rarely intervene?

Does the stormy girl's beauty suggest something about the captain?

Why do his arrows ricochet wildly just before the target?

Meanwhile, what does the girl's fear become when she turns around?

Which constellation best fits the story?

Though the captain arrests the ice horse, what fantasy freezes the dark around him?

When does it matter? When can you deceive?

Why do the men take the tusk and shank inside?
Does the narrator gain sight by his frustration, humiliation, torture, and debt?

Which prophesies help the girl court the ship?

Is anything more grotesque than the face of human ecstasy?

Major Jackson

Major Jackson was born in 1968 in Philadelphia. He is a graduate of Temple University and holds an MFA from the University of Oregon. His poems have appeared in *The Best American Poetry 2004*, *American Poetry Review*, *Boulevard*, *Callaloo*, *The New Yorker*, *Post Road*, and elsewhere. Jackson is the recipient of a Whiting Writers' Award, a Library of Congress Witter Bynner Fellowship, a Pew Fellowship in the Arts, a fellowship from The Fine Arts Work Center in Provincetown, a commission from The Chamber Orchestra of Philadelphia, and other honors. His debut collection, *Leaving Saturn* (University of Georgia, 2002), won the Cave Canem Poetry Prize for the best first book by an African American poet and was a National Book Critics Circle Award Finalist. Formerly the Literary Arts Curator of Philadelphia's Painted Bride Art Center, Jackson lives in South Burlington, Vermont, and teaches at the University of Vermont and the low-residency Creative Writing MFA Program at Queens University of Charlotte. His second book of poems, *Hoops*, is forthcoming from W.W. Norton.

Blunts

The first time I got high I stood in a circle
of boys at 23rd & Ridge tucked inside
a doorway that smelled of piss. It was
March, the cold rains all but blurred
our sight as we feigned sophistication
passing a bullet-shaped bottle of malt.
Johnny Cash had a love for transcendental
numbers & explained between puffs resembling
little gasps of air the link to all creation was
the mathematician. Malik, the smartest
of the crew, counterargued & cited the holy life
of prayer as a gateway to the Islamic faith
that was for all intents the true path
for the righteous black man. No one disputed.
Malik cocked his head, pinched
the joint & pulled so hard we imagined
his lips crazy-glued into stiff O's. It was long
agreed that Lefty would inherit his father's
used-car business, thus destined for a life of wrecks.
Then, amid a fit of coughing, I broke
the silence. *I want to be a poet.* It was nearing
dinnertime. Jësus lived here. His sister was yelling
at their siblings over the evening news & game shows.

The stench of hot dogs & sauerkraut drifted
down the dank hallway. A prespring wind flapped
the plastic covering of a junkman's shopping cart
as Eddie Hardrick licked left to right, the thin strip
of glue at the edge of a rolling paper, then uttered,
So, you want the tongue of God. I bent double
in the blade of smoke & looked up for help.
It was too late; we were tragically hip.

Euphoria

Late winter, sky darkening after school,
& groceries bought from Shop-Mart,
My mother leaves me parked on Diamond
To guard her Benz, her keys half-turned
So I can listen to the Quiet Storm
While she smokes a few white pebbles
At the house crumbling across the street.

I clamber to the steering wheel,
Undo my school tie, just as Luther Vandross
Starts in on that one word tune, "Creepin'."
The dashboard's panel of neon glows,
And a girl my age, maybe sixteen or so,
In a black miniskirt, her hair crimped
With glitter, squats down to pane glass

And asks, *A date, baby? For five?*
Outside, street light washes the avenue
A cheap orange: garbage swirling
A vacant lot; a crew of boys slap-boxing
On the corner, throwing back large swills
Of malt; even the sidewalk teeming with addicts,
Their eyes spread thin as egg whites.

She crams the crushed bill down
Her stockings, cradles & slides her palm
In rhythm to my hips' thrashing,
In rhythm to Luther's voice, which flutters
Around that word I now mistake for "Weep"
As sirens blast the neighborhood &
My own incomprehensible joy to silence.

Out of the house my mother steps,
Returned from the ride of her life,
Studies pavement cracks for half-empty vials,
Then looks back at bricked-over windows
As though what else mattered—
A family, a dinner, a car, nothing
But this happiness so hard to come by.

Pest

I heard the terrible laughter of termites
deep inside a spray-painted wall on Sharswood.
My first thought was that of Swiss cheese
hardening on a counter at the American Diner.
My second thought was that of the senator
from Delaware on the senate floor.
I was on my way to a life of bagging tiny mountains,
selling poetry on the corners of North Philly,
a burden to mothers & Christians.
Hearing it, too, the cop behind me shoved me
aside for he was an entomologist
in a former lifetime & knew the many
song structures of cicadas, bush crickets &
fruit flies. He knew the complex courtship
of bark beetles, how the male excavates
a nuptial chamber & buries himself—
his back end sticking out till a female sang
a lyric of such intensity he squirmed like a Quaker
& gave himself over to the quiet history
of trees & ontology. All this he said while
patting me down, slapping first my ribs, then
sliding his palms along the sad, dark shell
of my body.   How lucky I was
spread-eagled at 13, discovering the ruinous cry
of insects as the night air flashed reds
& blues, as a lone voice chirped & cracked
over a radio; the city crumbling. We stood
a second longer sharing the deafening hum
of termites, back from their play & rest,
till he swung suddenly my right arm then my left.

Don Pullen at the Zanzibar Blue Jazz Café

Half-past eight Don Pullen just arrived
from Yellow Springs. By his side
is the African-Brazilian Connection.
If it were any later, another space,
say "Up All Night Movie Hour"
on Channel 7, he might have been
a cartel leader snorting little mountains
of cocaine up his mutilated nostrils
from behind his bureau as he buries
a flurry of silver-headed bullets
into the chests of the good guys:
an armlock M-16 in his right hand,
a sawed-off double barrel shotgun
in his left, his dead blond
girlfriend oozing globules of blood
by the jacuzzi. No one could be cooler
balancing all those stimulants. No one.

She said she couldn't trust me,
that her ladybugs were mysteriously
disappearing, that I no longer
sprinkle rose petals in her bath,
that some other woman left a bouquet
of scented lingerie and a burning
candelabra on our doorstep, that she
was leaving, off to France—
the land of authentic lovers. In this club
the dim track lights reflecting off
the mirror where the bottles are lined
like a firing squad studying their targets
make the ice, stacked on top of ice,
very sexy, surprisingly beautiful & this
is my burden, I see Beauty in everything,
everywhere. How can one cringe upon
hearing of a six-year-old boy snatched
from a mall outside of London, two
beggarly boys luring him to the train
tracks with a bag of popcorn only to beat
his head into a pulp of bad cabbage!
Even now, I can smell them
holding his hand promising
Candyland in all its stripes & chutes.

Nine-fifteen, Don & the African-
Brazilian have lit into Capoiera.
The berimbau string stings my eyes
already blurring cognac, my eyes
trying to half-see if that's my muse
sitting up front, unrecognizable,
a blue specter. Don's wire fingers
scrape the ivory keys, off-
rhythm. It doesn't matter, the Connection
agrees there's room as they sway
& fall against the ceiling, a band
of white shadows wind-whipped
on a clothesline. Don's raspy hands—
more violent than a fusillade of autumn
leaves pin-wheeling like paper rain
over East River Drive in blazing reds
& yellows—hammer away, shiver in
monstrous anarchy. Don's arms arch like
orange slices squirting on my mouth's roof,
juice everywhere. His body swings up
off his haunches. The audience, surveying each
other's emotions, feel the extensions; their
bodies meld against the walls, leaving
a funeral of fingerprints as they exhale back
to their seats. Ten minutes to twelve,
I'm waving a taxi through holes
in the rain. I will tell her about tonight,
tell her how a guy named Don & his crew
The Connection hacked harmonies,
smashed scales, pulverized piano keys,
all in rhythm as each brutal chord
exploded in a moment's dawning.

Lisa Jarnot

Lisa Jarnot was born in 1967 in Buffalo, New York, and attended SUNY-Buffalo and Brown University's Graduate Creative Writing Program. Her work has appeared in *Bombay Gin*, *The Chicago Review*, *Five Fingers Review*, *Grand Street*, and elsewhere. Formerly the Editor of *No Trees*, *Troubled Surfer*, and *The Poetry Project Newsletter*, Jarnot has taught at Naropa University, the University of Colorado at Boulder, Long Island University, Brooklyn College, and elsewhere. She is the author of *Some Other Kind of Mission* (Burning Deck, 1996), *Ring of Fire* (Zoland, 2001), and *Black Dog Songs* (Flood Editions, 2003), and a coeditor of *An Anthology of New (American) Poetry* (Talisman, 1998). Jarnot now lives in New York City and is completing a biography of San Francisco poet Robert Duncan.

Poem Beginning with a Line by Frank Lima

And how terrific it is to write a radio poem
and how terrific it is to stand on the roof and
watch the stars go by and how terrific it is to be
misled inside a hallway, and how terrific it is
to be the hallway as it stands inside the house,
and how terrific it is, shaped like a telephone,
to be filled with scotch and stand out in the street,
and how terrific it is to see the stars inside the radios
and cows, and how terrific the cows are, crossing
at night, in their unjaundiced way and moving
through the moonlight, and how terrific the night is,
purveyor of the bells and distant planets, and how
terrific it is to write this poem as I sleep, to sleep
in distant planets in my mind and cross at night the
cows in hallways riding stars to radios at night, and
how terrific night you are, across the bridges, into
tunnels, into bars, and how terrific it is that you are
this too, the fields of planetary pull, terrific, living
on the Hudson, inside the months of spring, an
underwater crossing for the cows in dreams, terrific,
like the radios, the songs, the poem and the stars.

The New Life

I eat steak and live on the big neon avenue and fear strangers,
admire my neighbors, the drug store, and the bus,

I as an addict live addicted to the avenue, in the dark folds
late at night, addicted to sleep and lavender,

I went into the liquor store to buy a bottle of wine,
loving you and the liquor store, the lavender bottles, the
many directions in which the hairs on my lover's head
fall at twilight reading Roland Barthes,

I went into the sidewalk to reconstruct the broken glass,
loving sleeping I went into dark folds late at night loving my lover
but also addicted to fearing and loving my neighbor and the
types of wine,

I crawled in through the window and loving my neighbor
I loved my lover and counted the hairs on his head,

I as an addict am an addict and the street below is below
and my lover has countless hairs on his head and the poise
of living on the big neon avenue where I cut myself and
cooked the dark steak, emerging from the folds of lavender,

I cut myself and then my lover cut himself, and someone
puked on the side of a van

I fear the fears my lover fears and fearing strangers fear
the steak and twilight reading Barthes

I love him steadily reading fears and quiet the twilight reading
and quiet my lover and quiet my fears, admiring lovers and fearing
handsome strangers in the drug stores near the puked on van,

I run toward him in a bus in a dream, my lover puked on by the
children on the bus,

Coveting the drug store hip-hop lavender flowers, never quite
understanding what's been said, I admire cutting my steak,
the street below is filled with all the neighbors' heads and lovers
close behind the window weightless eating steak

I read the newspapers about the avenues and my lavender
photographed next to the wine,

I think my lover will be photographed and I am concerned about
the avenue itself, assuming neon characteristics, sometimes
casting shade,

I shade my eyes from the avenue where my lover and I make
love and the neighbors love their neighbors and the neon
characteristics of nightclubs shade the photo's eye, expecting
too much of the avenue like an unfinished painting
contrasting churches and contrasting love

I walk backward toward the street and love to be so backward
and love the lover's neighbor and casting shadows backward cast
the wine and types of love,

I close slowly avenues of poise assuming love and folds of
lover's hair,

I close slowly the sidewalk to find the broken glass, going toward
my lover to find the folds of likeness in the mirror made of glass and
waiting slowly close,

And loving how we meant to be sleeping I love the avenue
where we sleep and love the neighbors, vigilant, never quite asleep,
near the sides of vans,

I, slowly, closed with lavender, wake the lover waiting on the
avenue of glass.

Song of the Chinchilla

You chinchilla in the marketplace in france
you international chinchilla, chinchilla of the
plains and mountains all in fur you fur of the
chinchilla of the pont neuf, selling wrist
watches, on the oldest bridge of evolution that
you are, you, chinchilla, going roadside towards
the cars, the dark arabian chinchilla of the
neutral zone with pears, you still life of
chinchilla, abstractions of chinchilla, aperitif
chinchilla, lowing in the headlands in my mind,

dark, the cliffs of dover, dark chinchilla, tractor
of chinchilla, chili of chinchilla, chill of the
chinchilla, crosswalk of chinchilla of the dawn,
facilitator you, chinchilla, foodstuffs for the
food chain dressed in light.

The United States of America

I'm going to ask you to transition into a new theme
about the war. The thing that comes to mind now
is the war—the big war, the little war, the war that's
in my head, the war all around the edges of my ears,
the war to kill the troops, the war to kill the cows,
the transitional war, the bloody war, the not-bloody
war, the semi-bloody war, the figure of the neighborhood
with war, running toward the herds of cattle in the war,
not good at war, awash in war, the war-to-mores,
the more and more to war.

The Girl Who Couldn't Be Loved

> *"In every human breast there is a fund of hatred, anger, envy, rancor*
> *and malice, accumulated like the venom in a serpent's tooth, and*
> *waiting only for an opportunity of venting itself, and then, to storm and*
> *rage like a demon unchained."*   —Nietzsche

My name is Lisa Jarnot and I am a terrorist. I can tell you how it happened
to me and how I think that it occurred, thinking of myself as a terrorist,
wanting to murder and to bludgeon and to die, liking sharpness, surfaces of
sharpness and of blood. I can tell you that maybe I was born this way and
maybe I wasn't, maybe of this terror I am possibly innately so endowed,
and maybe there are other reasons too, in my training in the sciences of
sadness which is where it all begins, and if you ask me I remember certain
things, the gulf of red and white checked tiles upon the floor, the voices
overhead, the stupid son of a bitch my father was, the freaking stupid cock
sucker who was my mom, with the sounds in the air, of scissors, and canned
food, and jars of instant coffee, as they struck against the wall, of the
snowflakes flying against the porch light, and let me tell you what is good
about me, which is that I was born in 1967 in a small town near a lake and
I liked to watch the deer, and the horses, and I danced in puddles in the
springtime showers after ice storms when the crispness of the trees was
fairly new and I had these redeeming qualities, that I could read and write,

that I learned how to cook very quickly, tomato soup, and cans of beans, potatoes sliced so thin like the layers of ice upon the lake when it broke up in the springtime and we hopped from flow to flow in thick boots and thick coats in the thickness of the wind, that I wanted to live on the frontier, that the shopping center hosted a Kmart and an ice cream store, in the fields beside the highway, desolate and gray, full of briars and the sharp-edged grass, dense with nothing, spotted with the rusted tin beer cans, and I stretched out in the back of the car, chained in the hold of a slave ship, on the way to the new world, with the spiny winter treetops against the metal colored sky and the road salt making noise against the tires of the car, at night when I sat alone in my log cabin in the woods with the wind howling across the snow across the roof, with the sound of the television in the other room, when the springtime came and I built my campsite out along the side of the same house, with lawn chairs and a blanket and some boxes to keep warm, foraging for roots, jumping from chair to chair in the dark red room and barefoot down the river on a raft, raised by wolves, like the wolf boy who I saw, hiding in the tree-light on my haunches with my matted gnarled blonde hair, not a vampire or murderer or thief, but just a simple wolf, unable to sleep at night because of the sound of the airplanes overhead and the raccoons in the garbage, and the creaking on the stairwell in the dark, and what is good about me are these things, that I exist in all the forms I am, purely good, like I was then and like I am now, tenacious, in the form that my tenacity tends to take, which can be hopeful and can sometimes be obsessed, trying to be separate, alone and wide awake, trying not to get hit by a car or a bus, trying to get drunk, trying to run down the street as fast as I can, with my bicycle, red, white, with a basket on the front, trying to get somewhere quickly, and going nowhere on the way, hiding in the shadows of the house and in the shadows of the corn rows in the field, almost within reach, flailing like an animal at the gaping mouths of doors, the door to the school, the door out of the house, the door to anyplace with other people, where I couldn't go, sleeping all day, with my head down on the floor, deeply depressed, the twelve-year-old who wrecked the family known as Jarnot.

A. Van Jordan

A. Van Jordan was born in 1965 in Akron, Ohio. He is a graduate of Wittenburg University, Howard University, and the Warren Wilson College MFA Program. His poems have appeared in *Callaloo, Crab Orchard Review, Ploughshares, Seneca Review,* and elsewhere. He is the author of *Rise* (Tia Chucha, 2001), winner of the PEN/Oakland Josephine Miles Award, and *M-A-C-N-O-L-I-A* (W.W. Norton, 2004), a cycle of poems about the life of the first African American teenager to advance, in 1936, to the finals of the National Spelling Bee. Jordan is the recipient of a Whiting Writers' Award, among other honors. He has taught at the College of New Rochelle and is currently an Assistant Professor at the University of Texas, Austin.

Beggar's Song

I don't remember the last time
I was touched.
In a dream, a tongue—
Or, just breath—
Outlined my navel
With flute music
And I curled up,
Rolled to an empty beach,
Burrowed into wet sand.

When I woke,
My life was full of contradiction.
I trusted no one   not
The one who loved me   not
The ground that held me   not
The sky that caressed my cowling back.

My only fear is love;
I have a defense against all others.
My only friend is my skin;
I send letters to myself.

If I could dream now,
A dark woman would obsess
Over my hands.
She would stalk

Through brush and trees and other earth
To corner me on my back,
Stab me with her tongue,
Dance with all the forbidden steps
That my heart kept secret.

In my life, I've hid from everything above my head.
I knew my life was empty, yet I lived long.
We all come from dust. I rub my belly to the ground.
Every man has a song. I like guitars; they're full of emotion.
We all must die,
But in my death, let me live.
Take my husk and make a *charango*.
Open me up and throw away my armor.
Let blood and tears mingle with music.
Let my naked body be a mirror to the world.
Smell what lack of love does to the flesh.

Kind of Blue

How I tried to explain
the love I heard between
the notes, how I reached
for you when he played,
how when a man's heart splits open
in the middle of a song—
whether playing or just connecting—
it is not unlike a gasp
for air, at the close of sex,
at that moment, how wondrous
our faces seem when we hear
a soul speak through a horn,
how perfect the grammar
between the notes.

And it was not because I knew
I would leave you years later,
in D.C.—once I found you
in bed with another man—
that I took you downtown
to see Miles Davis in concert
at Cincinnati's Music Hall;
it was just because you could leave me

and I knew—even then when I knew
nothing, when I had just bought
my first Miles Davis album—
I knew that good memories haunt us
as much as the bad ones.
And that night in '85
I think it was because I loved
him that you hated Miles Davis.
Oh, you wore that short skirt—
your legs pouring out
like two high Cs from a trumpet's bell—
but you still had an attitude.
You said he was a heroin addict,
a junkie, that his skin stretched
like leather because of drugs.
And I was reminded
of my neighbor who was on crack
and the night he came to beg for some money,
this guy who had a wife and two kids,
I asked him why he got high,
as if it were my business.
With his head turned from me he said,
Man, it's like you're havin' sex
and you come and you just keep
comin' and comin', 15 to 20 minutes straight.
And then he looked at me and asked
Have you ever known love like that?
I gave him five dollars that night.

And despite your rolling eyes,
and the Tsssst you made with your teeth,
I bought you a ticket to the concert.

Remember how we sat on the front row
and how, in the middle of the first set,
Miles walked across the stage
on that tightrope invisible
to all but him, how he stopped at its edge,
and how he played "Time After Time"
and broke it down to you
and stared first at your legs
and then straight into your eyes.
I wasn't jealous, you see,
because he made my point for me.
And to this day, because of that night,

I know for certain
that you still love one of us.
And look at you now, years later,
getting high in your apartment,
your stereo spinning a Miles Davis disc.
You no longer question
what kind of blue pulls a man's skin
so tightly over the face.
Yes. What do the uninitiated, who can only listen,
know about this kind of love?

Public Radio Plays Eddie Harris

Clouds stand in protest of morning.

I wonder should I cross this picket-line sky and go to work.

The 70 bus stood me up for our 8:32am date.

Headlines say I voted for a man who cheated on his wife.

By 2:00pm my body's at war with a virus.

I am now blue fire.

My throat is lined with cactus.

There was no mention of this in the morning paper.

I crawl back home to my room; my bedsheets are cold.

At 10:00pm a call of bad news from my family:

Something about a car and my brother.

Doctors say he may never dance again.

This chord of bad news accompanies today's riff.

Folks *have* gone on strike in heaven.

Sweat pours off the shoulders of the night.

No need for liquids and drugs, I'm already dead.

If WPFW FM can't resurrect me, Lazarus was a liar.

Thank God, they're playing Eddie Harris.

I have friends who are atheists.

I have ammunition for our next argument:

They play four Eddie Harris tunes in a row!

Faith healers are tuning in.

I'm all but cured when they make the announcement:

Eddie Harris died today.

Thoughts tornado over my bed.

It pirouettes over the city with hips like my mama's.

Eddie always said there's no such thing as a wrong note,

Only bad connections to the next.

I put the alarm clock under the sheets.

In the morning it will sound like music.

Ilya Kaminsky

Ilya Kaminsky was born in 1977 in Odessa, in the former Soviet Union, and immigrated with his family in 1993. He earned his BA at Georgetown University, and received a law degree form the University of California at Berkeley. His poems have appeared in *American Literary Review, Gulf Coast, The Jerusalem Post, The New Republic, Salmagundi,* and elsewhere. His poetry in English has been recognized with a Ruth Lilly Fellowship from *Poetry* magazine and the Metcalf Award from the Academy of American Arts and Letters, and his poetry in Russian was featured at the Venice Biennial festival. Kaminsky is the author of a chapbook, *Musica Humana* (Chapiteau Press, 2002), and a full-length volume, *Dancing in Odessa* (Tupelo, 2004). A former George Bennet Writer-in-Residence at Phillips Exeter Academy, Kaminsky lives in Berkeley, California, and works as a law clerk at Bay Area Legal Aid.

Author's Prayer

If I speak for the dead, I must leave
this animal of my body,

I must write the same poem over and over,
for an empty page is the white flag of their surrender.

If I speak for them, I must walk on the edge
of myself, I must live as a blind man

who runs through rooms without
touching the furniture.

Yes, I live. I can cross the streets asking "What year is it?"
I can dance in my sleep and laugh

in front of the mirror.
Even sleep is a prayer, Lord,

I will praise your madness, and
in a language not mine, speak

of music that wakes us, music
in which we move. For whatever I say

is a kind of petition, and the darkest
days must I praise.

Dancing in Odessa

We lived north of the future, days opened
letters with a child's signature, a raspberry, a page of sky.

My grandmother threw tomatoes
from her balcony, she pulled imagination like a blanket
over my head. I painted
my mother's face. She understood
loneliness, hid the dead in the earth like partisans.

The night undressed us (I counted
its pulse) my mother danced, she filled the past
with peaches, casseroles. At this, my doctor laughed, his granddaughter
touched my eyelid—I kissed

the back of her knee. The city trembled,
a ghost-ship setting sail.
And my classmate invented twenty names for Jew.
He was an angel, he had no name,
we wrestled, yes. My grandfathers fought

the German tanks on tractors, I kept a suitcase full
of Brodsky's poems. The city trembled,
a ghost-ship setting sail.
At night, I woke to whisper: yes, we lived.
We lived, yes, don't say it was a dream.

At the local factory, my father
took a handful of snow, put it in my mouth.
The sun began a routine narration,
whitening their bodies: mother, father dancing, moving
as the darkness spoke behind them.
It was April. The sun washed the balconies, April.

I retell the story the light etches
into my hand: *Little book, go to the city without me.*

Maestro

What is memory? what makes a body glow:
an apple orchard in Moldova and the school is bombed—

when the schools are bombed, sadness is forbidden
—I write this now and I feel my body's weight:

the screaming girls, 347 voices
in the story of a doctor saving them, his hands

trapped under a wall, his granddaughter dying nearby—
she whispers *I don't want to die, I have eaten such apples.*

He touches her mouth as a blind man reading lips
and yells *Shut up! I am near the window, I*

am asking for help! speaking,
he cannot stop speaking, in the dark:

of Brahms, Chopin he speaks to them to calm them.
A doctor, yes, whatever window

framed his life, outside: tomatoes grew, clouds passed and we
once lived. A doctor with a tattoo of a parrot on his trapped arm,

seeing his granddaughter's cheekbones
no longer her cheekbones, with surgical precision

stitches suffering and grace:
two days pass, he shouts

in his window (there is no window) when rescue
approaches, he speaks of Chopin, Chopin.

They cut off his hands, nurses say he is "doing OK"
—in my dream: he stands, feeding bread to pigeons, surrounded

by pigeons, birds on his head, his shoulder,
he shouts *You don't understand a thing!*

he is breathing himself to sleep, the city sleeps,
there is no such city.

Sally Keith

Sally Keith was born in 1973 in Charlottesville, Virginia. She holds a BA from Bucknell University and an MFA from the University of Iowa Writers' Workshop. Her poems have appeared in *American Letters & Commentary*, *Conjunctions*, *Denver Quarterly*, *New England Review*, and elsewhere. She is the author of *Design* (Center for Literary Publishing, 2001) and *Dwelling Song* (University of Georgia Press, 2004). Keith has previously taught at Rhode Island College and served as the Emerging Writer Lecturer at Gettysburg College. Currently, she lives in Rochester, New York, and teaches at the University of Rochester.

Orphean Song

Dear smoke: It puzzles

    and it shuts me in my room where I dream
of home—a folder full of flowers, not pressed.
Your photograph, I've caved it
for the keeping jar and I'm afraid: I've bent
the brow, the hair not meant to move again.

Dear you: Confess

    How many ways am I missing?
I've lost our final folding doll, so stole
a splash of night to hold it in this vacant pear.
I fear the viceroy wing I've framed
tacked in glass, hung where I stare on the pane.

    The sky keeps coming.
And if color will, I am, but if the wing is split
again, I'm wrong—the filaments will splinter
and yellow open so glints go glitter and this
I'll brush away—deceived before.

Dear law: I got caught

    I was singing when they spied me.
The peasants got scared and dropped their forks
leaving the fallow fields, leaving
light stuck on the metal and the sound
of that song got stopped there in the stones.

The details do not improve.
Me muscle, me skin, and me bones,
But once a land and it grew. The wind turned white,
the undersides of leaves, they bled with the sun
on the tops of the others and here is the sound—

Dear one: Name this

   a stair dug for the day, a song
so it beckons and it pulls me through
the holes in the leaves. They've found me
glancing through to the base of the mound.
I found swarthy-like torches of red.

   I was willing then to sing again.
I'm out for my walk on the line.
When I reach the top of the road
the blackness lifts. It turns and in turning
it's swelling to two large clouds—

Dear love: A ladder

   in between. One falling to
the other. One drops
a flight of stairs. These are bones
in the sky. Fossils. A broken
cage. Washboard prayer.

   A missing tongue, pressing
its only word. Sad and
stammering on—Dear dear:
free, I'm free,
free, I'm asking

Mechanics

The truss cuts early Autumn's blue plane
   into uneven strips. Loss—
merging
color, darkness into this
            widening line, this blurred

frame. It holds, but the holding heavy
the frame not straight. We can never

touch the trusses. (They are a strong math.) Though

I do not doubt.

The leaves are (still) green. Fish still slip
    especially in the fishhouse
                                    the eye (still) stares
on the bed of crushed ice.

    Is this a need (for interruption)?

(And) the frame is not
    straight (and) the car moves on (and)
the mind goes back (and) the hand
                        still waves.

    Learning to find the moment, she said, is something solid

we can build ourselves on. The moment

(I know) is not, it is
                the division of water, seeing this once
or: I will forget my eyes and see the thing doubled. I need
                                    to understand

(the mind is divided, but) the passing
                            we never see.
What is (need)
            watching?

        Consider that the car moves at an average speed.
        The river is the Rappahannock
                            and cantilevers hold us (here).
        The town behind us empties out. Small houses (I do not know—

        what is their name?) fall from the center, teeter
        in a nervous line. Trailers grid the top of the bank.
        The whitewash of the fishing boat (below) reflects

        noon's straight glare. But (I want)
        to touch the wood. Each existence
        extends. It is precarious

        or: it grows—it moves
        forward (from the edge to bank
        with fish) with the straight

truss and time. Speak or hear—
There are two halves.
This part is not involved.

Units of words/mystery/faulting/folding/the history of calling

What is it we cannot see?

And how then shall we begin?

The moment necessary for crossing—
    it is not easy
to find. I know nothing about physics,
    mystery is finding each moment, struggling—
each axis—every point.

The man, below, reels in the fish, holds
    its fat body in his bare hands, stopping
the struggle, stilling it, lifting it
    off the hook—there is a hole
(now) below the fish's lip
    but the fish still slips. We keep supposing
moving depends on this. The shadows
    of the trusses (now) cut the sun into strips.

And consciousness—named (mind)
                                        (named) space?

Now whitecaps, because wind. Shadows faster
    and less and less sun. Or:

Which pieces would you choose to carry over?

I was standing in the middle
                        of the hill (the voice (still)
                                stands). The eyes looked
with persuasion. I turned
                (missed ascent) did not achieve—
                        the eyes too full (the voice)

    too heavy.

The view best from the top? I will never—

(see)/fingers/figures/penciled/paper
with grids. The grids for keeping
the lead in straight lines. The arrows (also)

arcs of precision, and rows upon rows and pages.
To stack the pale green grids, to hold them
in my hand. The grid for the numbers—

for the safety of line. Memory—
                      I will cross
                           the bridge. The words—
move around the room.

  Live crabs
          in summer. Raw oysters
in Autumn—their gray mass (in)
                     a punch bowl (and)
the small cup holds almost
                 twelve two-tined forks.
Brazil nuts fall, triangular (from)
                the shell. The shell
is empty. (It is)
         hollowed out. We can
know (touch)
        the inside. It is rough. (It is)
sculpted.
     Will you
          not come again?
     I will go—
there soon.
     Will you
          not come again?
     I will cross—
the river twice

         (The fishing boats are gone
            the water is strange and gray.
         She sits inside and stares
            at rough pages of a book.
         She moves her fingers
            down the margins
         thinks of empty space
            names the space)
the bridge.

The Gallery

I'm sitting in the kitchen and
    I've thought to list the things
that line the little town
      in me. I've thought to hang
my portraits on these walls, where
      light is stretching, already, though
it seems, at three, too soon. One,
    a door ajar. But the strokes are too thick
and if inside it's night, some lighter hue is
      leaking in. In Two
you left and the fog fell. Didn't I write
      to tell you? This painting is gray. There were shapes
underneath. I can't read them,
    now. It doesn't rise. Wet and it doesn't rise.
I'm taking notes on this envelope because
      the concerto adds to a slowness
in the leaves, blown off, see, and digging
    shallow trenches in the snow.
Three, where no color was
      the willow wisps to yellow were
stripped, and the willow in front of
      the grander, brownish-black trees. Underneath
a pail. In it stones. I picked one up
      and still damp from the snow
it shone.
    I write: it is currently seven degrees. In this
gentle after-breeze the body of
      the trenched leaf mechanically blows
open, falls closed like a lid. Four,
    the footprints in the frozen snow, false
tracks. I write it: Who is this cozening
    hidden lord who leads me? Five,
a drowning and a line.
    It is I. And you must
never cross nor ever trust beyond it.
    My legs are hidden and kicking. Salt
still burns in my lungs. The concerto then
    was not to be played and we didn't want
that portrait to be seen. Six, then,
    is in the form of a dream
where the earth went white and into the sky
    a magnificent fiery red. It is seeing what

I'm not supposed to see. Inside the closet, if I open
   the door, a pool of burning light.
Seven, it may have been the ocean
   an infinitude of wave-framed plates that catch
each bit of sun from the day, unfailingly. So caught
   it's carried, collided. This is where I can't
believe. It must have been a prayer. Eight, it could have been
   the field covered in snow, but broken by
the stalks—a metal collage where
   the can's sharp edge folds
against a bar of heavier lead. Where the edge juts.
   Where we should not touch. We should not—
Nine, you know this. Here nothing crept.
   The violinist plays exactly how
she meant to play. We keep pushing. But
   light roils until it is thin and then
it goes away. We should not—
   You know this. The door shuts.
And in Ten it shuts so it slams.

Subtraction Song

My real name got lost in the letter
I kept trying to write. There I was.

I'd sketched the field with Queen Anne's lace
the radial heads I'd given in
mathematical light. Two then:

I use a ruler to extend the planes.
Pullied and chained, they intersect.
They build me this crosshatched house.

I had an addressee.
I have a tangled house.
Two then: I'm making this object

and it equals a song. And the song's to be sung
in the church. And the roof of the church is to house
the song. And the house is what we'll offer up.

One: are you leaving?

(Two then: I reread my museum note:
Skeleton-cage, what is empty?)

The object, here, a handmade wooden box.
Extend the planes. Examine the arrows.
Study the torque.

Is light in there? It matters.
It matters like the candle's steel flames
still brief, the soft sound

dominoes make falling in a line
if the floor is made of wood.

Two then: don't speak for now.
And One is off to sleep.
Two then: are they stuck inside you?

I answered: stone ghosts.
I answered: congealing.
            (Two then: then fly away, fly away all.)
I answered: thick throat.

            (One: I reread my note from June:
                A man and a woman stand in a clearing
                their shadows drop in the hands of a clock.
                Their shadows stop and the couple slips
                into the circling trees.)

Two then: stop flying.
And One.
Two then: help me through

the fact of you.
And One whispers:
open the box.

            (Two then: I reread my note from May:
                Where gnats hurry in patches of slow pond air
                the world shuts—a quaking lid. Consider this fact:
                I'm sitting here. Here things don't leave.)

And I didn't know then. I'd called the stone
my final proof, sunk in the center of the field,
sunk at the foot of the tree. And there I'd leaned

singing you the song as you sat
in your box, singing once the shadows
lifted off and went away—

The elegy sang itself blue for the rock.
Two then: I've studied how we're meant to act.
And One. He cried himself to sleep.

> (In my notes the sand crabs were dusty white
> the white of no reflection, the white in which
> things sink. And by moonlight, the crabs
> slipped from the sand to the sea.)

Two then:
Love-veil, what color are you?
One, in silence, went white.

> (Two then: I reread my notes to find fragments of letters:
> *Dear One—Today is.*
> *And the sun for the first time in weeks.*)

Two then: if you can pry the planks
call my name. Apprentice me there.
There in the chance of that light.

One calls:

> (Two: I reread my notes that label the box:
> *A carpet rolled up.*
> *An ocean pulled out. Tangles and chokes.*
> *All pulling. Frays at the edge.*
> *The sound you make falling after me.*
> *That crashing sound the fact makes.*)

Two then:

One.

Suji Kwock Kim

Suji Kwock Kim was born in 1968 and grew up in Poughkeepsie, New York. She received her BA from Yale University and her MFA from the University of Iowa Writers' Workshop. Kim was subsequently a Fulbright Fellow in Korea and a Wallace Stegner Fellow at Stanford. Her poems have appeared in *The New York Times, The Los Angeles Times, The Washington Post, The New Republic, Open City, The Paris Review, Ploughshares,* and other major newspapers and journals. She is a past winner of the "Discovery"/*The Nation* Prize and has been awarded fellowships and grants from the NEA, The Fine Arts Work Center in Provincetown, the New York Foundation for the Arts, the Blakemore Foundation for Asian Studies, and elsewhere. Her first book, *Notes from the Divided Country* (Louisiana State University Press, 2003) won the Academy of American Poets' Walt Whitman Award and the Bay Area Book Reviewers Award, and was a finalist for the PEN Center USA award and the Griffin International Poetry Prize. Kim is currently Chair of Writing and Assistant Professor of English and Asian Studies at Drew University. She lives in New York.

Occupation

The soldiers
are hard at work
building a house.
They hammer
bodies into the earth
like nails,
they paint the walls
with blood.
Inside the doors
stay shut, locked
as eyes of stone.
Inside the stairs
feel slippery,
all flights go down.
There is no floor:
only a roof,
where ash is falling—
dark snow,
human snow,
thickly, mutely
falling.
Come, they say.

This house will
last forever.
You must occupy it.
And you, and you—
And you, and you—
Come, they say.
There is room
for everyone.

Monologue for an Onion

I don't mean to make you cry.
I mean nothing, but this has not kept you
From peeling away my body, layer by layer,

The tears clouding your eyes as the table fills
With husks, cut flesh, all the debris of pursuit.
Poor deluded human: you seek my heart.

Hunt all you want. Beneath each skin of mine
Lies another skin: I am pure onion—pure union
Of outside and in, surface and secret core.

Look at you, chopping and weeping. Idiot.
Is this the way you go through life, your mind
A stopless knife, driven by your fantasy of truth,

Of lasting union—slashing away skin after skin
From things, ruin and tears your only signs
Of progress? Enough is enough.

You must not grieve that the world is glimpsed
Through veils. How else can it be seen?
How will you rip away the veil of the eye, the veil

That you are, you who want to grasp the heart
Of things, hungry to know where meaning
Lies. Taste what you hold in your hands: onion-juice,

Yellow peels, my stinging shreds. You are the one
In pieces. Whatever you meant to love, in meaning to
You changed yourself: you are not who you are,

Your soul cut moment to moment by a blade
Of fresh desire, the ground sown with abandoned skins.
And at your inmost circle, what? A core that is

Not one. Poor fool, you are divided at the heart,
Lost in its maze of chambers, blood, and love,
A heart that will one day beat you to death.

On Sparrows

1
You are the song that lies beyond the ear.
Nothing gnaws like you. Wing-thrash. Bloodbeat.
     A mockery of air.

Here among woodrot and dung,
I hear sparrows churring beyond the creosote-soaked fence,
beyond the dump guttered with toxins and tar,
     beyond my eye.

They are not
what is not. If they cannot
lead me to you, they carry me
beyond myself—a faint whistling
whirring through locust roots, their far-off trills
thrumming through loam and scum, three low-pitched calls
gristling through husks, bark scabbed with moss or mold.
Shreds of unbodied voice bleed off the wind—
     sweet, sweet, sweet.

Now I am afraid
my listening will erase all that is
not you. How to stay faithful
to earth, how to keep from betraying
its music—each note soaking bracken and thorn,
now burring mulch and scurf, each chur growing louder
as the birds fly closer, across a barbed-wire lot in sodium light,
across the slop-gorged pit where sewers pour,
until a swarm of bodies scatters through the sky like shrapnel, exploding
     into sight.

2

Are not two sparrows sold for a farthing?
And one will not fall to the ground without your Father.

(King James Bible)

2

Without your Father's will.

(New Oxford Bible)

3
In the air

but not of it.

At dawn I glimpse them, simmering

like flies above a corpse-dark field.

Tinder for the eye—

black forms grating

my glance, each shape scraping

sclera and nerve like a match,

until the sparrows become

themselves.

Sunrise strikes

the horizon's strip of fuel—

until earth

ignites, the visible world spreading

like a spark thrown into gasoline

and leaping into fire

———

Now each steel-streaked sparrow

arrows toward me

in a whistling arc.

Bullet without a gunner.

Aircrack. Forethirst.

Of smoke and umber wings.

Their flock a blur

of blades, a shattered

grid, shreds ripping farther apart

as the birds come closer.

Now they light

on a leafless oak,

filling its arms

with coal-and-ochre leaves.

Suji Kwock Kim   207

Now I feel my eye

        tear. I want to know what they can't

———

resemble, these birds, what my retina

        retains

of their bodies. What is burned

        into the gaze's maze of nerves,

and what

        is changed?

I want to hold them. I see

        I will never hold them unharmed.

Now something leaps across

        each synapse intact,

to fire

        the engine of dreaming within.

And something is broken down,

        consumed in its furnace

of wish

        and will.

4
There's a special providence in the fall of a sparrow.
        (Hamlet)

4
My thoughts are lesions in my brain. I want to be a machine.
        (Hamletmachine)

5
One sparrow catches
        my eye.
Crown
    the hues of charred iron and mud,
plump head jerking back and forth after it perches.
I love the way it never soars
        too far from earth.
Nor does it land
        for long, scudding from branch
to lichen-crusted branch, each one
        a temporary ground.
I love how this sparrow appears
        to have no love

for the vertical—how it skitters across thicket and scrub,
or away,
       to flit up or down.
No grid of thought seems
                searced into its brain,
freeing it to fly without aim but not without
pleasure, claws ungrasping the limb it leaps from,
bough snapping back with the sound of meathooks creaking
when smoked slabs, scabbed with salt, are unhung.
O flight and joy, this ancient dance of flesh and wind,
the sparrow's bloodwinged body beating through the air—
and yet, if seen only with the eye,
not much, a machine of meat and bone,
dirt-colored, small, stricken with lice.

6
CLAY-COLORED SPARROW. *Spizella pallida* 5 1/4" (13 cm) A pale sparrow of
       midcontinent; plain-breasted. Note the cream crown stripe and
       sharply outlined brown ear patch.
VOICE: 3 or 4 beats: *bzzz bzzz bzzz*. Unbirdlike.

6
SWAMP. SAVANNAH. SEASIDE. FIELD
LARK. GRASSHOPPER. FOX. AMERICAN TREE.
WHITE-THROAT. GOLD-CROWNED. VESPER. SONG.

James Kimbrell

James Kimbrell was born in 1967 in Jackson, Mississippi. He attended Millsaps College, the University of Southern Mississippi, the University of Virginia, and the University of Missouri-Columbia, where he received his PhD. His poems have appeared in *The Kenyon Review*, *The Nation*, *Poetry*, and elsewhere. Kimbrell's two books of poems are *The Gatehouse Heaven* (Sarabande, 1998) and *My Psychic* (Sarabande, 2006). With Yu Jung-Yul, he translated *Three Poets of Modern Korea* (Sarabande, 2002). The recipient of a Ruth Lilly Fellowship and a Bess Hokin Award from *Poetry* Magazine, a "Discovery"/*The Nation* Award, an NEA Fellowship, and a Whiting Writers' Award, Kimbrell lives in Tallahassee, Florida, and is Director of Florida State University's Creative Writing Program.

Empty House

Every few nights I walk over here, screen door opened
And springless, leaves now up to the second step,
No one watching out the window but me with my elbows
On the ledge, my face staring back at my staring in.

What if all along, I'd been waiting in there? What if
The bird left its nest behind the mantel and built
Another beside this glass? I still wouldn't know
How to read something so physical as any moment is,

Something as known as a crooked stick, as the look
Of one wing in the other. Maybe it's true that everything
Leads to this, a night in which silence displays its own

Hidden architecture, the hewn gables, the untranslatable
Syllable of moon in a tilt above the roof, only to show
How absent the self is. How picked of words. How near at hand.

Letters to a Vanishing Fiancée

1.
The night you left I hooked my heart to that silver
Train's caboose, so to become, to be, if not
Together, at least passionately dismembered

There among the creosote ties and the rust-spiked
Rails that led, more and more, to you. How quickly
The past became a movie I fell salty-lipped and

Fast asleep in. How walking from that station
Was like waking in a theater, bewildered, the music
At a mawkish end. (What was that woman's name?

And who was the man she called "My Scientist"?
And why the telescope in the revolving door?
And what did she believe when she said she believed

In him? And why did that city look dark blue?)

2.
You loved me, you loved me not the moment
We split beside the Hudson. We had one map
To the gallery marked X, and two ways

Of arriving, apologetic, so famished
For one another that we would've laid down
On the wide marble steps were it not

For the bed of pigeon droppings. We took
The first thing agreed upon—the wrong
City bus. And though it drove us far from home,

How could we have argued, stunned
As we were by evening, by the pier pasteled
With dusk, our window-glazed reflections

Rising in the surface of each other.

3.
A momentary stay: that night, for instance, we slipped
Beneath the barrier chains, waltzed across
The viewing deck and assumed our table

At the abandoned café. If anyone had seen us
They would have known that we'd
Just made the grand decision to marry

No later than the fall. But the bay looked rugged
From that jagged height, and the moon nested
Like a hangnail hooked in the wind-bent trees.

And though we strolled through that darkness
As if through a curtain parted for applause,
If we'd not shown up to see our own appearance

It would hardly have existed at all.

4.
What we mistook for love was love replete
With silences we kept falling through.
Our first date: a failed attempt at biking. Our second:

A night at the planetarium, a heaven we couldn't help
But give in to once we'd reached your room;
Your dress draped on the chair-back, and cricket sounds

Bending through the window screen surrounded
The crooked space between my body and yours,
An absence which outlasted us. Such was our

Beginning, and such would be our end: two friends—
One adrift amidst the platform bustle, the other
Stepping into the passenger car's interior glow,

Glancing at the numbered seats, walking down the row.

Salvation

It's not that I harbor a weeping willow
Shadow's worth of longing for those cloaked
        Turns and straightaways, or that swampy
South Mississippi was ever half as tragic
        As I dreamed it could be, but that I still cruise
From time to time in the dope-ripe
        Ford Fairlane of the mind where nothing
Has changed, where we remain hopelessly
        Stoned devotees of the TOWN OF LEAKESVILLE
Emblazoned upon the graffitied water tower's

Testimonies to love. We believed speed
Would save us, would take us fast
      And far away from the junkyard wrecks
Stacked in their mile-long convoy to nowhere.
  And though losing the way should
Have seemed the worst of divine betrayals,
      We took it as a minor fall from grace,
Tail-spun over the embankment rail, rocking
      That flung steel body down as if to play
A barre-chord on the barbed-wire fence.
    I'll never know what angelic overseer
Was bored and on duty that night, but we
      Rose up and climbed out of the warped last
Breath of that car, no one with so much
      As a scratch on his head, not a drop
Of beer spilt, and the radiator hissing
      Like a teapot in hell when someone yelled
She's gonna blow! and each of us
      Standing there, starving for something more,
Something other than the back wheel
      Spinning that sudden dark, cricketed quiet.

My Psychic

has a giant hand
      diagrammed in front of her place
on West Tennessee.
    It towers above a kudzu hill as if
  to offer a cosmic *How!*
           as in *Hello!* from a long
way off, as in how

she already knows
      the sundry screwed up ways a day
can go days before
      I park my wreck on the hill again beside
  her white Mercedes. O
         little slice of Lebanon!
O cedar scented

cards fanned like feathers
      of a Byzantine peacock! Tell
me again how I

might have been a fine lawyer, that I'll raise
four kids in Tallahassee, how
            I married—it's true—on
my lunch break—*Yez*

she took you to lunch
        okay a zeven year lunch ha ha!
Incense. Mini-shrine.
        A wagon train of chihuahuas snoozing by
her slippers. *You have anxious*
        about a future...I do. But
lately I've grown cold,

unconsoled by her
        extrasensory view. I think
—no need to speak—across
        the black tabletop, I don't want to know
if I'll find a bright city,
        a room by the river, a love
I will recognize

by her dragonfly
        tattoo. O narrative of ether!
O non-refundable
        life facts! say that what happens may not matter,
    or that it matters as any
            story does when two fresh lovers
embrace the old pact

(her bra on the chair,
        his socks in the kitchen) that says
their love is level,
        unfabled, new. Level with me, tell me why
    the dogs on the floor, little
            moon-fed hounds of Delphi, seem
so over it, so

done with the fleas of
        destiny. Maybe that's the right
attitude, no need
        to ask why I'm here on a perfectly blue
    Friday, content with
            what the thin air, what the dust
motes in the light say

near the high window. I
   should've learned that music long ago—
O soundless number!
      O jukebox of being that the dogs dream to! No
   faux crystal ball, no tea leaves
            or terrace in the nether
reaches of my palm

will make her answers
      less like hocus pocus in a purchased dark.
It's time to pay, to drive away
      from telepathic altitudes, to say adieu
   to why love ends. How
               a heart opens again. Why
anything is true.

Joanna Klink

Joanna Klink was born in 1969 in Iowa City, Iowa. She attended Carleton College, the University of Iowa Writers' Workshop, and Johns Hopkins University, where she received her PhD in Humanities. Her poems have been published in such journals as *Boston Review*, *Denver Quarterly*, *Gulf Coast*, *The Kenyon Review*, and *Ploughshares*, and have been recognized with a Rona Jaffe Writer's Award. Her first book is *They Are Sleeping* (University of Georgia Press, 2000). Klink is at work on a second book of poems, *Circadian*, and a book on Paul Celan called *You*. She lives in Missoula, Montana, and teaches in the University of Montana's MFA Program.

And Having Lost Track

And having lost track, I walked
toward the open field. Now transparent,
now far, the day-moon burned through the waste
air. I passed the scientists, their gentle hands
holding cinders to the light.
I passed a pile of corroding metal,
a young girl with a ring of keys.
The sound of a flute came and went.
I passed a garden under snow, a half-open book,
a man unaccustomed to grief.
And thought: what must I do differently.
And could not avoid the scraps of glass,
the fog at my knees. I, like you,
am irreparable. And aware that
when the cold clouds lift, there may be nothing.
And having lost track, I walked by the high
gold grasses, a softness I could not reach to
feel. And came upon a table laid out
with wine and winter shadow. We shall
grow heavy. And felt the signature of light,
of sound and people, laid bare within me.
And I would give it up: this weight,
this concentration. Would gladly
be mistaken, or rebuild by force what
cannot hold. I passed the slow autumn light
as it moved through the branches,
the terrible spread of deserts, the leap

of a bleeding deer.
To be outside the classifiable world,
and having lost track, and having heard
no message. As when a single existence
vanishes and the flute does not warp,
or sounds like the inside of a shell,
and the word for shell means
too many things. As if this were the last
mile, a path blooming with cold roses.
And chose the science of extraction,
the science of snow.
And walked in the dark world,
everywhere shaking with light.
That we only exist. That we do not
have the means. And are free to take place.

Porch in Snow

There you are, snow filling the air,
in the midst of quiet. The porch still with ice
and the distances shifting in us, winds
that cross as silently as the words we cannot use.
In darkness snow falling like stars over the streets,
I have always wanted this, comes quietly into the garden.
Winter, there is no prayer but this,
to be done with suffering, to hold fast
in the time of few choices. An animal
moves through the backyards, its eyes
precise and lit, the premise of everything I believe,
a whiteness that measures the sadness
of the creature unsure where it will sleep.
And every conviction that you held of what it means
gone, the evening long gone. And I think
you suffer pain. And it may be a shining
in your eyes as other sleepers enter homes.
Restless with ice, an animal crosses the wide field
in you, a darkness that asks
everything for measure, spacious world,
the animal moves against all winter,
a grace of feeling we had not imagined.
This also, comes quietly upon the winter garden
while a car starts, snowlight falling across the alley
in radiant extension of everything I cannot

see. As if the night were utterly changed,
as if you would turn to enter the rooms again,
lit against cold, and there were no further sorrow
possible for you, in any form.

Mariana Trench

35,827 feet

Palpable, principal, unearthly, is alive. Marianas, a stillness gathering

in the unrecognizable deep, cumulative, pressured, like pleasure again and

again ripped from a body. A look you give me, broken understanding,

and you know it will take hours, networks of words to begin again,

kettle and tray, truant pull of the pupil as it takes in my protests, hopes,

span of shoulders, the gauze of light and oil on these arms, birds grazing

sheets of surface burning over the trench, as if to trespass for seconds into

the blackness below, an endless inwardness beneath the bright explosions

of their wings, now gliding in some far sense of light, a boundary bathed in dusk

leaning beachward, some trust in coast at the end of day when the sweater

pulled over skin still pulses with sun, flowers set in sills to gather light

as a hand passes over the serrated stems, griefless bending and diving

in the summery breeze, sorting through conflict or simply given to motion,

my body shut in your arms, refusing conclusions, feeling the bones spread

beneath skin, an apology forming near the boundary, tense, lost, veins

full of salt-vapor, the story undisclosed, descending in the soft bluegray

of your eyes, the slow spread of depth toward some unfelt, soundless

sediment, and unraveling toward sea, in need, in everything we can spare.

Orpheus. Eurydice. Hermes.

How is it with you, that you do bend your eye on vacancy,
and with the incorporeal air hold discourse?

I

Huge birds flap through the toxin dark.
She would prefer it on the whole if he spoke in a whisper.
In the air, feet floating over the smooth porphyry path,
Orpheus in a blue wool coat, Eurydice shaking.
Hermes flits between them.
If he were more inclined to speak he would say *it works*
first upon sensation would say *it shimmers*
through the natural arcades and alleys of the body
would say *then leaks slowly back into fact.*
God of this and god of that with beating wings at his ankle joints.
Huge birds murmur in the scrawny pines.
Her hair films with ice then hardens into sticks.
Bits of zero paper up her throat.
The sound so weak it hardly reached his ears.

II

Eurydice there's been talk—
I am supposed to look straight ahead.
Eurydice take my hand—
I have been instructed to look straight ahead.
Are you hurt—
When you say today you mean
This bridge, *this* bedroom—
I would prefer it on the whole if you spoke in a whisper.
Have you—
I have, yes. I think so, yes.
Are you saying—
I am saying it.
…it's been one continuous accident…
What did you say?—
I think it's lovely the color of it.

III

Hermes likes things to come easily. He didn't ask for this job.
He pulls the hood over his shining eyes. Technically,
if you count the business about the stolen cattle, God of Herdsmen
and Fertility of Herds, God of Luck, Furtiveness and Trickery,
Patron of Oratory with a General Interest in Literature
(some ghosts congregate by the brink) God of Roads
and Boundaries, Sleep and Dreams, God of Faring and The Distant

Joanna Klink   219

Message (their shuffling drops down the gorge, half-mile below
a fish leaps) Patron of Travelers and Rogues Vagabonds and Thieves,
also Patron of Gymnasts....They move across a windless meadow.
Bright unshaken place. Hurry.

IV
He forgets that he can't—he forgets the condition.
He forgets himself.
He forgets her.
He wants assurance she is still there.
He is afraid she might disappear again.
After all she was suddenly gone.
He thinks she may be blushing.
He would like to address her.
He would like to touch her small shoulder bone.
This is a generation before Troy.
His feet hurt his head burns. He is concerned,
undisciplined, seeks recognition—she is a room full of paintings—
As her foot drags behind him bits of star chip off the iron rock.
And they are going unnoticed—nothing but the unresisting air—
Hermes herds them forward, touching her on the temple, pushing
flat against his back. Ceaseless prologue, return him
more violently, there is no ordinary life, perception
is thirsty. In the claustral dark, bracken grind against his leg.

V
I can think of three ways in which an accident might happen.
(Eurydice opens her mouth and suggests)
You were exasperated with what you had done.
You were impatient.
You were absent-minded—your attention was wandering.
(He lowers his eyes) It's a technical problem—
(Hermes growls *It's not a technical problem*)
Do you realize
It does
For example
O but they wilt like other things.
After all I'm behind you.
On condition
On condition Sir I'm behind you.
(Sir, Angel of the Upper Air, Unnatural Officer, Minister of What
Keeps, Illustrious Bishop, Jewel of Clerics, Floating Mirror of the Church)
(Whatever brings it up into the nervous system more suddenly)
(Whatever nails the salt-flesh onto the bed).

VI
Would this be pointless for you—
I think probably.
You prefer to be alone—
I like the impersonality of it.
Is this because the memory is more interesting or because the
    presence is
disturbing?—You've stopped. Have you stopped?
(Love anywhere but in me)
Does this irritate you?
(Anywhere but in me take this)
If I could play for you now (Cries Hermes *O play for us now*)
Don't be silly even Tantalus has not gone back to his waves.
Is this not…?
(Proceed heavenward)
(Shudders her bone-colored skin)
You practice injury. You comment on the thing you love.
Sometimes I hardly know what I am doing, sometimes it disappears completely.
Of course you lose the damaged forms more easily in darkness.
(Reaches his arm back)(Into the robber speech)

VII
Do you feel it when I take hold of your hand?
Hermes, they are becoming free—concordance of nerves
along the walking spine, her soft clipped leg
leaning into the freakish outline
(Sisyphus sits on his rock to listen)
(For example the snow understands the orchard as it buries it)
Do you feel it when I take hold of your hand?
(Frost burns in bits between her shoulder bones)
She would prefer it on the whole if he spoke in a whisper
(His voice is dry)(Does she feel it)
Something cracking there are bridges over voids—
When I take hold of your hand
(Up ahead a ray of natural optic light)
(Whose feet, whose bodies do they wear)
Hermes semaphores wildly in the dark.
Zero of the bone.
Then her wide soul squints and the thought
grafts easily onto the animal air.

Noelle Kocot

Noelle Kocot was born in 1969 in Brooklyn, where she lives today. She holds a BA from Oberlin College and an MFA from the University of Florida. Her books are 4 (Four Way, 2001), *The Raving Fortune* (Four Way, 2004), and *Poem for the End of Time and Other Poems* (Wave, 2006). Kocot's poems have appeared in *The Best American Poetry 2001, Conduit, Fence, The Iowa Review, New American Writing,* and elsewhere. The recipient of grants from the NEA and The Fund for Poetry, as well as *American Poetry Review's* S.J. Marks Poetry Award, Kocot writes, "For a living, I am a total bottomdweller, teaching part-time at LaGuardia College, John Jay College, and various GED and LSAT prep courses in neighborhoods where there's gunfire going off as I'm teaching. I barely make ends meet. I will soon be teaching part-time at St. Francis College and The New School. My husband/mentor, composer Damon Tomblin died in 2004, after which I took religious vows in the Catholic Church. Everything I do in life is a monument to his memory and the relationship we continue to have. My hope is that someday I will quit being a poet and be a pure philosopher on the subject of death and the afterlife but dammit, I just started my sixth book the other day and I have to finish it."

Bad Aliens

They're really here, spreading their ideas
Like vulture droppings, conniving to sow
Their brazen ontologies like bone-encrusted wheat
Along our field of vision yellowed like an almanac,

Stringing our thoughts into a syzygy,
Until we cannot move them and feel instinctively
That we never will. The few, the very few,
Who escape become spokespeople for our cause,

And although their identities remain unknown
To even them, surely they will turn a phrase
Or two that will make the bastards think again
Before they steal our fluids in the night,

Suck the breath from our livestock, tearing
Off their very flesh, leaving a metallic aroma
In the air as if from singed, mineral-soaked hair.
The world is becoming a giant crematorium

Before our eyes. Next thing you know,
It'll be your big toe shot up with morphine
At your family reunion,
It'll be your child slurping blood

At First Communion, it'll be a havoc
Of suburban cannibalism bursting into flames
At the mere suggestion of an accident.
Meanwhile, the flowers hang like open mouths

As we walk around relishing
Our wisdom of refracted light.
The neighbors lounge outside the warehouse playing cards
While inside the aliens are at it again,

Warning the boy strapped to the steel table
As in a dream that he will find his end
In a myriad of abandoned mines.
And no one will come to look for him,

And no one will even think to, because by then
All will have been erased, by then we will have forgotten
Him as we have forgotten
The name of the druggist's Seeing Eye dog.

And we'll go on with our house-painting,
And we'll go on with our affairs
Of negligence, and we'll go about with our heroics
Of tin foil, and all the while the aliens

Will be waiting for the perfect hour
To land on the non-referential velvet of our lawns,
Bending each blade of grass perfectly
To match the charred feathers of the baby chicks

Still lining the barn walls from two Easters ago
Where they probed our insides brilliantly
For signs of redemption and were satisfied.
The aliens are here,

Permanently confirmed to walk among us
And because they're here already,
There will be no possession, no redeemer
Yet to come. Instead, a triangle in the sky

Reflects the sober landscape, a reminder
That angles are the highest fate of form
Like the beaten metal of shell-cases stabbing
The corners of the pulpy world.

The imprints of their ships
Reveal a plastic sincerity, as if all along
They were only here to help, as if stealing
Our children, their faces plastered

Permanently onto milk cartons, were an intergalactic feat
Worthy of a stellar bow. We know they hold
The inevitable ace, we know they wear
The hereditary apparel of extinct, misty grasses

Overgrowing the sepulchral cloth
Of the earth. We stand frozen before their badness,
We are a smoky restaurant full of soldiers
That can fly off the globe at any moment,

Leaving their beams to bisect our newest footprints
With the mockery of some season's malingering death.
The three-sided pyramid of the occipital
Can deflect only so much into geometry

Of our collective breath. I would gouge
Out the insides of this sleep so big,
I would start my own crusade if I thought I had a chance,
But they're *bad*, they're bad for *real*.

And in the word *Bad*, bordered by flashing air,
I see the wheat spin a numeral's fiery dance,
And this leaves me with two questions:

—Why all this irony?
—Are you enjoying the view?

An Ordinary Evening

There I go again shoving my wheelbarrow
Of pain across the filthy streets
Of the dimly-lit city. No one stops me,
No one says anything like, "Here let me,"

Or "Jeez, what a wonderful thing
You have there, do you know where
I can get a thing like that?"
Instead we trundle along,

My wheelbarrow and I, dodging
The strollers and shimmering cars
Which look beautiful under the orange
Streetlamps, and everyone seems as blessed

As a holy star, and I forget
My wheelbarrow for a moment,
As one might forget a warning
In a dream, and in my mind, I gather

Various items: A net crammed with the scales
Of invisible fish, the wind that passes,
Singing, and all of my widowed beliefs
Lost in a language full of storms,

And I remember just what makes my garlands
Of solitude sway like the sea
In front of a lighthouse.
Then, in the crisp rottedness

That lines the question marks of steam
Coiling out of the potholes
Which I manage to avoid for the most part,
I ponder my wheelbarrow, and all

Of its inner-meaning, which is far sweeter
When trembling on the lips of a stranger
At the end of a thin day
That sheds its shadows like a dress,

And tosses them into the flames of sunset
Blazing up from the gasoline
Shrouding the asphalt, setting
The whole sidereal sidewalk of trees on fire,

And while the others have already fled,
You and I remain caught
In this conflagration, yet I can say nothing
And only observe the melting scene

Flashing across your beatific eyes,
And it is there, only there
That I can finally bring myself to say,

"Yes, I think I would like some help
With this. Here you go."

Gypsy Summer

There is a votive X tattered like a chewed card,
A duck swaying in the rainless morning on a lake,
And in the brain-balancing streaks of moonlight,
A trapeze crumples to the floor,
Long or oblong, a kind of addition.
I am looking at my credit

Report, bad, very bad credit
I have. I held about twelve cards
At once "for an emergency," twenty-five years old, rolling in my addition.
I was living in a lacustrine
City, camping out at night on the green floor,
Dreaming of tiny alligators in the moonlight

On a serial killer campus, how the moonlight
Flecked a victim's hair as her head spun on a turntable, a credit
To Danny Rollins' sick imagination, how he wept on the floor
After stealing her student ID card
From her headless pocket. The owls on the lake
Were silent that night, in addition

To puffing into phantom letters of NY Times want ads
In my sleep. The moonlight
Came and went, but still I spoke in the vocabulary of lack
When I told the Brooklyn gypsy three months later of my spanking credit
And how, if she removed my god-awful curse, I would renounce reading Tarot cards
For good. She smiled, made me lie down on her polished wood floor,

And danced around me counter-clockwise, flooring
Me with her predictions of my imminent demise, in addition
To her prediction of me as the wild card
Who, for $45,000, would prevent all my friends' souls from dispersing in the moonlit
Night forever and forever. I gave it to her. People wonder how the credit-
Ratings of manic-depressives get so fucked up, and I can tell you, it doesn't take a lake

Around a temple of proverbs to tell the tale, no lake
Of infernal fire to help the story along, although the fluorescent
Gates of hell are far from strangers. The false nodes of that summer don't discredit
The season five years later, where, added
To my thinking the future mayor of NY was the antichrist with a plan, the moonless
Midnight spoke to me in tongues and the bloated transparency of angels carded

Me for liquor I'd tried to buy on credit but couldn't. The addition
Of ducks to the lake in Central Park failed to floor
Me like the Bellevue moonlight. It bleated, pick a card, any card, any card but
    this card.

Civilization Day

It is nearly always an excuse, never to have done this,
Never to have done that, and it's easier to say
I have this or that to do instead of simply,
I am always in pain. It's true,

If you look at it long enough, (look at anything),
It's true. And the suffering that seems
To come from elsewhere, well, this is
Only the day absurdly hanging its head,

The day that takes the solar road
Past the eulogies that dream us, and it is sad,
Very sad, to think that the flesh is so stupid
That it doesn't even care.

Because vanity is a silver falling forward into life
With its tight jaws and expiating teeth,
A garage to hide its febrile daydreams in while it feeds
On the burning that is besieged. And the false

Vows which destroy me, and which nonetheless,
I carefully pronounce, crowd around to lick
The sores of evening, while someone else
Pulls the lion from the thorn-green sound.

But today is a day to be civilized,
It is Civilization Day! The heat rises
Off the table, the glass moves sideways,
And I run into the rain, of which I speak

So familiarly, and I don't have to do anything
Per se. The Northern Lights still clinging
To my fingers, somewhere I live out my double life,
Yet without the tomorrows hurling through the loops,

And that which has frightened me is dragged
Over the raped earth into the whiteness of spring.
Because time ends in the vagueness of legends,
As my sovereign thoughts remind me that it is the light

That defines us, subtly seeking its own.
That time I was so helpless—it rises up
In the unmade sheets while my eyes
Go numb across the pleasant plant.

"Poetry is made in bed like love,
Poetry is made in a forest,"
But today is Civilization Day, and my demolished
Dynastic cravings and the statements that are heir apparent

Say, "It depends upon how well one rides
A bucket into the saving grace of wind,"
And so it all goes on in the dangling of a mind.
I could walk up and down this tree-lined

Street for hours and point out what I see:
There are fetuses strung together underground like cans,
Infinitely regressing, there are burning bridges,
There are other things I can't help anybody with.

But today, oh you know what it is,
Today the sky opened up and poured out Kierkegaard,
And his quiet fire dressed my hair, and somewhere I lived
Out my double life; such is the inventiveness of absence.

Meanwhile, I am living a life not to be believed
With a nearness that hurts my eyes, a bird seeking
Successive autumns across the stinging snow.
At other times I'll say, "Press the stop button, press it!"

With the vexed exclamation of the noisy deaths that wake the world.
Mostly I just sit around and watch the rain,
A book of vowels underneath my elbow, and I work in this empty room
Toward some enlightened dawdling, listening for the drill

That will fill the cavity in my heart,
And for the fear that almost broke it open but could not
Or would not make me fall face down upon those inroads
Of infernal mystery to that which has fully come through.

And when evening breathes again into this kitchen
Onto a stack of plates, I will lift up my candle
And join with those who've prayed, I will still myself
And wait for my portion of the brainfood of my surviving days,

Because today itself is Civilization Day,
And though I walk in the valley of the shadow
And though I walk in the valley of the shadow
I have the right to be mortal, and I do what I have to do.

I Am Like a Desert Owl, an Owl Among the Ruins

The alpha You. The omega You.
My grandmother's ghost, its girlish snafu
Basking in the waters of urgency.

But I want the coolness of snow.
I want pairs of hands that speak to me cleanly,
Sutras to resuscitate what reigns

Over warped celluloid and heirlooms I can't touch.
There are no family photographs.
Once I was ordinary.

I rattled around with arms, with legs,
With a damp remembering that served me well.
Then, a little sleep, a little slumber,

A little folding of the hands to rest.
I asked myself, don't you just love it?
And then, why don't you just love it?

And then, from what grace have I fallen?
As I Sisyphus with his mtue rock
Unsettling the topsoil, dissolved now

Into brandied battle shouts and pages that breathe like people?
There are hazards here, more so than before
The Furies struck and scarved the white night sifting

The bright waterlights blinking
And grieving over a mash of ice.
Like them, I wanted only to die, moon-dark, blessed,

Poised beneath the driest arrows of my suffering,
Far from the flocks of burning, singing gulls,
Face to face with the God of my childhood.

Katy Lederer

Katy Lederer was born in 1972 in Concord, New Hampshire. Educated at the University of California at Berkeley and the University of Iowa Writers' Workshop, she edits the journal *Explosive* and serves as a Poetry Editor of *Fence*. Her poems and prose have appeared in *American Poetry Review, Boston Review, Harvard Review, GQ,* and elsewhere, and have been recognized with a grant from the New York Foundation for the Arts. Lederer is the author of the book of poems *Winter Sex* (Verse, 2002) and of the memoir *Poker Face: A Girlhood Among Gamblers* (Crow 2003), which was included on *Publishers Weekly's* list of the Best Nonfiction Books of 2003, named one of *Esquire's* Best Books of the Year, and honored with a Discover Great New Writers citation from Barnes & Noble. She currently works for a quantitative trading firm and lives in New York City.

Sympathy and Envy

Until my friends abducted me
The world was a cubicle
The point where the passage runs east to west puzzles me
Your world
It is you and, it seems, through you
I see myself
To the south is a portent
An asking for work and a shower
A cubicle
Benched
Over the horizon is the greatest writer ever to have lived
He is not blind nor sure
He is nothing and has never written anything
We care about
As we do about ourselves
If we write
As the world will go
We'll go
And we will
Pretend
In the presence
Of delinquency and parody
There are animals bursting and lacerated
By the strokes of bells
There are lashings of the soul, a trill

The movements of assassins and hunger
The world is formidable and proud
It is angry
The four points of laughter recede into heaven
We stand and listen
We know them we
Know ourselves
This advance should not now be the last
In our last breath the gleaming reminiscent teeth the scrotum
And disgust—it was rotund
It was extemporaneously pleasant
It was legal and menial
Our shoulders will leave us
Our voices will bleat
Help us the world is lost
Help us
We get what we want.

A Dream of Mimesis

It is duty and not hospitality that has diverted the ancient guest.
It is the whispered threat of sentiment and ignorance.
There is a plenitude of foresight. Before the diversion of the light.
The light is now spilling over. We now recognize him by his scar.
The feelings are being externalized. No contour is blurred, but of light
There is only the thin throat of it that hits his head. He rises—
Is seen through the curtains. Now lax—with the wind, made more solid. They are lying
Open. Their mouths are opening and closing, glistening
Slick in the yellow light. He is wanting to fuck.
The thigh is clean. The scar on the thigh is newly healed.
In the episode's chaste entrée ("once...when a boar...")—here—
He must straddle her ass. We are patient. Here, his organs begin to swell—
Lest they are spiritual, his courage will fail him. His organs are swelling—we have, here
Great depths—trimmed by delicate vulvic folds. Flesh dangles, cut.
They talk. Her hand, fraught, grabs at his clean, polished cock.
Gradually, historically, the choice has befallen him. Idols aged rot on the verge
Of legend. It runs too smoothly. The river beside her. Angst. The river is blue.
The river is not very wide. He is raping her. The situation is complicated.
The scar on his thigh is newly healed. Let's not see it just yet—let's see
Both of their bodies illuminated in a uniform fashion. He slaps her. She grabs
At his ass. A suggestive influence of the unexpressed. The separation of styles.
Light hits her throat. The thighs of each swell—then abate. The sublime action dulls the

He "persecutes" her. He is not afraid to let the realism of daily life enter into his
   sublime.
There are clearly expressible reasons for their conflict. The human problem has
   dealt with them
In this fashion. They are using two styles. The concept of his historical becoming
   has disturbed him
Into action. The episodic nature of her pain is obscured by the sublime action of
   his cock.
He is the simile of the wolf. He is seeking her nipples with his mouth ("A god
   himself
Gave him…"). The introduction of episodes. An eloquent foreground. A uniform
   present
Entirely foreign to the story of his scar ("The woman now touched it…")

In Las Vegas

1.
When I write a novel in Vegas, I ask myself what other people will think.
When I write a novel, I think a lot about eating.
When I call my friend, he gets very excited.
Out of my window I see a huge mountain.
Its striations make it look as if the rain has fallen sideways on it. Over the years
I have danced a lot. I have thought to become a novelist.
I see a mountain that looks as if drenched by the rain. I see a sky
wherein clouds drift by slowly and unendingly.
Pistons go up and down. Pendulums swing back and forth.
If a person who is in love with me reads this, they will care.
If someone who hates me reads it, they will dismiss me as an imposter.

2.
Trees are like cairns. The yard is clean. The door is opened
to let in air. I have driven great distances and listened to a lot of music.
I read things that make me jealous. Alone.
I read about people I know. All women want to be beautiful.

3.
The pool's light like moonlight.
The idea is to exercise caution and not give it up to them.
To say love and not be determined to show it then makes one a bastard.
To make proclamations as these are very pretty things to make

and to script them out and cause ugly havoc in the universe
we then must know. Over the hills there are lights.
Over the hills there are lights and this heat.
You have been the measure of all greatness.
It is pleasant of you in my mind to have been so.
You please god to love then if measuring greatness within me
found succubus to be fled, sent out, and adored.
Pray for me, I be less wholesome when trees sway.
Winds. Winds go these everywhich way.

4.
I like the sky. And I do not do
the opposite of what the trees do.
Interesting. I love you
is like sitting on a bench and you don't
mean it when you say it.
Someone else has made you say it.

Dana Levin

Dana Levin was born in 1965, grew up in Lancaster, California, and graduated from Pitzer College and the Graduate Creative Writing Program at New York University. Her poems have appeared in many national magazines, including *The Atlantic Monthly, The Kenyon Review, Ploughshares,* and *Poetry.* Levin's first book, *In the Surgical Theatre* (American Poetry Review, 1999) was honored with the Witter Bynner Prize from the American Academy of Arts and Letters, the Great Lakes College Association New Writers Award, the John C. Zacharis First Book Award from *Ploughshares,* and the PEN/Osterweil Award. Her second book of poems is *Wedding Day* (Copper Canyon, 2005). Levin has received three Pushcart Prizes, an NEA Fellowship, a Lannan Foundation Residency, a Witter Bynner Fellowship from the Library of Congress, and a Rona Jaffe Foundation Writers' Award. She lives in Santa Fe, New Mexico, teaches in the low-residency MFA program at Warren Wilson College, and directs the Creative Writing Program at College of Santa Fe.

Ars Poetica (the idea)

would it wake the drowned out of their anviled sleep—

would it slip the sun like a coin behind their eyes—

*

The idea, the teacher said, was that there was a chaos
left in matter—a little bit of not-yet in everything that was—

so the poets became interested in fragments, interruptions—
the little bit of saying lit by the unsaid—

was it a way to stay alive, a way to keep hope,
leaving things unfinished?

as if in completing a sentence there was death—

Chill Core

Are you becoming enslaved
    to a bad idea? That it all

just *happened*
  like wind or sky,
that there was nothing human in it—it was just
    part of the elements, an abuse
cosmic
    in its inevitable rounds—

I know, they were like lights, the moon bitter and the sun furious
    in a single sky,
you the dumb substance
    lodged in the alfalfa waving in acres,
bound to the rage,
    the shriveling light—
Can you see that you're not there anymore?
    You're here,

in this dream, at the shore of a vast and slow-petalled sea,
    the top of your skull perched
on your open palm—
    The wind is moving
through the convolutions, a frost dusting
    the gray ridges
of your open brain, glinting in the frigid
    light—

The white question is opening
    in your left hand,
the bone you can dig with, that can upend
    the memory
of being human
    locked in the brain's chill core—
that being of grief and terror
    I will help you assemble here.

Glass Heart

could the West creep in to your idea of happiness—abundance
    which gave no comfort,
        in which your loneliness was spared—

                    *

The student wrote: she wipes tears from her heart.

Forgotten, on the kitchen table—glassy, beaded with sweat—

The line is too sentimental, said the teacher, unless I see it literally: taking
a sponge to the anatomical heart, wiping and wiping the tears off it—

glass heart, so transparent—the tears drove around its autobahn

Then the kids came home and found it pulsing there. Like in a
washing machine, you could see the grief go round and round—

The student wrote: sucking tears out of her aorta with a straw—

*a bitterness so pronounced it was a kind of ammonia, a world
in which one could lose one's parents and be put on a train alone—*

Her grandfather had owned a little store for years. They can shoot
out the windows, he would say, wagging a finger, as long as they
don't set the street on fire—

glass heart, so transparent

Was it their mother's, their father's? It lay weeping in the heat.
But they had to leave, to help deliver groceries—

The student wrote: in my left my heart my right my bone, beating my heart
like a bloody drum—

Ovens, the grandfather muttered. In Russia they ate us raw.

so transparent

Meal after meal no one claimed it. After awhile no one saw it,
though it ticked at the center of the table like a clock—

singing O, this sack of water, swaying on its hook of bone.

Cinema Verité

And the lights go down—
hush.

And a light comes up—

the screen.

          That brightens, so well, our dark day.
That brightens

          to a fountain in a square,
dolphins without their tails—
          without their heads.
Just their arched backs
          crowning a chaos of broken nymphs, what's left
of the government
          of the sea—
The light shifts.
          Widens.
Black-and-white

          necklace of fires
erupting from the gas line, buildings bereft
          of façades—

          strangers picking through a desolation, passports,
lovers,
          gone—

          then weeping in French.
Then credits in French in Czech in Deutsch then
          the Village cafés, *joie*
to the nth
          degree—

          trumpeting out, like loud flowers,
along Bleecker Street.

          After which there's a drink.

          Then a toke, beside the garbage cans—

          And then a late train and a key in the lock and the lights going up
in the den of the metropolitan
          twelve o'clock
with its last
          hopeful seconds, that we won't
go to bed bored—

*

Hush.

Thoughts everywhere taxiing hurriedly.

A little like New York, isn't it,
ceaseless hive, humming despite a historical
            exhaustion—Outside

        the sky's
apartment panorama. Every twelfth window blued
            with light—

        beacons of the bag-eyed tribe called
Who Bricked the Doorway to Sleep—

        3 A.M., slumped on the couch, to surf
the blood
            and promise:

        dances to banish the hunch'n'shiver
the Claritin the Klonopin new
            kind of soap for an old kind of stain, channels
surging toward the sea—

                        *

        Wire of light.

        Dawn sheen
thin along the river.

        Burrowing
into every screen in your single room
            like an I.V.,
feeding the face that will medicate
            the blood in the day,
anchor
            tethering you
to *news*—

        until you step out
into the afternoon glare,
            snap on the dark lenses,

foam of gray speakers into your ears and pump up
        a perfect noise
to soundtrack the filmed-over day—

        thinking, What time does it start.

        thinking, I am so late.

        thinking, Not the 6 but the B, the B to the N, the N
to the light
        flooding the stairs up to Union Square and opening out
onto a kind of joy, the escape into the art
        of another country's pain,
and then the screen fades and the people stand and the bright suffering
        comes to an end—

        No.

        Yes.

        How.

Maurice Manning

Maurice Manning was born in 1966 in Lexington, Kentucky, grew up in Danville, Kentucky, and attended Earlham College, the University of Kentucky, and the University of Alabama. His first book, *Lawrence Booth's Book of Visions* (Yale University Press, 2001) was a Yale Series of Younger Poets selection. His second book, *A Companion for Owls* (Harcourt, 2004), is a verse sequence written in the voice of Daniel Boone. Manning's poems have appeared in *The New Yorker*, *Poetry London*, *The Southern Review*, *The Virginia Quarterly Review*, and *The Yale Review*, and have earned him writing fellowships from The Fine Arts Work Center in Provincetown and The Hawthornden International Retreat for Writers in Scotland. Manning teaches in the writing program at Indiana University in Bloomington.

First

Arriving, we walked down as if we were hill-born
and bred to know only hills, so that the end of hills
was surprising, rolling out before us like a woman's
skirts gathered and fanned across her lap, like loosely
folded fabric, like calico: spotted and patchworked
as if some big-fingered god had gently smudged
the world he made. Our horses and our dogs paused.
We had not expected glory and it stopped us dead,
which is not altogether uncommon: Moses spying
Canaan, for example, must have first stood silent
before waving his people ahead, the land smothered
in half shadow, half-light like velvet, and steadied
himself, one hand firm on his staff, the other reaching
to his brow, wiping his gray hair back. So I walked
into Kentucky barefooted and clumsy as if I had
sneaked out of school to cheat my lessons and come
upon a girl waiting for me behind a beech tree,
wondering where on earth I'd been. I stood still
on the invisible line and spit across it onto the new
map, making my first mark, wondering if I could
keep such a dark and bloody secret to myself.

A Condensed History of Beauty

1907: A man digs a deepwell on a hilltop, harnessing
       gravity, resulting in free indoor plumbing.

1926: A man and a woman sit in a country parlor by a fire;
       she reads *Sonnets from the Portuguese* out loud; he falls alseep.

1937: A boy rides a chestnut gelding twenty-six miles
       to town and twenty-six miles back without bouncing once.

1939: A boy cracks sixty-three hickory nuts with a hammer;
       a woman proceeds to bake a legendary cake.

1944: A boy takes a shotgun to a freightyard and blasts
       lead patterns on the sides of boxcars.

1945: A man picks up a coal bucket and his heart explodes; two mules
       drag his casket up a hill; the preacher recites "The Crossing of the
       Bar."

1951: A young man writes his mother from Korea:
       It has been turrble colt in this Godforsaken two bit place, ha!

1965: A gambler wins thirty-seven rocky acres and a rough-hewn house
       in a card game; he hangs a sign by the road: *Trespassers Will Be
       Shot in the Knee.*

1972: A boy climbs a tree with a slingshot in his teeth; he has a powder
       horn full of pea gravel and shoots at a washtub; it sounds like a
       church bell.

1973: A boy listens to a transistor radio while lying in a burned out car;
       that night, he tells his sister: *Today I heard you singing from a
       little silver box!*

1976: Two boys take the foot-brake off of a bicycle. One boy sits
       on the handlebars. The pedaling boy says: *Let's close our eyes.*

On Death

The best thing about dying is it frees you
from the fear of death; you get it over with,

that fear you spend your whole life dancing
around, as if it were a fire and you were
a wild, ink-streaked Indian, kicking sparks
into the heavens. But death is not anything
like a fire. Death is like the wind: it is air
once held back and now released. Death
is not a buffalo calf half eaten by wolves—
that is an example of life. A man sleeping
in the dog-trot between two cabins, or
a woman raising her skirts in the weeds,
or a collapsed trio of hoops and rotten
barrel staves, the barrel no longer a vessel—
death is like these; it has a still foreverness.
I think of death as the king of quiet falling,
in that, dying we fall, maybe off of a horse,
or maybe into a daughter's arms, but it is still
falling, like a leaf loosed from a tree, never
to hit the ground. But once we die, the sense
of falling stops because there is nothing
that we are falling from. We become plain
stones in the bottom of a river, unnoticed,
life teeming above us, sometimes someone
peering down at us but seeing a face instead
of a stone, which is not death, but the false
image of death which comes from living in fear.
So death is the one who drops stones into
the water, shattering the image, as we sink,
and we look up from our river of foreverness
at life, painted and wild and scared to death,
and above that is a fire, bound by a rough circle.

On God

Is there a god of the gulf between a man
and a horse? A god who hovers above the trench
of difference? Not a god who makes us notice;
but a god who rakes his hand through the air and makes
a space neither can enter. What about
a god of animal innards? Some god
whose sole creation cleans the blood of an elk?
Perhaps there's a god of petty disaster
who breaks wagon wheels and paints clouds across
an old man's eyes. Consider the gods of flint

and primer who work side by side with the gods
of spark and steel; then there's the god of aim
and the god of near death—a god commonly praised.
Consider a god of small spaces, a fat
man's misery god, who lives in the shadow
between two rocks and sleeps on moss, content
with the smallness of his task; the god who bends
rivers, the god who flecks the breast of a hawk,
the god who plunders saltworks. I once thought
one god looked over my shoulder and measured
my steps, but now I believe that god is outnumbered
and I am surrounded by countless naked gods,
like spores or dust or birds or trees on fire,
the song, the grit, the mean seed of nakedness.

"[O boss of ashes boss of dust...]"

O boss of ashes boss of dust
you bother with what floats above
my chimney what settles to the ground
you wake the motes from sleep you make
them curtsey in a ray of sun
they hold their tiny breath as if
they're waiting for the little name
of the dance that's coming next then they
will take their places Boss if I
were smaller I would join them O
I'd cut a rug or two I'd slap
my hand against my shoe if that's
the kind of fuss you're raising Boss
you know I never know for sure
I only know you bother me
from time to time you've caught my breath
a time or two you've stirred me up
before which makes me want to tell
you Boss I wouldn't mind it if
you bothered me a little more

Sabrina Orah Mark

Sabrina Orah Mark was born in 1975 in Mexico, and grew up in Brooklyn. She holds a BA from Barnard College and an MFA from the University of Iowa Writers' Workshop, where she was awarded a postgraduate Glenn Schaeffer Fellowship. Mark's poems have appeared in *American Letters & Commentary, The Canary, Conduit, Denver Quarterly, Gulf Coast, Indiana Review,* and elsewhere. Her first book is *The Babies* (Saturnalia, 2004), a collection of prose poems. Her essay "Mark Levine: The Poetics of Evidence" appears in the anthology *American Poets of the 21st Century: The New Poetics.* A 2002-2003 fellow at The Fine Arts Work Center in Provincetown, Mark lives in Athens, Georgia, where she is pursuing her PhD at the University of Georgia and working on her second book, *Tsim Tsum.*

Hello

I am one anatomy and take turns. Sometimes after dinner I wrap them up in newspaper. Before they grow cold or one is still sleeping. Hello. They call me Zillah. I fell in love on the night train to Warsaw. Every human situation strikes me as a terrific joke. I am a torn off blouse in that red river. Ha ha holocaust. I can't complain. There are rules and there are onions and there are beautiful outer skins. Is that you, little darling? Let me see your visitor's pass. Some workmen from the gravel pit found Zillah holding an open umbrella, waving goodbye to her fans and singing "she fell in love on the night train to Warsaw." Hello. They call me Zillah. I touch them as they try to climb the wall. Let us tell you what it's like to be Zillah, they say, as they part my wig down the middle. It's like

The Babies

Some thought it was because of all the babies I suddenly seemed to be having. Others, that I should pay for the damages. Fact is, I wasn't getting any older, so I bought a small aquarium, and skipped town. Took up with a toy store owner until he left me for a more beautiful robot. Took up with a reader of instructional booklets. Never mind. I was lost. By the time I arrived at Mrs. Greenaway's, it was clear I was nowhere at all. In exchange for room and board, I'd rearrange her furniture, her birthmarks, her quiet animals, until they took on more satisfying shapes. Sometimes the shapes were simple, like a mustache or a pipe. Sometimes they were more complicated arrangements, like the one of dead Mr. Greenaway's closed barbershop. Over the years, as Mrs. Greenaway and I became more and more vague, the shapes did too. For identification purposes, we'd give them names like *She Wasn't Fooling Anyone*, *She Was Hurt* and *She Was Hurt Bad* or *The Insides of Doctors*. One night when I was working on a piece I thought I'd call *Symphony, Symphony,* the shapes began to slip out of my hands. At first, as Mrs. Greenaway remembers, the sound of broken glass. Then the trumpets. Then the terrible music of all those babies I once seemed to be suddenly having, marching, like soldiers, in rows. Then their round wet bellies coming toward me. Mrs. Greenaway still talks about how expertly they gathered me into their tiny arms. And how they took me away not like a prisoner. But like a mother. Into a past I still swear I never had.

The Mustache

Everything about the young foreign taxidermist was overdone. Did he absolutely have to wear the apron with the tiny red castles in the shop? Or weave, at night, in and out of the trees? I don't think so. I would bring him buckets of ice water day after day hoping he would just cool off a bit. Fact is, he never did. But to be fair, he really was practicing what the papers called "heroic medicine." It was love. I admit it. It was *fancy* love. I was the envy of the world, being hitched up with such a genius, and that felt good. Of course, these days, I can't touch rope or a small child without thinking of him. Without expecting his large hands to come out of nowhere. We were, as mother said, both "slowly losing our minds." He'd talk for hours about hygiene, the Water Cure for example, and wrote an award-winning essay on the Electric Bath as a way to treat hysteria in the female fox. "Too many foxes," he would say, shaking his fist, "too many foxes running around like chickens with their heads cut off." In the winter months we would ride our bicycles down to the scrap-metal yard where he would make love to me in devout silence. The delight in his eyes when he found that small cage! He was both tender and rough, and I had never, and will never again, be as touched by another man. I didn't notice the black mustache growing slowly but unmercifully on his left shoulder until two or three years into the affair. At first it seemed harmless. A small patch of dead grass. But eventually I couldn't help but only see the large dark field. Its silent twitching. By then it was already early fall, and the fact is, it tore us apart.

Transylvania, 1919

"It's good to be back," they say, lifting up the trap door and peeking in. It is early. I was not expecting visitors. I slip off my grandfather's dead lap and smile shyly. Holding hands, they tiptoe down the stairs. Like a long dark draft. Like a century. They are wearing my galoshes. They push their thumbs into my cheeks and pinch my wrists. "Isn't this romantic?" they hiss, pointing at my grandfather until his mouth opens. They circle him and pull the dark zippered stitching from his arm. Upstairs, Mama is ashamed. Mama is shouting at us to go home. Her glasses are mended with string…which reminds me: I climb the stairs. My grandfather coming loose in my arms. I climb the stairs to where Mama is sweeping the swallows into her large brown skirt. She is very old. I kiss my grandfather and gently place him down. As Mama once had. When I first met her. Among the gravel and the circus trailers.

The Experiments Lasted Through the Winter

We asked, what is this? It rustled. We dug a hole. What is this, we asked, a nocturama? No, we agreed, the thing was not a nocturama. A nocturama is when you cannot catch their breath. We nodded. We dug a hole. Our white hair warmed around the thing, we asked, is this a genesis? No, we agreed, the thing was not a genesis. A genesis is when he sweeps across the water. We nodded. It rustled. We stood closer to each other, we asked, what is this, a stillness? We watched it from a distance, we agreed, the thing was not a stillness. A stillness is when their legs come close. We dug a hole. We climbed the tree to watch it from below. What is this, we asked, to look at the boy? We touched our instruments and agreed the thing was not to look at the boy. To look at the boy is when there is no boy. We dug a hole. We weakened. We could no longer touch the thing. The thing, we were afraid, had lied to us. What is this, we asked, a father? We dug a hole. No, we agreed, the thing was not a father. A father is when you raise the cloth to his lips. What is this, we asked, we leaned against each other, what is this, a war? No, we agreed, the thing was not a war. A war is when you cannot hear the animals.

Corey Marks

Corey Marks was born in 1970 and grew up in southwestern Michigan. He holds a BA from Kalamazoo College, an MFA from Warren Wilson College, and a PhD from the University of Houston. His poems have appeared in *The Black Warrior Review, New England Review, The Paris Review, TriQuarterly, The Virginia Quarterly Review,* and other journals. His first collection of poems, *Renunciation* (University of Illinois Press, 2000) was a National Poetry Series selection. In 2003, Marks received an NEA Fellowship. Presently, he lives in Denton, Texas, and teaches at the University of North Texas.

Portrait of a Child

When I'm ready to think of something else, finally,
I think of wind that runs like a river along a river,
and trees bending into themselves with a will for breaking,
a will to break from the soil and leave the lap of the horsefield
where death has laid its head, its fire-red curls.

I think of the young painter who finds the body of a child,
drowned in the river and cast on stones that rattle
in the white hands of the water.

At first, the painter thinks all the right things.
He thinks of his own infant son.

But then he notices the child's beautiful blue lips
like the blue rim of a bowl, and the wine of its blood
spilled on a stone, and the dark loaves of its closed eyes
resting on the table of its face,

like the meal Christ rises over, sweeping his hands apart
while around the table the Apostles all lean against each other,
whispering, waiting, posing, even, for the thousands of painters
not yet born,

all but Judas, who looks away,
who has already broken the heavy bread and chews the grain,
not thinking of betrayal, of kissing sour wine from Christ's lips,

but of walking in a narrow street and hearing the song
of one bird that flew a hundred miles to rest in a tree
and pull its meal from a tent of worms.

The painter begins a portrait of the boy.
For a long time he stands beside the river, the brushes in a jar
near his hand, the sun turning lower in the sky,

and after a while he doesn't look at the child on the stones
but only at the boy lying in the soft bed of paint,
the dead boy at the end of his brush.

Then the boy by the water wakes
and climbs from the stones to the riverbank.
He walks to the painter and asks him, What are you painting?
You, the painter says, But you're dead.

No, the boy says, That boy is dead,
and he points to the painting.

Three Bridges

When the rains came I was, for my own purposes,
on the far side of the river. Who could've known
the drizzle would ratchet to torrent, or the river
unbuckle, swallow its banks, ring the scattered trees
like so many necks trying to stay afloat, strip boats
from their moorings on the village shore and batter
them out of the river's throat into the mouths
of other rivers? Or that it would wash out the town's
three bridges: the one too narrow to walk two abreast,
the one beyond the last houses already ruined,
abandoned by all but reckless boys and swallows,
even the one, story goes, someone made a pact
with the devil to build. When I crossed in the morning
I could feel the bridge arch in the uneasy air like a wing.
Hours later I had to leave what I'd come to do
half-done. The rain made it hard to see; everything
bleared, went pallid and indistinct, the rain
coming down and never done with falling.
Soon my clothes weighed as much as a child.
I fell, and the rain struck me clean. I lost my way

and found a river I didn't recognize in its frenzy,
whitecaps shearing its surface like teeth.
Even when the rains died, the flood kept on,
worrying the absent bridges, the water thick with silt,
its current full of animals coiled in the rush. I couldn't
dare it. Where's the devil when his deal falls through
its own reflection? Now the bridge is half of what it was,
reversed in the river bottom leading nowhere
I want to go. At least from here I can see my house,
my daughter when she walks into the yard with a pail.
She looks up by chance, and though she must wonder
what's become of me, she doesn't see me waving.
I'm unrecognizable motion in a landscape she knows
she should know but doesn't anymore. Or she sees me
in too many places to keep track; I'm the one missing
thing missing everywhere…But then her eyes catch
on the swallows sweeping the bloated river—no way
back to their roosts now, they lift away to take an eyeful
of everything that isn't what it was. And move on…
This must be what death is like: those left behind
look up sometimes where they think you should be,
but if they see you at all it's from too far to make sense
of what you've become—a blear, a color bled briefly
into sight through a whirl of silt. And then—who can
blame them, there's so much to do to reclaim the house,
to live in it again—they look away, and you're left
waiting for the river to settle back between the banks
that held it in place all your life and become itself again.

After the Shipwreck

How long beneath water-spun sand, silt,
the shifting saturations of light and dark?
One bird or another drifted its year-long shadow,

then you, come down from the house
that appeared one day on the wooded bluff,
pause over the panting waves where they lick clean

what they'd buried: a stone-pocked fretwork impossible
to make seaworthy again. But how you stare!
Each day you outstrip your mother's fear,

caught like a flag in the trees behind you,
to try the rust-scored slick of blackened timber
turned out by the lake, to imagine it whole again...

There!, the point of its sail a blunt brilliance flared
among the horizon's clouds like the glint
of a coin mid-turn, halfway to a fountain's bottom.

You'll reach after, pluck it from the slipknot
of someone else's wish, imagine the whelming again,
the rending of wood that spilled goods and bodies

into the cold, and wish to be lost yourself, overboard
into some other life larger than your small house
and the flutter of your mother's worries.

If you'd listen, I could tell you...
what? The captain called out to us in the storm
but we couldn't hear him in the windswept

garble. His mouth moved as though he spoke
from outside a glass pane. Funny, almost,
to see him calling there without voice,

without anything he could say that would make
its way to us, words stunned, broken-necked
as your mother's behind the storm window.

We didn't know we were lost until we were:
one day the lake had been clear and still,
and our tasks coiled within us like rope

we hauled fist over fist whether told to or not.
Then the water became a thing with hands
for mouths: the under reached through, the captain

all the while parting his lips for the ventriloquized storm.
But your mother calls to you each time you trail
down to the slack-jawed water; she knows

the world is there to take you from her. *Careful*,
she mouths, but your ears turn to glass. You hear
everything but her—the waves turning, the distant breaking

of a boat. Already you've become a transparence
splintered from the wooded dark. Beyond the trees
the lake shifts like a mouthful of coins.

Khaled Mattawa

Khaled Mattawa was born in 1964 in Benghazi, Libya, immigrated to the United States in 1979, earned Bachelor's degrees in Political Science and Economics at the University of Tennessee at Chattanooga, and received an MA in English and an MFA in Creative Writing from Indiana University. His poems have appeared in *The Best American Poetry* anthology and such journals as *The Black Warrior Review, Callaloo, Crazyhorse, The Kenyon Review,* and *Poetry.* He is the author of two books of poems, *Ismailia Eclipse* (Sheep Meadow, 1995) and *Zodiac of Echoes* (Ausable, 2003), as well as the translator of five books of Arabic poetry and the coeditor of two anthologies of Arab American literature. He has been awarded a Guggenheim Fellowship, a NEA Translation Fellowship, an Alfred Hodder Fellowship from Princeton University, the PEN American Center Poetry in Translation Prize, and two Pushcart Prizes. Mattawa teaches in the Creative Writing Program at the University of Michigan, Ann Arbor.

I Was Buried in Janzoor

is what I keep telling them, but they hook me
up to monitors, point to screens and show
flashes of my pulse. They draw blood from my arms,
smear my face with warm dabs. I say, listen:
June, two years after the war, a hundred
and four degrees in late afternoon, they prayed
for me without kneeling, arms lifted to the sky,
chanted "God is great." A plain cedar coffin,
unvarnished, used, the shroud made of Egyptian gauze.
Six cousins settled me on cool dirt,
and a man, the son of a slave, the one
who washed my body placing a rag on my waist,
the one who did not want to insult the dead,
he heaped the world over me, pressing dirt
with small feminine feet. I'd like to say that
my wives mourned my death for years, that my children
did not fight over my inheritance—forty hectares,
two houses, seven cows, a mule. I'd like to say
that when my name is mentioned in the village
teahouse, no one spits on the sidewalk, no one
curses the day of my birth. I'd like to say
that a grandson is named after me, my picture
on his desk as he eyes foreign words. He thinks of me
rarely, but always as an example of the decency

and apathy that made us prey to strangers from abroad,
that I'm remembered by a woman from Milan, who as a girl,
pressed me to her in her father's tobacco shed.
We stared at each other knowing no words
for the misery that bound us, the nuances
of skin that tore us apart. I'd like to say
I feared or betrayed no one, that I taught
my children all they deserved to know,
that I did not desire the neighbors'
daughters and sons. I'd like to say that you
made me happy, that I would love to return.
I looked at the sky on holy nights and saw
no palm fronds flaming copper gold, no pit for me
to shake Satan's hand. I visited a thousand weddings,
gave rice and pearls; I fed beggars from my table
and helped the blind find their way home;
I sacrificed she-goats and roosters
for local saints; I built a mosque. Stupid
were most of my thoughts, listless most my days.
I loved nothing more than my mother's coffee,
I loved a spoon of her lentil soup more than
I loved the truth. I'm still buried in Janzoor.

Growing Up with a Sears Catalog in Benghazi, Libya

Omar pointed to a pink man
riding a red lawn mower,
rose bushes, yellow tulips,
orchids framing slick sod.
Owners of villas in Jilyana,
my brother's friends
desperately needed
"the grass machines."
He planned to charge triple
his cost, build a house
by the sea. Eyes half-shut,
cigarette clouds above him,
he snored leaving unfinished
a recitation of truncated schemes.
In my room I gazed
at the pink man again,

marveled at pictures
of women in transparent bras.
How I loved their black nipples
and full gray breasts!
I fancied camping
with the blue-eyed one
in the $42 Coleman tent,
the two of us fishing
at a lake without mosquitoes,
sailing the boat on page 613.
After watching soaps
on our mahogany-cased
(27 inch) color TV,
we galloped lime green scooters
on "scabrous terrains,"
returned to our 4-bedroom home,
mud up to our knees,
to make love on the mattress
on page 1219.

***

One morning,
my brother and I landed
in New Orleans, in the heat.
The city's stench nauseated us,
mosquitoes slipping through
our window screen.
At the Lake Shore Sears
he caressed lipstick
red fenders, sank fingers
in the comfort of seats.
The smallest model
was striped with silver,
and he hugged it
like a long lost niece.
In a patois of his own,
he bargained, told
universal dirty jokes.
We rode two on a nearby lawn,
sunshine, cool morning breeze.
We parked them outside
Morrison's where our waitress
said she bought all

her clothes from Sears.
That night I undressed her
gently, stroked her breasts
with my cheeks.
She sighed, and I heaved,
the air in her room
scented with my dreams.
In the morning she said
I talked in my sleep,
raved at someone,
kept asking
"What kind of flower
you want planted
next to your grave?"

Echo & Elixir 1

It shines through clouds and rain.
It dyes the streets with its pink blossoms.
The day crawls through its tunnels.
The roads are long and long.

City without words. Night without night.
Somewhere I remember
these clothes are not my clothes.
These bones are not my bones.

I forget and remember again.
Ships in the harbor which is the sea
which is the journey
that awakens a light inside my chest.

Look at the hands turning the knobs.
The hands that haul the machine.
The man on the phone calling,
hanging up, calling again.

Dust and twisted nails, pebbles
and pieces of broken china,
and all the sweeping that goes on in the world.
No help.

No use saying "I will wait."

It flowers into decades of May.
It shines the windows with your passing gaze.

Echo & Elixir 2

Cairo's taxi drivers speak to me in English.
I answer, and they say your Arabic is good.
How long have you been with us? All my life
I tell them, but I'm never believed.
They speak to me in Farsi, speak to me in Greek,
and I answer with mountains of gold and silver,
ghost ships sailing the weed-choked seas.
And when they speak to me in Spanish,
I say Moriscos and Alhambra.
I say Jews rescued by Ottoman boats.
And when they speak to me in Portuguese,
all my life I tell them, coffee, cocoa,
Indians and poisoned spears.
I say Afonsso king of Bikongo writing
Manuel to free his enslaved sons.
And Cairo's taxi drivers tell me
your Arabic is surprisingly good.
Then they speak to me in Italian,
and I tell them how I lay swaddled
a month's walk from here. I tell them
camps in the desert, barbed wire, wives
and daughters dying, camels frothing disease,
the sand stretching an endless pool.
And they say so good so good.
How long have you been with us?
All my life, but I'm never believed.
Then they speak to me in French,
and I answer Jamila, Leopold, Stanley,
baskets of severed hands and feet.
I say the horror, battles of Algiers.
And they speak to me in English
and I say Lucknow, Arbenz. I say indigo,
Hiroshima, continents soaked in tea.
I play the drum beat of stamps. I invoke
Mrs. Cummings, U.S. consul in Athens,
I say Ishi, Custer, Wounded Knee.

And Cairo's taxi drivers tell me
your Arabic is unbelievably good.
Tell the truth now, tell the truth,
how long have you been with us?
I say my first name is little lion,
my last name is broken branch.
I sing "Happiness uncontainable"
and "fields greening in March"
until I'm sad and tired of truth,
and as usual I'm never believed.
Then they lead me through congestion,
gritty air, narrow streets crowded with
Pepsi and Daewoo and the sunken faces
of the poor. And when we arrive, Cairo's
taxi drivers and I speak all the languages
of the world, and we argue and argue about
corruption, disillusionment, the missed chances,
the wicked binds, the cataclysmic fares.

Jeffrey McDaniel

Jeffrey McDaniel was born in 1967 in Philadelphia, and holds a BA from Sarah Lawrence College and an MFA from George Mason University. His poems have appeared in numerous journals and anthologies, including *The Best American Poetry 1994*. An acclaimed performance poet and the recipient of an NEA Fellowship, McDaniel is the author of three books: *Alibi School* (Manic D, 1995), *The Forgiveness Parade* (Manic D, 1998), and *The Splinter Factory* (Manic D, 2002). He lives in Brooklyn and teaches creative writing at Sarah Lawrence College.

Logic in the House of Sawed-Off Telescopes

I want to sniff the glue that holds families together.
I was a good boy once.
I listened with three ears.
When I didn't get what I wanted, I never cried.
I banged my head over and over on the kitchen floor.
I sat on a man's lap.
I took his words that tasted like candy.
I want to break something now.

I am the purple lips of a child throwing snowballs at a taxi.
There is an alligator in my closet.
If you make me mad, it will eat you.
I was a good boy once.
I had the most stars in the classroom.
My cheeks erupted with rubies.
I want to break something now.

My bedroom is so dark I feel like an astronaut.
I wish someone would come in and kiss me.
I was a good boy once.
The sweet smelling woman used to say that she loved me
and swing me in her arms like a chandelier.
I want to break something now.

My heart beats like the meanest kid on the school bus.
My brain tightens like a fist.

I was a good boy once.
I didn't steal that kid's homework.
I left a clump of spirit in its place.
I want to break something now.

I can multiply big numbers faster than you can.
I can beat men who smoke cigars at chess.
I was a good boy once.
I brushed my teeth and looked in the mirror.
My mouth was a brilliant wound.
Now it only feels good when it bleeds.

Lineage

When I was little, I thought the word *loin*
and the word *lion* were the same thing.

I thought *celibate* was a kind of fish.
My parents wanted me to be well-rounded,

so they threw dinner plates at each other,
until I curled up into a little ball.

I've had the wind knocked out of me
but never the hurricane. I've seen two

hundred and sixty-three rats in the past year,
but never more than one at a time.

It could be the same rat, with a very high
profile. I know what it's like to wear

my liver on my sleeve. I walk in
department stores, looking suspicious,

approach the security guard, say *What?*
I didn't take anything. Go ahead, frisk me,

Big Boy! I go to funerals and tell
the grieving family *The soul of the deceased*

is trapped inside my rib cage and trying
to reach you. Once I thought I found love,

but then I realized I was just out
of cigarettes. Some people are boring

because their parents had boring sex
the night they were conceived. In the year

thirteen hundred thirteen, a little boy died
who had the exact same scars as me.

Opposites Attack

I walk on tiptoes, so as not to disturb
the blindfolded elderly couple, sleeping

quietly on the floor. Outside the sky
is the color of a drowned man's face.

The birds are still on strike. The local
children build a snow transvestite.

The trees have rolled up their long sleeves.
They're cousins with the octopus.

I remember packing snowballs in the ice box
and dreaming of beaning sunbathers

in July. I was never good at sunbathing.
I used to climb the fire escape and recline

on the roof's rough blanket at midnight,
pretending the house was a wedding cake,

as I covered my limbs with cooking oil
and offered myself to the moon.

Those were the good cold days, when
a Peeping Tom was worth something,

and a wisecrack got you a swift kick
in the pants. Nowadays you need a Glock

in the glove compartment and a cavalry
of narcotics galloping through your veins,

just to get a cop to spill coffee on you,
and sometimes even that isn't enough.

I'll see your cross-eyed pigeon
and raise you a jar of epileptic brains.

Put your business cards on the table.
Read the palm trees and weep.

Roman orgies weren't built in a day.
I bet you an opera singer's esophagus

that my apocalypse can beat your
apocalypse—even on an off night.

The Archipelago of Kisses

for Sarah Koskoff and Todd Louiso

We live in a modern society. Husbands and wives don't grow
        on trees like in the old days. So where
does one find love? When you're sixteen it's easy—like being
        unleashed with a credit card
in a department store of kisses. There's the first kiss.
        The sloppy kiss. The peck.
The sympathy kiss. The backseat smooch. The *we shouldn't*
        be doing this kiss. The *but your lips*
taste so good kiss. The *bury me in an avalanche of tingles* kiss.
        The *I wish you'd quit smoking* kiss.
The *I accept your apology, but you make me really mad*
        sometimes kiss. The *I know*
your tongue like the back of my hand kiss. As you get older,
        kisses become scarce. You'll be driving
home and see a damaged kiss on the side of the road,
        with its purple thumb out. Now if you
were younger, you'd pull over, slide open the mouth's ruby door
        just to see how it fits. Oh where
does one find love? If you rub two glances together, you get
        a smile; rub two smiles, you get
a spark; rub two sparks together and you have a kiss. Now
        what? Don't invite the kiss
to your house and answer the door in your underwear. It'll get
        suspicious and stare at your toes.
Don't water the kiss with whisky. It'll turn bright pink and explode

into a thousand luscious splinters,
but in the morning it'll be ashamed and sneak out of your body
without saying goodbye,
and you'll remember that kiss forever by all the little cuts it left
on the inside of your mouth. You must
nurture the kiss. Dim the lights, notice how it illuminates
the room. Clutch it to your chest,
wonder if the sand inside every hourglass comes from a special
beach. Place it on the tongue's pillow,
then look up the first recorded French kiss in history: beneath
a Babylonian olive tree in 1300 B.C.
But one kiss levitates above all the others. The intersection
of function and desire. The *I do* kiss.
The *I'll love you through a brick wall* kiss. *Even when
I'm dead, I'll swim through the earth
like a mermaid of the soil, just to be next to your bones.*

Dear America

I am but a riverboat—hopelessly in touch
with my inner canoe. On the first day of nursery

school, I cried in mother's arms. It wasn't
separation anxiety. I was scared she would

come back. In high school, I was voted *most likely
to secede.* In college, I took so many drugs

the professors looked at samples of my urine
just to know what books I'd been reading.

I'm a narcissist trapped in the third person.
The sound of my own head being shaved

is my all-time favorite song. I stop people
on the street, show them pictures of myself

as a child, ask *have you seen this boy?
He's been missing for a long time.* His eyes

are the last swig of whisky before stumbling
out of a bar on a sunny afternoon. His cheeks

are twirling ballerinas. His cheeks are revolving
doors. I'm all out of cheeks to turn. I'm all

out of cheeks. My ego is a spiral staircase
inside a tornado. My eyebrows are that furry

feeling you get in your gut when you're about
to tell a lie. My tongue is a dolphin

passed out in an elevator. My tongue is a red carpet
I only roll out for you. My penis is a wise ass

in the back of a classroom who doesn't know
the answer, but sticks his hand up anyway.

My heart hangs in my chest like a Salem witch.
My heart is a turtle ripped from its shell.

My heart is a street so dark nymphomaniacs
are afraid to kiss. My heart, America, my heart.

Joyelle McSweeney

Joyelle McSweeney was born in 1976 in Boston. She attended Harvard University, Oxford University, and the University of Iowa Writers' Workshop. Her poems have appeared in *Colorado Review, Crowd, Denver Quarterly, Fence, Gulf Coast, Poetry,* and elsewhere. McSweeney's two books of poems are *The Red Bird* (Fence, 2002) and *The Commandrine and Other Poems* (Fence, 2004). The cofounder of Action Books and a staff critic for *The Constant Critic,* she lives in Tuscaloosa, Alabama, and teaches in the MFA program at the University of Alabama.

Still Life w/Influences

I stood at the modern knothole,
my eyes on the pivoting modern stars and naphthalene green
turfs and surfaces.

Behind me the stone fleur-de-lis
sank back over the horizon,
carving a fleur-de-lis-shaped track in air
that spread into a bigger hole.

                    Up on the hill,
a white tent had just got unsteadily to its feet
like a foal or a just-foaled cathedral.
Down on the beach, ten black whales were crashing

slowly, through themselves,
draped in wet bedsheets.
The bedsheets smoked into the air.

I opened my palm. A green edifice opened there.
It seemed to breathe but that was air breathing for it,
lifting a corner or a column.

Goodbye, my thirteenth century.
                    I folded the money away.
What do ye do when ye see a whale?
                    I sing out.

The Wind Domes

Everyone knows that time unfolds
as events into the particular. His shredded shirt

floats down as cloud ripples. These are his motion-
and his power-lines

receding through the valley.

His shoulders one shade greener than the sky.
The valley two shades greener.

go back after—songs waft from the box
encouraging us to go through with it.

>To be a worthy continuum.
>To be a moral compendium
>in the dark green chickpea glade—

>>I'm a kid so I can't   go anywhere.
>>You'll have to   bring it to me.

>—in the frosted flakes of grain
>in the rushes where, if you pull one up,
>they scream or interrogate you.

>Emptied of their po-et-ree
>they lie in the potters' field.

>The vessels, I mean. The protest of the dog
>in the throat of the evening
>makes the evening suddenly deep.

The Problem of Knowledge is
what to do with it,
        once you have it.
(Sign this form.)
(Paste a picture of your skiff, here)

        gamboling debt
on the rambling see.
The little deck shifting

like a slopéd glen (Paste
your thumb to it. Thumb*print*, you clod!)

a-clearing. The buck's rack glinting in retreat.

I lift it like a flashcard and it gathers no _____.
Lift it like a fish from life.

> and how am I to convince you, if you aren't here to convince?
> Those people just aren't here anymore.
> They split. They left the club. I told you
> (I woulda told you) like a bathmat or a bathroom's drudge
> -light to make do with. To make
> right by. There is no second life.
>
> Plutonium wristlet appears as a circle of fireflies
> as she crosses the humpéd lawn.
> The closer they get,
> you can see the holes between them.
>
> Slipped from her wrist, plunged to toss in the bed
> that ran from the summer capitol.
> The river, I mean. Sunk down
> to surface again
> in the cluster. Magnified.
>
> How it gave off a summery light.

Persuasion

Others were more economical than I. But I
had my red marble. I had action
figures weighting down the drapes
on tiny threads. That twisted and got smaller.
One door led
to a more economical room.
Perhaps a more economical view. The girl
across the hall was the same girl.

I climbed out across the telephone wires. I thought
they'd hold me, like the webbing of a lawn chair,
and like a wedding or a lawnchair they didn't. I kept

pulling chunks out of the hummock. I fell with my
fists full of humus. Into, of course.

At home the state-painter was painting the ghost oak. And
the window around the oak. The room around

you-know-who.
She came from the same
town in Iceland.
Whither and whence I
came. O-ho!
With her eye
she came and came.
With her weather
eye she came.

I saw the damage this was doing to the van
would *not* cost six hundred dollars.
I pedaled off in my car.
My car got smaller.
It wouldn't fit my littlest brother!
It fell over.
Fell, of course, into.

Back at the ranch, it was a tenement.
I was a tenant of the studio-apartment.
I was building a house in French.
Expectorant—I was self-enlightened,
my efforts self-directed and sustained.
To the tune of eighty-seven dollars
I debated a suitable depth. A squirrel
at each level of the fence

with an apple for a face looked on blandly.
I mean red. Red-faced. Blindly.

Heavenly stage set comes
in on wheels and wheels around.
The fish wind up the concrete ladder
because they believe it's better
to reach a higher part of the *rive*
to pour themselves out
while I pour myself into

the form that has survived
My father leaves tomorrow
and he leaves this
afternoon. This is before
I set fire to my room,
pouring water into the electric baseboards
trying to wash a tiny brine shrimp
off the wall. It might have lived.
This is after my mother,
her father dead. Lay in bed.
Heard the Skylark song.

Sarah Messer

Sarah Messer was born in 1966 in Boston. As a teenager, she was a Burger King employee, a 4-H horse judge, a platform diver, and a ballerina. Messer attended Middlebury College and the University of Michigan, and has won fellowships from The Fine Arts Work Center in Provincetown, the Wisconsin Institute for Creative Writing, the Andrew Mellon Foundation, the NEA, and the American Antiquarian Society. Her poetry has appeared in The Journal, The Kenyon Review, The Paris Review, Post Road, Third Coast, and elsewhere. Her short fiction has been published in Story and Provincetown Arts. Messer is the author of a collection of poems, Bandit Letters (New Issues, 2001), and a history/memoir hybrid, Red House (Viking, 2004), which was named a Barnes & Noble Discover Great New Writers pick. She is currently an Associate Professor of poetry and creative nonfiction at the University of North Carolina-Wilmington.

Look,

this is not the West, this is
the 21st century but still as desolate—
cottonwood pollen blowing through
abandoned mansions, the ball-bearing factory,
strikers with their flap-jack placards
waving at the glance of traffic.

At the discount cinema, gunfighters name
a young Cherokee guide "Look"
because of the way she stares, because
of the way they look at her. And everyone
keeps their eyes on the horizon.
Look, you've won a set of false teeth.

Look, you've won a ghost town.
When Look closes her eyes, she sleeps
like an abandoned shopping mall,
she sleeps like the crawl space under the stairs.
She wants to inhabit the veins of a leaf,
she wants to sleep in the ear of the city's great giant.

But all the gunfighters are torch singers;
they are street lights in the wilderness.

Look does not lead them over the mountain pass.
Like Annie Oakley, she aims with mirrors
and shoots backward. Wagon trains slow
like conches moving through conch grass.

Barns and blacksmith shops bloom
beneath the hoof of the clouded moon.
Pieces of horses, news clippings are carried off
by dogs. Cannot. Couldn't. Continue.
Some stayed, like food dropped from a plane,
and survived. Some consumed each other.

Look tries to forget her husband killed
at the trail-head—how the horizon rolled
violently in his skull hitting ferns and roots
and lichen. His skin like dried pine needles,
the blank, wagon-grease eyes. Memory is a tool
dropped in the ocean.

A cowboy rubs dirt from his neck, just off
the assembly line. He looks at her skin, thinks:
darker than saddle leather. Hindsight is the best
kind of oppression. Our children will
push up the anachronistic skyline, he says,
Step closer to the fire, let me look at you.

With this change to indoor lighting,

with this new Zoloft prescription, your eyes have become pools
of oil in the back field the century before kitchen appliances

were invented, before the sky seeped turquoise like something
withdrawn, before spy satellites stapled down the horizon.

Now the air smells like steak, after-shave and gasoline,
like my father's slow slide into adultery, a faucet dripping

in the back of my mind. The man selling coffee at the campus
kiosk is a secret outlaw. He cuts himself for decoration—

thousands of tiny mayflies at his wrists.
Unmoved by the trend of punk teenagers and their designer dogs,

he percolates the end of the century in a spoon.
He is a pie without filling, a photograph of a whipped

man, an empty sandwich. His wounds are healing
into marks of brown crayon, into curling iron burns.

In this light my skin is the color of corsets, jars of old bust cream.
When I was sixteen, my father built a disco in the basement

with speakers that flashed lights the color of grenadine, maraschino
cherries, while in my mother's kitchen, a bowl of oranges

covered itself with a green shawl. It isn't so difficult to understand
why women over the centuries mixed their own medicine.

Why not kiss me for real, as if for the first time?
Why not write me an opera? I'm sick of your guitar strings

and that tattoo of Lacan under your arm. Let's make
ourselves famous or else get drunk. If you want, you can find me

sitting on the frozen fountain in my 19th-century clothes,
with my Judy Jetson hair, with my scarification vendor,

and my Rottweiler waiting as dutiful as a pot roast, his head in my lap.

Rendered Dog

I have held the man in my mouth
all day, trying to find a place
to bury him, dig him up later.
Mailboxes gape, trees fling
their arms in the air like bad actresses,
a child in a driveway unfolds
her palm like an anemone under
a wave, her face watery
above the training wheels.

Everywhere I walk, he is cat fur,
orange peel beneath my tongue: a tincture
of needles, the taste of liver salving
the gray earth. Once, in a quarry we

slathered silt beneath shirts, bodies
in the girth of plateau, morass
of limestone scapula, backs of flat rock.
We rolled our mud-flanks
across continents. A plane glazed
the dark monitor of sky, blinking red
heartbeat, *we are still alive.* I wondered
what it would be like to hold
the earth inside me, and worried
about being interred too early, lying
naked in mud, the simple sheath of seeds.

Yet technology impedes impulse, and this
is the industrial age. In the marketplace
flesh is sucked in airtight plastic, renamed
meat. Shoppers stare at my matted
hair, my swollen mouth, the crenellated
edges of lip-flap billowing with each
breath. My painted toenails click
on asphalt. They call me
bitch with a bad mouth. But I only
translate the man who trained me: *speak,*
fetch, and *come.* Once, everything owned
itself, and roots were dug out of meaning.
Now, even the dirt can be sold.

Marriage Proposal

Our love rhymes with: cub scout, clod-hopper, trouble-shooter, sore
thumb. Sitting in the kitchen with our fruit cocktail skin.

Who says love can't last? A little syrupy, yes, a little soft;
a can of exploding snakes, yes, a dissolving eros-aspirin. Yes,

I could be your silent auction—all that old lady furniture
delivered from the house on the hill: velvet drapes, china poodles,

chintz, chamber pots on your doorstep. Now & Forever, like
an interstate. Why not jackpot everything—imagine

those satin pockets in the dead ancestor's tuxedos. Imagine
the cool slide of your hand entering—imagine yourself dressing

before gilt mirrors, the wool seams unthreading, the smell of wet
sheep, and your hands moistening like pudding cake

on fine bone china—it isn't proper, but could you please
pass me that candelabra? I need to check the laundry in the basement.

Meanwhile, try to imagine a mansion of fabric against your skin.
Already the branches of the family tree have forgotten the itch

of your amputated limb. As a precaution, I've welded the keys
to all our doors into matching bullet-proof vests. Did I say

forever? Yes, I guess, so then you'd better
sew all my openings shut with thread pulled from the bed sheets—

you'd better bury me beneath you, our hands
and feet tied. I want to be trapped by the cage of your ribs

as it slowly sinks into mine.

Ethan Paquin

Ethan Paquin was born in 1975 in Nashua, New Hampshire, and educated at Plymouth State College and the University of Massachusetts. His poems have appeared in such journals as American Letters & Commentary, Boston Review, Boulevard, Colorado Review, New American Writing, and elsewhere. Paquin's three books of poems are The Makeshift (Stride, 2002), Accumulus (Salt, 2003), and The Violence (Ahsahta, 2005). He is the editor and publisher of the online journal Slope and the small poetry press Slope Editions, and an Assistant Professor of Humanities at Medaille College, where he directs the undergraduate creative writing program. Paquin resides in Buffalo, New York.

Hearing Music Through Dark Trees

I imagine this is a movement the owl loves!

    He's off delighting in the fluttery notes,
the way they nuance from silence to moonlight,

fluttering upward like beetles in sunlight,
which left us some hours ago.

    *

Sunlight's a miniature trawler that plows through the nothing
God handed us, willed us,

which He meant for us to fill with hazy notions and the words

and sometimes, as by a camp fire with friends and guitar,
    laughter

and sometimes, as in a broken room,
    the scrape of screaming

and all the time, little blissful owls, or other animals and birds
    I can't imagine at this moment.

    *

I can't imagine the other animals, birds....– my apologies.

The owl has had its way with me;
   it has drawn over me a musick irrevocable,

    humming of an hour of moonlight,
humming of an hour of moonlight.

Capstone

        "We're all frauds"
           —anonymous

One of those back roads, the day you wanted to go to the diner, the best
diner you'd eaten at, on one of those winter days when sun goes for the eyes
(knock-out punch), glaring, gritting its teeth, readying, daring us to drive
right into it—we did—yet welcoming enough with its veil of slurred white,

    was, I think—I think it had to have been around one of the bends,
where they built that controversial bike path (remember the town meeting,
Special Session? so many turned up in homemade knit-wear)—the exact
location of my Leap Into Manhood, which is to say my first moment of
cynical actualization—

    Hey maybe I'll teach with a Don't Ask Don't Tell policy

Don't ask if I'm married / don't tell me if you're a dirty dirty
    "Dirty Girl" or Lolita,

        Riot Grrrl, political girl

We can party all night I know this abandoned tree house near...

Bring the booze I'll bring my professor-mentor We'll get with the ski bum
and the German and the newspaper staff and the bearded one (did you know
Americans are still talented enough to restore colonial barns?)

Why, you ask? We want to celebrate, we've pulled off our disguises, we
owe it to frank discussions over cold coffee on various and sundry side
roads throughout local mid-sized ranges of hills in a mid-size sedan, soulful
enough to adore the veil of white all around, desperate enough to want to
hide behind it forever,

desperate beauty

we can't do anything with it.

Where Were You

through an infernal _____ and sea
where were you

through rainless orange seasonal
where were you

through burn cycles and fealty
where were you

through plant and reap and germinal
where were you

through scree in mountainside fall
where were you

through mixed or extended metaphor
where were you

through threshers and silos and sów
where were you

through man and the death of violence toward beast
where were you

where were you
though man and his beast and his violence did die?

where were you
though threshers and silos and sów pitch-perfect in sun?

where were you
though metaphor wither'd for your stare categorizable's not?

where were you
though scree whispered to the mountainsides, "Fall"?

where were you
though planted were things of regrettable harvest?

where were you
though burn cycles took out the canopy in which [your eyes]?

where were you
though rain-drownings quelléd orange burn of sun and nightly?

where were you
though an _____ sea toss'd you, stopped you,

whereas my harbour you'd have sought,

whereas my hand to drowning sun offered,

whereas my water to singe the sides of leaves,

whereas my scythe and seeds and immutable hunger,

whereas my pulley to raise any and all of the peaks as a god,

whereas my stare to meet yours, for if not mine, then whom,

whereas my brush to auric light digest and mirror your eyes,

whereas my gravestone to the violence of language,
                    insufficient and stupid in the line of a gaze

so heavily levied,

and readily,

and in levity

in levity am I constant   and   in energy   yours
—touch   where were you   touch   this
life can not   stand   length
of shadow   of shadow and nightly
and nightly your   shadow   stand   close
in   please   where   to see.   to
see no   more shadow   but
the woman   she stands   essence
but   always dissolvéd   some-
how.   and come   closer   sea,   sea-
scape's   all   we have   got,
reminder
of hunger   auric light
eat
sun offered   shadow a   form   of
sun,   she a form   of   frozen light,   dis-
solvéd   little   leaf in   field
of vision   field   of   leaves   each a
future   each a   harbour   as
are those   her   eyes

Alan Michael Parker

Alan Michael Parker was born in 1961, grew up on Long Island, and attended Washington University in St. Louis and Columbia University, where he received his MFA. His poetry has appeared in *American Poetry Review, The Gettysburg Review, The Kenyon Review, The New Yorker, The New Republic, The Paris Review,* and elsewhere, and has been recognized with a Pushcart Prize and the Lucille Medwick Memorial Award from the Poetry Society of America. Parker is the author of the novel *Cry Uncle* (University of Mississippi Press, 2005) and three books of poems—*Days Like Prose* (Alef Books, 1997), *The Vandals* (BOA, 1999), and *Love Song with Motor Vehicles* (BOA, 2003). He is a contributing editor to the journals *Boulevard* and *Pleiades.* Parker is also the coeditor (with Mark Willhardt) of *The Routledge Anthology of Cross-Gendered Verse* (Routledge, 1996), the North American Editor of *Who's Who in 20th Century World Poetry* (Routledge, 2001), and editor of *The Imaginary Poets: 22 Master Poets Create 22 Master Poets* (Tupelo, 2005), a compilation of the work of fictional poets invented by prominent American writers. Parker is a member of the core faculty of the low-residency MFA Program at Queens University of Charlotte and an Associate Professor of English and Director of Creative Writing at Davidson College. He lives in Davidson, North Carolina, with his wife, the painter Felicia van Bork, and their son, Eli.

Driving Past My Exit

Yes, my Captain, I was there.
I was the one punching the buttons of the radio

until the right commercial came on
and commerce was my friend.

I was happy as a full wallet.
No sir, acceptable losses

did not yet concern me,
and the unnatural colors of the clouds

were barely noticeable in the glare.
No sir, I could not claim to be

aware of horns blaring, or of
my heart

stopped at the light;
and when the signal changed and my blood

seemed to still, at ease, and the road
moved around me, and the foothills shone

like the store windows of home
lit by artillery fire,

I was not of two minds, even then.
Yes, my Captain, I contend

I acted alone. My lieutenants?
Of the fates of others I know not:

a soldier is what a soldier does.
And yet, yes my Captain, I admit

that war is unforgiving, and our advances
in night vision have shown us

what we feared. Yes, my Captain,
I gave myself

to singing, invested in the production
of goods, of prosperity jingling.

Yes, my Captain, I now believe
I was only following orders,

good weather and green lights for miles.
Yes, Captain, I was

happy as a new shirt,
and the music on the radio was for me.

The Vandals

In the poem about the vandals, the vandals
Back their Dodge 4 x 4 up to the door

Of the abandoned town hall and theater.
In untied boots, they carry canvas bags

And carry off the oak wainscoting.
Above the wings and pit and stage, the ghosts

Of two starved porcupines command
Twin mounds of scat, respectively,

The prickly hats of king and fool.
(The chairs don't care, bottoms up, attentive.)

As the vandals stomp inoutinoutinoutinout
All in one breath because poetry

Is an oral tradition, the ghosts of the porcupines
Fill the air with rhyme: Visigoths and mishegas,

Gerkin and curtain, howitzers and trousers.
The vandals stomp inoutinoutinoutinout:

In their arms the split and pocked wood,
In their wake the porcupines

Are unaware of God's universal love.
In the poem, no one is free:

The ghosts of the two porcupines
Got in but they can't get out,

Starving over and over. The vandals—
Who sometimes look like you

And sometimes me—will never
Go home to cozy vandal homes

To make of their deeds a poem.
In the poem about the vandals,

Because a poem is an abandoned theater,
The porcupines have eaten the scenery:

Padua, Venice, Alexandria, Verona, gone;
Love prostrate on its pyramid.

And the vandals stomp inoutinoutinoutinout,
And the vandals stomp inoutinoutinoutinout.

The Vandals Dying

In the poem about their dying
The vandals bellow for their nurses,

Slather all the smoke alarms
With Jell-O, rip every goddamned

Tube from every goddamned arm.
Where's the sawbones? they holler.

Bring on the leeches and the MRI!
A candystriper, just fifteen, beleaguered

In her future body, colors in each "O"
In *Cosmopolitan*. She knows already

That the dying never die by yelling.
Deal, the vandals roar, enthralled;

Two hearts, the bidding opens.
Because a poem can do no more

Than deny its expectations,
The candystriper dozes, dreams

The Scream by Edvard Munch, colors in
The mouth. In their semiprivate rage,

The vandals play and play,
Each gesture vaguely ceding to its ghost.

The candystriper wakes, bleary
—Where am I?—at the nurses' station,

Her candystripèd cuff
Soaking up a cup of soup,

The callboard lit before her,
Buzzing, blinking, calling

Someone, anyone, even God above,
Who's busy in another poem, busy dying.

Practicing Their Diffidence, the Vandals

Fill their bodies with their ghosts
The way a poem fills itself with words.

It's yet another Sunday, church-rush brunch,
Everyone festooned, all the vandals

In their wingtips, boaters, and seersucker suits
Tapping ashes from their Cuban cheroots

Into the rubber trees and potted ferns, all the ferns
Burgeoning despite the blinding light

Of art. The vandals are out
To eat again, yoo-hoo-yoo-hoo-yoo-hoo!

They wave Italian breadsticks in the air,
Spin tiny tropical umbrellas seized

From complimentary Mai Tais. Looks like
A lousy musical, mutters the assistant chef,

As he peeks through the window of the kitchen door
And wipes his favorite cleaver on a dirty rag.

I'm cooking for the chorus of "Easter Parade."
The vandals menace him with twenty orders

Of the broiled eel, hold the teriyaki;
They clutch their chests in mock arrest,

Feign heart attacks as social unrest, happy
To make a scene. He's unperturbed,

The assistant chef: he knows the vandals
Have to go, he knows which hostess peddles dope.

Water, water, everywhere, the vandals call—
And then, as if the lights had suddenly

Gone down and the audience walked out,
The vandals look around, see themselves

Grown older, see their ghosts
In every empty glass. It's only a poem,

They whisper to each other.
It's only a poem, it's only a poem, it's only a poem.

D. A. Powell

D. A. Powell was born in 1963 in Albany, Georgia, and grew up in the rural South and California's Central Valley. He holds Bachelor's and Master's degrees in English from Sonoma State University, and received his MFA from the University of Iowa Writers' Workshop. His poems have appeared in such journals as *American Letters & Commentary*, *The Canary*, *Chicago Review*, *Colorado Review*, *Gulf Coast*, and *Pleiades*, and have received awards from the Academy of American Poets, *Boston Review*, the James Michener Foundation, the NEA, the Poetry Society of America, and *Prairie Schooner*. His three books—*Tea* (Wesleyan, 1998), *Lunch* (Wesleyan, 2000), and *Cocktails* (Graywolf, 2004)—form a trilogy, partially autobiographical and partially elegiac, chronicling life in queer America. Powell has taught at Columbia University, Harvard University, Sonoma State University, and the University of Iowa Writers' Workshop. Presently, he lives in San Francisco and is part of the English faculty at University of San Francisco.

[when you touch down upon this earth.little reindeers]

when you touch down upon this earth.   little reindeers
hoofing murderously at the gray slate roof: I lie beneath
dearest father xmas: will you bring me another 17 years

you gave me my first tin star and my first tin wreath
warm socks tangerines and a sloppy midnight kiss
I left you tollhouse cookies.   you left me bloody briefs

lipodystrophy neurosthesia neutropenia mild psychosis
increased liver enzymes increased bilirubin and a sweater
don't get me wrong: I like the sweater.   though it itches

but what's the use of being pretty if I won't get better?
bouncing me against your red woolies you whisper: *dear*
boy: unzip your enormous sack.   pull me quick into winter

[sleek mechanical dart: the syringe noses into the blue vein marking the target of me]

sleek mechanical dart: the syringe noses into the blue vein marking the target of me
haven't I always looked away.   don't want to see what's inside me.   inside me or coming out
older than balder: older than I'd planned to be.   aliveness jars me.   what's sticking what sticks

in my dream the haruspex examines my entrails.   glyphs of the ancient chitterlings transcribed:
highballs. speedballs. chirujos. chickens. lues. spora. blasphemy. butter. bitters. epicac.
highrisk behavior posterchild: come reeve.   a thousand happy tourists in-&-out me. I matterhorn

how much frivolity does the hypodermic draw away: does it taste men waferthin who blest my tongue
does it know knees I've dandled on. I feel taken in: darts in the waist of a coat I'll bury in

for I have husbanded recklessly: wedding daggers.   holes in my memory of holes: danaidic vessels
the needle quivers.   sickens.   I spill names an alphabetsoup of hemoglobin.   someone cracks the code

in a fortnight of waiting I draw up a will.   develop false symptoms.   how will I survive surviving

I'll throw parties where death blindfolded is spun: won't someone be stuck.   and won't I be missed

[tall and thin and young and lovely the michael with kaposi's sarcoma goes walking]

tall and thin and young and lovely the michael with kaposi's sarcoma goes walking
and when he passes each one he passes goes "whisperwhisperwhisper."   star of beach blanket babylon

the sea washes his ankles with its white hair.   he sambas past the empty lifeguard tower
days like these who wouldn't swim at own risk: the horizon smiles like a karaoke drag queen
broad shoulders of surf shimmy forth as if to say "aw baby, sell it, sell it."   he's working again

towels lie farther apart.   the final stages: he can still do a dazzling turn *but each day*
smiles grow a little sharper.   he blames it on the bossanova.   he writes his own new arrangements

[writing for a young man on the redline train: "to his boy mistress"]

All the bodies we cannot touch
Are like harps. Toucht by the mind
—Robert Duncan, "Fragments of a Disordered Devotion"

writing for a young man on the redline train: "to his boy mistress"
first to praise his frame: pliable as hickory. his greasy locks waxy ears
I'll stop the world and melt with you brustling through a nearby headset

if I had time to ride this monster to the end I would: hung by handstraps
jostle through the downtown stations. each stop bringing us closer
to what? gether? perhaps: or that exit of the tunnel where I look back

and *poof*:   no lover. men have led shameful lives for less proportioned fare
tossing greetings thick as rapunzel's hair: "anybody ever told you that you
[ugh, here it comes lads, stifle those chortles]   resemble a young james dean?"

why *fiddle-dee-dee*, he bats his lids: the fantasy already turning to ruin
what if he debarked at my destination of pure coincidence? followed
through the coppice of the square: fox and hound, fox and hound

I'd lead him on a merry chase: pausing every few: admire a fedora
check the windows of the haberdashers and cruise the sartorial shops
until I felt his winded breathing on my neck: yawned and departed again

we could while away the afternoon just so. but at my back, etc

fresh and sprouting in chestnut-colored pubes is how I'd want him
not after the dregs of cigarettes. the years of too many scotch sours
why, I wouldn't even know what to say to one who drinks scotch sours

except, "sir." and "tough luck about those redsox" [which it always is]
now I've spent myself in lines and lost. where is that boy of yesteryear?
let him die young and leave a pretty corpse: die with his legs in the air

[coda & discography]

a song of paradise

to enter that queer niteclub, you step over the spot: sexworker stabbed
reminds me of the chalk outlines on castro street or keith haring's canvases

missing. beaten. died at the end of a prolonged illness. a short fight

phantoms of the handsome, taut, gallant, bright, slender, youthful: go on
the garment that tore: mended. the body that failed: reclaimed

voyeurs, passion flowers, trolls, twinks, dancers, cruisers, lovers without lovers

here is the door marked HEAVEN: someone on the dancefloor, waiting just for you

> *so many men, so little time* [miquel brown]
> *calling all boys* by the flirts. patrick cowley's *menergy*
> *only the strong survive* [precious wilson] or *I will survive* [gloria gaynor]

> the flirts' *passion* and roni griffith's *desire*
> *the boys come to town* [earlene bentley]
> gloria gaynor's *I am what I am*. eartha kitt's *I love men*

> *runaway* [tapps]. *seclusion* [shawn benson]. *helpless* [jackie moore]
> eria fachin *saving myself* and the three degrees *set me free*
> *goodbye bad times* [oakey & moroder]. *keep on holdin' on* [margaret reynolds]

> oh romeo's *these memories* and *the heart is a lonely hunter* [bonnie bianco]
> real life's *send me an angel*. *earth can be just like heaven* [two tons of fun]
> yaz: *situation* and *don't go*. and *why* by bronski beat

> *give me just a little more time* [angela clemmons]
> *unexpected lovers* by lime and *mercy* by carol jiani
> *let's hang on* [salazar] and *maybe this time* [norma lewis]

> vivien vee's *give me a break* and her haunting *blue disease*
> ashford & simpson's *found a cure*. *doctor's orders* [carol douglas]
> sylvester singing *body strong*.   sylvester singing *stars*

Kevin Prufer

Kevin Prufer was born in 1969 in Cleveland, Ohio, and attended Wesleyan University, Hollins University, and Washington University in St. Louis. He is the author of three books of poems: *Strange Wood* (Winthrop/ Louisiana State, 1998), *The Finger Bone* (Carnegie Mellon, 2002), and *Fallen from a Chariot* (Carnegie Mellon, 2005). He is also editor of *The New Young American Poets* (Southern Illinois University Press, 2000) and, with Joy Katz, coeditor of *Dark Horses: Poets on Overlooked Poems* (University of Illinois, 2005). Prufer has received two Pushcart prizes, the *Prairie Schooner*/Strousse Award, the Poetry Society of America's Emily Dickinson Prize, and two George Bogin Memorial Awards. He lives in rural Missouri, where he teaches at Central Missouri State University, serves as codirector of Pleiades Press, and edits both *Pleiades: A Journal of New Writing* and *American Book Review*. For 2004–2006, he has been Vice President/Secretary of the National Book Critics Circle.

For the Unfortunates

Forgive me, insomniacs. I dozed off. I fell into a dream. I slipped, here at the kitchen counter, with the apples, looking over the lawn.

And you, the wounded. Will you forgive me? I cut my finger on this paring knife. It stains the sink, but not so badly. I bit my lip to keep from crying and now the water washes the basin clean.

You, who haven't room in your heads for a new thought: I live in a windmill. All day long, the blades swing round, the hundred cogs above the roof clicking away like excellent ideas. Forgive me. My ears are full of cotton, but it does no good.

Wood bugs in my walls, wasps in my bread box—they aren't laughing at you, who have no feeling in your thumbs, the numb at heart. Their mouths are full of woodchips, their eyes blind with paint.

Won't you all be kind? I have so many gentle thoughts. Forgive me, unfortunates: there is a little knife in my hand.

The End of the City

Now only the dying and as the sky closes its shutter I say
I walked with them I talked with them I speak their names again
and count them on my fingers I count back on my fingers.

And now the trees drop their leaves into the avenue
and the cars have stopped so the leaves billet the windshields.
Now the sun is beautiful as a tear rolling down the sky.

When the Romans came Carthage dropped through the trees
and when the Visigoths came Rome fell like an old coin
and with the plague Antioch tripped in its boots.

Cities fall and sometimes like old men rise on their joints
so as my city stumbled I was on the phone saying
Thank you for calling please ring me up again to the dead air

my words failing and my hands growing cold.
And as the dying turned in their beds I was saying
Lord lord raise them up and keep their feet from sliding

but from the west where the wind comes *dead air*
and from above where the street lamps nod on their posts *no light*.
I do not remember a war I do not remember a pestilence

I did not provoke the avenues into such silence.

A Car Has Fallen from a Bridge

There is the death of the car, which was quiet and signifies little, ticking gently in a
field of snow.

And there is the death of the body, which was quick, the body unaware and cooling
against the dash.

Of course, there is snow, which wants so badly just to sleep, surrounding the car
and the body where they came to rest.

How gentle the snow seems from the car, like a gauzy curtain the wind blew from
a window on a fall day perhaps years ago. How sweet,

the little paw prints where the sprung glass scattered.

People drive over the bridge not noticing the rail has torn away, not noticing the
car which rolled into the field and, moments ago, just died.

I want to be younger than I am.

I want to say to my mother, *no*. To cry in the back seat because I am bored and hungry and we are still one hundred miles from home.

The car lay in the field and the head slept on the dash. An ambulance pulled to the edge of the bridge

but could not figure out how to descend to the frozen field and the car, which was already dead.

Sometimes, I think I understand death, my mother whose heart just stopped while she spoke to a friend on the phone. *Painless, painless,*

I say then. And *merciful*, the receiver dangling from its cord. How nice to go that way, like a car which one moment is happy and, another, suspended in flight where the bridge broke loose.

To the body, the snow is neither cold nor gentle. To the body, there's a zero where a field should be.

If I only had a cell phone, I would try to call her.

The Rise of Rome

Rose like a fog off a lake at dawn as the bus rolled past, a young man nodding
  sleepily against the glass.

Rose from the runway like an airplane that has not long to live.

Rise, the pastor told us, and we rose from our pews and fingered the books because
  we knew

our time was short. We sang and bowed our heads, then kneeled.

It was a gorgeous empire in its brick and marble. Gorgeous,

like a new car, all windshield and chrome. I wanted to touch it, to slide my finger
  along the headlight's bee-eye of glass

and not think about it overturned in a field, the wheels slowing and the cockpit just
  smoke.

Rise, the gods said in their wisdom and rings. *Rise*, in their fingers nettled over
with scars, in their whimsical and gratuitous

anger and love. Rome rose and rose like a fog

and we said *yes* to the gods and played out guitars. *Yes* and boarded our planes, or
drove the long roads outside of the city

where the sun came down and no one plowed it away. It was a marvelous time,

faster and faster like smoke. The baths and the aqueduct, the opulent quarter and
the less

opulent. I swam in perfume while my servants ate mice, while the borders
  collapsed

and planes crowded the skies. *Oh give me, give me*, I said to the gods who
  grinned around their crystal balls.

It was always summer while Rome was rising. The pastor said *kneel*. The gods
just laughed.

We spread our beach towel on the sand and collapsed.

On Finding a Swastika Carved on a Tree in the Hills above Heidelberg

Later, on the Neckar's oil-slick banks,
I fed a two-headed swan a stale bread crust.
The healthy head ate;
the other, featherless, eyes closed or undeveloped,
dragged from the end of its garden-hose neck
in the mud on the shore.

Meanwhile, all along Schwartz Strasse,
as they do every day, the citizens sat
In pairs at their outdoor café tables
swallowing schnitzel, sighing at the sun's descent.
They shredded their napkins
then rubbed the rims of their wine glasses

until the evening was filled
with a crystal air-raid siren sound.

The night floated down like a thousand allies
lashed to black parachutes.

Srikanth Reddy

Srikanth Reddy was born in 1973 in Chicago. He holds a BA from Harvard University and an MFA from the University of Iowa, and is currently a doctoral candidate in English literature (writing a dissertation on digression in 20th-Century American poetry) at Harvard. His first collection of poetry is *Facts for Visitors* (University of California, 2004), and poems from this collection have appeared in journals such as *American Poetry Review, Fence, jubilat, Ploughshares,* and *Verse.* A former fellow at the Wisconsin Institute for Creative Writing, Reddy now lives in Chicago, where he is an Assistant Professor of English at the University of Chicago.

Corruption

I am about to recite a psalm that I know. Before I begin, my expectation extends over the entire psalm. Once I have begun, the words I have said remove themselves from expectation & are now held in memory while those yet to be said remain waiting in expectation. The present is a word for only those words which I am now saying. As I speak, the present moves across the length of the psalm, which I mark for you with my finger in the psalm book. The psalm is written in India ink, the oldest ink known to mankind. Every ink is made up of a color & a vehicle. With India ink, the color is carbon & the vehicle, water. Life on our planet is also composed of carbon & water. In the history of ink, which is rapidly coming to an end, the ancient world turns from the use of India ink to adopt sepia. Sepia is made from the octopus, the squid & the cuttlefish. One curious property of the cuttlefish is that, once dead, its body begins to glow. This mild phosphorescence reaches its greatest intensity a few days after death, then ebbs as the body decays. You can read by this light.

Scarecrow Eclogue

Then I took the poem in my hand & walked out
past the well & three levelled acres
to where the sugarcane built itself slowly to the songs of immature goats
& there at the field's shimmering center

I inserted the page
into the delicately-woven grass of the scarecrow's upraised hand

where it began to shine & give a little in the gentle
unremitting breeze sent over from the east.

I stepped back several paces
to look at what I'd done.
Only a little way off & the morning light bleached out my ink
on the page so it simplified

into a white rectangle against a skyblue field
flapping once, twice
as if grazed by one close shot after another.
The oxen snorted nearby

& there was a sense of publication
but not much else was different, so I backed off all the way
to the sugarcane's edge until the poem was only a gleam
among the fieldworkers' sickles surfacing

like the silver backs of dolphins
up above the green crop-rows into view, then down from view.
How it shone in my withdrawal,
worksongs rising

over it all. So then I said the poem aloud, my version
of what the god dressed up as a charioteer said
to the reluctant bowman
at the center of the battlefield.

How he spoke of duty, the substance
of this world,
& the trembling armies ranged.

Second Circle

Now, darling. It's time you strapped me back on that wheel.
Strap me on, my salt girl, O sweet Lady Slip—
I'm down on my knees. At last I've learned how to kneel.

It's turning without me. One misses the halo, the steel
gear-teeth at the spine, the way the world flips
now, darling—it's Time. Strap me back on that wheel.

Two scarecrows faced each other across a dark field.
How do they do it? I asked the front seats, inflatable globe
on my knees. At last I've learned how. To kneel

without touching the earth, mouthing O as one reels
past the urinal doors to the dancers with whips…
Grave darlings of the times, you strapped me to that wheel

& I ripped myself free. Mother, you wept for a while
under the golden-red plectra of Fall & then stopped.
I'm on my knees. At last they're knees. I need them to kneel

but can't rise without you. O tie these hands, they feel
so cold they must be my hands, old things that grip
in the Now, darling. Strap me back on that wheel.
I'm on my knees at last. I've learned how to kneel.

Evening with Stars

It was light. Whoever it was
who left it under the gumtree last night
forgot to close the gate. This morning when I stepped
out on the breezeway I had to shoo off a she-pig
& three rag-pickers before I could tell
what it was they were carting away
through the leaves. I had the houseboy bear it
into the sunroom. After attending to my & my employer's
business, I returned sometime after midnight
to examine it. A pair of monkeys
were hoisting it over the threshold
toward a courtyard of fireflies. When I shook my fist
they dropped it & I settled down at last.
It was gilt. It was evening with stars.
Where a latch should have been, a latch ·
was painted on. Over the lid, a procession.
Chariot. Splintered tree. Chariot. Chariot.
In the lamplight the hollows
of the footsoldiers' eyes were guttering.
I'd say they looked happy.
Tired & happy. Their soil-flecked boots
sank down to the buckle in weeds

& lacquered nettles, six men to a burden.
It was light. I could see
in the middle distance a bone priest
picking his way through crop rows
toward the wreckage of an iron temple.
Scarlet clouds moving out. Jasper clouds moving in.

Here, on a cistern, a woman
keeps nursing her infant.
She is unwell.
The workmanship is astonishing.
You can pick out every lesion on her breast.

Mostly, I am alone.

Burial Practice

Then the pulse.
Then a pause.
Then twilight in a box.
Dusk underfoot.
Then generations.

*

Then the same war by a different name.
Wine splashing in a bucket.
The erection, the era.
Then exit Reason.
Then sadness without reason.
Then the removal of the ceiling by hand.

*

Then pages & pages of numbers.
Then the page with the faint green stain.
Then the page on which Prince Theodore, gravely wounded,
   is thrown onto a wagon.
Then the page on which Masha weds somebody else.
Then the page that turns to the story of somebody else.
Then the page scribbled in dactyls.
Then the page which begins *Exit Angel*.

Then the page wrapped around a dead fish.
Then the page where the serfs reach the ocean.
Then a nap.
Then the peg.
Then the page with the curious helmet.

*

Then the page on which millet is ground.
Then the death of Ursula.
Then the stone page they raised over her head.
Then the page made of grass which goes on.

*

Exit Beauty

*

Then the page someone folded to mark her place.
Then the page on which nothing happens.
The page after this page.

Then the transcript.
Knocking within.

Interpretation, then harvest.

*

Exit Want.
Then a love story.

Then a trip to the ruins.
Then & only then the violet agenda.

Then hope without reason.
Then the construction of an underground passage between us.

Spencer Reece

Spencer Reece was born in 1963 in Hartford, Connecticut, and attended
Wesleyan University. His poems have appeared in *Boulevard*, *The New
Yorker*, *Nimrod*, and elsewhere. His first book, *The Clerk's Tale* (Houghton
Mifflin, 2004), which won the Katherine Bakeless Nason Literary
Publication Prize, was written over the course of fifteen years. Reece lives in
Juno Beach, Florida, and works as an assistant manager at Brooks Brothers
in Palm Beach Gardens, Florida.

Portofino

Promise me you will not forget Portofino.
Promise me you will find the trompe l'oeil
on the bedroom walls at the Splendido.
The walls make a scene you cannot enter.

Perhaps then you will comprehend this longing
for permanence I often mentioned to you.
Across the harbor? A yellow church. A cliff.
Promise me you will witness the day diminish.

And when the roofs darken, when the stars drift
until they shatter on the sea's finish,
you will know what I told you is true
when I said abandonment is beautiful.

Autumn Song

The muscular sky of Minnesota is more than I can fathom,
    full of salmon-colored promises of just how expansive love can be
at a time like this where the growing slow hunger of fall hushes
    and sounds in the footsteps of squirrels whirling like dervishes
and in the slopping slough-sound of mad cows crazy in love.
    The human being naked in love is lovelier in the autumn dusk
than on a summer's day. Most blowhards lead you to believe

romance hangs itself most astoundingly in the summertime,
        but I am here to say fall is lovelier still for falling in love,
for a love that stills the heart, that rustles our dust with good news —
        when the maple sweats and saps at the corners of his mouth
and when the oak shakes his leaves like a thousand horseshoes
        is the time my heart bangs with barn-joy and I breathe in the subtle
approbation of death coming as I recognize the Byzantine look

of the trees emptying themselves of themselves. The leaves fall
        like leaflets in a relentless war and the architecture of skeletons
becomes more and more apparent and the water wavers, the water cracks,
        and everywhere this upturned look, the look of one last kiss,
and on such a night as this, I feel dignity, I feel survival; in the nude
        descent of the earth shedding its sweat, its passion, my breath,
my shimmering cargo, is eager to dawn and break free from its hold.

The Clerk's Tale

I am thirty-three and working in an expensive clothier,
selling suits to men I call "Sir."
these men are muscled, groomed and cropped—
with wives and families that grow exponentially.
Mostly I talk of rep ties and bow ties,
of full-Windsor knots and half-Windsor knots,
of tattersall, French cuff, and English spread collars,
of foulards, neats, and internationals,
of pincord, houndstooth, nailhead, and sharkskin.
I often wear a blue pin-striped suit.
My hair recedes and is going gray at the temples.
On my cheeks there are a few pimples.
For my terrible eyesight, horn-rimmed spectacles.
One of my fellow-workers is an old homosexual
who works hard and wears bracelets with jewels.
No one can rival his commission checks.
On his break he smokes a Benson & Hedges cigarette,
puffing expectantly as a Hollywood starlet.
He has carefully applied a layer of Clinique bronzer
to enhance the tan on his face and neck.
His hair is gone except for a few strands
which are combed across his scalp.
He examines his manicured lacquered nails.
I admire his studied attention to details:
his tie stuck to his shirt with masking tape,

his teeth capped, his breath mint in place.
The old homosexual and I laugh in the back
over a coarse joke involving an octopus.
Our banter is staccato, staged and close
like those "Spanish Dances" by Granados.
I sometimes feel we are in a musical—
gossiping backstage between our numbers.
He drags deeply on his cigarette.
Most of his life is over.
Often he refers to himself as "an old faggot."
He does this bemusedly, yet timidly.
I know why he does this.
He does this because his acceptance is finally complete—
and complete acceptance is always
bittersweet. Our hours are long. Our backs bent.
We are more gracious than English royalty.
We dart amongst the aisles tall as hedgerows.
Watch us fade into the merchandise.
How we set up and take apart mannequins
as if we were performing autopsies.
A naked body, without pretense, is of no use.
It grows late.
I hear the front metal gate close down.
We begin folding the ties correctly according to color.
The shirts — Oxfords, broadcloths, pinpoints—
must be sized, stacked, or rehashed.
The old homosexual removes his right shoe,
allowing his gigantic bunion to swell.
There is the sound of cash being counted—
coins clinking, bills swishing, numbers whispered—
One, two, three, four, five, six, seven...
We are changed when the transactions are done—
older, dirtier, dwarfed.
A few late customers gawk in at us.
We say nothing. Our silence will not be breached.
The lights go off, one by one—
the dressing room lights, the mirror lights.
Then it is very late. How late? Eleven?
We move to the gate. It goes up.
The gate's grating checkers our cheeks.
This is the Mall of America.
The light is bright and artificial,
yet not dissimilar to that found in a Gothic cathedral.
You must travel down the long hallways to the exits
before you encounter natural light.

One final formality: the manager checks our bags.
The old homosexual reaches into his over-the-shoulder leather bag —
the one he bought on his European travels
with his companion of many years.
He finds a stick of lip balm and applies it to his lips
liberally, as if shellacking them.
Then he inserts one last breath mint
and offers one to me. The gesture is fraternal
and occurs between us many times.
At last, we bid each other good night.
I watch him fade into the many-tiered parking lot,
where the thousands of cars have come
and are now gone. This is how our day ends.
This is how our day always ends.
Sometimes snow falls like rice.
See us take to our dimly lit exits,
disappearing into the cities of Minneapolis and St. Paul;
Minneapolis is sleek and St. Paul,
named after the man who had to be shown,
is smaller, older, and somewhat withdrawn.
Behind us, the moon pauses over the vast egg-like dome of the mall.
See us loosening our ties among you.
We are alone.
There is no longer any need to express ourselves.

Paisley Rekdal

Paisley Rekdal was born in 1970 in Seattle, Washington. She studied as an undergraduate at the University of Washington and Trinity College in Dublin, completed an MA in Medieval Studies from the University of Toronto, and received her MFA in Poetry from the University of Michigan. Her poems and essays have appeared in *The Black Warrior Review, Denver Quarterly, The New York Times Sunday Magazine, Ploughshares, Poetry, The Virginia Quarterly Review,* and elsewhere. Rekdal is the author of a book of essays, *The Night My Mother Met Bruce Lee* (Pantheon, 2000; Vintage, 2002), and two books of poetry—*A Crash of Rhinos* (University of Georgia Press, 2000) and *Six Girls Without Pants* (Eastern Washington University Press, 2002). Her work has been recognized with a *Village Voice* Writers on the Verge Award, a Fulbright Fellowship to South Korea, an NEA Fellowship, a Wyoming Council for the Arts Fellowship, and the Laurence Goldstein Poetry Prize from *Michigan Quarterly Review.* She lives in Salt Lake City, Utah, and teaches in the University of Utah's Creative Writing Program.

Strawberry

I am going to fail.
I'm going to fail cartilage and plastic, camera and arrow.
I'm going to fail binoculars and conjugations,
all the accompanying musics: *I am failing,*
I must fail, I can fail, I have failed
the way some women throw themselves
into lover's arms or out trains,
fingers crossed and skirts billowing
behind them. I'm going to fail
the way strawberry plants fail,
have dug down hard to fail, shooting
brown runners out into silt, into dry gray beds,
into tissue and rock. I'm going to fail
the way their several hundred hearts below surface
have failed, thick, soft stumps desiccating
to tumors; the way roots wizen in the cold
and cloud black, knotty as spark plugs, cystic
synapses. I'm going to fail light and stars and tears.
I'm going to fail the way cowards only wish they could fail,
the way the brave refuse to fail or the vain fear to,
believing that to stray even once from perfection
is to be permanently cast out, Wandering Jew
of failure, Adam of failure, Sita of failure; that's the way

I'm going to fail, bud and creosote and cloud.
I'm failing pet and parent. I'm failing the food
in strangers' stomachs, the slender inchoate rings
of distant planets. I'm going to fail these words
and the next and the next. I'm going to fail them,
I'm going to fail her—trust me, I've already failed him—
and the possibility of a *we* is going to sink me
like a bad boat. I'm going to fail the way
this strawberry plant has failed, alive without bud,
without fruit, without tenderness, hugging itself
to privation and ridiculous want.
I'm going to fail simply by standing in front of you,
waving my arms in your face as if hailing a taxi:
I'm here, I'm here, please don't forget me,
though you already have, I smell it, even cloaked
with soil, sending out my slender fingers for you,
sending out all my hair and tongue and brain.
I'm going to fail you
just as you're going to fail me,
urging yourself further down to sediment
and the tiny, trickling filaments of damp;
thirsty, thirsty, desperate to drown
if even for a little while, if even for once:
to succumb, to be destroyed,
to die completely, to fail the way I've failed
in every particular sense of myself,
in every new and beautiful light.

Stupid

> In Detroit, a 41-year-old gets stuck and drowns in two feet of
> water after squeezing his head through a narrow sewer grate
> to retrieve his car keys.

A joke? Tell me

the story of Job, that book of the pious man
who suffered because the devil wanted to teach God
faith kills through illusion. *Sub*
+ *ferrere* = to carry, to wear boils

like a string of pearls around the neck
and watch son, wealth, house turn
into a sootfall of ash. *Suffer*

the little children I thought was an imperative
not to love but to disdain.
Tell me the one about Santiago Alvarado
who died in Lompoc, having fallen

through the ceiling of the shop
he burgled when the flashlight he carried in his mouth
rammed into his skull.

How Nick Berrena was stabbed to death
by a friend trying to prove a knife couldn't penetrate
the flak vest Berrena wore,
or Daniel Jones dug an eight-foot hole in the sand
whose broad shelf buried him alive.

Hast not thou made a hedge

about him, and about all he hath on every side?
Skin for skin, yea, all that a man hath
he will give for his life.
Tell me what the foolish

should make with their small faith
in roofing, keys just a fingerhold away. This world,
shimmering with strange death in which we know
that to trip on the staircase, wreck the lover's car
is perhaps also to sit covered with ash eating
one's own white heart.

Why doesn't the universe turn a lovelier face to me?

A woman runs to a poison control center
after eating three vaginal inserts while a man
has a cordless phone pulled from his rectum.
I comfort friends

badly, curse the stove for my meal,
live with the wrong man for years.   Faith
for me extends just as far as I'm rewarded; if I laugh
about the mouth foaming with nonoxynol
I'm also awed at the woman's belief propelling her *toward*
not *away from* fear, contrary to skepticism or evidence.

Are there not mockers with me?

and doth not mine eye continue in their provocation?
Bildad begged Job take the smarter path of self-blame:
the sinner must be punished with sin, the stupid destroyed
by stupidity. *Shall the earth be forsaken for thee?* he asked.

How long will ye mock me? Job cried. God waits
and his words blush furiously up to heaven.

Stupid. Job is stupid for believing.
And I am one of the false mockers chastising
endlessly the faith of one who suffers,
who produces no great thing but shame: to wait

is to destroy the organ and a rash act
must mar this soul. *Stupid,*
how could you love me when everything I give you hurts?

Satan is an old joke to us who don't know

how many temptations lurk
in the commonest household:
the knife, the flashlight. But Santiago knows

and if stealing is the thing that brings one closer
to happiness, and keeping one's hands
free means the difference
between this life and death, that's one line he'll cross.

Few people die intelligently,

the mind gone, shit or urine trickling
between sheets: why not be stabbed
believing yourself protected from the physical indignity
of a knife? *The Lord,*
he destroyeth the perfect and the wicked.

Stupid, listen to me: I'm dying

and everywhere there are azaleas and people speaking French,
so many cups of tea I'll never drink!
Job, you are stupid for your faith as we are stupid for our lack of it,
snickering at the stockbroker jogging off the cliff, though
shouldn't we wonder at all a man can endure
to believe, like this one

whose wife said was so in love
with the world how *could* he look down
while running when he knew
(or should he) all his soul

went up?

What Was There to Bring Me to Delight But to Love and Be Loved?

I declared, and immediately rejected this. For instance:
a man I loved once liked to hurt women and would tell me
what he did to his lovers. The sight of a woman's slight hips
as she was knocked over a television might give delight. Or the way
bones sounded in skin that bumped or scraped against a wall.
He used to claim he could hear things like this, not
the scratch of a woman's back on a wall, but actual
bone rubbing muscle, skin, joint, the sound
as if sticks rattled in cloth. It frightened him, he said, he found himself
pushing other women to prove he couldn't really hear the sound.
And I loved him. I loved forgiving him. I must admit this
though he never laid a hand on me,
I knew enough about this kind of loss.
There were more significant things
to demand from the world. Such as how
a word could call up more than violence, idea, person, become
reality with only the finest limitations
of meaning. Such as *monster*, perhaps,
or *grave*, or *delicious*. I could say, for instance, that this man
was a *delicious monster* with his strap-colored hair and soft mouth
though where does that place me
in the universe of word? Perhaps you could say *I*
was the monster, searching not for where rivers ran but to the source
of rivers, the frozen nugget of an idea of river: so cold
it almost burns the rock around it. I was the one willing to sacrifice
so many others of my kind; I could listen for hours
to his stories of women whose bones itched within them
and all I could think was *hand, eye, mouth* as if to say the words
was to take his fingers into my mouth, to suck
the warm pink nails between my teeth, or lick the egg taste
from his eye with my tongue. These were more real to me
than the fact he would cry out on the phone or in my bedroom

where we would talk. He would cry and all I could think was
More, let my thighs be another casing for you
if this is the kind of grave you want. I almost thought *grace.* I almost
gave in once but, and this is the truth, he was afraid of me. I
was the coldness of rivers, he said, I was the source
and when he looked down at me lying on the sheets rumpled
like ruined skin, he called me his destroyer.

Perhaps the real question in the world is not
what to love, but how to forgive.
What does it take for the monstrous
to be delightful in the eye of God? As if beauty itself
wasn't also obscene—a hand really fleshed claw, a peony
a flowering of blood. Or perhaps a word is really all it signifies, all
we can trust in fact; to name a thing
is to make it so. When I called this man a *man*, you must believe
he became one for me. The source of the river,
not its oceangrasp. What happened to the man I loved
is that eventually he choked a woman almost to death.
We weren't speaking then. Even I, it seems, have my limits.
But I can imagine how he would have told me he could hear her spine
crying out to him, an accusation of the flesh. *What more is there*
but to love like this and to be loved? he asked me once.
You are my source of delight,
an eternal search for grace, I answered. I almost said *the grave.*

A Crash of Rhinos

What's your pet name? Collective noun?
What will Snookums do today? Your bedmate
pulls quarters magically from behind your ear, one
for each hour you've spent together. When he stops
there's fifty cents sliding into the sheets and his tongue
covering the pink cauliflower of your nipple. "Beautiful
defects," he whispers into your body. "Ah, Nature." Roll away,
don't care when he calls you "Thumper." By noon you'll be
nose to nose anyway, a sloth of bears, snoozing
your way into this relationship.

Ah, Nature. You could tell him its startling fact
is not its defects but its sameness. A uniformity
suggestive of some single-cell prototype, our Adam/Eve
genome plucked, as scientists think, from the thread

of a lightning bolt. Darling, today you're more
than anonymous, one sexy blip among the thousand
couples grunting in each other's arms; defined by Loving,
your action. Flying geese only recognized
by the form they make in the sky.
A crash of rhinos, piece of asses. Stinkhead:
everything comes in boring droves of hogs.

This is how you got here. Mid-morning he tallies your union
in terms of snakes, tarantulas, the evolutionary needs
of common flagellates till you scorn science: its primal
urge to pair like scared cows shoved ass to ass in circles
for defense. A clutch of penises! What is love but fear?
That soft storm at your periphery, sudden hand
pushing you below surface? Thoughts, as you age or sicken,
sifted from consciousness like dusts of starlings: Love me,
little lamb. No one should die alone.

Sweetheart, all your friends are married.
Packs of teazles? Kerfs of panters? A multiplicity of spouses.
Today only two quarters protect you
from loneliness. It's out of your hands. The job
didn't pan, checks bounce, 2 A.M. is its own
worst child. This is your last magic trick.
"Kumquat," he whispers. Lover. Loved one.
And the soul begs always, *Leave me leave me*
while the body says simply, *Stay.*

Matthew Rohrer

Matthew Rohrer was born in 1970 in Ann Arbor, Michigan, and grew up in Michigan, Alabama, and Oklahoma. He holds a BA from the University of Michigan and an MFA from the University of Iowa Writers' Workshop. His poems have appeared in many journals, including *Boston Review*, *Conduit*, *Crowd*, *Open City*, *Ploughshares*, *The Village Voice*, and a journal made out of a matchbook called *Matchbook*. His first book, *A Hummock in the Malookas* (W.W. Norton, 1995), was a 1994 National Poetry Series selection. His other books include *Satellite* (Verse, 2001) and *A Green Light* (Verse, 2004), which was shortlisted for the 2005 Griffin International Poetry Prize. With poet Joshua Beckman, Rohrer collaborated on the book of poems *Nice Hat. Thanks* (Verse, 2002) and released an audio CD of their live collaborations, *Adventures While Preaching the Gospel of Beauty* (Verse, 2003). Rohrer is a founding member of the journal *Fence*, and served as one of its poetry editors until 2005. He writes, "For the past five years I have been an Adjunct Instructor at the New School while also holding various unpleasant full-time jobs. I live in Brooklyn and besides teaching adjunct courses, I am a full time stay at home dad for a two-year-old. I am fully domesticated."

Childhood Stories

They learned to turn off the gravity in an auditorium
and we all rose into the air,
the same room where they demonstrated
pow-wows and prestidigitation.

But not everyone believed it.
That was the most important lesson
I learned—that a truck driven by a dog
could roll down a hill at dusk
and roll right off a dock into a lake
and sink, and if no one believes you
then what is the point
of telling them wonderful things?

I walked home from the pow-wow
on an early winter night in amazement:
they let me buy the toy tomahawk!
As soon as I got home I was going
to hit my sister with it, but I didn't know this.

from *The World at Night*

I went out one night with people from work
to an editor's apartment. I drank
a glass of poison. She served me poison
and everyone else was either immune
or politely refused. In the subway
I didn't know the meanings of any words
and my sweat stung me. People on the car
pushed me off at the next stop when I puked
in my hands. Without any meaning, time
accreted to things in funny shapes—old,
asymmetrical hobbledehoys
tormented me, a stern but benevolent
lizard gave me counsel. My stomach contents
spilled around me. My mind was actually
seven or eight minds, all but one of them
composed of helicopters. The other one
was sad. Satellites could tell I was sad.
When another subway came I crawled on
and technically I passed into death, but
passed through and awoke at Coney Island
and saw black cowboys galloping on the beach.
Hungry, mentally defeated, I stared
at The World's Largest Rat—for fifty cents.
Really, it was only the same color
as a rat. "It's from the same family,"
the barker explained. I felt vulnerable
illuminated by neon and fried light.
Everyone had to use one big toilet

and the sky was orange with satellites.

And satellites know everything.

My Government

The history of the world
is the history of rural malcontents
rising up against the capital.

Each night I hear something scratching
to get in my fortress
which can only hold out so long.

The cat thinks something lives in the radiator
and puts his mouth to the vent—its breath.

No man is an island. Also, no one is interested
in excessive indeterminacy. The French
will eat the horse right out from under you. That,
and so much more, have you taught me, World.

Your products will collapse after a short time
and we will be forced into the streets for more.

It is possible to live only on what you grow yourself
if you eat little and lie very still.

We Never Should Have Stopped at Pussy Island

There is this desire to resurrect
the young grandfather
in his salt-stained fatigues,
but the fatigue of even pretending
to accompany him on the troopship
across the flat pale oceans
of the world sinks me
into the depths of the deep green couch.
There he was—riding into Manila
in the back of a jeep to restore communications,

surrounded by topless women
running non-stop in circles around him.
Huge American planes lay fallen
into the very buildings
they had been attacking.
There was no stopping this thing.
In the photographs on the kitchen table
I look down the barrels of the ladies'
enormous dark areolas.
He never took off his boots there.
This heat presses me against the floor.
In Manila, long ago,
his sweat dissolved his clothes.
My wife is wearing his fatigues
tonight, and no bra; she is his size,
smooth and skinny legs.
They had to fuck up that whole island
to get it back and they were glad to have it.
The cows there were thinner than ours,
and hated both sides equally.
Boys were getting their bones ripped out
by bombs but it was also a safer time
to be alive—my grandfather's troopship
just swerved all over the sea and they were safe,
the enemy couldn't find them,
the only ones who knew where they were
were covered in scales, and the truth
could not be got from them.
And every move they made was a secret.
We do not know if they stopped
at any particular island.
The heat here turns into hot rain
as it did on his head
and the eviscerated boys
from Charlevoix blown back
into the trees. We do not know
why he did not call home, when he returned.
I do not even know what goes on
in the apartment upstairs.
We only know what the Army censors tell us.
Some boys simply disappeared,
never to wear ankle-high leather boots
with zippers, never to wake up
on a day that those were in fashion.

Tessa Rumsey

Tessa Rumsey was born in 1970 in Stamford, Connecticut, and lived on Harmony Ranch, an artist's commune, for four years, before moving with her parents to San Francisco, where she was raised in the Haight-Ashbury neighborhood and also lives today. She holds a BA from Sarah Lawrence College, an MFA from the University of Iowa, and an MA in Visual Criticism from the California College of the Arts. Rumsey's poems have appeared in *Boston Review*, *Conjunctions*, *The New Republic*, *Verse*, *The Washington Post*, and elsewhere. Her two books of poems are *Assembling the Shepherd* (University of Georgia Press, 1999) and *The Return Message* (W.W. Norton, 2005), winner of the 2004 Barnard Women Poets Prize.

More Important Than the Design of Cities Will Be the Design of Their Decay

Loneliness is a laboratory; its territory is forever defined; for reasons
    beyond our conviction
It cannot be lessened; only *redirected* and made to resemble *a crumbling
    heaven* or the year's
Grand delusion: *I shall no longer want for that which left me long ago*—
    go slow, said the soul,
That you may know the streets of your abandoned city more intimately
    than any joy
Or cherished season. We were in collusion, this city and I, creating
    a mythology of desolation;
Feeling utterly evacuated; yet methodically structured; in a post-Roman
    Empire; previously
Doomed sort of way—and what did the soul say, but *know it better,* then
    in a fever, *go deeper.*
There are days, I told the translator, when the veil drops and I am
    no longer inside the No-
Place most familiar, built by me long ago, and I walk through the world
    as if made real
By the existence of others and the casual way a crowd pauses together
    on a concrete curbside—
Perhaps one of them is weeping, perhaps another will gently reach out
    and twist a knife

Into my heart and we will lock eyes, and I will fall to my knees, and
    for a moment
He will hold me. What will I remember? The cold blade's cruel
    demeanor? My body
As it seizures? Or the gesture of my destroyer, showing me that in this
    life, I was not alone.

Man-Torpedo-Boat

If he had loved me he would not have designed
the land mine the land mine
that jumps up from black matted soil
to the level of a heart the land mine
that explodes while floating in the air
like an iron cherub like the blameless conjunction
between *man* and *killing machine*

If he had loved me he would not have written
the executioner's list for Tuesday the list
spotted with jam and breadcrumbs and the hubris
of early morning coffee
tucked away into the trousers of a messenger
holding one end of a rope the rope tied
to the last name on the list

If he had truly loved me he could not have delivered
the letter bomb the letter bomb
wrapped in luminous paper of onion skin bejeweled
by the riddling stamps of Egypt the letter bomb
addressed in the goldblack songlines of Arabic and pushed
through the mailslot like the suggestion of new love
and its necessary language

If he loved me like bread and water like air like thinking
he would have reinvented his speech
like the poet Marinetti in Italy
on the eve
of World War I
searching for a new grammar
to capture the velocity of the machine gun

Every noun should have its double
that is

the noun should be followed
with no conjunction
by the noun
to which it is related
by analogy

Man-torpedo-boat.
Darling-land mine-heart.
Hand-list-executioner.
Messenger-rope-prisoner.
Letter bomb-mailslot-last breath.
Lover-machine gun-corpse.
Corpse-lover-me.

Assembling My Shepherd

Thrown out of a third story window on acid late spring.
And I put my hand to his forehead to say: listen. Be still.
I am here. Sitting calmly on the sidewalk breathing glass
stuck to his broken body, transformed by sudden flight
so I held him. And was an unseen protector in the rarefied
atmosphere of an unsteady city. I get scared. I get

terrified and really it was my mother standing over him
as I watched from curtained windows—
how she wrapped him in a blanket. How she said: breathe.
How I sequenced my arms around my torso and saw
him coming through a crack in the window to take me with him,
she was all that stood between us, I built her a village

and hid behind the cistern when weather came, and when
I was a worm there was sun, and when I was a lion, sun,
her land had a quality of time that steadied me under the sun.
I get scared. I get so you slip in through a crack seeing I
saw your face, you had to be feared before you could be loved,
my mother held my shoulders and said *you are a shepherd,*

the village, torn down, I listen for your instructions

Never Morocco

I

The limits of our language are the limits
of our world coo-cooeth the philosopher
into my love's tin ear (Tangier? But I was nowhere

near Morocco—) as he sucks a luminous
alphabet of smoke from the crack pipe,
as the alley weather turns from inadequate

to oceanic, as the picture is bamboozled
toward a more tented-Saharan-tea-party-
meets-nomadic-American-junkie motif—

to his east, neon Casbah blinks pistachio
and shocking pink, camels ache aimlessly
along the duned horizon, Where oh where

is my orange tree? my *casablanca*? In ruins—
here, he ignites—hermaphrodite
city folds in upon itself, spelling

swarms of retarded bees gone ritalin
among his inner trees *you are not what*
you say you are not what you say you are not—

II

You could be barefoot and heroic, addicted
to chain guns and rocket launchers
and still the desert would not need you

funny to be dying for the mirage's
deranged marriage of distance
and liquid and realize everything

you've ever uttered is the projection
of a picture—*sea of sand, flying*
camel, sandstorm, Bedouin—you

are not where you say you are, epileptic
beneath the city's dank and fogbanked
dawn, the book will kill the minaret

the alphabet will kill the icon, what
did the philosopher say that night,
beneath the never and the phantom

orange trees (pornography for the bindles,
rubberbands for the bucks?)—whisper *lover
dying* whisper again *not breathing*

III
And what is a "tree"? And what is "seeing"?

Big Rig the Baroque Sky

Stand still. Places move within us.
There was the impulse to flee and then there was
New Hampshire, with A, and our refugee vision
of being made more. Connected. Part of
as opposed to dismembered from the nature

program on public television. Once inside
we hoped it would be less of a reunion and more
a realization, *your exile was self-imposed*
or *the door to the garden never closed*
an oiled click would unlock the loamy frame—

in the futuristic city A and I described
a firefly dictatorship. Where meadows
would make us childlike. Beside a cult
of delphinium. Blessed. Following the simple
orientation of the sun. It was our prodigal vision:

forgotten reams of river will embrace us.
Feeling generally cast out, not knowing where
from. We drove in a big rig for days. Over water
of asphalt, Manhattan silver, then white, then
theoretical behind us, and above our big rig

the baroque sky, thickening with decoration
as we spoke of its "sandstone plates" and "Taj Mahal."
At dusk swallows rose over the highway
like black questions of panic, cries—
where will I rest—dip, *will my wings end*

where the wind begins—
rise, do machines dream of spring,
of clouds perplexing their screens?
I objectify what I desire so I can feel
superior and arrived at a maple cathedral,

pledged allegiance to a hierarchy of back roads
and a lilac-green anarchy of light.
At the wet wood shack where syrup was made
A did not cut the wood vein
but he held the blade, beneath custodies

of palmate leaves and long-winged fruits.
We drank straight from the jug. Put our feet
in the river. Decoration disintegrated
as our toes became clear in the water,
what you've been all along

my trigger-finger stroked the channel
changer. And the impulse to flee was a waking
trance state of a sacred order, my Machiavellian
vision: there is no secure mode to possess us
without ruining us, and so the acquisition

turned to loss, say "exiled. And we never even
arrived." Say "dismembered. And the baroque sky,"
say "new principality," say "New Hampshire"
where everything we did was accompanied
by commentary from the leaves—

we can explain back roads and your impulse
to flee in terms of a single substance: water:
the blackest answer: we are never at rest:
and swallows: and factory machines: and
questions: arise

Robyn Schiff

Robyn Schiff was born in 1973 and raised in Metuchen, New Jersey. She holds a BA from Sarah Lawrence College, an MA in Medieval Studies from the University of Bristol, and an MFA from the University of Iowa. Her poems have appeared in *The Black Warrior Review*, *Court Green*, *Denver Quarterly*, *Kiosk*, *VOLT*, *Verse*, and elsewhere. Her debut collection, *Worth* (University of Iowa Press, 2002), was recognized with an award from the Greenwall Fund by the Academy of American Poets. Schiff is an active Contributing Editor of the poetry journal *The Canary*. Formerly a Visiting Assistant Professor at the University of Oregon, she recently moved to Chicago with her husband, the poet Nick Twemlow, and is a Visiting Assistant Professor of English at Northwestern University.

At Shedd Aquarium

Watch them be themselves
in habitats contrived
in dark rooms with openings
like televisions broadcasting
a dimension where Pigment rides
in its original body
and metaphor initiates impractical
negotiations with Size and Color
and Speed and Silence
too thoroughly forward
but to feel
the self an excess.

Fastness, I am tired of resting.
Isn't it indecisive not to be smaller
driven through waters barely perceivable
but where a wake scribbles
a line like a Chinese character
abandoning its construction box
to slip as line only
into an opening
smaller than its shoulders?

Each fin scores the air
as it opens the surface.

A sliver of a fish circles
forever that day
as if to turn something over
in its skinny head keen
to resolve a difficulty
I have.

It is an opera with a lonesome
heroine pacing revolving moors
engineered to seem panoramic.
The diva opens and closes
the tragic mouth singing
deliberate, even breaths
intuition hears.

Theater of false proportion. Theater of constellations reconfiguring. Theater
of readjusting the reception. Theater of missing appointments. Theater of
driving into the ocean with the headlights turned lowest green and the theater
of the engine shifting into oceanic-overdrive. Theater of hearing something
coming closer over theatrical fields of theater set crops. Theater of this can
not be my life, for which, it is too quiet. Theater of seeing something moving
in the one light in the distance which is darkness. Theater of stopping. Theater
of my mistake: not coming forward, going further, the something moving in
the theater of lighting in the theater of the hour between the theater of
morning and the theater of night in the theater of years in which the theater
of regret is keeping the secret theater of the revision.

Theater of slipping between
two points in a simulated rock-mountain.

Theater of who will not tell
casually follows.

Chanel Nº 5

Waterfall gown with water-
fowl sleekness embroidered so as to rise
the speed of light while
not in motion; slit placed
to stride from standstill to escape
as a leopard, monkey, or fox might hear an en-
emy in the dark brush

before she sees it (the coat
is lined) and try deception. These Exiled
Russian Princesses em-
broidering with Pari-
sian seamstresses learned the over-
under stitch in which the end is drawn beneath the
fabric. In photos, fire

in the fireplace a blur on
a log—the shutter was slow—workers pose
as fire beyond betrays
the presentation. If
The Grand Duke Dimitri had moved
suddenly to kiss Chanel's mouth this also would
be recorded as a

blur. Yes, he who pushed Rasput-
in from the bridge pressed and held his mouth to
hers until light sufficed
to keep the exiled Duke
loving her. Action mustn't take
place on the surface but in illusive spaces.
Hesitant Princes of

no domain line up on a
gold chain upon the black drop of her dress
in the dark room. Her neck-
lace is all that shows up.
Patterns of points into inde-
pendent linear shapes transformed by Perspective
on which the cold light of

her jewelry surfaces
like the searchlights of a search-boat, body
in the river decom-
posing, murderer, free.
"At my age, when a man wants you
you don't ask to see his passport," she answered re-
porters about fucking

the Nazi called "The Sparrow"
(his language) in 1940 when in-
vited back to Paris
to fuck him at the Ritz.
Emptiness is innocent? Not

so as Ruth Greenglass described a hollow in the
stereo-console in the

sitting room of her in-laws
in which a lamp was installed. For use in
microfilming, a bulb
affixed on the secret
documentation of the bomb
delicately renders that which is put before
it; reiterating,

smaller, in the Rosenbergs'
console, the atom bomb assembling
and assembling in
silent darkness. Visit-
ors want to hear a record, the
Rosenbergs say the stereo is broken. We've
been waiting on repair-

men almost since we bought it.
There's no workmanship. Mrs. Rosenberg
who unscrewed the transmitt-
er herself says something
must be missing under the lid,
I lifted it and it looked lost.

The Rosenberg testimon-
y admits an ordinary living-
room, a stereo they
paid $21
for. Inside, nothing unusu-
al. A maid they paid too much dusted it every
second Friday morning.

Vampire Finch

Roosting in a crater with one
red foot on either side of her stony egg,
the red-footed booby endures the finch
feeding on her tail in which the
finch has inserted its intravenous
bill to drink the blood. The red-footed booby
knows what happens if she steps

from duty to shoo the finch. The
finch's bill the ages perfect with use will
pierce the egg with one thrust and leave the egg,
should someone come along, fit to
paint an easter meditation upon
that can never spoil. A lacquer developed
by the Japanese who had

no easter, also uses egg
shell and no egg. Cracked beyond recognition,
the fragments are inlaid so as to seem one
continuous flat surface of
a tabletop on which one writing home
never knows one leans one's elbows on that which
stood balanced alone on its

smallest point, vernal equinox
momentarily drawing the whole egg up;
likewise, darkly drawing, the vampire finch
draws on the red-footed booby's
tail-blood; it attaches itself in the
air like Spanish moss, is already feeding
when it puts its feet down on

the feathered back of its warm source.
Pictured feeding itself, iconography
perfect for an island flag or stone-cut
sculpture through which water runs off
the roof of a church through the open beak
of one bird into the beak of the vampire
into the courtyard spouting

black rain filthy from the carved gut
of both ugly birds, finch tense with appetite,
victim-bird rigid with patience and blood
loss, the weakening stance of its
roost captured in Peter's Basilica
where Jesus firmly droops across Mary. The
inevitability

of the finch's thirst darts into
the arrowy point of the beak that stands in
nature for Dracula's two pointed teeth
inscribing a sleepy neck with
marks a prisoner makes to count two more

days with the tine of a fork. When he doesn't
hunt his own, slaves bag village

children and leave them struggling on
the Count's floor, beds empty when parents check them
in the morning. How do they get in? There was
no disturbance but a storm in
the distance rocking a cargo ship in
and out of the beam of the lighthouse. The Count
was in the hold of that ship

raising the coffin lid off the
coffin he traveled in. On land in a train
racing the ship, Mina raises her arms
in a trance in which she gestures
emptily as the Count eats through
the unsuspecting watchmen of the ship's crew,
the smell of shit in the air

makes Mina too sick to eat her
own meal her companions offer. On the ship,
flies breed in the wet muck. More beautiful
than the flower petal in the
prismatic bubble the male fly brings the
female, the empty bubble he sometimes brings
instead. Revolving in the

glassy glare like a globe Vermeer
would dangle, it would make you sick to see things
as fast as they happen like locking your
gaze on a passing train you have
to look away. Loeb did when Leopold
practiced passing ransom from the 3 o'clock.
He looked away from train to

cigar box to marsh grass searching
for the empty box which would contain ransom
if this wasn't practice. Leopold knew
a good place to hide the body
from his days of bird-watching where the train
cut through the still marsh and "From the air vents we
could see civilians laughing."

Woodpecker Finch

That bird named for the bird twice-size itself
has a twig in its mouth or would not be called
the woodpecker finch, extending its reach the length of a twig,
it probes the bark for ants

with the twig in its mouth it would not be called
the woodpecker finch without.
It probes the bark for ants
in darkness where the dead were brought—

woodpecker finch, without,
ruts of ants, within, collapsed
in darkness where the dead were brought
down on the living like salt

salting salt. Being stealthy,
being invisible,
poking with a puppet like a hyphen into
the colony while the finch is yet in the transept of the church,

machine-tragedy in which God cranked from rafters
is not the Japanese black-cloaked puppeteer walking among the living
story of a wife whose devotion to her husband is such she throws herself
from a cliff. The woodpecker finch

sticks the stick-faced stick into the sappy bark,
naked, jerking from the beak of the finch,
picking at the sand with its one foot,
what god is this without a mask

coming or going
like a snake
that won't bend?

Goddess of Mercy
mercifully intervened
and saved the wife.

A bobby pin in an electric socket
plugged into the current
without being dropped
in front of the outlet.

Plugged into the current,
Bridge of Emergencies
from the outlet
to the outer

colony? No. The finch's extended beak
jutting from its given beak,
temporary, light enough to lift in flight,
resolved: *look look* (the theater is dark)

look look (finch taps prop).
A play using multiple sets
provides contrast when a god
causes one place to vanish

mid-act. Flying machines,
trapdoors, hidden stairs,
plot twists, tricks of light,
gloved hands,

promptbooks.
There is music.
There is little conversation.
Wife escapes singing

through the stage door
where the stagehand leans between acts.
Who will fill the wineglass for the love scene?
Who will fall in love?

The final configuration of the B-2 Stealth Bomber
"flies by wire,"—flies by computer—while the pilot takes
a scheduled nap in the 17th hour of the 2-day flight,
5 minutes before the midair refueling of the clean burning engine

time for one short dream
in which your mother opens the screen door.

The facty heart, indiscernible
in graphite that absorbs trap-signals.
How will she find you?

Goddess of Mercy: I thought I saw Wife jump from this cliff

Wife: I jumped

Goddess of Mercy: I thought I saw Wife jump from this cliff
but the Valley is clean

House of Dior

Now we are on the chapter of pleats.
The impatience to fold, the joys of having folded,
the pleasures of folding them again.
Fabric enough in the sleeve to drape the dress,
in the skirt to drape a chest of drawers,
in the dress to drape the view of trees blacked-out
along the walk from here to the next
house. Walking in the dark inside the house
this is the black we black the windows with.
I have hung the last square of cloth.
Good-bye porch. Good-bye midnight postman
with your sack of envelopes. My love sings
to himself. Each pleat steps into the seam
with a pin in its mouth. Crease upon crease,
a fan on which an embroidered rowboat sits
at the far edge of a lake. The lake is deep enough.

Patty Seyburn

Patty Seyburn was born in 1962 and grew up in Detroit, Michigan. She earned a journalism degree from Northwestern University, an MFA in Creative Writing from University of California at Irvine, and a PhD in Creative Writing and Literature from University of Houston. Her poems have appeared in *Crazyhorse, Field, New England Review, The Paris Review, Poetry, Quarterly West, Seneca Review, Swink, Third Coast*, and other journals. Seyburn is the author of two books of poems, *Diasporadic* (Helicon Nine, 1998), winner of the American Library Association's 2000 Notable Book Award, and *Mechanical Cluster* (Ohio State University Press, 2002). Coeditor of the poetry journal *Pool*, she lives in Newport Beach, California, and teaches literature and creative writing courses at the University of Southern California.

The Alphabetizer Speaks

I have my reasons

have never known starvation nor plenitude
and unless the order of the world
changes, I won't.
If the order of the world changes, I will
disappear, the way some vowels
elide into their word-bodies
or an individual blade recedes
into a field each season.

Will my daughter carry on this way?
I cannot yet tell her qualities—
if she prefers scale to chance, sequence to random.
And this may mean nothing.
I find chaos theory appealing, and eavesdrop on talk
of black holes, chasms, any abyss
that fetters sense. I relish
the desultory in many matters,
am slovenly, a slacker, a slave to caprice.
Except with the letters.

There is such thing as a calling
though I cannot speak for prophets or martyrs.
I have been summoned
by people of stature and the low-stationed,

comrade and debutante alike.
My eyes suffer, and my hands, my back.

I am my profession. It is no whim.
I do not want the world a certain way.
The world is that way, and I am a vehicle
on the road of nomenclature. I tend the road.

In my dream, all events coterminous—
no linear narrative, preceding or next.
The odd vignette, lone scene, an image
in isolation, no neighbors.
Then I awaken and pace
my thin balcony, calculating
how much of me waits above, how much
lives below, and I pose
the question of balance. My name
cues the turn home.

First Bookshelf

There is a duck lost at sea when
his crate breaks after the boat is
destroyed. Tossed, overturned,
claimed and buoyed by a frigid
ocean, he observes the moon and
stars, knows loneliness, isolation
and lack of purpose. He wonders
if he'll find a home. There is a
monkey who makes countless,
thoughtless errors and manages
to redeem himself with friendly,
anonymous counsel. He makes
great messes and never seems
to gain an awareness of what
others endure on his behalf. He
is not held accountable for his
mistakes. A royal elephant has
appropriate adventures and an
extended family. A huge dog
with morals means well but his
size often inhibits his ability to
reach his goals. He frequently

learns to compensate for his errs
by giving rides, providing shelter,
protecting the meek. There is a
mouse with balletic grace, while
her tiny cousin has nothing but luck
and the charm of the weak: you
can't choose your family. There is
another mouse, crudely drawn in
primary colors, whose exploits are,
at best, prosaic. She keeps company
with an elephant, an alligator, and
a female of ambiguous species.
She drives a bus, cleans house,
bakes gingerbread, takes a bath,
attends the fair. She is middle class.
And yet another mouse, with many
paid friends and a girlfriend, sister
or cousin, also paid. They used to
keep silent but have, of late, learned
language, which has increased their
popularity but drained the pathos
from their exploits. A company of
pigs, an obdurate spider, a ravenous
caterpillar that endures change and
sheep: lost, defiant, naked. The duck
story is somewhat true except that
we are given the duck's perspective,
which must be questioned, as we have
no small stake in believing that we
are the only ones who understand
that we exist, with little notion of why.

What I Disliked About the Pleistocene Era

The pastries were awfully dry.
An absence of hummingbirds—
of any humming, and birds' lead
feathers made it difficult to fly.

Clouds had not yet learned
to clot, billow, represent.
Stars unshot, anonymous.
Moon and sun indifferent.

No one owned a house, a pond,
a rock on which to rest your head.
No are, no here then there. Beginning
meant alive. The end was dead.

Art still a ways away—no lyre.
Beauty, an accident. Needs
and wants bundled like twigs
then set on fire. Except, no fire.

Candles had no wicks. Fruit
lacked seed. Books bereft of plot.
Ornament and condiment
were empty cisterns. There *were* pots.

It was pure act. No motivation,
consequence, imagination.
Sometimes, a flare, a glow, a gleam.
No questions asked. No revelation.

And I was not yet capital I.
Still just an eye. No mouth,
no verb, no AM to carry dark
from day, dirt or sea from sky—

God not God until one dove
called out "where the hell's dry land?"
An answer formed. A raven shrugged
and toed a line across the sand.

New, the sand. New, the vast
notion of this long division.
New, the understanding that
this time, there would be no revision.

Brenda Shaughnessy

Brenda Shaughnessy was born in 1970 in Okinawa, Japan, and grew up in Southern California. She attended the University of California-Santa Cruz and received her MFA from Columbia University. Her poems have appeared in *Boston Review, Conjunctions, Jubilat, The Paris Review, The Yale Review,* and elsewhere, and have been recognized with a fellowship from the Japan-U.S. Friendship Commission and a Bunting Fellowship from the Radcliffe Institute for Advanced Study. Her first book of poems is *Interior with Sudden Joy* (Farrar, Straus, and Giroux, 2000). Shaughnessy lives in Brooklyn, where she teaches at Lehman College, CUNY, and serves as Poetry Editor of the magazine *Tin House.*

Your Name on It

Let this one clear square of thought be just
like a room you could come to in. An attic room,
after you've swiveled over to the wrecked
corner of the champagne. After you

hand-rolled cigarettes and ass and sold
your best midnight speech to a slick jack
of clubs. For a stingy cut: a wet, bony
kiss. You have nothing left to say

and nothing to say it with. Mouths,
whole faces even, have been pilfered
in prettier ways. For everyone who ever
looked at you and thought *that one thinks*

it's so damn easy, you don't have to look
back at them. Ha! It is easy. This room
has no mirror, no leap-leer to strain
or stylize the fuzz of your body through

the razor of your eye. This room is dark,
and high. If you spit out the window
you could kill a bug. There's the document.
There's always the window, your signature.

Epithalament

Other weddings are so shrewd on the sofa, short
and baffled, bassett-legged. All things

knuckled, I have no winter left, in my sore rememory,
to melt down for drinking water. Shrunk down.

Your wedding slides the way wiry dark hairs do, down
a swimming pool drain. So I am drained.

Sincerely. I wish you every chapped bird on this
pilgrimage to hold your hem up from the dust.

Dust is plural: infinite dust. I will sink in the sun,
I will crawl toward the heavy drawing

and design the curtains in the room
of never marrying you. Because it is a sinking,

because today's perfect weather is a later life's
smut. This soiled future unplans love.

I keep unplanning the same Sunday. Leg
and flower, breeze and terrier, I have no garden

and couldn't be happier. Please, don't lose me
here. I am sorry my clutch is all

tendon and no discipline: the heart is a severed
kind of muscle and alone.

I can hear yours in your room. I hear mine
in another room. In another's.

Postfeminism

There are two kinds of people, soldiers and women,
as Virginia Woolf said. Both for decoration only.

Now that is too kind. It's technical: virgins and wolves.
We have choices now. Two little girls walk into a bar,

one orders a shirley temple. Shirley Temple's pimp
comes over and says you won't be sorry. She's a fine

piece of work but she don't come cheap. Myself, I'm
in less fear of predators than of walking around

in my mother's body. That's sneaky, that's more
than naked. Let's even it up: you go on fuming in your

gray room. I am voracious alone. Blank and loose,
metallic lingerie. And rare black-tipped cigarettes

in a handmade basket case. Which of us weaves
the world together with a quicker blur of armed

seduction: your war-on-thugs, my body stockings.
Ascetic or carnivore. Men will crack your glaze

even if you leave them before morning. Pigs
ride the sirens in packs. Ah, flesh, technoflesh,

there are two kinds of people. Hot with mixed
light, drunk with insult. You and me.

You Love, You Wonder

You love a woman and you wonder where she goes all night in some tricked-
out taxicab, with her high heels and her corset and her big, fat mouth.

You love how she only wears her glasses with you, how thick
and cow-eyed she swears it's only ever you she wants to see.

You love her, you want her very ugly. If she is lovely big, you want her
scrawny. If she is perfect lithe, you want her ballooned, a cosmonaut.

How not to love her, her bouillabaisse, her orangina. When you took her
to the doctor the doctor said, "Wow, look at that!" and you were proud,

you asshole, you love and that's how you are in love. Any expert, observing
human bodies, can see how she's exceptional, how she ruins us all.

But you really love this woman, how come no one can see this? Everyone must
become suddenly very clumsy at recognizing beauty if you are to keep her.

You don't want to lose anything, at all, ever. You want her sex depilated, you want everyone else not blind, but perhaps paralyzed, from the eyes down.

You wonder where she goes all night. If she leaves you, you will know everything about love. If she's leaving you now, you already know it.

Panopticon

My bedroom window can be seen from the viewing deck
of the World Trade Center. I've seen it.
What I saw?

My roommate experimenting with my vibrator.
She looked lovely through sheer curtains
on my creamy bed. Is she thinking of me?

I am thinking of her and I left bread crumbs on the telepath.
She can feel it, my seeing, even through a trance of fog.
I've lit her with it.

It is her blindfold, her sweet curse, her ration
of privacy spilled like flour as she imagines
the miraculous bread is rising.

I decided on three possible reactions:

To keep watching her and, when I go home, to mention
the strange vision I had, describing
what I saw in detail.

              To feed the telescope with quarter
after quarter, and read a book while the time ticks.
I have been blessed with seeing, as with a third eye,
without the compulsive mimesis of appearing. The luxury
of an octopus is never using any legs for walking.

              Or, to stay home with my own
pair of binoculars, in the dark, watching whoever is
watching me, watch me.

Richard Siken

Richard Siken was born in 1967 in New York City, and says he moved to Tucson, Arizona (where he currently resides) at age two-and-a-half because "he wanted to wear western shirts with pearly buttons and ride horses (which he did and does)." He holds an MFA from the University of Arizona and has published poems in such journals as *Conjunctions; Forklift, Ohio; Indiana Review;* and *The Iowa Review.* He is the recipient of an NEA Fellowship and Editor of the literary journal *spork.* Siken's first collection of poems, *Crush* (Yale University Press, 2005) was a Yale Series of Younger Poets selection.

Boot Theory

A man walks into a bar and says:
                              Take my wife—please.
                                                  So you do.
            You take her out into the rain and you fall in love with her
                                    and she leaves you and you're desolate.
You're on your back in your undershirt, a broken man
                  on an ugly bedspread, staring at the water stains
                                                            on the ceiling.
            And you can hear the man in the apartment above you
                        taking off his shoes.
You hear the first boot hit the floor and you're looking up,
                                                you're waiting
      because you thought it would follow, you thought there would be
                  some logic, perhaps, something to pull it all together
      but here we are in the weeds again,
                                                here we are
in the bowels of the thing: your world doesn't make sense.
            And then the second boot falls.
                              And then a third, a fourth, a fifth.

      A man walks into a bar and says:
                        Take my wife—please.
                                    But you take him instead.
You take him home, and you make him a cheese sandwich,
            and you try to get his shoes off, but he kicks you
                                    and he keeps kicking you.
      You swallow a bottle of sleeping pills but they don't work.

Boots continue to fall to the floor
in the apartment above you.
You go to work the next day pretending nothing happened.
Your co-workers ask
if everything's okay and you tell them
you're just tired.
And you're trying to smile. And they're trying to smile.

A man walks into a bar, you this time, and says:
Make it a double.
A man walks into a bar, you this time, and says:
Walk a mile in my shoes.
A man walks into a convenience store, still you, saying:
I only wanted something simple, something generic...
But the clerk tells you to buy something or get out.
A man takes his sadness down to the river and throws it in the river
but then he's still left
with the river. A man takes his sadness and throws it away
but then he's still left with his hands.

A Primer for the Small Weird Loves

1.

The blond boy in the red trunks is holding your head underwater
because he is trying to kill you,
and you deserve it, you do, and you know this,
and you are ready to die in this swimming pool
because you wanted to touch his hands and lips and this means
your life is over anyway.
You're in the eighth grade. You know these things.
You know how to ride a dirt bike, and you know how to do
long division,
and you know that a boy who likes boys is a dead boy, unless
he keeps his mouth shut, which is what you
didn't do,
because you are weak and hollow and it doesn't matter anymore.

2.

A dark-haired man in a rented bungalow is licking the whiskey
from the back of your wrist.
He feels nothing,
keeps a knife in his pocket,
peels an apple right in front of you

while you tramp around a mustard-colored room
in your underwear
drinking Dutch beer from a green bottle.
After everything that was going to happen has happened
you ask only for the cab fare home
and realize you should have asked for more
because he couldn't care less, either way.

3.

The man on top of you is teaching you how to hate, sees you
as a piece of real estate,
just another fallow field lying underneath him
like a sacrifice.
He's turning your back into a table so he doesn't have to
eat off the floor, so he can get comfortable,
pressing against you until he fits, until he's made a place for himself
inside you.
The clock ticks from five to six. Kissing degenerates into biting.
So you get a kidney punch, a little blood in your urine.
It isn't over yet, it's just begun.

4.

Says to himself
The boy's no good. The boy is just no good.
but he takes you in his arms and pushes your flesh around
to see if you could ever be ugly to him.
You, the now familiar whipping boy, but you're beautiful,
he can feel the dogs licking his heart.
Who gets the whip and who gets the hoops of flame?
He hits you and he hits you and he hits you.
Desire driving his hands right into your body.
Hush, my sweet. These tornadoes are for you.
You wanted to think of yourself as someone who did these kinds of things.
You wanted to be in love
and he happened to get in the way.

5.

The green-eyed boy in the powder-blue t-shirt standing
next to you in the supermarket recoils as if hit,
repeatedly, by a lot of men, as if he has a history of it.
This is not your problem.
You have your own body to deal with.
The lamp by the bed is broken.
You are feeling things he's no longer in touch with.
And everyone is speaking softly,

so as not to wake one another.
The wind knocks the heads of the flowers together.
Steam rises from every cup at every table at once.
Things happen all the time, things happen every minute
that have nothing to do with us.

6.

So you say you want a deathbed scene, the knowledge that comes
before knowledge,
and you want it dirty.
And no one can ever figure out what you want,
and you won't tell them,
and you realize the one person in the world who loves you
isn't the one you thought it would be,
and you don't trust him to love you in a way
you would enjoy.
And the boy who loves you the wrong way is filthy.
And the boy who loves you the wrong way keeps weakening.
You thought if you handed over your body
he'd do something interesting.

7.

The stranger says there are no more couches and he will have to
sleep in your bed. You try to warn him, you tell him
you will want to get inside him, and ruin him,
but he doesn't listen.
You do this, you do. You take the things you love
and tear them apart
or you pin them down with your body and pretend they're yours.
So, you kiss him, and he doesn't move, he doesn't
pull away, and you keep on kissing him. And he hasn't moved,
he's frozen, and you've kissed him, and he'll never
forgive you, and maybe now he'll leave you alone.

Saying Your Names

Chemical names, bird names, names of fire
and flight and snow, baby names, paint names,
delicate names like bones in the body,
Rumplestiltskin names that are always changing,
names that no one's ever able to figure out.
Names of spells and names of hexes, names
cursed quietly under the breath, or called out

loudly to fill the yard, calling you inside again,
calling you home. Nicknames and pet names
and baroque French monikers, written in
shorthand, written in longhand, scrawled
illegibly in brown ink on the backs of yellowing
photographs, or embossed on envelopes lined
with gold. Names called out across the water,
names I called you behind your back,
sour and delicious, secret and unrepeatable,
the names of flowers that open only once,
shouted from balconies, shouted from rooftops,
or muffled by pillows, or whispered in sleep,
or caught in the throat like a lump of meat.
I try, I do. I try and try. A happy ending?
Sure enough—*Hello darling, welcome home.*
I'll call you darling, hold you tight. We are
not traitors but the lights go out. It's dark.
Sweetheart, is that you? There are no tears,
no pictures of him squarely. A seaside framed
in glass, and boats, those little boats with
sails aflutter, shining lights upon the water,
lights that splinter when they hit the pier.
His voice on tape, his name on the envelope,
the soft sound of a body falling off a bridge
behind you, the body hardly even makes
a sound. The waters of the dead, a clear road,
every lover in the form of stars, the road
blocked. All night I stretched my arms across
him, rivers of blood, the dark woods, singing
with all my skin and bone *Please keep him safe.*
Let him lay his head on my chest and we will be
like sailors, swimming in the sound of it, dashed
to pieces. Makes a cathedral, him pressing against
me, his lips at my neck, and yes, I do believe
his mouth is heaven, his kisses falling over me
like stars. Names of heat and names of light,
names of collision in the dark, on the side of the
bus, in the bark of the tree, in ballpoint pen
on jeans and hands and the backs of matchbooks
that then get lost. Names like pain cries, names
like tombstones, names forgotten and reinvented,
names forbidden or overused. Your name like
a song I sing to myself, your name like a box
where I keep my love, your name like a nest
in the tree of love, your name like a boat in the

sea of love—O now we're in the sea of love!
Your name like detergent in the washing machine.
Your name like two X's like punched-in eyes,
like a drunk cartoon passed out in the gutter,
your name like two X's to mark the spots,
to hold the place, to keep the treasure from
becoming ever lost. I'm saying your name
in the grocery store, I'm saying your name on
the bridge at dawn. Your name like an animal
covered with frost, your name like a music that's
been transposed, a suit of fur, a coat of mud,
a kick in the pants, a lungful of glass, the sails
in wind and the slap of waves on the hull
of a boat that's sinking to the sound of mermaids
singing songs of love, and the tug of a simple
profound sadness when it sounds so far away.
Here is a map with your name for a capital,
here is an arrow to prove a point: we laugh
and it pits the world against us, we laugh,
and we've got nothing left to lose, and our hearts
turn red, and the river rises like a barn on fire.
I came to tell you, we'll swim in the water, we'll
swim like something sparkling underneath
the waves. Our bodies shivering, and the sound
of our breathing, and the shore so far away.
I'll use my body like a ladder, climbing
to the thing behind it, saying farewell to flesh,
farewell to everything caught underfoot
and flattened. Names of poisons, names of
handguns, names of places we've been
together, names of people we'd be together.
Names of endurance, names of devotion,
street names and place names and all the names
of our dark heaven crackling in their pan.
It's a bed of straw, darling. It sure as shit is.
If there was one thing I could save from the fire,
he said, *the broken arms of the sycamore,*
the eucalyptus still trying to climb out of the yard—
your breath on my neck like a music that holds
my hands down, kisses as they burn their way
along my spine—or rain, our bodies wet,
clothes clinging arm to elbow, clothes clinging
nipple to groin—I'll be right here. I'm waiting.
Say hallelujah, say goodnight, say it over
the canned music and your feet won't stumble,

his face getting larger, the rest blurring
on every side. And angels, about twelve angels,
angels knocking on your head right now, hello
hello, a flash in the sky, would you like to
meet him there, in Heaven? Imagine a room,
a sudden glow. Here is my hand, my heart,
my throat, my wrist. Here are the illuminated
cities at the center of me, and here is the center
of me, which is a lake, which is a well that we
can drink from, but I can't go through with it.
I just don't want to die anymore.

Tracy K. Smith

Tracy K. Smith was born in 1972 in Falmouth, Massachusetts, and was raised in northern California. She attended Harvard University and Columbia University, and was an active member of the Dark Room Collective. Smith has held a Wallace Stegner Fellowship in Poetry at Stanford University and is the recipient of a Rona Jaffe Writers' Award. Her poems have appeared in *Callaloo*, *Gulf Coast*, *The Nebraska Review*, *Post Road*, and elsewhere. Her first book, *The Body's Question* (Graywolf, 2003), was awarded the 2002 Cave Canem Poetry Prize for the best first book by an African American poet. Smith has taught at Stanford, Marymount Manhattan College, the Gotham Writers Workshop, and Medgar Evers College of the City University of New York, and is currently a faculty member at the University of Pittsburgh and Princeton University. She divides her time between Pittsburgh and New York.

Self-Portrait as the Letter Y

1.
I waved a gun last night
In a city like some ancient Los Angeles.
It was dusk. There were two girls
I wanted to make apologize,
But the gun was useless.
They looked sideways at each other
And tried to flatter me. I was angry.
I wanted to cry. I wanted to bury the pistol,
But I would've had to walk miles.
I would've had to learn to run.

2.
I have finally become that girl
In the photo you keep among your things,
Steadying myself at the prow of a small boat.
It is always summer here, and I am
Always staring into the lens of your camera,
Which has not yet been stolen. Always
With this same expression. Meaning
I see your eye behind the camera's eye.
Meaning that in the time it takes
For the tiny guillotine
To open and fall shut, I will have decided
I am just about ready to love you.

3.
Sun cuts sharp angles
Across the airshaft adjacent.

They kiss. They kiss again.
Faint clouds pass, disband.

Someone left a mirror
At the foot of the fire escape.

They look down. They kiss.

She will never be free
Because she is afraid. He

Will never be free
Because he has always

Been free.

4.
Was kind of a rebel then.
Took two cars. Took
Bad advice. Watched people's
Asses. Sniffed their heads.

Just left, so it looked
Like those half-sad cookouts,
Meats never meant to be
Flayed, meant nothing.

Made promises. Kept going.
Prayed for signs. Stooped
For coins. Needed them.
Had two definitions of family.

Had two families. Snooped.
Forgot easily. Well, didn't
Forget, but knew when it was safe
To remember. Woke some nights

Against a wet pillow, other nights
With the lights on, whispering
The truest things
Into the receiver.

5.

A dog scuttles past, like a wig
Drawn by an invisible cord. It is spring.
The pirates out selling fakes are finally
Able to draw a crowd. College girls
Show bare skin in good faith. They crouch
Over heaps of bright purses, smiling,
Willing to pay. Their arms
Swing forward as they walk away, balancing
That new weight on naked shoulders.
The pirates smile, too, watching
Pair after pair of thighs carved in shadow
As girl after girl glides into the sun.

6.

You are pure appetite. I am pure
Appetite. You are a phantom
In that far-off city where daylight
Climbs cathedral walls, stone by stolen stone.
I am invisible here, like I like it.

The language you taught me rolls
From your mouth into mine
The way kids will pass smoke
Between them. You feed it to me
Until my heart grows fat. I feed you
Tiny black eggs. I feed you
My very own soft truth. We believe.
We stay up talking all kinds of shit.

History

Prologue:

This is a poem about the itch
That stirs a nation at night.

This is a poem about all we'll do
Not to scratch—

(Where fatigue is great, the mind
Will invent entire stories to protect sleep.)

Dark stories. Deep fright.
Syntax of nonsense.

Our prone shape has slept a long time.
Our night, many nights—

This is a story in the poem's own voice.
This is epic.

*

Part One: Gods and Monsters

There is an eagle.
The Eagle.

The Eagle dreams light,
Dreams molten heat, dreams words

Like *bark, fir,* and great mountains
Appear under the shadows of great trees.

The Eagle dreams *fox*, and that amber shape
Appears in a glade. Dreams *egg*,

And the fox is cradling
A world between sharp teeth.

All gods do this.
Flesh is the first literature.

There is Pan Gu. Dog-god.
His only verb: to grow.

And when he dies, history happens.
His body becomes Word:

Blood, eye, tendon, teeth
Become river, moon, path, ore.

Marrow becomes jade. Sperm, pearl.
The vermin of his body, you and me.

Elsewhere and at the same time,
Some scrap of first flame,

Of being ablaze, rages on,
Hissing air, coughing still more air,

Sighing rough sighs around the ideas
Of *man, woman, snake, fruit.*

We all know the story
Of that god. A story written in smoke

And set down atop other stories.
(How many others? Countless others.)

There is the element of Earth to consider:
Fast globe driven by the children of gods.

Driven blind, driven with fatigue, fear,
With night sweats and hoarse laughter.

Driven forward, stalled, dragged back.
Driven mad, because the ones

Who drive it are not gods themselves.
Because the children of gods are not gods.

*

Part Two: The New World

There were always fragile fingers
Winding cotton and wool—
Momentary clouds—into thread.

Was always that diminishing. Words
Whittled and stretched into meaning.
And meaning here is: line.

What the fish tugs at. What is crossed.
Thin split between Ever and After.
And what, in going, is lost.

Was always the language of pigment:
Indigo, yolk, dirt red. This meant
Belonging. What the women wove:

Stark wonder. Hours and hours.
Mystery. Misery. On their knees.
A remedy for cold.

There were houses not meant to stand
Forever. But not for the reasons
We were told.

*

Part Three: Occupation

Every poem is the story of itself.
Pure conflict. Its own undoing.
Breeze of dreams, then certain death.
Every poem is a world.

This poem is Creole. *Kreyol.*
This poem is a boat. *Bato.*
This poem floats on the horizon
All day all night. Has leaks
And a hundred bodies at prayer.
This poem is not going to make it.
But it must.

And this poem is the army
left behind when the *bato*
Sails. This poem is full
Of soldiers. *Soldas.*
When the *bato* is turned back,
The people it carries,
Those who survive, will be
Made to regret leaving.
The *soldas* know how to do this.
How to make a person
Wish for death. The *soldas*
Know how to do this
Because many of them believe
They have already died once before.

There are secret police
Who don't want the poem to continue,
But they're not sure
It is important enough to silence.
They go home to wives

Who expect to be taken out,
Made love to, offered
Expensive gifts. They are bored,
The police and their wives.
They eat, turn on the tv, swallow
Scotch, wine. In bed, they say nothing,
Feigning sleep. And the house,
A new house, croons to itself
Its voice seeps out and off,
Marries with the neighbors',
Makes a kind of American music
That holds everything in place.

Of course there are victims in this poem:

victim victim victim victim victim
victim victim victim victim victim
victim victim victim victim victim
victim victim victim victim victim
victim victim victim victim victim
victim victim victim victim victim
victim victim victim victim victim
victim victim victim victim victim
victim *you are here* victim victim
victim victim victim victim victim
victim victim victim victim victim

*

Part Four: Grammar

There is a *We* in this poem
To which everyone belongs.

As in: *We the People—*
In Order to form a more perfect Union—

And: *We were objects of much curiosity*
To the Indians—

And: *The next we present before you*
Are things very appalling—

And: *We sailed in the big sea for a month and a half*
Until we came to a place called Charleston—

And: *We find we are living, suffering, loving,*
Dying a story. We had not known otherwise—

We's a huckster, trickster, has pluck.
We will draw you in.
                    Look at your hands:
Dirty. You're already in:

        Your starched shirt is wet under the arms.
        Your neck spills over the collar, tie points—

        Repentant tongue—toward your bored sex.
        There is a map on the wall. A trail

        Of colored tacks spreads like a wound
        From the center, and you realize (for the first time?)

        The world is mostly water. You are not paid
        To imagine a time before tanks and submarines,

        But for a moment you do. It's a quiet thought,
        And a cool breeze blows through it. Green leaves

        Rustle overhead. Your toes sink into dark soil.

Or:

        You unwrap foil from around last night's rack of lamb.
        It sits like a mountain of light next to the sink.
        Something inside you wants out. You calculate
        Minutes and seconds on smooth keys.
        There is humming, and a beeping when the food is hot.
        Above your head, a bulb hangs upside down
        Like an idea in reverse, tungsten filament
        Sagging between prongs. Your heart sways
        Like a tattered flag from the bones in your chest.
        You don't think of Eisenhower, long dead,
        His voice flapping away on a scrap of newsreel
        From decades ago. But the silence around you
        Knows he was right:
                        You have a row of dominoes set up,
                        You knock over the first one,
                        And what will happen to the last one
                        Is the certainty that it will go over
                                        very quickly.

Or:

> You settle into the plush seat
> And the darkness swells, the screen
> No longer silent, white. Outside
> No longer today, no longer now.
> Place names and years appear,
> disappear like forbidden thoughts.
> *Chile. Cambodia. Kent State.*
>
> Why, when the lights come up,
> Does a new part of you ache?
> Was that you this whole time,
> Running, hands in the air?
> You all these years, marching
> Under the weight of a gun?

We, petty tyrant, has swallowed *Us* and *Them*.
You will be the next to go. *We* smiles,
Leans back in its chair.

*

Part Five: Twentieth Century

Sometimes, this poem wants to let go awhile,

Wander into a department store and watch itself
Transformed in a trinity of mirrors.

Sometimes this poem wants to pop pills.

Sometimes in this poem, the stereo's blaring
While the tv's on mute.

Sometimes this poem walks the street
And doesn't give a shit.

Sometimes this poem tells itself nothing matters,
All's a joke. *Relax*, it says, *everything's
Taken care of.*

> (A poem can lie.)

Part Six: Cosmology

Once there was a great cloud
Of primeval matter. Atoms and atoms.
By believing, we made it the world.
We named the animals out of need.
Made ourselves human out of need.
There were other inventions.
Plunder and damage. Insatiable fire.

*

Epilogue: The Seventh Day

There are ways of naming the wound.

There are ways of entering the dream
The way a painter enters a studio:

To spill.

Duende

1.
The earth is dry and they live wanting.
Each with a small reservoir
Of furious music heavy in the throat.
They drag it out and with nails in their feet
Coax the night into being. Brief believing.
A skirt shimmering with sequins and lies.
And in this night that is not night,
Each word is a wish, each phrase
A shape their bodies ache to fill—

> *I'm going to braid my hair*
> *Braid many colors into my hair*
> *I'll put a long braid in my hair*
> *And write your name there*

They defy gravity to feel tugged back.
The clatter, the mad slap of landing.

2.
And not just them. Not just
The ramshackle family, the *tios*,
Primitos, not just the *bailaor*
Whose heels have notched
And hammered time
So the hours flow in place
Like a tin river, marking
Only what once was.
Not just the voices scraping
Against the river, nor the hands
nudging them farther, fingers
like blind birds, palms empty,
echoing. Not just the women
with sober faces and flowers
in their hair, the ones who dance
as though they're burying
memory—one last time—
beneath them.
                    And I hate to do it here.
To set myself heavily beside them.
Not now that they've proven
The body a myth, parable
For what not even language
Moves quickly enough to name.
If I call it pain, and try to touch it
With my hands, my own life,
It lies still and the music thins,
A pulse felt for through garments.
If I lean into the desire it starts from—
If I lean unbuttoned into the blow
Of loss after loss, love tossed
Into the ecstatic void—
It carries me with it farther,
To chords that stretch and bend
Like light through colored glass.
But it races on, toward shadows
Where the world I know
And the world I fear
Threaten to meet.

3.
There is always a road,
The sea, dark hair, *dolor*.

Always a question
Bigger than itself—

> *They say you're leaving Monday*
> *Why can't you leave on Tuesday?*

Juliana Spahr

Juliana Spahr was born in 1966 in Chillicothe, Ohio. Her poems have been published in such places as *The Baffler*, *Chicago Review*, *Conjunctions*, *The Village Voice*, and *The Best American Poetry 2002*. Spahr's three full-length collections are *Response* (Sun & Moon, 1996), a National Poetry Series Selection; *Fuck You—Aloha—I Love You* (Wesleyan University Press, 2001); and *This Connection of Everyone with Lungs* (University of California Press, 2005). She is also the author of the book of criticism *Everybody's Autonomy: Connective Reading and Collective Identity* (University of Alabama Press, 2001), the coeditor (with poet Claudia Rankine) of *American Women Poets in the 21st Century: Where Lyric Meets Language*, and the coeditor (with Joan Retallack) of *Poetry and Pedagogy: The Challenge of the Contemporary* (Palgrave Macmillan, 2006). With poet Jena Osman, Spahr coedits the journal *Chain*. She frequently self-publishes her work at http://people.mills.edu/jspahr) and lives Oakland, California.

localism or t/here

for Susan Schultz

There is no there there anywhere.
There is no here here or anywhere either.
Here and there. He and she. There, there.

Oh yes. We are lost there and here.
And here and there we err.
And we are that err.
And we are that lost.
And we are arrows of loving lostness gliding, gliding, off, and off, and
      off, gliding.
And arrows of unloving lostness getting stuck even while never hitting
      the mark.
And we are misunderstanding fullness and emptiness.
And we are missing our bed and all its comforts that come night after
night without end and sometimes during the day also and are singular
even when coupled, doubled, and tripled and have something to do with ie
comforter's down coming from the duck.

Oh here, you are all that we want.
Oh here, come here.
You are rich and dark with soil.
And you are encouraging of growing.

And you are a soft rain without complaint that refreshes and stimulates.
And you are full of seeds.
And you are as accepting of the refrigerator as you are of the bough loaded
    with fruit.
And you and you and you are here and there and there and here and you are
    here and there and tear.

December 1, 2002

Beloveds, yours skins is a boundary separating yous from the rest of
yous.

When I speak of skin I speak of the largest organ.

I speak of the separations that define this world and the separations
that define us beloveds, even as we like to press our skins against
one another in the night.

When I speak of skin I speak of lighting candles to remember
AIDS and the history of attacks in Kenya.

I speak of toxic fumes given off by plastic flooring in a burning
nightclub in Caracas.

I speak of the forty-seven dead in Caracas.

And I speak of the four dead in Palestine.

And of the three dead in Israel.

I speak of those dead in other parts of the world that go unreported.

I speak of boundaries and connections, locals and globals, butterfly
wings and hurricanes.

I speak of one hundred and fifty people sheltering at the Catholic
Mission in the city of Man.

I speak of a diverted Ethiopian airliner, US attacks on Iraqi air
defense sites, and warnings not to visit Yemen.

Here, where we are with our separate skins polished by sweet
smelling soaps and the warm, clean water of our shower, we sit in

our room in the morning and the sounds of birds are outside our windows and the sun shines.

When I speak of yours skins, I speak of newspaper headlines in other countries and different newspaper headlines here.

I speak of how the world suddenly seems as if it is a game of some sort, a game where troops are massed on a flat map of the world and if one looks at the game board long enough one can see the patterns even as one is powerless to prevent them.

I speak of the memory of the four floating icebergs off the coast of Argentina and the thirty thousand dead salmon in the Klamath river this year.

I speak of how I cannot understand our insistence on separations and how these separations have nothing and everything to do with the moments when we feel joined and separated from each others.

I speak of the intimate relationship between salmons and humans, between humans and icebergs, between icebergs and salmons, and how this is just the beginning of the circular list.

I speak of those moments when we do not understand why we must remain separated or joined only in the most mundane ways.

I speak of why our skin is our largest organ and how it keeps us contained.

I speak of the preservation of a balanced internal environment, shock absorbers, temperature regulators, insulators, sensators, lubrications, protections and grips, and body odor.

I speak of the Pew study on Anti-Americanism and the three C's of the IRA—Columbia, Castlereagh, and Stormont Castle—and I speak of the unconfirmed dead in Iraq from the bombing of a refinery at Basrah.

When I speak of skin I speak of a slow day in the forces that are compelling all of us to be brushing up against one another.

When I speak of skin I speak of the crowds that are gathering all together to meet each other with various intents.

When I speak of skin I speak of all the movement in the world right now and all the new boundaries of the right now that are made by all the movement in the world right now and then broken by the movement in the world right now.

But when I speak of skin I do not speak of the arbitrary connotations of color that have made all of this brushing against one another even harder for all of us.

Beloveds, yours skins are of all colors, are soft and wrinkled, blotchy and reddish, full of blemish and smooth.

Our world is small, contained within 1.4 to 2 square meters of surface area.

Yet it is all the world that each of us has and so we all return to it, to the softening of it and to the defoliating of it and to the moisture that we bring to it.

December 4, 2002

Embedded deep in our cells is ourselves and everyone else.

Going back ten generations we have nine thousand ancestors and going back twenty-five we get thirty million.

All of us shaped by all of us and then other things as well, other things such as the flora and the fauna and all the other things as well.

When I speak of yours thighs and their long muscles of smoothness, I speak of yours cells and I speak of the British Embassy being closed in Kenya and the US urging more aggressive Iraq inspections and the bushfire that is destroying homes in Sydney.

And I speak of at least one dead after rioting in Dili and the arrest of Mukhlas, and Sharon's offer of forty percent of the West Bank and the mixed results of Venezuela's oil strike and the overtures that Khatami is making to the US.

When I speak of the curve of yours cheeks, their soft down, their cell after cell, their smoothness, their even color, I speak of the NASA launch and the child Net safety law and the Native Linux pSeries Server.

When I speak of our time together, I speak also of the new theories of the development of the cell from iron sulphide, formed at the bottom of the oceans.

I speak of the weight of the alien planet.

And I speak of the benefits of swaddling sleeping babies.

Beloveds, all our theories and generations came together today in order to find the optimum way of lacing shoes. The bow tie pattern is the most efficient.

I want to tie everything up when I speak of yous.

I want to tie it all up and tie up the world in an attempt to understand the swirls of patterns.

But there is no efficient way.

The news refreshes every few minutes on the computer screen and on the television screen. The stories move from front to back and then off the page and then perhaps forward again in a motion that I can't predict but I suspect is not telling the necessary truths.

I can't predict our time together either. Or why we like each other like we do.

I have no idea when our bodies will feel very good to one of us or to all of us together or to none of us.

The drive to press against one another that is there at moments and then gone at others.

The drive to press up against others in the same way.

January 28, 2003

Yesterday the UN report on weapons inspections was released.

Today Israel votes and the death toll rises.

Four have died in clashes in the West Bank town of Jenin.

Yesterday, three died in an explosion at a Gaza City house.

Since last Monday US troops have surrounded eighty Afghans and killed eighteen.

Protests against the French continue in the Ivory Coast.

Nothing makes any sense today beloveds.

I wake up to a beautiful, clear day.

A slight breeze blows off the Pacific.

It is morning and it is amazing in its simple morningness.

I leave the house early so I miss the parrots but outside the door I stop to listen to the ugly song of the red-bottomed bulbuls.

It is so calm here and yet so momentous in the rest of the world.

Amid ignorant armies and darkling plains, the news has momentarily stopped trying to make sense and the stories appear with a doubleness.

Israel said the four killed today were armed men and were killed in a series of clashes.

Palestine claims they were shot in running battles.

Palestine claims the bomb explosion in Gaza was caused by a missile from an Israeli helicopter.

Israel claims it was a Palestinian bomb that exploded prematurely.

In the Ivory Coast some school boys sing, "France for the French, Ivory Coast for the Ivorians. Everyone go home. We are xenophobes and so what."

Others carry signs that say "Down with France, long live the US" and "No more French, from now on we speak English" and sing "USA, USA, USA" against the French.

Later today Bush will speak.

How can we be true to one another with histories of place so deep, so layered we can't begin to sort through it here in the middle of the Pacific with its own deep unsortable history?

I left our small apartment that is perched at the side of a dormant volcano that goes miles down to the ocean floor, perches on layer after layer of exploding history.

It wasn't just our history of place but the contradiction of the US taking unilateral military action to rid Iraq of its weapons of mass destruction that entered our two small rooms and we just wanted to leave and get on with the day's mundanenesses—email and photocopies and desk chairs and telephones.

While driving away from our small apartment, beloveds, I turned on the radio.

Today on the radio, Christie Brinkley exists and her worries about Billy Joel's driving abilities exist.

A lawsuit exists where Catherine Zeta Jones and Michael Douglas are suing *Hello!* magazine for poor-quality wedding photos.

U2 spy planes exist flying over the Koreas.

Supermodel Gisele Bundchen's plan to eradicate hunger in Brazil exists.

Heart disease in women exists.

John Malvo's trial exists.

Aretha Franklin exists and a subpoena for her exists.

Hackers of the Recording Industry Association of America website exist.

Thalidomide exists.

Zoe Ball exists.

And Fatboy Slim exists but now without Zoe Ball.

Bronze Age highways in Iraq, Syria, and Turkey continue to exist.

Renee Zellweger and Richard Gere, lead actors in *Chicago*, exist.

Cell phones and tunnel vision exist.

Cable problems exist in a crash in Charlotte.

A dismembered mother, the shoe bomber's letters, Scott Peterson's wife and girlfriend, Brian Patrick Regan's letters to Hussein and Gadhafi, nineteen thousand gallons of crude oil in the frozen Nemadji River, all of this exists.

The world goes on and on, spins tighter and then looser on a wobbling axis, and it has a list of adjectives to describe it, such as various and beautiful and new, but neither light, nor certitude, nor peace exist.

Larissa Szporluk

Larissa Szporluk was born in 1967 in Ann Arbor, Michigan. She attended the University of Michigan, the University of Iowa, the University of California at Berkeley, and the University of Virginia. Her poetry has appeared in *Black Clock, Hayden's Ferry Review, Salt Hill, The Virginia Quarterly Review, The Best American Poetry* anthology, and elsewhere. The recipient of a Rona Jaffe Writer's Award and grants from the Ohio Arts Council and the NEA, Szporluk is the author of *Dark Sky Question* (Beacon, 1998), which won the Barnard New Women Poets Prize, *Isolato* (University of Iowa Press, 2000), and *The Wind, Master Cherry, The Wind* (Alice James, 2003). Szporluk currently resides in Ithaca, New York where she is a visiting Professor at Cornell University. Her permanent residence is in Bowling Green, Ohio, where she and her husband Carlo Celli are Associate Professors at Bowling Green State University. With their children Marco and Sofia, they spend summers in northern Italy, climbing mountains.

One Thousand Bullfrogs Rejoice

It is dark inside the body, and wet,
and double-hearted. There are so many ways
to go, and not see, and lose
the feeling of the thread, which was alleged
to be invisible, and lose the man,
the fast Athenian, to someone with less rootage,
and never reach the fabled center,
afraid that if you did, you would find the hybrid,
not the hero, beautiful.

If you want to jump ahead,
Chapter Two just tells you how you erred
in Chapter One, taking his hand first
and being honest. Chapter Three says never mind,
you won't get another chance
to guide him—no one loves a volunteer.
No one loves a savior.
Chapter Four is set along the shore
where you are hiding, where life outside you
changes surface hourly.
Chapter Five: A skeleton is tangled
in a hyacinth. Their intimate clutch,

only for a minute, weirds you.
Tide is always bringing those reminders.
But here you keep in tune with rhythmic raging.
You open like a mussel made of gold
to anything in want of shelter,
anything with devious or laudable intentions.
Chapter Six. You open like a song
and bellow in the ear of second guessing.

Meteor

I chose this. To be this
stone, grow nothing. I wanted this
absolute position in the heavens
more than anything, than you,
my two, too beautiful, my children.
A man I knew once
muttered in his terrors of the night,
no, no, no, instead of yelling.
It was this, this dismal low,
that made me leave him. I will leave them.
All the butterflies the lord above
can muster, all their roses.
I will leave whatever colors
struggle to be noticed. To leave,
to leave. That's the verb I am,
have always been, always will be,
heading, like a dewdrop,
into steamy confrontation,
my train of neutral green
lasting half a second
before casting off its freight—his arms
outside the sheet, how warm they were,
like Rome the year it burned,
Nero at the window, loving no one,
fusion crust. I fly because
my space is crossed
with fear and hair and tail and hate,
the bowels of a lioness,
iron in her roar.

Holy Ghost

All my thoughts of you are good ones.
The horse whose neck is clothed with thunder—
they are good ones.
*The voice that shakes the wilderness—*good ones.
I think about how, if I could wake up,
I could go to your life,
how that would be good, if I could wake up.

But where I am is so large.
You are a fly.
You are impossible.

Where I am is so large, like a dark saying,
repeating. Where I am
is repeating. I don't know where it begins.

Where I am is the same,
but the light just takes you away, and I
am the only one here.
It's mine, like a dark saying—
Hide them in the dust together.

Bind their faces in secret.
You see how it's mine? You see how I try
to wake up?
The horse whose neck is clothed with thunder—
they were good ones.

I am the only one here, a giant,
asleep on the damp floor.
I am on the floor
of my invention, my forest
of dark sayings—
the Lord shall hiss.

My forest is always the same.
I am asleep on the damp floor.
My lids are down. Your face is a secret.
Hiss, hiss.

Eohippus

Wooded area has wed itself
to crime, and sometimes *alley*
binds with molestation, and then a tiny clue,
the treadmark of a shoe, yarn hair
of a doll, will carry on the language
like a fossil, *shallow grave*,
the way a hoofprint of a mammal with four toes
broadens the whole epoch of the horse,
connecting time and place and suspect
in a brand-new constellation.

The chief detective starts to find them:
sidelong angle of a neck
suggesting one-way struggle,
like surrender to an ancient warrior
or athlete, what Greeks might call
gorgeous boy with javelin;
dandruff on the welcome mat
with matching DNA…

A *fall* comes burning down from heaven,
a meteor, an iron, pounding the young corn
in this or that dark county.
A fall is classified as actual
and named for where it fell—*Gallup,
Petaluma, Kettering.*

A *find* is just the fall
unwitnessed. A find is picked up later.
We take the finder's word for it,
but reserve a little room for doubt.
We test the find. We put the finder
in the line-up, in a row of men
who stare beyond the viewing lens
like otherworldly musicians.

Glass divides the witness from the pederasts.
The notes she hears are streaming from their hands,
impossible to cipher, bamboo snares
that pluck a tiny wing, then softly play the body
that is lying still, *piano, piano,*
so as not to rouse the consciousness,

but let it linger in its wilt,
the wounded bird, half-asleep,
returning to a paradise, free of all taxonomy,
of narrow paths, of artifacts—
of water-bearers and their centaurs
in a midnight saturnalia.

Elsewhere

Did you hear, *I heard,*
that I flew, *you flew,*
at dusk, like the foxes,
my eyes, *your eyes,*
silver-white, like foxes,
and flew, *you flew,*
over things, *what things,*
in there, *in where,*
the trees, *what trees,*
reached up, *reached what,*
for me, my fur,
your fur, I heard,
they pulled, *pulled what,*
our love, *a ruse,*
was rare, on earth,
like stars that fall,
like ice, and spread,
spread what, my legs,
your legs, were white,
silver-white, like ice,
and shook, *shook what,*
my heart, *what heart,*
in truth, our love,
a ruse, on earth,
was caught, *by what,*
by things, *what things,*
my tongue, *your tongue,*
was white, *silver-white,*
like leaves, and split,
split what, in two,
like ghosts, at dusk,
like wings, *they whisht,*
not hurt, in truth,
just lost, *a ruse.*

Brian Teare

Brian Teare was born in 1974 in Athens, Georgia and grew up outside Tuscaloosa, Alabama. He attended the University of Alabama, Indiana University, and Stanford University, where he held a Wallace Stegner Fellowship. The recipient of a fellowship from the NEA, Teare has published poetry in *Boston Review, Ploughshares, Seneca Review,* and *Verse,* among other journals. His first book, *The Room Where I Was Born* (University of Wisconsin Press, 2003), won the 2004 Triangle Award for Gay Poetry. Also the author of a recent chapbook, *Pilgrim,* Teare lives in Oakland, California, and is a member of the graduate writing faculties of the New College of California and the California College of Arts.

First person plural is a house

where I put myself in third person in a bed I know
his older brother's hands will visit. It's no mistake incest starts

with an eye: at this distance they're theoretical as dolls, rhetorical
as pain imagined, but they can't see the word they create

with their bodies, can't know such bodies won't stop speaking,
always that word on the tongue in the mouth of another.

In the kitchen stands Mother, wringing her hands,
wet laundry: no: rubbing their stained fabric together

to clean them of song. Living room geometry: Father's face acute;
a bottle of whiskey: his arithmetic kisses. How many fingers, sucked

down, will fill him? How many until the bottle's clear?
On the porch, outside the poem, I smoke a cigarette, note

how a narrative's ending denotes another beginning, how
no bottle remains empty, no hands, no mouth or hips. I'm not worried;

no one else watches his story being written. I want to know:
with what grammar he'll enact it, with which line, breaking,

he'll hold the slip of syntax between him
and me. When I say "I" I mean eye, sum of my watching.

Set for a Southern Gothic

From here, this poem a neon pall over the tarry asphalt,
it's too cliché to be sympathetic, really, the black Caddy
the boy spills out of in stacked heels and hot-pants, the man
plump in the word *seersucker*—suit, straw hat, white oxfords—
the boy—it's sad—young enough to think such a get-up
original. If I had to, I'd start with the motel before they screw
everything up, the boy and his "companion." Or maybe
the sign, *Moon-Winx*, ironic only for its regulars who joke,
Girl, *shit*—even the Man-in-the-Moon has to turn a trick.
Sure as hell ain't no shut-eye going on in there.

*

"It's hot," I could start, "It's 1989." But it's only Alabama,
July, a town where *this time* the man hasn't worn underwear;
he's wearing too much cologne. This time, he's nervous.
The boy snaps grape Bubblicious.Trouble with the key,
the man's palms swampy—bad sign. The boy checks
his memory in the shine on the car's hood: yep, he *is* cute.
From his jacket pocket, the man takes a silver flask flashy
as a sports car, drags a deep draught. Sets to work again,
jimmying the door. It gives like a sigh. It startles them both.

*

                              I'd start with anything
but what they have, that room's air, interior scrubbed raw
with the smell of sex, accordion noise of the overtaxed a/c,
mildew filming the bathroom with spoor, I'd give them
anywhere else. Start five months back when they meet
at a bar, boy starry-eyed with poppers, man sleek with liquor,
the Dollar Inn after. Start at the Moon-Winx in March
April May June, the scandal of the boy's oral precocity,
the man's wedding band, how they make "missionary"
an anachronism. The bills in the boy's back pocket as he leaves.

*

What in this cheap scenery is equal to what they have? There
a cigarette burns, improbable, propped on the busted tv;

burn marks blossom on the bed-sheets instead of flowers;
the ashtray clots with offal. I'd like a better set, words
to help pretend it's not rank as ever in here, but the boy too
knows oily condoms coil in on themselves, spent beneath
the unmade bed. What can I say? The boy likes the idea, fucking
in someone else's filth, but the man opts for some dignity
tonight: they'll do it in the shower instead.

*

          I don't want it at all, not again, not
this 4th of July, not this boy who skipped family fireworks
spitting his gum into the ashtray, this man who made excuses
to miss the fiftieth annual Episcopal picnic slipping his jacket
onto the one wire hanger by the door. Don't want the man
unknotting his tie, the boy sucking in his stomach before
the mirror warped with water. But it all happens anyway,
the man behind, the kisses he gives so careful, complex
and timid, the boy's confused. He only understands how
to play war, siege that opens its fields in trick affection,
all subterfuge and foreplay, I watch it start in him, beloved
tripwire skin—

          it's what he feels best. Has to think of it this way
to feel anything at all.

*

          There's a way the room looks
before the man sets it loose (the ending I don't have to make),
a way memory retouches the tawdry with compassion: the man
maudlin and soft with drink (graying, if you hadn't guessed—
his daughter's a year behind the boy in school); the boy naked
and angry with pleasure, his body's betrayal. They look hopeful
maybe, unpunished, but for certain there's a moment fraught
with grace, the whole room getting lucky, the air ragged
with kisses before the man whispers into the boy's neck his mistake
(the moment I would give up to change), before the man, bent
over the boy's neck, lets go the slip always in check, words
unsheathing the knife in his voice, shucking its shiver deep
in the flesh, and how do I know it isn't—
          "I love you," he says.

Detail from "Set for a Southern Gothic"

On the spread the boy unbuckles like an old leather belt.
Burn marks blossom on the bed-sheets instead of flowers.

A last long swallow and the man caps his flask. I come back
to this, how the boy knows the man feels whiskey secure

a door behind which his wife and daughter sleep. The way
he lights a cigarette and laughs (crack of the glass ashtray

smacked down) when the man asks, "Aren't you too young
to smoke?"
                    Now I will say it: the boy *does* think about the word

"love," wonders if what he feels (hot ash flaring at the cherry)
as the man's pants tent, is that something like it? The man undoes

his shirt's pearled buttons (fingertips square, nails cleaned
and clipped) down to the slight furred swell above his belt

where the boy knows the man will guide his head. I could tell you
what I once thought led the boy here, but I'm not sure I believe

the clear theorems now, in this room again: can I say "victim"
as the man's pants unzip, "perpetrator," as the boy kneels

at the bed's edge? I permit, now, the sound of one word only: *Power.*

*

Forgive me—it's how I feel best, how I have to think about it
to feel anything at all. Isn't it easier if *The boy unbuckles on the spread?*

If *The man undoes his shirt's pearled buttons?* If "power" is the sole word
the boy can own? I didn't want to make it difficult, but: the sink

dingy where he spit out the cum, three of four condoms they'll leave
in the trash, the ashtray's clotted offal, the man sobbing *please, please*

into the boy's arched back, the ribs whose curl his fingers follow into
as if into touch-closed mimosa leaves, don't you see how the plot turns

374   Brian Teare

on the word "love"? The boy's vertebrae unbuckle in the man's hands,
the angle of the last sweet thrust. And the man empearling his back, *please*

please, arias cramped and final in the throat, the thick sweet salt-reek
rich in air and on skin. The boy, his cinched mouth a flat-line of pleasure.

*

Where I love the man, this moment, 1 never expected to.
Here, as the neon *Moon-Winx* sign draws its appalling wash

over the scene, Man-in-the-Moon winking as if anything
might be bought for the price of a room, in this mean

blue light of memory, I'm able to love the leathery stretch
of the man's testicles, the vulnerable little cinch between,

the rings seaming his bent neck, the silver filaments he's proud of
wiring his temples and chest, the hard square reach of his thumbs,

and as the boy gets up to wash himself, as the man lights
the story's familiar post-coital smoke, as the man waits, watches

steam steal into itself, rain-sound roiling from beneath the door,
I allow the sound of only one other word: *Expense.* "I love you,"

the man says, VACANCY the light his skin blues beneath,
and how does the boy know it isn't true as he counts greenbacks

in his head, distance, how close to New York they could get him…

*

Water corrects the errors, softens the small smeared pears, bruise-
prints picked one and one and one from his ribs. When he breathes,

the ribbed pears swell and beat against their skins, seconds until
their noise subsides back into blood. His breath catches at the man's touch

(he didn't hear—) and his mind, a child's room shaped by the sound
of rain, dissipates as the man enters him. The boy starts down the long

thin hallway of sex, and I follow, naked linoleum echoing. On the walls,
the bulbs' lumens pin flickering shadows like wings of caught birds—bare

bulbs and bent wire cages, pale blue walls lined with barred windows
where men stare and stroke the dark toward an ecstasy of salt. No one

is safe. Not here. Not the boy who walks always toward the ending
I no longer have to make, not the man as he hastens over the vacancy

of his labor. I use the men who watch and stroke the dark to measure
the distance between us; they are the price of that distance: with each one

he was the door to a room shaped by the sound of rain, and each one
was for a little while the applause of water on a tin roof: with each

he could briefly think: I'm beneath summer rain; I've never been touched.

Dead House Sonnet

house of each sentence endlessly hinged, house of each phrase opened elegy
entirely latches, exactly latches, hasps, proliferant, endlessly opened, of doors,
termini effigies, each noun in a house a nova of votives, wicks ashen, burnt
them, syntax like bark that smoldered the garden in winter, nasturtiums
come summer undone verbs, burnt them, burnt tense, the present's past, burnt
that, house of ash, house a tinge, a reek of eucalyptus oil, burnt the wild,
burnt the intractable, weedy, deep-rooted tufts of thistle's purple furze, made
house to come down, trashed, screens slashed, jambs unplumbed, without
doors, made drained porcelain the old forms, gave chip, gave to stain
structure, made gone what touched him, stripped paint, grain of floor, made
gauged the gouge of form, form the firmament fallen, made whiteness
a wall, made framed the fallen lavish tragedian shadow where a picture hung,
made what's left a nail, nib, of shadow, made it mine tongue unto nothing,
made it quite, it query, quisling, quietude's quill, that silence: writing: then sirens

Trick Noir

Close your eyes and you're stoned, child, here on River Road
where the city on the banks begins, fished quick like river-trash
up from the water. Imagine. Follow the water-silt and stink,

valley laid out ribboning black and fog-licked up hills
from the riverbed. Imagine wet asphalt wheezing beneath tires
as he drives, gin-bottle rattling on the floor. Sitting shotgun,

you're stoned. Don't panic—grin at his jokes. Try not to think:
the minister's too-sweet son, locker-room jocks, Daddy's .38,
or the girlfriend you can't get it up for. You're sixteen, sweet

Jesus, don't you get it?—his fingers easing up the cuff of your
shorts, curving in over your thigh—he's married. Imagine
the cool metal as he says *Nice—is this for me?* and, go ahead,

what stoned boy wouldn't smile, first-time high and happy
he's hard for once? He's not handsome, this man, not anyone
you'd want to see again but you will: he's got a truck and a place

to fuck, and that's what the city likes, wheels and sex between men
discreet. Open your eyes. Roadside trailers laid out end-to-end
repeat like railcars in the rain. Could be your life, his, imagine—

scrub pines leak sap into the truck-bed. The white detonations
of oncoming cars etch error into each windshield-streak, play up
the fracture inherent in glass. Believe me, in time you'll look back

on these moments when you're drunk or stoned and he's taking you
back to his place where he'll pay you after, but not yet, no, now,
please, forgive yourself of the future—of his hand; of the ring bright

on his finger; of the river moaning in pine-wet wind; of velocity;
of how you'll bend in his bed; of the honkey exotic in his gold-tooth
smile; of moist dark green bills; of the need they'll leave behind—

and I too will forgive you, briefly, here where the city's beauty begins
by touching you. The day he asks *It's our secret?* you'll swear *Yes* to him
and ten others just like him and it will never stop again, touch.

As for me, I'm no one you know; I exist only in future tense.
Don't imagine me, please, there where you are, hard beneath
a stranger's hands. Close your eyes. The wind is thick, awake

where the kudzu chokes the creekbeds that follow the road.
Listen: know that I think of you and the city, its green river-
stink, black asphalt giving rise to mist at the rank apex of evening.

All beauty, its excess and rot, begins here, at the end of River Road
where the city slides its lights into water slow beneath the bridge,
and there's beauty, too, in the tinny chuckle of his belt unbuckling,

in the crushed corsage his underwear makes on the floor,
in the tick of bills he counts out after. Remember it's the same
for us all: you wouldn't believe the life you'll be asked to live.

For seven months of tenth grade you'll feel stubble burning,
bruises pitted black from skin like cherry-stones, pinched nerves
singing against school desks and your mind lost to knowledge

because the city's secret touches you all day and no one can know.
Each algebraic equation halved by his having you, metaphor
a vehicle—its engine idles in your mind—imagine the distractions

of geography: by night the city'll spread himself out on greasy sheets
creased like a map where his cock is compass—rose, and risen,
dizzy with fixity—and his mechanic's hands engineer the scale

on which you're laid. His lessons will teach you this much:
there are only two ways to fuck a boy and be a man—drunk,
or paying for it—and anything else, he'll say, is less than a man

and worse than a woman: a faggot. Which would be you.

Ann Townsend

Ann Townsend was born in 1962 in Pittsburgh, attended Denison University, and received her MA and PhD from Ohio State University. Her poetry, fiction, and criticism regularly appear in such journals as *AGNI, Five Points, The Georgia Review, The Nation, The Paris Review, Ploughshares, Poetry,* and *Witness.* Townsend's two books are *Dime Store Erotics* (Silverfish Review Press, 1998) and *The Coronary Garden* (Sarabande, 2005). Her work has been recognized with the "Discovery"/*The Nation* Award, the James Dickey Prize in Poetry, an NEA Fellowship, and other honors. Townsend, a gardener and trained vocalist, has taught at Denison University since 1992. She lives with her husband, the poet David Baker, and their daughter Kate on a small farm in Granville, Ohio.

They Call You Moody

Such proneness to sadness, such little fits
of life-grinding-to-a-halt:
today three diet cokes can't erase
the jack-pine limbs that dance maniacally
outside the window. All the world's
a pathetic fallacy where willows weep
and the two crows striding across the turf
freeze-frame into death's heads
with every snap of the camera's
imaginary stutter. Ha ha ha they caw
and carried on the updraft they soar and dip
against the sky's umbrella. Oh chemicals rich
in the blood, oh minor turbulent despair,
the sky unfolds, rinsed with bluing,
the crocuses snap open on their crazy
hinges. I hear it all, even through glass,
the loosening, the ticks, the groan.

Touch Me Not

*"Rembrandt went to extraordinary lengths to fix the
precise tone and bluish pallor of dead flesh...."*
—Simon Schama, *Rembrandt's Eyes*

They took my glasses and laid them

on a table. They took what rings
I wore. They raised my arm
above my head and I rocked against a pillow
that smelled sweet, like anesthesia,
like meat. I hoped to stay awake
for the operation, to see my thumb
flayed and spread apart
on the table, and pieced back together.
My arm was pinned and held
and treated kindly, rinsed and dried
and spoken to like a fearful dog.

That spring my father's hand in its death

looked like a claw, unhappily white,
and if I thought I saw a tremor,
a border flexing, it was just a shadow
resting on his finger's underside
and not his dumb hand beckoning to me.

I must have been crying by then.

His instrument raised the flexor tendons
from my wrist, and with swing music
in the background, the Vercet-induced
vapor and bright lights, I dreamed
"The Anatomy Lesson of Doctor Tulp"
as seen from below, from the dead man's
view, until finally my flayed hand and wrist
resembled a stringed instrument,
a tiny mandolin, tendons and ligaments
glistening in their residency.

For months before, chill air

surrounded my fingers like a traveling halo,
those I embraced flinched and said
touch me not. A marvel,

a magician's trick, a whiteness so dead cold
the doctor's temperature strip failed to register
at all. My love called me little ice cube.
My love opened jars for me
and brushed my teeth.

I wanted to reach in and I did,

to his thumb, flushed with embalming fluid.
I measured my own against it,
and like a paradox of motion and stillness,
Achilles running fast, and faster, going nowhere,
I floated my pulse upon silence
despite his pallor, every line of paint that brought him
forward, despite the unconstructed, awful hands
formed around a block, and pinned there.

Modern Love

The rain streams past the gutters, overflowing
        a drain clogged with leaves. From inside
the sound is cool and precise, and though
        the door lies open and the light
spills out, the kitchen keeps its warmth.
        The refrigerator hums, the girl works on
beneath the pools of light, and the man
        outside her window sees her pull
on a cigarette; his eyes follow
        the orange-bright tip; he flicks water
from his eyes and wonders what to do next,
        how to proceed, whether to use the knife
or his hands to open the latched screen door.
        He has never been so wet.

She studies the list on the table, decorum
        of crossed-out items—the few that remain.
The rain slows, and the last crickets begin
        a feeble song from the pond next door.
So far away, each thinks. He watches her mouth open
        in concentration. He must make her
hear him as he meant to be heard:
        what they have done has not been wrong.
His hands know their way past the buttons of her dress.

She lifts her eyes to the window and catches
sight of her own likeness in the glass.
  She can never stop herself: smiling
at the ghost reflection before her.
  He believes she is looking at him.

Natasha Trethewey

Natasha Trethewey was born in 1966 in Gulfport, Mississippi, and attended the University of Georgia, Hollins College, and the University of Massachusetts at Amherst. Her poems have appeared in such journals and anthologies as *American Poetry Review, Callaloo, The Gettysburg Review, The Kenyon Review, The Southern Review, New England Review,* and *The Best American Poetry 2000* and *2003.* She is the author of *Domestic Work* (Graywolf, 2000) and *Bellocq's Ophelia* (Graywolf, 2002). Her third collection, *Native Guard,* is forthcoming from Houghton Mifflin. Trethewey has received fellowships from the the the Bunting Fellowship Program of the Radcliffe Institute for Advanced Study at Harvard, the Guggenheim Foundation, the NEA, and the Rockefeller Foundation Bellagio Study Center. She lives in Decatur, Georgia, and is Associate Professor of English and Creative Writing at Emory University. For the 2005-2006 academic year, she holds the Lehman-Brady Joint Chair Professorship of Documentary and American Studies at Duke University and the University of North Carolina at Chapel Hill.

Miscegenation

In 1965 my parents broke two laws of Mississippi;
they went to Ohio to marry, returned to Mississippi.

They crossed the river into Cincinnati, a city whose name
begins with a sound like *sin,* the sound of wrong—*mis* in Mississippi.

A year later they moved to Canada, followed a route the same
as slaves, the train slicing the white glaze of winter, leaving Mississippi.

Faulkner's Joe Christmas was born in winter, like Jesus, given his name
for the day he was left at the orphanage, his race unknown in Mississippi.

My father was reading *War and Peace* when he gave me my name.
I was born near Easter, 1966, in Mississippi.

When I turned 33 my father said, *It's your Jesus year—you're the same
age he was when he died.* It was spring, the hills green in Mississippi.

I know more than Joe Christmas did. Natasha is a Russian name—
though I'm not; it means *Christmas child,* even in Mississippi.

Genus Narcissus

Faire daffadills, we weep to see / You haste away so soone.
—Herrick

The road I walked home from school
was dense with trees and shadow, creek-side,
and lit by yellow daffodils, early blossoms

bright against winter's last gray days.
I must have known they grew wild, thought
no harm in taking them. So I did—

gathering up as many as I could hold,
then presenting them, in a jar, to my mother.
She put them on the sill, and I sat nearby,

watching light bend through the glass,
day easing into evening, proud of myself
for giving my mother some small thing.

Childish vanity. I must have seen in them
some measure of myself—the slender
stems, each blossom a head lifted up

toward praise, or bowed to meet its reflection.
Walking home those years ago, I knew nothing
of Narcissus or the daffodils' short spring—

how they'd dry like graveside flowers, rustling
when the wind blew—a whisper, treacherous,
from the sill. *Be taken with yourself,*

they said to me; *Die early*, to my mother.

Countess P——'s Advice for New Girls

—*Storyville, 1910*

Look, this is a high-class house—polished
mahogany, potted ferns, rugs two inches thick.
The mirrored parlor multiplies everything—

one glass of champagne is twenty. You'll see
yourself a hundred times. For our customers
you must learn to be watched. Empty

your thoughts—think, if you do, only
of your swelling purse. Hold still as if
you sit for a painting. Catch light

in the hollow of your throat; let shadow dwell
in your navel and beneath the curve
of your breasts. See yourself through his eyes—

your neck stretched long and slender, your back
arched—the awkward poses he might capture
in stone. Let his gaze animate you, then move

as it flatters you most. Wait to be
asked to speak. Think of yourself as molten glass—
expand and quiver beneath the weight of his breath.

Don't pretend you don't know what I mean.
Become what you must. Let him see whatever
he needs. Train yourself not to look back.

Native Guard

> *"...if this war is to be forgotten, I ask in the name of all things sacred*
> *what shall men remember?"*
>
> —Frederick Douglass

November 1862

Truth be told, I do not want to forget
anything of my former life: the landscape's
song of bondage—dirge in the river's throat
where it churns into the Gulf, wind in trees
choked with vines. I thought to carry with me
want of freedom though I had been freed,
remembrance not constant recollection.
Yes: I was born a slave, at harvest time,
in the Parish of Ascension; I've reached
thirty-three with history of one younger

inscribed upon my back. I now use ink
to keep record, a closed book, not the lure
of memory—flawed, changeful—that dulls the lash
for the master, sharpens it for the slave.

December 1862

For the slave, having a master sharpens
the bend into work, the way the sergeant
moves us now to perfect battalion drill,
dress parade. Still, we're called supply units—
not infantry—and so we dig trenches,
haul burdens for the army no less heavy
than before. I heard the colonel call it
nigger work. Half rations make our work
familiar still. We take those things we need
from the Confederates' abandoned homes:
salt, sugar, even this journal, near full
with someone else's words, overlapped now,
crosshatched beneath mine. On every page,
his story intersecting with my own.

January 1863

O how history intersects—my own
berth upon a ship called the *Northern Star*
and I'm delivered into a new life,
Fort Massachusetts: a great irony—
both path and destination of freedom
I'd not dared to travel. Here, now, I walk
ankle-deep in sand, fly-bitten, nearly
smothered by heat, and yet I can look out
upon the Gulf and see the surf breaking,
tossing the ships, the great gunboats bobbing
on the water. And are we not the same,
slaves in the hands of the master, destiny?
—night sky red with the promise of fortune,
dawn pink as new flesh: healing, unfettered.

January 1863

Today, dawn red as warning. Unfettered
supplies, stacked on the beach at our landing,
washed away in the storm that rose too fast,
caught us unprepared. Later, as we worked,
I joined in the low singing someone raised
to pace us, and felt a bond in labor
I had not known. It was then a dark man
removed his shirt, revealed the scars, crosshatched
like the lines in this journal, on his back.
It was he who remarked at how the ropes
cracked like whips on the sand, made us take note
of the wild dance of a tent loosed by wind.
We watched and learned. Like any shrewd master,
we know now to tie down what we will keep.

February 1863

We know it is our duty now to keep
white men as prisoners—rebel soldiers,
would-be masters. We're all bondsmen here, each
to the other. Freedom has gotten them
captivity. For us, a conscription
we have chosen—jailers to those who still
would have us slaves. They are cautious, dreading
the sight of us. Some neither read nor write,
are laid too low and have few words to send
but those I give them. Still, they are wary
of a negro writing, taking down letters.
X binds them to the page—a mute symbol
like the cross on a grave. I suspect they fear
I'll listen, put something else down in ink.

March 1863

I listen, put down in ink what I know
they labor to say between silences
too big for words: worry for beloveds—
My Dearest, how are you getting along—
what has become of their small plots of land—
did you harvest enough food to put by?
They long for the comfort of former lives—

I see you as you were, waving goodbye.
Some send photographs—a likeness in case
the body can't return. Others dictate
harsh facts of this war: *The hot air carries*
the stench of limbs, rotten in the bone pit.
Flies swarm—a black cloud. We hunger, grow weak.
When men die, we eat their share of hardtack.

April 1863

When men die, we eat their share of hardtack
trying not to recall their hollow sockets,
the worm-stitch of their cheeks. Today we buried
the last of our dead from Pascagoula,
and those who died retreating to our ship—
white sailors in blue firing upon us
as if we were the enemy. I'd thought
the fighting over, then watched a man fall
beside me, knees-first as in prayer, then
another, his arms outstretched as if borne
upon the cross. Smoke that rose from each gun
seemed a soul departing. The colonel said:
an unfortunate incident; said:
their names shall deck the page of history.

June 1863

Some names shall deck the page of history
as it is written on stone. Some will not.
Yesterday, word came of colored troops, dead
on the battlefield at Port Hudson; how
General Banks was heard to say *I have*
no dead there, and left them, unclaimed. Last night,
I dreamt their eyes still open—dim, clouded
as the eyes of fish washed ashore, yet fixed—
staring back at me. Still, more come today
eager to enlist. Their bodies—haggard
faces, gaunt limbs—bring news of the mainland.
Starved, they suffer like our prisoners. Dying,
they plead for what we do not have to give.
Death makes equals of us all: a fair master.

August 1864

Dumas was a fair master to us all.
He taught me to read and write: I was a man-
servant, if not a man. At my work,
I studied natural things—all manner
of plants, birds I draw now in my book: wren,
willet, egret, loon. Tending the gardens,
I thought only to study live things, thought
never to know so much about the dead.
Now I tend Ship Island graves, mounds like dunes
that shift and disappear. I record names,
send home simple notes, not much more than how
and when—an official duty. I'm told
it's best to spare most detail, but I know
there are things which must be accounted for.

1865

These are things which must be accounted for:
slaughter under the white flag of surrender—
black massacre at Fort Pillow; our new name,
the Corps d'Afrique—words that take the *native*
from our claim; mossbacks and freedmen—exiles
in their own homeland; the diseased, the maimed,
every lost limb, and what remains: phantom
ache, memory haunting an empty sleeve;
the hog-eaten at Gettysburg, unmarked
in their graves; all the dead letters, unanswered;
untold stories of those that time will render
mute. Beneath battlefields, green again,
the dead molder—a scaffolding of bone
we tread upon, forgetting. Truth be told.

Pimone Triplett

Pimone Triplett was born in 1965 in Oakland, California, and grew up in Maryland. She holds an MFA from the University of Iowa Writers' Workshop. Her poems have appeared in *AGNI, The Paris Review, Poetry, Triquarterly, The Yale Review,* and other journals. She is the author of *Ruining the Picture* (Northwestern University Press, 1998) and *The Price of Light* (Four Way Books, 2005). Triplett is currently an Assistant Professor of Creative Writing at the University of Washington, and also teaches in the low-residency Warren Wilson MFA Program for Writers.

Story for the Mother Tongue

(Bangkok to Chang Mai)

Went to see the *there* that was, for me, full
latitudes, umpteen tracks of world away.
On a train, as it happened, sputtering-to-brake
half our time up the country's question mark coast,
feeling beneath my feet a churn of steam and tin can,
hiss of dithyramb, bike spoke, whole gutter balls
in the aluminum beast. A full car hummed
with that one tongue not mine, but almost.
Since it was my own aunt, after all, who sang
out from the platform that morning not to be
kidnapped—*lukpa*—by anyone, nor taken
into the jungle for who knows what.
And so I knew a little of this music, falsetto
bounce and stutter up from the lungs of my mother
often enough. It came to nothing against
that din in the aisles, boxes and loose seat straps
jostling, the rise and fall pitch of two kids wrestling
their plastic bags, curry-slick. A boy beside me,
teen-aged, kept coughing the way
a kitchen timer ratchets backward.
He fed his dog mangoes clumped in sugar
and red pepper, the cage rapping for miles
on the window smear of rust and whiskey light.

Until finally something happened so that this couldn't
be the one about the exotic anymore, but instead
I had to brace myself as the train lurched forward,

suddenly stopped. And how standing in line
for the bathroom the boy pushed himself into me
then, put his hand hard on my chest, high I don't
know, booze on his breath maybe, I don't know.
I couldn't get free when he whispered into my ear
in English *jesus christ* and then *slut*, his lips moving
slow like words he'd just learned, like reciting after
the teacher in class.
                    Later alone in the WC at last,
gray waves of fluorescent power buzzing off, then on,
then off again, one fist-sized window, one way to look out,
I stared down, awful batter in the hole, a grid
near the feet grinding one blackness up against
another. Longer I stared the more I could feel
space shrinking all around, the crowd of us skimming
the river of tracks we rode on and no still point
in any of us by then, I thought, the water running
with no quiet under the blood and tissue, face and bone,
door jammed, and then just sounds bouncing in the small box—
the two syllables—*kap khun*. Which in Thai means
person, though I thought it was *please* when they
came from out of me at last, words I must have made
while pounding on the walls just then—*kap khun*—locked
in place, the seconds breaking open, mine
and endless and the train moving slowly on.

Next to Last Prayer

1.
Dear God, in shadows now and nothing but, come to think of it—
          shape of a woman's dark
          laid down against rocks,
her hair split by wind, then let to be whole, and back again.

As somehow it used to matter that in St. Louis a few
          thunderheads could crowd
          an oval plot of sky
toddler side of the apartment pool just before the others,

women and children, barefoot or flipflopped, riddled the turnstyle.
          My mouth was Mother's mouth.
          The daily materials, innocent,
still in motion: offerings of Doublemint and spear-,

bags of sponge yellow bunnies, Fresca, warm, a brass-lime
        aftertaste that faded.
        So okay God,
either the bits come back, or swim up in pictures,

the seconds grabbed. My father, more than often then,
        camera-ready, saying: *look*
        up, look out (snap).
I could hold myself right in the light so it finished

looking as though I'd held my breath. Something like swimming,
        which he also taught,
        mouthing: *you hold your breath,*
seconds before I went under for the push and flail,

that slick privacy. And so from now on I'd like to know
        what's to be made
        of this life between
the mind's swing on memory's hinge (Father's

splashing at the deep end) and this shadow, wavering,
        falling down over
        and over again
(dear Mother) against dirt, concrete, shade of the body

that won't stay put—I know the point we never mentioned
        was home, dark spot
        on a kitchen curtain
where someone threw the bowl of hot soup, spot where the shouts

seemed to come from. I know our shapes graced in and out, faces
        in a slow float
        of underwater evenings,
shifting in a pool light's cone through the frankly blue....

2.
But then you know already, don't you God, the way the year
        went on pulsing
        toward a single day,
she and I suddenly in Chang Mai, Thailand, in her country,

because (they said later) she needed to get away. There in heat,
        in dark, small houses,

her family's portraits—
no one I knew—hung in arches over doorways. A pretty woman,

dead, a blue-eyed old man. Mother and I walked for hours under
        the awning of an outdoor market.
            Again, the things of this,
no, that, world, moving and absurdly "beautiful": hills

of glass eyes and "whiteout," bowls of plastic-wrapped pastry,
        whole tables lined
           with imitation pinecones
tied to miniature cacti, red seahorses in watery globes beside

a spinning pig topped by spiders under their golden goblets
        that turned and turned,
           until I turned
and she was gone. Then, rising up from the dark ground,

I saw him, half a man, really, his hand open, outstretched.
        The eyes, blue,
           the eyes, up at me.
A mouth, moving, and his syllables—*Kor tow* (you hold your breath).

Black in the palm lines and him up at me—*Kor tow*...
        It was too hot. The human shadows
           passed by, one then another, each
broken by a tangle of table legs below me, water in troughs, something

swimming at the edges of the aisles. The human, a pant of bodies
        pressed to pay for linens,
           silver, cameras, someone
(you hold your breath, *snap*) above me then reaching for a picture

of a woman naked, and then somewhere else, a voice
        floating out
           from under, but mine,
saying I wasn't him, I was let to be whole,

saying *don't stare and aren't you ashamed of yourself*....
        Until suddenly
           she was back,
of course, and the haggling and our own relieved cries

came through. Later, she told me how his words were ones
        of asking, a way

of saying *please*.
That night, when she must have held her body to me

(*snap*), it was one of the blanks, god, like mine by then, as we stood,
        stilled, caught in the shadow's
        fix-in-place (*snap*), frozen
with the light behind us—our darks divided, falling to the floor.

Portraits at the Epicenter

1
Here's the one where the sun
        is thin as through fish bones,
late day in the picture, a girl standing
        in the kitchen, hearing: fix
your hair, let's hear your whistle, what
        are the dolls' names, say,
"potatoes."
        She's young, at home,
wearing the sweater threaded with the shapes
        of fifty states,
looking straight into
        the camera's flash of light.
Behind, a slackness in the curtain,
        no, dark spot on the curtain where
they say one parent took aim at the other,
        spot they made
larger than her body.
        The camera light flashing *now*
back then, a present she'd been offered,
        and *snap*, the future, everyone looking back
into the distance, the framed picture that was theirs,
        hers now.
A bus carrying girls on the one side,
        boys on the other.
An air raid siren sounding,
        the beginners lining up for
a game of *miss mary mac,*
        chalk on a thumbnail
lit by a match,
        followed by the pledges of allegiance.

2.

       Dark enough so that those shapes blackening
and seeming underneath
       the surface must have been
the ducks not flying on the opposite bank
       at the picnic that day, appearing flat, bloodless,
but moving, pagelike, no longer,
       as we'd once thought,
weighted with our kind of living.

Flash, the day was done, we left the place.
       Or then again maybe
nothing
       like this happened, maybe
there was no *place*, only the distance
       asking something of us.
I know there was an old man I loved,
       Mother's father, his battle stories
coming in like a voice-over
       from outside the frame, whispering
Guernica, London,
       Hiroshima…"They wanted,"
he said, "one light to marry
       all the others."

       Here's the one where he spills water
from a wooden bucket, swinging the mirror
       round his neck again, to remember
the hour his air caught fire. *Stop*.
       He spread an arm over the family plot,
as if the land could be taken like a bride.
       Stop. What was the flash of light
like? Says he woke to walk away
       from cast-off paneling, corrugated tin.

3.

Between there and here, I picture
       the story of the mistress:
"It was murder,
       Mother, taking your place.
At first they came because I looked like you,
       later because I looked like them.
I had to practice
       everything you said,

from lips berry-bright with opium,
        to faking the one quiver that made them proud.
I held a match
        so close to my eyes
half of them believed I blinked it out,
        the fire lasting just long enough.
Some, burned like me, wanted
        to show the flames of what remained still graceful.

        Over the bed I've hung the painting
you left of yourself,
        the mass light behind you
searing skin—arms—excoriated
        to rags, wings.
How I must have loved you, Mother,
        just before I was born,
before I had to be given
        a name."

4.
Once Grandfather wrote that he knew "This Is Your Life"
        ranked high among viewers
in America. "They sent me an invitation
        embossed with Hazel Bishop long-lasting
lipstick, nail enamel, cream.
        The band played when I entered.
Applause came at unusual
        parts. 'The morning was perfectly
clear,' I said (*clap*),
        and suddenly the on-set air-raid siren
sounded (*clap*). A stranger entered.
        Said he flew over
us, and sorry, my God…
        and I said (but whispered), 'a flash
of light, then I dropped…'

I remember the camera's surge,
        its collapsing one mirror onto another.
Say something, they said.
        I said, 'We came back out,
look at us.'
        Say something, they said.
I said, 'Re-member, this word you use
        as if the body can be

repeated.' (*Cut!*)

     'As the limbs of the dead
come back out of the distance.' (*Cut.*)

     'Don't look at me like I'm not here,'
I said, then,

       'Don't look at me.'"

Karen Volkman

Karen Volkman was born in 1967 in Miami, and received degrees from New College of the University of South Florida and Syracuse University. Her poems have appeared in many journals and anthologies, including The Best American Poetry, The Pushcart Prize Anthology, Boston Review, Chicago Review, New American Writing, and The Paris Review. She is the author of Crash's Law (Norton, 1996), a National Poetry Series Selection, and Spar (University of Iowa Press, 2002), winner of the James Laughlin Award from the Academy of American Poets. Volkman has received awards and fellowships from the Akademie Schloss Solitude, the NEA, and the Poetry Society of America. She has taught at Columbia College Chicago, The New School, the University of Alabama, the University of Chicago, the University of Pittsburgh, and elsewhere. Volkman now lives in Missoula, Montana, and teaches in the University of Montana MFA Program.

[Now I promise...]

Now I promise the shriek that the pressure of days, the pressure of days will be weapon. We drive and we drive, we blare music, we go on. On the highway of our lost intentions, all signs are strident, all exits goodbye.

Who's that voice? A wound in a wheel-spin? Speed—which I love like an orphan, dear dazed infant of my most *present* caress. Lord, I am loving your children, the antic and plastic and plausive, the caustic and restive, the everyway raw.

Think: our limbs are straight, our wings tattered, our tempers *blade*. Still—a starling rustles in your temple, mutant mystic. Still—a something shudders in your fingers, when you sing. That there are—yes, no, then, never—pieces of plan and purpose. That they stay.

[If it be event...]

If it be event, I go toward and not back. I go tower, not floor. I listen but rarely learn, I take into account occasionally, but more often there are lips to kiss, words to pass from tongue to mouth, white entire. It knows a few names about what I am, it goes door to door saying *She is* or *Her ire*. But when the rainbows are handles I hold dragging earth to more vivid disasters, oh swinging by the strap. You thought she was a dimwit flapper, really she's a chemist with a taste for distress. You thought she came with guarantees, really she's your nightmare hatcheck has a vagrant head. I sort of sometimes go by the book, the need to move being visage, mask you wear like dark sky or water (water that boils or breaks or scares the flame). We don't need a nest to grow in, a bed to sleep. In the clairvoyance of loving wrongly, o glass pillow o swallow, is dream is dare is dagger. Your turn.

The Case

Old wolf, I said,
leave a tatter
for my family,
a scrap, a rag,
a bone, a button—something
to bury.
          Because, I said,
I've chased
the fast fox from
the henhouse, and twisted
the livid blossoms
from failing stems,
mercy, spare a rag,
a bone, a button,
for my family.

And because, I said, I sang
the names of saints
on Sunday, and lay
with another woman's
husband Monday eve, leave
a scrap, a rag,
a bone, a button—
to bury.

And he said:
It will take
whatever it is given. It will
be still.

May

In May's gaud gown and ruby reckoning
the old saw wind repeats a colder thing.

Says, you are the bluest body I ever seen.
Says, dance that skeletal startle the way I might.

Radius, ulna, a catalogue of flex.
What do you think you're grabbing

with those gray hands? What do you think
you're hunting, cat-mouth creeling

in the mouseless dawn? Pink as meat
in the butcher's tender grip, white as

the opal of a thigh you smut the lie on.
In May's red ruse and smattered ravishings

you one, you two, you three your cruder schemes,
you blanch black lurk and blood the pallid bone

and hum scald need where the body says *I am*
and the rose sighs *Touch me, I am dying*

in the pleatpetal purring of mouthweathered May.

Kiss Me Deadly

1.
How do they get so close to the window,
a tree in figment, arithmetic moon?
Summer broke you, winter builds you—
a lofty leafage in the prism, a pure
empire. Where they've ghosted roofs
on the drawings of infants—
because I *did* leave a letter, small map,
semblance. Tarnish the mirrors,
they will not shield. And wound
this ribbon round my fingertip,
to keep you.

2.
Should it be better, going off, grim-
visaged indigents, tinny mimic stars?
Two things love a third—hosting a harbor
in the brokenest guitar.

Two things leave a remnant—its sound
and space and silence shrill and wide.

3.
Two things torch a fragment.
When did the moon grow an eye?
I speak from a shameless seance,
a blue-lipped winter that mutters and broods.
I move in a blowsy specter,
a gap-toothed slattern with a curse and a cry.
Let's give the lily a scissor.
Let's smash the cup and saucer,
spill the wine.

4.
She moves, she means, she masters.
She deems, she dooms, she stammers.
Schools, and schemes, and skitters,
rumors, raptures, rathers. She *aspires*.
She did, she don't, she daren't.
She shall, she shan't, she shouldn't.
Hooped and looped and latent,
she doth, she loath, she mightn't.
She make, she moan, she silent.
She gave, she grieve, she amn't.
She behave.

5.
Though intentions erode like the moon,
they are still as ghostly, as noble.
Someday to sing it with champagne and sherry,
in a gauze gown, tonic,
stippled with perfume.
An opera of Edens. A synaptic how-come.
In this boomtown boudoir, baby
you always wrong.

G. C. Waldrep

G. C. Waldrep was born in 1968 in South Boston, Virginia. He attended Harvard as an undergraduate, took his MA and PhD in American History from Duke University, and, in 2005, received an MFA from the University of Iowa Writers' Workshop. Between 1995 and 2000, he was a member of the New Order Amish community in Yanceyville, North Carolina, where he worked as a carpenter's helper, baker, and window-maker. Waldrep's poems have appeared in such journals as *American Letters & Commentary*, *Boston Review*, *Conjunctions*, *Denver Quarterly*, *Gulf Coast*, *New American Writing*, and *Ploughshares*. His first book of poems is *Goldbeater's Skin* (Center for Literary Publishing, 2003). Waldrep is also the author of the nonfiction book *Southern Workers and the Search for Community* (University of Illinois Press, 2000). His work has received awards from the Academy of American Poets, the Poetry Society of America, and the North Carolina Arts Council. For the 2005-06 academic year, Waldrep is serving as a Visiting Professor of History and Poetry at Deep Springs College in Inyo County, California.

The Miracles of St. Sebastian

Stooping in the dooryard the boy saint picks up the body. He is curious, he begins to massage the tissue around the eyelids; begins to pluck, feather by feather, then the skin—a deeper massage—pulling away from the cranium. It is not his firm pressure that accomplishes anything, he is merely part of a larger process that would take longer were it not for his assistance.

He does not think *sparrow*.

He thinks, vaguely, *bird*. He thinks, more specifically, *skull*: it's the bone he wants, near shimmer, its pallid shoal.

His own hand is a skeleton reaching after a skeleton. This is the first lesson of desire: like to like. The fruit comes later.

Time passes. He thinks it is wrong to laugh at clowns because his grandmother tells him they were born that way, delivered from the hospital with bulbous noses and orange hair. Later he paints clowns, faces copied from financial magazines, glossy inserts, *TV Guide*. He dresses them up in his mind, applies the pancake and mascara, the outrageous prosthetics. He tells himself he chooses these faces because they are strong faces. They are all male.

He paints women too, many women, first as nudes, then as flensed, then as skeletons. He paints hominids, he paints apes. He paints hominids painting. He paints painting apes. He paints a male chimpanzee bent over his easel and palette, sketching a female nude.

He does not think of painting a female chimpanzee sketching a male nude.

He paints a woman from the neck up. He paints a woman from the neck down. He paints three women as they pass a peach from hand to hand. He etches a woman cast upright in snow: sex, navel, eyes, breasts.

He becomes a teacher. He argues that all art is figurative; that the figure ceases to matter only when we cease to be human. He is very sure of this. He thinks all art occurs in its own time. He memorizes: fossae and tibia, coccyx and acetabulum, calcaneus and teres.

He paints his wife slipping out of the musculature of her upper back as from an evening gown. He paints himself holding his own skin.

He paints a python, curled around a branch, straining to draw a hunter's shaft from its body with its own bloodied mouth.

What Begins Bitterly Becomes Another Love Poem

The earth has a taste for us, in its unknowing
appetite there yet resides a hunger, incompletion
that draws all life to its dark self. What, then,
shall we say of the flesh's own desire, distal
thumb-brush at evening? There is nothing to say,
the vowels cluster uncertain in the beautiful vase
the throat makes, fricatives corralled behind
ridge of gum and bone-splinter. Flesh and earth:
fire is an illusion, to which water is the antidote.
The day was a bright one, there seemed no need
to move about with mirrors, the usual circumspection
and indirect approach. The abundance of small life
argued some measure of clemency, likewise
the Jerseys lowing in the paddock breeze, tender
shoots of cress and sweetpea spiralling upward.
But fire is a cruel hoax: now you see it,

now you don't, the object of your affection
cast in carbon on the hard ground which will,
in time, receive. Roadside the irises bloomed
two or three feet max above soil's surface,
rough tongue resting lightly on each leaf, each
violet exclamation. In full sun your hand guided mine
to the wound. A small one. Water and blood,
like the nurse said: prestidigitation of the body.
We stood without shadows on asphalt at midday.
What we call patience is only fire again, compressed.
I remember: your face flushed, stray petal lodged
in the damp whorl of your disheveled hair.

Hotel d'Avignon

The religious cry in their patois of sand and dusk.
If I could find the portico I would repaint the columns.
No one has left the key with me
so I sketch one on scratch paper.
I am a handy artist, so this is easy:
the notches are precise, there is a sense
of perspective in the hatching of the brass,
as from a light source.
Through the corridors I walk
with my paper key held before me.
Night is always the same here. Outside
the religious fragment slowly into the tall grasses.
My paper key is a fine instrument
and yet they are afraid of it.
All night, from their crusts of earth,
the religious mutter curses: They hope I will lose the key,
that I will crumple or erase it, at least
that I will never use it.
Listen, I call to them through the grille,
Everything in the world is a knife,
everything in the world cuts a little from you.
But they do not listen. I do not speak their language.
Through the night as through the day
I walk, perform small tasks.
Some days I think about drawing a new key.
Some days I do.
Light is untidy, my mother used to say, clucking gently.
You must collect the rays scattered about you.

O Canada!

There were these enormous Canadas, shaved & bedridden, all along the border: some on this side, some on that, some we weren't sure about or which straddled, some we had to cross to get to, some that were the means of our crossing, some that were simply in the way, small Canadas, dumpy Canadas in which the locals once carved cells for meditation, or beekeeping, none of the authorities of our (limited) acquaintance were quite sure which, these (cavities) which we dubbed "the empty Canadas," quixotic, inquisitive, quisling (some whispered), a bevy of Canadas, a cantonment of Canadas, such splendid Canadas!

& we were stopped on our return & our bags searched, every pocket turned out to seam, to hem, to orifice & centrifuge, had we stolen, had we cozened, had we lusted for, or against these, the smallest of Canadas, had we in fact imagined more diverse, even more exotic Canadas, had we, in touching the many Canadas of our (collective) acquaintance, so much as scraped from their sleeping hides the slenderest crescent of Canada, beneath a nail, say, and breathing hard in the dry cold of that enormous room could we swear, & avow, & affirm, that we in the future would leave those Canadas alone, that we would not so much as think of writing to those Canadas, much less cohabiting with them or engaging in minor (though illicit, & therefore profitable) trade, that we might not pirate the microecologies of those Canadas, nor duplicate for any purpose beyond the instructional, i.e. neither love, nor money, nor for the thrill of the thing itself, *le frisson, le frottage*,

& soon it was night & we were on our way again, and you were limping, a little, from a pebble that had lodged in your boot, & Megan was saying something about the excellent tea we'd had at the roadhouse a few villages back, & Stuart had bought a new blank journal from the Fassbinder boutique, & he was trying to write in it, while we walked, which we all, even Stuart, agreed was not particularly efficacious, but he wanted to get as much down, he said, as he could, while these memories were still fresh, which we agreed was an excellent idea, if poorly timed, & though we kept watch among ourselves, even at night (for this was the summer of the comet), we saw no more Canadas, heard no more Canadas, smelled no more Canadas (that plush & glacial nidor), ran our hands over, or across, or beneath no further Canadas, tasted no additional Canadas (but had we tasted?), until we began to wonder

had we ever been there, to Canada, or had we merely imagined the voyage, & what would it be like to go back, or rather, in the face of this growing uncertainty, to go, as if for the first time, what might we find there, and this was all we talked about as mile passed into mile, among the elk and the water buffalo, and the walk was pleasant, and the scenery was agreeable, and there was a certain balm or bite to the air which we could not name, but which made us hopeful, the azure Canadas, the wounded Canadas, the missing Canadas, the emphatic Canadas, the marsupial Canadas, the recrudescent Canadas, the vigilant Canadas, the piñata Canadas with their sugared eggs,

—every bright & yearning Canada to come—

Joe Wenderoth

Joe Wenderoth was born in 1966, grew up in Baltimore, and attended Loyola College, New York University, and Warren Wilson College, where he received his MFA. His poetry, fiction, and nonfiction has appeared in many journals and anthologies, including *Great American Prose Poems*. Wesleyan University Press published his first two books of poems: *Disfortune* (1995), and *It Is If I Speak* (2000). Verse Press published *Letters To Wendy's* (2000), a work of fiction, and *The Holy Spirit of Life: Essays Written for John Ashcroft's Secret Self* (2005). Wenderoth's latest book, *Agony: A Proposal*, is forthcoming from Verse in 2007. He is Associate Professor of English at the University of California, Davis, where he lives with his wife and daughter.

As Hour and Year Collapsed

We were a whole army underground;
we did not move.
We were replicas, at first,
but the army above,
that which we were shaped to resemble,
moved, spoke, faded, and came
to rot
in shallow graves above us.
We were never them;
even as the workers painted our eyes
the colors of their eyes,
even as they hauled us by torchlight
into the vast royal burial chambers
and made us to stand the way they stood,
once, above,
we were never them.
When our faces were finally finished
and our ranks were formed,
we stood guard over the absence
of the one who required us.
No one was allowed to look.
The chambers were sealed
and the last few torches burned down.
We stood suddenly alone in silent darkness.
We knew, though, that someone above
could imagine us,

and we could sleep standing up
in that image.
The workers, who painted our eyes
and carved our horses' manes,
could imagine us—the priests,
who looked into our faces and blessed us
before and for this dark, could imagine,
and knew that we were there.
But then they moved, faded, and came to rot.
We were still spoken of, as time passed,
but only as an *idea*, as though
we did not actually stand here
inside the earth, in these colors,
these unseeing eyes, this dark.
No one any longer imagined us as real;
we had to imagine ourselves—
the way we looked, the way we stood—
from the inside,
from the stillness of our own hearts.
And we did learn to see ourselves in this way:
blind, colorful, standing guard over nothing.
And we came to accept,
as *hour* and *year* collapsed
into one dull drizzle of dust,
that we would not be found—
our guard would never be relieved.
There are worse fates than this,
we told ourselves,
without speaking, without moving,
without anyone above us in this darkness.
But we were wrong—what we told ourselves,
the way we stood, for years, in this darkness,
was wrong—all wrong.
And you, you bring how wrong to light—
you alone let the sharp light that forged us
fall hard on our faces again.
You alone remind us that what we have understood
has never been what we are.

Send New Beasts

These beasts will not do.

1. Their bleeding is decidedly inadequate—from a distance they appear not to bleed at all. Considering the likelihood of distance in today's spectator, this is not a small problem.

2. While they are exotic enough in appearance—and I assume this is why they were selected—they have a tendency, and an ability, to hide themselves in plain view. I don't claim to understand this ability—I only know that it is widely felt that, even at close range, they are difficult to get a good look at, and this is especially true when a blow is being struck upon them. It's almost as if they're immune to isolation—as if they are able to always appear, no matter how alone they are, in the noise and confusion of a herd.

3. They are far too obedient and willing to receive blows. Indeed, they seem to sense when a blow is coming and to move intuitively into it. If this movement was desperate—graceful or graceless—it might generate some interest, but it seems to fall, tragically, somewhere in between. That is, they seem able, at every point in their torture, to collapse in a reasonable fashion, as if the collapse was being dictated by their own will. No one enjoys—I don't think I even need to tell you—a reasoned collapse. It is this aspect of the beasts that most deeply defeats us, our simple want of a show.

4. Their attacks—and I hesitate to even call them attacks—are largely indistinguishable from the active reasoning of their own collapse. It is as though they seek above all to expose us to this activity of theirs—to infect us with their will to reason, and in so doing, reduce us to the unvarying rhythm of their irreducible herd. I would like to say that we are immune to this reduction, but I am not sure. In any case, I see no good reason for continuing to subject ourselves to these attacks. It would be better to have no beasts at all—to live altogether outside of shows—than to sink numbly into tolerance of a spectacle which fails to clarify what it is that distinguishes us from beasts.

Narrative Poem

Gradually I got to aching so bad
that I couldn't lie still.
I had a fever every day for a few years.
I took out school loans.
I watched a little tv in a little room.
I came into some pills—
friends were having back problems, dental work.
I moved my little tv from city to city,
watching with delight, with loathing.
Gradually the ache withdrew
into the foundation, lapping more softly
at my bones.
My girlfriend and I drove to Canada
and bought codeine.
We watched a tv movie
in a resort motel in the off-season.
We drove back and rented a house in Baltimore.
We got credit.
We bought a 32-inch tv and a new couch—
two-thousand dollars, all told.
I kicked out the driver's side window of our car
in a Denny's parking lot.
I filed an insurance claim;
many valuable objects had been stolen from the car.
We ran out of codeine.
I couldn't afford to get the window fixed.
We drove all winter with the window down.
Our neighbor gave us a ten-gallon aquarium
and I bought two piranha.
I feed them a goldfish every morning.
Sometimes one will get its head and tail torn off;
even so, it swims around the tank a while.

Where I Stand with Regard to the Game

At first, I played the game as I was given to play the game. I played without
grace, without pretense—I played with pure joy, and with a brutality all my
own. I played the game without understanding that there was a game. This
could not go on. I could not help but be taken in by the others, by the
warmth of their constant measure, in which, it was said, I had a considerable

potential for grace. So I gave myself to them. I learned how to hold a pretense, how to hold myself in check, and in my play, it was said, there gradually arose a new grace, an understanding of the game. This could not go on. Pretense gave rise to grace, I gathered, and so I held myself in check. I withdrew as powerfully as I had first played. The game went on and I taught myself to keep out of it—I taught myself to watch. To demonstrate my detachment, I described the game. At first, the lay of the field, the way the weather came and how the light in the field endured it. Then the way the players moved, the waxing and waning of their graces, and the shouts that seemed, alternately, the achievement of complete fullness and complete vacancy. These shouts defied description. I turned away from them—I turned away from my whole project, and turned to the rules of the game, which everyone had to admit had never been made sufficiently clear. Why was the field marked in this fashion? Clearly there are boundaries, but what of these zones within the area of play—what could they signify? Even the movement of the players—what is legal, what is not? What moves should the children emulate? There was room here for an understanding such as mine to do good work. In clarifying the rules of the game, I did not feel graceful, exactly, but I did feel as though I was developing a clarity in which the various graces of the players would have to be more apparent. I also felt that, so long as I was clarifying the rules of the game, I could not be blamed for my failure to describe the shouts of the players. As I worked, the game went on, untouched by my efforts. As I poured forth my eloquent logics and settled fine points never before addressed, it was as though the players were not listening. I felt, at first, that this was not of consequence— the players, in the midst of play, could not be reasonably expected to listen to me. I realized, however, as time went by, and as my work on the rules of the game became an increasingly undeniable success, that even those who were not playing, those who, like myself, watched—even these were not listening to me, and were not at all interested in making the amendments to the rules that my work made logical. This irked me. I began to ask myself why I continued with my work. I began to write less about the rules of the game and more about why I felt the need to write about said rules. The question of play arose—the question, that is, of whether or not I should have ever stopped playing, and whether or not it would be possible to play now. I began to speculate, from the incredible distance I had worked years to create, on the benefits of a life of play. Such speculation proved only the distance I had worked years to create. If I was to play—if I was to abandon everything I had ever worked for in favor of resuming a life of play—there could be no graceful approach. There could be no speculation. There would have to be something new, something defying description. There would have to be a complete and hopeless destruction of every grace, every distance. And that is where I stand.

Greg Williamson

Greg Williamson was born in 1964 in Columbus, Ohio, and grew up in Nashville, Tennessee. He attended Vanderbilt University, the University of Wisconsin, and the Writing Seminars at Johns Hopkins University. His poems have appeared in AGNI, The New Republic, The Paris Review, Poetry, Sewanee Review, Southwest Review, and elsewhere, including The Best American Poetry 1998 anthology. Williamson is the recipient of a Whiting Writers' Award and an Academy Award in Literature from the American Academy of Arts and Letters, among other honors. His two collections are The Silent Partner (Story Line Press, 1995) and Errors in the Script (Overlook, 2001). He teaches in The Writing Seminars at Johns Hopkins University and divides his time between Baltimore, Maryland, and Duluth, Georgia.

Italics, Mine

Hello, up there. Thank God you happened by.
    I'm touched. I've been beneath the covers
  For so long now the light is stark,
Where honestly I thought that I might lie
    Alone forever in the dark,
      And this is a place for lovers.

By night I dreamed about the day you looked
    And read my thoughts and would agree
  To spend some time with me, and talk.
Since all the flights to Paris have been booked,
    Perhaps you'd settle for a walk
      To see what we shall see.

You see that oak leaf there? I always sense
    A kinship with the leaves. To me
  Each one portrays a little oak,
A fragile replica of an immense
    Black oak, itself a lush, baroque,
      Green forest of a tree.

And at the shore let's walk the water line,
    The ocean's flexing, outermost
  Advance, where the seawater laps
A sandy beach, plotting a jagged line

Whose every subdivision maps
A continental coast.

Or looking backward toward the mountain range,
We see the ridge line's collarbone,
Comprising summit and ravine,
And holding up a rock we find a strange,
Profound affinity between
The mountains and the stone.

If I seem to be beginning to repeat
Myself, it is because the world
Repeats itself in hidden laws
Whose figurings and fractals the exegete
Tries to articulate because
In the beginning was the word.

As with the sense of humor in a laugh,
In every word a poem survives,
Abundantly rich in ways and means
To build the sentence and the paragraph,
The rise and fall of little scenes,
The stories of our lives.

The coming home of walks and talks and stories
Discloses what we came to know,
Where the changing fortunes of a day
Become a lifetime's sadnesses and glories,
A stranger's face to which we say,
As to the mirror, "Hello."

Hello. I hope you pardon my conceits,
But I have dreamed on my nightstands
From all these little rooms to build
A home where we might lie between the sheets,
And I declare myself fulfilled
When I am in your hands.

But this has all been talk, I know, and I
Can tell you are about to turn
And go your way, while I repair
To darkness and a dateless night. Goodbye.
I will be saying a silent prayer
That one day you return.

Nervous Systems

And the crack in the tea-cup opens
A lane to the land of the dead.
                                        W. H. Auden

Not many trees survive our satellite
Communities. But here by a quiet house
And fanned by warm midmorning breeze, daylight
Flares in a living ash, where dark birds light
On ramifying, migratory routes.
And then this warning flashes on the light
Meter: Inside the house a pilot light
Is always burning in the oven's eyes,
And the low roof is pulled down over the eyes
Like a hat, and underneath the morning's leit-
Motif networks of subterranean lines
Run like the nervous system, or bloodlines,

Or fractures spreading from tectonic lines
Of fault. From distant coasts, heavy and light
Petroleum is piped across state lines,
And gas, electric, oil, and water lines
Convey their vital humors to the house.
The greatest threat to all these bottom lines
Remains the operator who declines
To call for information about their routes
But sinks the backhoe's teeth among the roots.
An accident explodes in the headlines,
Rattling the suburb's glassy eyes,
Or seeps into the ground beneath our eyes,

Avoiding, for a time, the public's eyes.
The leak spreads like reticulating lines
Of thought, which thinks of crow's-feet at the eyes,
Or secret guilt dilating in your eyes,
Something you hope is never brought to light,
Or mysteries behind your neighbor's eyes,
To dark forebodings lurking in the house-
Hold phrase, our faults that may bring down the house.
There's a screw loose, blown fuse, fire in the eyes,
Frayed nerves, live wires. Like words out of taproots,
The pipes break off on long, anfractuous routes.

Bearing in mind the origin of "routes"
Is *rumpere*, "to rupture," cast your eyes
On the thriving industry of thrift, which roots
In the cracked sidewalks, cracking with the roots.
There's something going on between the lines,
Below our feet, baring along their routes
Whatever's buried with the bitter roots.
Across the seeded lawn, by a floodlight,
A sassafras is spreading toward the light,
But it has "stone" and "breaker" in its roots.
It's growing at the corner of the house,
Derived from *hydan*, "to hide," which gives us "house."

Thus, rarely do we see an open house.
Like Huntington's stalking in genetic roots—
Who can be sure what's growing up in-house,
In living rooms, in broken homes? They house,
Perhaps, deft infidelities, black eyes,
Crude violence to the children playing house.
The oven's eyes are burning in the house.
And you can almost hear, in the phone lines,
The hubbub that entreats, retracts, maligns.
A work truck sidles up beside the house.
Two men in hats and uniforms alight.
They have a pickaxe and a trouble light.

The underground is booming. Traveling light,
The pipelines work their way from house to house,
Operating among our darkest roots,
Like nervous systems tingling behind the eyes,
Conveying a threat, or something, along those lines.

Junkyard

Where the tall towers of the city rise
Deep in the distance across a river bend,
The fading traces of a gravel drive
Run off the county highway through a field
Of all the usual grasses to the banks,
Where hidden in Queen Anne's lace and goldenrod
A junkyard lies at the end of the road, unused
And gone to grass in the shadow of the city.

Or else it is the shadow of the city,
Whose time has come and will not come again,
Except for what we make of it from these
Twice ruined ruins. Down in the dumps of Troy
Cracked urns and ornate scraps of fired clay
And broken bits in turn reflected Troy
Beyond the walls, and testify that they
Were crafty artisans and horsemen and
Indeed they were besieged for many years.

Down here blue flies and butterflies and bees,
The water's running thump against its banks,
The sunlight glimmering in shattered glass
As the yard explodes with crickets every step,
All deepen the stillness of a burned-out stove,
Radiators, a listing water heater.
(In a cold world they were a people who
Had trouble keeping warm.) And one sees tires
And tractors here, a dozen diesel drums,
A concrete mixer, bales of barbed wire,
Blank televisions, box springs, a commode.
(They farmed and built and played. They carried on.)

But mostly what one notices are cars.
Flamboyant chrome, the engines and the fins,
The size and extra racks say much about
The people who possessed them, but in the names
We see the way they must have seen themselves:
DeSoto, Coronado, Phoenix, Bel Air,
Roadmaster, Nomad Wagon, Maverick
Rambler, Galaxy, and Eldorado.
(They yearned for going more than getting there.)

These are the easy emblems of our race:
Of fire and forge and factory, of long
Assembly lines, emblems of oil and speed,
Of city and suburb and the rush to work,
Of traffic jams and of the wanderlust
We've always loved about ourselves. (They were
Romantic, reckless, migratory people.)

Under the sun in the lively yard, how slowly
Smolders the inexorable decay.
The grills grin on insanely with chrome teeth.
Hoods gape. There is no light in the deadman stare

Of headlights, no faces in the empty mirrors,
Where bonelike struts and pipes are scattered among
The skeletons of mice and the spent shells
Of cicadas. A brittle snakeskin suns itself
On a rock, and one thinks of all the absent souls
Who wore their bodies out.

                              No doubt there was
Great sadness in these wrecks, happiness too.
Possibly because I am young, I think
Of them as young, the kids of another time
Who turned the keys and brought the behemoths
To life, who cruised the parties and midnight roads
And went to work and drove away to school.
Despite the somberness of smashed front ends,
Cracked windshields and a bullet-riddled door,
How dated and naive those children seem,
Behind the wheel or taken for a ride,
Now that ivy has climbed in the back seats
And water stagnates in the pickup beds
Where, once, in parking lots or country roads
Our discontinued parents ground their gears.

The great chimneys burn across the river.
Whatever we are, we will become whatever
Is said about us. That goes without saying,
Although one could be wrong about a place
Where wind in dry grass sounds like rain. Time comes
To go. And I leave under the stewardship
Of crickets and flies and pollinating bees
The reclamation project of the weeds.

Emily Wilson

Emily Wilson was born in 1968 in Cleveland, Ohio, and grew up in Scarborough, Maine. She holds degrees from Harvard College and the University of Iowa Writers' Workshop. Wilson has worked as a grantswriter and copyeditor, and has taught poetry at the University of Iowa, Colby College, and the University of Montana, where she served as the Richard Hugo Visiting Writer in 2005. Her poems have appeared in such journals as *Boston Review, Colorado Review, TriQuarterly,* and *Volt.* Wilson is the author of *The Keep* (University of Iowa Press, 2001). She lives in Brooklyn.

[Wind in bare vines…]

Wind in bare vines
rifling the flowerpot

someone extracted
the shattered pine from

the tulips thrust
standards out of walnut

trash and what now
crazes the gardenside

elms a neighborhood
you come to starved

animal standing
shy at the door I

wish for this
world I did not welcome

Relict

This is the ocean
dead-reckoned into

autumn estuarial
grounds in which drift

an aberrance of terns,
the few barrier

cottages closed up.
The small vowel-shifts

we have been through.
This trend toward hometowns

that are evermore
strange. The textures

eccentric in mud.
Not figuring your end.

You become the lone trove
of whole kingdoms.

Coal Age

trunks budded and scarred
summer experience on the loess edge of the moraine

fallings out between elders
beautiful forestations of made language

sister puts forth her little finger
on the tip in composite relief the damselfly structure exacted

a storm floats over the purchase
neither you nor I neither one of us

mass interlockings of leaves tiny waxed tabs interlapping
the false pines the puzzling pines

it has not yet occurred along the limb it has not yet determined to be spurlike
it is not yet done it lingers in the pattern of its advancement

are you long of this world I
am delivered into casting my bit among us

are you a being of more than one measure
ruffed at the back of the neck so none may hold me

The Fossil Garden

Some spare relief
of sedges so many

million years old.
As if articles

of faith were
unnumbered. As if

the seminal
mind could be prized

from its berth.
In the intricate

underworld birds
are abstracts of

collapse without ground.
You come to some end.

And love that season
travels hungry.

Suzanne Wise

Suzanne Wise was born in 1965 in Rutland, Vermont, and grew up in Killington, Vermont. She received her BA from Middlebury College in Vermont and her MFA from the University of Michigan in Ann Arbor. Her poems have appeared in *Boston Review, Denver Quarterly, Fence, Tikkun, Volt,* and elsewhere, and have been recognized with two fellowships from The Fine Arts Work Center in Provincetown and a Barbara Deming Memorial Fund Award, among other honors. Her first book is *The Kingdom of the Subjunctive* (Alice James, 2000). Wise has served as the literary events planner for Small Press Distribution in Berkeley and Poets House in New York City, and has taught creative writing at Middlebury College and in the Publication, Performance, and Media Program at Pratt Institute. She lives in Brooklyn.

Testimony

Because that heckler was a joke,
(she was no lady), we forced her to behave
like a sheep, beat her, forced her
to enter a hole in front of her house,
ordered her to bend her head,
riddled her. We stitched her good.
She could not move or cry.

Later we paid for what we did.
Her father got 8,000—she had not yet bled.
After the first real customer, the price dropped
to 4,000, then 200 for an hour.
After months of effort, our gynecologists
examined her, proclaimed her barren.
The current ransom is 300 or five jugs of oil.

It is important to be accurate, to measure results,
to learn from mistakes, to continue to do what is right,
correct what is wrong and improve what is imperfect
so as to avoid great losses.

Especially these days, as we pass through
the most unfortunate events, overwhelming our country
and friends as if one had happened upon them
by chance, on some secret errand.

To write down our passionate thoughts
at all is already, in some measure, to command
and have our way with them.

Our inspiration comes out of that dreamy
atmosphere in which men have things
as they will. We regret we were forced
to omit so much.

Confession

I had my faults.
I had my so-called desires.
I remained open to temptation.
I argued with my colleagues.
I did not reach 100 percent
in my assignments. But I was no pry
pole, I was subsidiary. I was aspiring
to cog. I wanted to be a gullible
sheep or a rowdy-dowdy shepherdess
or a shamefaced sheepdog.
When I learned what I had to be,
I sat down on my luggage set
and wept. Then I unpacked. I decorated.
I raised the roof. I flew my kite.
I removed all the skulls and thieves.
I told my wise leaders where to sponge.
I was less than resistant. I was more than bold.
I was beyond naked. I was technicolor.
I was a brilliant butcher, an innovative
streetwalker, a saucy sales manager.
I knew a good stogy, a fine lace teddy.
I lived for love. I erred accordingly.
I assumed the world condoned my stunts.
It's clearer today. I was misunderstood;
I was in the know everyone else wanted
out of. Today there are no traces
of erasures, and no qualms, no real
wrongs. I made judgments for the best
and by the standards of the time.
Now that it's over I must beg
for attention. I have been robbed
of the limelight that comes with

responsibility. I can only imagine
how hard it must be for you
to believe me, I mean, to hold
blame. I mean, to be you.

50 Years in the Career of an Aspiring Thug

1. Burned Christ to a crisp. 2. On the Betty Crocker burner. 3. Tied a body to the railroad tracks. It wore the clothes of a girl. 4. Later found naked and weeping in the fields. 5. It was a body of straw. 6. It wore a note that said: *I am God.* 7. Drove Father's golf cart into the pond. *My final hole in one,* said the note stuffed in the ninth hole. 8. Stole prize roses from Mother's garden. Wore them on the head, as a wreath, in secret, admiring the Romanesque profile in the bathroom mirror. 9. In the diary: *I will conquer.* 10. Dreamed of making the rank of Eagle Scout. 11. Stole Brother's BB gun. 12. Shot the lights out all over town. 13. Disappeared. 14. Didn't leave a note. 15. Got a job in the city working for the glass company. 16. Checking panes for cracks. 17. Etched curses into every self reflected. 18. Got a job working for the car company, answering the phone. 19. *I'm Henry Ford, on this earth to eat your soul.* 20. Got a job working for the baby food company, counting cans of mashed beets, broccoli, meats. 21. Kept that job. 22. Wrote neat columns. 23. Of numbers. 24. Added with precision. 25. Punched. 26. The. 27. Clock. 28. The. 29. Clock. 30. The. 31. Clock. 32. *One more spot in the spotty night,* scribbled on the forehead in the mirror. 33. Sad brow of the girl on the job in the boss's bed. 34. *I am beads on an abacus.* 35. *Clicked.* 36. *From left to right.* 37. Wore a crown. 38. Of sweat. 39. Bars of the headboard trapped in small hands. 40. Woke as the only one inside the body of mulch, the body of palm smears, the rewired body of blue veins and split hairs, the body of loose and multiplying terms. 41. Breathed zeros in the damp. 42. Monitored ceiling stain's spread. 43. Pondered the unwritten book of the distant. 44. Time card. 45. *That little priest hungry for sins.* 46. Wielded the stolen grease pencil. 47. Blackened the stolen roll of fish wrapping paper, a record. 48. Of hiding places. 49. *Because street lights got replaced.* 50. *Because fields grew parking lots.*

Advice

It is time for you to stop trying to be so smart.
It is time to abandon those plans for aqueducts,
canals, sewers. It is time to burn your boats,
to jump into the next free dingy, to run

yourself aground on foreign land. It is time
to smash every inhibition on the shores of progress,
then loll in the rubble, flinging shards of ship
at gulls as you build empires in the sand
beneath a beach umbrella. Basically,
it is time to stop trying so hard.
Instead, lie back and listen to the waves
smashing shells to bits. Think of it
as a chorus goading you to greater heights
or as wild beasts begging to be caged.
Basically, it is time for you to be heard.
Remember to enunciate. Pay attention
to vowels, the way they seduce
regardless of the words they inhabit.
Recognize how the names of things
slide off their thingness like fried fish
from an oily plate. Smell the fishy fragrance,
injected into the steamy air by the mere
mention of *dinner*. Fondle your imaginary
skillet. How hard and dark and hot it is.
This is just the beginning of your power.
You will find new oceans, you will reside
in a do-or-die mode. This is not necessarily
a problem and thus the ironic, absurdist tone
you have become accustomed to
must also be abandoned. You must be
patient. You must quietly await
your one authentic voice. As Pound said,
quoting Beardsley: Beauty is slow.

For me, on the other hand, it is over,
politically, and as a human being.
I will never talk about myself again.
I will be taciturn, modest.
You will continue to look at me
from the outside and not know
what I have suffered. Still,
it may be difficult to forget
that I have been your leader.
It is this indebtedness
that will define you
as my greatest joy.

Rebecca Wolff

Rebecca Wolff was born in 1967 in New York City, dropped out of Bennington College, received her BA from the University of Massachusetts at Amherst, and holds an MFA from the University of Iowa Writers' Workshop. Her poems have appeared in numerous journals, including BOMB, Boston Review, Grand Street, Open City, and The Paris Review. Wolff is the author of Manderley (University of Illinois Press, 2001), a National Poetry Series selection, and Figment (Norton, 2004), winner of the Barnard New Women Poets Prize. Wolff founded the literary magazine Fence in 1997 and its imprint Fence Books in 2001. Recently the Visiting Writer-in-Residence at Boise State University in Idaho, Wolff is a poetry instructor at The New School, a freelance editor, and the editor of The Constant Critic, a poetry review website. She lives in Hudson, New York, with her husband, the fiction writer Ira Sher, and their two children, Asher Wolff and Margot Sher.

Press Play

In your truck without a notion, fighting a lot of feeling
with a huge supply of answers, we are listeners.

By this dim lighting that we sometimes find disquieting
songs play, stiff vocal support for common
tears, *tears* rising fast
and falling down like the dysfunctional word it is.

Turn my cheek to you: fuzz, deflected angle. You see me.
My face toward you I see you, the gauzy lens of you.

Messenger, decrease the pressure of the song on me.

Lie down with me. It can't be that I don't love you.
Every second rocketing, summoned.
What will we have once our songs
are relegated to their place? *A rise*

in the level of substandard expectancy,
a fluttering without correction in the ear
of the candidate, an indigenous people gone
delinquent, marginalized.

You must guess and guess again. Terrible waters
break over my head. I hum opportunistically,
fantasizing several eventualities. We speak less, we
kiss and kiss until the kiss
falls meaningless.

Sybil

1. These are the vague demands you make on me

2. (that I) assemble
    (to) recollect
    (to) decode
    ( ) associate

3. that I admit, fraught with difficulty, reintegration
    is no day at the beach in eggshell tints
    "The inmates start to get brave and a little crazy"
    when they hear that friendly voice—the matron.

4. (But that's also my mind, lost)
    Her epic poem on the constraints society places on the

5. misunderstood.

6. Everything can't be…a product of imagination
    The reasons for doing this are many *and* variable
    and *I'm ready for my close-up…*

7. You know that scrimshaw's been outlawed
    Finally, they tried an antipsychotic on me
    This had an unexpectedly positive effect
    on the general population, the dissimulation,
    the oppression

8. the faint aroma of performing seals.
    With that same arrogant look on his face,
    a man related to you commits suicide
    in a dark room, tonight. I am "a psychic,"
    but she is psychic
    Sarcasm not in her repertoire.

9. If you are transparent it is for transcendence.
    A good friend, she hears herself telling me
    "there is more to my essential character,
    more that is most essentially me."

10. Don't think of how much time we've wasted
    blood on your protruding lower lip
    the dead hours are really dead
    (inchoate)
    (insensate)

11. with such good will and sex
    appeal young girls descend
    the staircase. My ears ring
    and my vision fails. I must be
    speaking the truth

12. ...the cat came back.
    Padding on sore paws over ninety miles
    to the old homestead,
    destroyed by fire

13. the bull moose lets out a roar.
    Making the music I'm famous for.
    Rope's indulgence gives

14. ...the void rushes in.
    Is that a musket mounted
    on the wide-planked wall?
    Or a yoke?

15. Something brainless about that half
    of the bracket.
    The registration
    of sound on my mind,

16. it was as though she'd placed them there for me to see.
    I am only in the picture at one end
    —this is probably more than you ever wanted to know
    about me. Men outside.
    I'm a woman
    in a pastel field.
    What I want out of a

fuck-scene: continuity. In
fear of you.

Lamb, Willow: An Arch Dolefulness Has Taken Me This Far

If you like Chance
and you think you might live forever
listen: They say death comes to us all.
They say: Tuesday Death comes to everybody.

Then if you really think about it,
it starts to seem unlikely,

dust the most forgiving
of all elements. Rinsed clean, I am, I say, through
no particular effort.

Once more I am in the right place but with the wrong feelings.
Festival of Mysteries, Carnival of Absolute Purchasing Power.

Damp-earth smell rises up
from the rigid enclosure,
terraced zone of eternal rest. I brought myself here
for one whole day; I bought an all-day
pass. Flashbulb pops off in the exclusive crypt:

You said you wanted to see...

Here is a machine that kills
cancer. By liquefying
cells and freezing them and then cracking the bad cells
into a million pieces and vacuuming them up with a tiny
nozzle. It's so effective, we are all
living long lives. You made your living

as a nurse in the old country.
Only the knowledge that I had done it before

allowed me to think that I could possibly
do it again. The demystification of meantime

into a magic circle—it is, essentially,
mine: my job to make it smarter, a dog
and puppy show. Illimitless

deep pathos of the infant cosmology;
amusement park of abbreviation.
More important the unlimited freefall
in the spot you bury your demon:

It goes down,
while you grow up, and last the centuries
as a lamb or willow

Lamb or willow,
wherever you go,

fear
the living *and* the dead
inertial and nocturnal
energies a winding shroud

(I was born
with a yellow brain
and cannot make up stories)

it can be as short as you want it
it can be as long as you want it.
That's not your temperature, that's
a homemade contaminant.

Spacious Sity of Eternal Rest
of rectangular shape wherein I will find

coagulate.

Rinsed clean, I am, I say, and
it hardly matters

Spring, Summer, Winter

From the land, the water
from the water, the land

instrument to medium in the meantime

stuck out here in the devastation in the forest
in the middle of fucking nowhere
between landmass and incontinence

camp and derangement, the more songlike
the further we row
from our figmented shore

Mark Wunderlich

Mark Wunderlich was born in 1968 in Winona, Minnesota, and grew up near rural Fountain City, Wisconsin. He attended Concordia College's Institute for German Studies, the University of Wisconsin-Madison, and Columbia University, where he received his MFA. He is the author of two books, *The Anchorage* (University of Massachusetts, 1999), winner of the 1999 Lambda Literary Award, and *Voluntary Servitude* (Graywolf, 2004). Individual poems have appeared in *Boston Review, Fence, New England Review, The Paris Review, The Yale Review*, and elsewhere. Wunderlich is the recipient of an NEA fellowship, an Amy Lowell Traveling Fellowship, a Massachusetts Cultural Council Fellowship, two fellowships from The Fine Arts Work Center in Provincetown, and a Wallace Stegner Fellowship from Stanford University. He has taught at Barnard College, Columbia University, Ohio University, San Francisco State University, Sarah Lawrence College, Stanford University, and Stonehill College. Wunderlich is currently a member of the literature faculty at Bennington College in Vermont, and lives near the village of Catskill in New York's Hudson Valley.

Amaryllis

after Rilke

You've seen a cat consume a hummingbird,
scoop its beating body from the pyracantha bush
and break its wings with tufted paws
before marshaling it, whole, into its bone-tough throat;
seen a boy, heart racing with cocaine, climb
from a car window to tumble on the ground,
his search for pleasure ending in skinned palms;
heard a woman's shouts as she is pushed into the police cruiser,
large hand pressing her head into the door,
red lights spinning their tornado in the street.

But all of that will fade; on the table is the amaryllis
pushing its monstrous body in the air,
requiring no soil to do so, having wound
two seasons' rot into a white and papered bulb,
exacting nutrition from the winter light,
culling from a complex chemistry the tints
and fragments that tissue and pause and build
again the pigment and filament.
The flower crescendos toward the light,
though better to say despite it,

gores through gorse and pebble
to form a throat—so breakable—open
with its tender pistils, damp with rosin,
simple in its simple sex, to burn and siphon
itself in air. Tongue of fire, tongue
of earth, the amaryllis is a rudiment
forming its meretricious petals
to trumpet and exclaim.

How you admire it. It vibrates
in the draft, a complex wheel
bitten with cogs, swelling and sexual
though nothing will touch it. You forced it
to spread itself, to cleave and grasp,
remorseless, open to your assignments—
this is availability, this is tenderness,
this red plane is given to the world.
Sometimes the heart breaks. Sometimes
it is not held hostage. The red world
where cells prepare for the unexpected
splays open at the window's ledge.
Be not human you inhuman thing.
No anxious, no foible, no hesitating hand.
Pry with fiber your course through sand.
Point your whole body toward the unknown
away from the dead.
Be water and light and land—
no contrivance, no gasp, no dream
where there is no head.

Voluntary Servitude

In a valley in Wisconsin there is a graveyard where the graves are flooded
   by a spring.

You say, Don't wreck me, and I say I won't, but how can I know that?

To see a man in shackles, how you feel about that, depends on whether
   the servitude is voluntary.

The bodies are intact in their graves, soaked in a bath of ice. Hair a net
   around them.

Music does not console me. Words in books rise up and scatter.

A friend told me of a snake that came into her room one night.

The house was in Pennsylvania. She lived there alone.

In the dark she could hear it—dry, slipping onto boards like a stocking
rolled from a leg.

It retreated when she turned on a light. There was a dark hole at the floor.

Residents disagree about the cemetery.

Some think to say the bodies are intact is wrong.

To suggest that there is anything abnormal is unfit thinking.

I have a new story to tell you.

In it, there is a girl. It's a story a friend once told me.

Some forms of servitude are voluntary. Some shackles too—

Some you can remove. But this story—

you start in the middle, in the thick and marrow of it.

I think you'll like it. Let me tell it to you.

Lying side by side. In the dark.

Fourteen Things We're Allowed to Bring to the Underworld

Did you get the photo I sent? The horse? I would take her with me. I used
to go to her stall and just press my ear against that swimming belly, the
liquid of her. I could sleep lying atop that animal, all iron smell, shifting
from foot to foot. All hay.

What would you take? What things? L. says Fire, and I understand that, and
would take that too. Architecture, fretwork for structure. The miniature tea

set for delicacy. Opera for blood. Iron for fortitude and weight. Linen as a reminder of skin. Crystal for simple music. Tin. Leather for harnessing. Paper. Milk. A boat. I'll stop one short.

Ron Vawter is gone, I imagine you've heard. He was on an airplane, over the ocean when he was taken. Imagine, in flight. Remember it, the Soho garage where we saw him, reclined on the dais, draping himself in strings of beads and wrapping his head in a silver turban, the turban's refusal. He was thin, I was shocked by that, and the lesion bloomed on the patch of his leg we weren't meant to see.

Give me this one thing. Summer is impossible, you must understand. I cannot survive there, that house. All day the muddy river pushes by, and you there watching it.

Predictions about a Black Car

Four boys have been arrested for killing geese. This is how it happened: The first pinned back the white-pinioned wings. The second stretched the neck, held shut the damaged and rubbery bill. The third bit through feather and esophagus, his mouth filled with its blood. The last boy kept the other geese herded in the corner, watched. I do not know what will become of them, though the town hopes for something extravagant.

By now I know you've heard of my accident—the black car stopped in front of me, my dramatic spin to the ditch. You were there when the psychic warned me about such a car, before she rubbed her hands with alcohol and set her palms ablaze. At the hospital they x-rayed my wrist, its club and piston flaring into the hand's calcium branch, the flesh translucent and ashy, an undersea picture.

I've been reading a book about a storm, folded into thirds, twisting its way north with a tropical fury. In it, the fishing boat, a moveable target, is pitched against the waves until its light is finally doused, hull pulled apart, another story with property at its center.

There was a morning this spring when the sky was washed of any choler. I could hear the ocean from my small yard, breathing in and out. Two gulls cried from their perch near the chimney. You weren't here, and I'm sorry for that; my heart was quiet, in need of no other.

Monica Youn

Monica Youn was born in 1971 in Berkeley, California, and was raised in Houston, Texas. She received her undergraduate degree from Princeton University, her Master's degree from Oxford University, a law degree from Yale University, and a Wallace Stegner Fellowship from Stanford. Her first book is *Barter* (Graywolf Press, 2003). She lives in New York City, where she is an entertainment lawyer.

Naglfar

she said   they are building the ship
the color of steam   the color of salt

the end of the world   she stopped
speaking   she was alone

she spent hours   cutting her fingernails
they won't take them   when I die

she said   for the ridged sides
of their ship   cutting off

the white crescents   they looked
like tiny boats   they collected

in her pockets   in the seams of her dress
I am trying   she said

holding out   her nailless hands
to prevent   the end of the world

Ragnarok   she said
if startled   her eyes strayed

to the notched petals of the dogwoods
the flecks of mica in the path

Night Ferry to Naxos 1

All your carefully cultivated notions of realism

come to an end here, where the sentimental pink
funnels into the Peloponnese

like a rum and grenadine cocktail
poured down a taut throat. Tourist,

this is how the peace drains into you.
Your fingers uncurl on the deck railings,

and over your head, a spiraling umbilical
of ship-smoke loops back to the brown air of Athens,

which only now, behind you, is beginning
to take shape: a smog-shielded dome.

The flattering breeze picks out your contours
in silverpoint—its insinuations

sweet as fresh-laid sheets, a bedtime story,
mother love. Already above you,

half-heard, a tattoo of wingbeats, bare feet
racing in circles on hard-packed dirt.

You will have to become a hero like the rest of us.

Night Ferry to Naxos 2

Another round of *Dona Nobis Pacem*

from the Italian ladies below deck and you know
you'll never be rid of it now.

You're still humming *sotto voce* at 3 A.M.
When the hold's thick wall falls away

to reveal this island, coy as a cameo
on a widow's black bosom.

Since April, a honeyed
habit-forming dew

has been collecting
in the hollows of the rocks,

and the local myths, freshly washed,
have been polishing their bare limbs.

All for you, wind-whipped
and shivering on the gangplank: the *deus*

ex machina in silver lamé,
a lobster on an enormous plate, a birth....

Nothing you can do will disappoint them now.

Flatlanders

Here the sky's all spreading belly,
postcoital, pressing the ground
deeper into the ground.

Rumors of incest: a folded
Rorschach, a mirror in love with a lake.

In fenced backyards across Fort Bend County
buttered-up high-school sweethearts
lie on sheets of tinfoil for a tan;

wake up crying, siren-red,
eyelids swollen into temporary lips.

*

We know no other shapes
than those that contain us;
we have built our zoneless city,

hub of freeways, a dark ètoile.
In Tony's, an ageless lady stirs

her iced tea till the ice cubes melt
to sharp-boned shadows of themselves;
a wink of lime slice, her gem-knuckled hand.

In the garage of St. Joseph's Children's Hospital,
shivering, an intern in short-sleeved scrubs

pulls a soft gold spot into the center
of his cigarette filter, an indrawn breath.

*

Hurricane season in the suburbs:
windows asterisked

with masking tape—crosshairs,
false-eyelashed eyes. We remember

when the whole city was a pavé brooch
most of us would covet.

Sometimes we feel lucky:
the hurricane's eye—

our shy neighbors emerge
into the ultramarine
spotlight, the settling leaves,

stand hushed, reverent,
peering up the skirts of the storm.

*

In the eighth grade we learned
a cone pushed through a plane
is a spreading circle to the Flatlanders.

There's no point in looking up.
From time to time a football drops

from the technicolor buzz of stadium lights
into the supplicant hands
of some misshapen archetypal hero.

And on the last night of every year,
the sullen boot-clad men of Pasadena

park on the feeder roads, sit for hours
on the roofs of their pickups,

trying to shoot the fireworks out of the sky.

C. Dale Young

C. Dale Young was born in 1969 and grew up in Palm Beach, Florida. He earned his BS at Boston College, and holds both an MFA and an MD from the University of Florida. His work has appeared in *The Best American Poetry 1996*, *The Paris Review*, *Ploughshares*, *Poetry*, *The Virginia Quarterly Review*, and elsewhere. He is the author of *The Day Underneath the Day* (Northwestern University Press, 2001). His second manuscript, *The Second Person*, was a finalist for the James Laughlin Prize from the Academy of American Poets and is forthcoming from Four Way Books. Young currently practices medicine, serves as Poetry Editor of the *New England Review*, and teaches in the low-residency MFA program at Warren Wilson College. He lives in San Francisco.

Proximity

I have forgotten my skin, misplaced my body.
Tricks of mind, a teacher once said: the man
with the amputated right arm convinced he could

feel the sheets and air-conditioned air touching
the phantom skin. There must be a syndrome
for such a thing, a named constellation of symptoms

that correspond to the ghost hand and what it senses.
This morning, I felt your hand touch me on the shoulder
the way you would when you turned over in your sleep.

What syndrome describes this? Not the sense of touch
but of being touched. Waking, I felt my own body,
piece by piece, dissolving: my hands, finger by finger,

then the legs and the chest leaving the heart exposed
and beating, the traveling pulses of blood
expanding the great vessels. The rib cage vanished

and then the spine. If your right hand offends you,
wrote Mark, cut it off and throw it away,
for it is better for you to lose a part than to lose

the whole. But I have no word for this phantom
touch, and the fully real feeling of the hair
on your arm shifting over my own as your hand

moved from my shoulder and out across my chest.
Desire makes me weak, crooned the diva,
or was it Augustine faced with his own flesh?

Whisper me a few lies, god, beautiful and familiar lies.

Torn

There was the knife and the broken syringe
then the needle in my hand, the Tru-Cut
followed by the night-blue suture.

The wall behind registration listed a man
with his face open. Through the glass doors,
I saw the sky going blue to black as it had

24 hours earlier when I last stood there gazing off
into space, into the nothingness of that town.
Bat to the head. Knife to the face. They tore

down the boy in an alleyway, the broken syringe
skittering across the sidewalk. No concussion.
But the face torn open, the blood congealed

and crusted along his cheek. *Stitch up the faggot
in bed 6* is all the ER doctor had said.
Queasy from the lack of sleep, I steadied

my hands as best as I could after cleaning up
the dried blood. There was the needle
and the night-blue suture trailing behind it.

There was the flesh torn and the skin open.
I sat there and threw stitch after stitch
trying to put him back together again.

When the tears ran down his face,
I prayed it was a result of my work
and not the work of the men in the alley.

Even though I knew there were others to be seen,
I sat there and slowly threw each stitch.
There were always others to be seen. There was

always the bat and the knife. I said nothing,
and the tears kept welling in his eyes.
And even though I was told to be "quick and dirty,"

told to spend less than 20 minutes, I sat there
for over an hour closing the wound so that each edge
met its opposing match. I wanted him

to be beautiful again. *Stitch up the faggot in bed 6.*
Each suture thrown reminded me I would never be safe
in that town. There would always be the bat

and the knife, always a fool willing to tear me open
to see the dirty faggot inside. And when they
came in drunk or high with their own wounds,

when they bragged about their scuffles with the knife
and that other world of men, I sat there and sutured.
I sat there like an old woman and sewed them up.

Stitch after stitch, the slender exactness of my fingers
attempted perfection. I sat there and sewed them up.

Infidelity

The sun hovering a mile above the edge
of the Pacific, the wind rifling through the sea-grass...
Early evening of the longest day of your life.

Vast is this water, vast and incapable of solace.
Beside you, the wind and an empty space
to be filled with a fistful of sand.

If knowledge is understanding which questions
to ask, and wisdom is knowing which questions
to ask again, then what is it you seek, you

who have questions for which there are no answers?
There is a sleeping god in heaven.
There is a sleeping god who lets the loved one

secretly poison you in your sleep.
Even your shadow wavers behind you in the grass.
Your heart beats slowly in your chest, in your ears.

For consolation, you carry a fistful of sand.
You carry yourself over the dunes with a fistful of sand
and a newly discovered love of the second person,

your shirttails small flags left in your wake.

Kevin Young

Kevin Young was born in 1970 in Lincoln, Nebraska, and grew up in Topeka, Kansas. He attended Harvard University, Brown University (where he received his MFA), and Stanford University (where he held a Wallace Stegner Fellowship). His poems have appeared in *Callaloo*, *Fence*, *The Kenyon Review*, *The New Yorker*, *The Paris Review*, *Verse*, *The Virginia Quarterly Review*, and elsewhere. Young is the author of the poetry collections *Most Way Home* (William Morrow, 1995; Zoland, 2000), a National Poetry Series selection and winner of the John C. Zacharis First Book Award from *Ploughshares*; *To Repel Ghosts* (Zoland, 2001), a finalist for the James Laughlin Prize from the Academy of American Poets; and *Jelly Roll: A Blues* (Knopf, 2003), winner of the Paterson Poetry Prize and a finalist for the National Book Award and *The Los Angeles Times* Book Prize. His most recent poetry collection, *Black Maria: Poems Produced and Directed by Kevin Young*, was published by Knopf in February, 2005. Young is also the editor of *Giant Steps: The New Generation of African American Writers* (HarperPerennial, 2000), *Blues Poems* (Everyman's Library, 2003), and *John Berryman: Selected Poems* (Library of America, 2004). Named a "Writer on the Verge" by *The Village Voice* and the recipient of fellowships from the Guggenheim Foundation and the NEA, Young has served on the creative writing faculties of the University of Georgia and Indiana University. He is now the Atticus Haygood Professor of English and Creative Wrtiting and Curator of the Raymond Danowski Poetry Library at Emory University in Atlanta, Georgia.

Soundtrack

Banging out a symphony
in a typewriter key, I didn't hear

My door creak open, only
her *Ah-hum* & perfume

My knocking knees

When, uninvited, she sat
herself down. Crossed

Her legs like the county line

& I, some boot-
legger driven far

For such strong lightning.

She leaned & asked
once more could I find—

A friend? her man?
something so valuable

She could not say?

Anythin,
was once my answer—

Had spent off-meter hours,
hundreds, snooping for her

Working under the cover—

Was left with only
a fake-mustache rash

& some prop glasses
without glass.

My heart twin
cufflinks then.

*

Tonight, her eyes welling
over like an oil rig.

I let my mind, like
a housewife, or eye, wander:

August again
    & I eleven, filled with Sunday

& early supper—
    hummocked, happy.

How the sycamores sang,
    the cicadas.

This is long before
    gunfire, before the Colt

& rope & a river
    I am still swimming.

Long before I arrived
    in our starved city, before derringer days

& nights even darker for all
    the streetlights…

Her hands tapped
an impatient Morse, fanned

Two lace gloves. *Well?*
Her veil smile.

Adam's-apple bob. Ceiling-fan swirl.

*

I thanked her for
her time, then sent her

Away packing, teetering
on unsheathed stilletos.

Her kisses tender, a resignation—

I may be back
to her like an undertaker

Whose scent no one can shake—

For now I'll ignore the lack
of knocking, the quiet

Except for wind
& tin-roof rain,

The phone's pleading ring.

The Rushes

I had everything arranged

I bought orchids
her favorite shade

Received this hot tip
from a dice-eyed snitch

Gave him something bottled up
in exchange

For her real name

This stoolie told me all
odds stacked against me

The 10-to-1 bookie

Who called her cookie,
trouble, doll

The gangster moll

Had sworn me legs
broke to match my heart.

I laughed & ordered up
another tall

Bottle of tales. Deal
me in. Suicide kings.

*

Planned she & I would meet
where the dead sleep, pretending

No one there knew me—

Beneath the morgue moon,
blue light tugging at seas

One day, I thought, that
will be me

In the godawful ground—

Our kisses cemeteries

The suicides coughing
in their restless deep

The moon autopsied
to find out if it waned

From natural causes.
Bulletproof hearses.

*

Soon my frame grew
hazy, swayed

As if memory
is not this etched thing

A useless machine

I dreamt the sleep that sews
the eyes up

Loan-shark chums
bobbing shallow water

Recall what happened last
time we held—

How like a trapped
parrot she talked

How soon she sang

*

I snapped back to see
her hushed beside me

Soft-focus frame fading

The fedoraed darkness moving—

Our arms open
as fire, we embraced

While bullets ricocheted
off stone angels

Worn down by weather
& winnowed by tears

Of red-clad widows
in crocodile heels

Who visit just one hour a year.

Negative

Wake to find everything black
what was white, all the vice
versa—white maids on TV, black

sitcoms that star white dwarfs
cute as pearl buttons. Black Presidents.
Black Houses. White horse

candidates. All bleach burns
clothes black. Drive roads
white as you are, white songs

on the radio stolen by black bands
like secret pancake recipes, white back-up
singers, ball-players & boxers all

white as tar. Feathers on chickens
dark as everything, boiling in the pot
that called the kettle honky. Even

whites of the eye turn dark, pupils
clear & changing as a cat's.
Is this what we've wanted

& waited for? to see snow
covering everything black
as Christmas, dark pages written

white upon? All our eclipses bright,
dark stars shooting across pale
sky, glowing like ash in fire, shower

every skin. Only money keeps
green, still grows & burns like grass
under dark daylight.

Song of Smoke

To watch you walk
cross the room in your black

corduroys is to see
civilization start—

the *wish-*
whish-whisk

of your strut is flint
striking rock—the spark

of a length of cord
rubbed till

smoke starts—you stir
me like coal

and for days smoulder.
I am no more

a Boy Scout and, besides,
could never

put you out—you
keep me on

all day like an iron, out
of habit—

you threaten, brick-
house, to burn

all this down. You leave me
only a chimney.

Errata

Baby, give me just
one more hiss

We must lake it fast
morever

I want to cold you
in my harms

& never get lo

I live you so much
it perts!

Baby, jive me gust
one more bliss

Whisper your
neat nothings in my near

Can we hock each other
one tore mime?

All light wrong?

Baby, give me just
one more briss

My won & homely

You wake me meek
in the needs

Mill you larry me?

Baby, hive me just
one more guess

With this sing
I'll thee shed

Matthew Zapruder

Matthew Zapruder was born in 1967 in Washington, D.C. He holds a BA in Russian Literature from Amherst College, an MA in Slavic Languages and Literatures from the University of California at Berkeley, and an MFA in Poetry from the University of Massachusetts at Amherst. His poems have appeared in such journals as *BOMB*, *Boston Review*, *Conduit*, *Fence*, *Harvard Review*, *jubilat*, *McSweeney's*, *The New Republic*, and *The New Yorker*. Zapruder is the author of *American Linden* (Tupelo, 2002) and *The Pajamaist* (Copper Canyon, 2006), and the co-translator of *Secret Weapon*, the final collection by the late Romanian poet Eugen Jebeleanu. He works as an editor with Wave Books, teaches creative writing at The New School in New York City, and is the co-curator of the KGB Monday Night Poetry Reading Series. Zapruder is also a member of the permanent faculty of the Juniper Summer Writing Institute at the University of Massachusetts in Amherst and was recently a Visiting Professor at the California Institute of the Arts. He lives in New York City.

Canada

By Canada I have always been fascinated.
All that snow and acquiescing.
All that emptiness, all those butterflies
marshalled into an army of peace.
Moving north away from me
Canada has no border, away
like the state its northern border
withers into the skydome. In a world
full of mistrust and self-medication
I have always hated Canada.
It makes me feel like I'm shouting
at a child for letting a handful
of pine needles run through his fist.
Canada gets along with everyone
while I hang, a dark cloud
above the schoolyard. I know
we need war, all the skirmishes
to keep our borders where
we have placed them, all
the migration, all the difference.
Just like Canada the Dalai Lama
is now in Canada, and everyone
is fascinated. When they come

to visit me, no one ever leaves me
saying, the most touching thing
about him is he's so human.
Or, I was really glad to hear
so many positive ideas regardless
of the consequences expressed.
Or I could drink a case of you.
No one has ever pedaled
every inch of thousands of roads
through me to raise awareness
for my struggle for autonomy.
I have pity but no respect for others,
which according to certain religious leaders
is not compassion, just ordinary
love based on attitudes toward myself.
I wonder how long I can endure.
In Canada the leaves are falling.
When they do each one rustles
maybe to the white-tailed deer
of sadness, and it's clear
that whole country does not exist
to make me feel crappy
like a candelabra hanging
above the prison world,
condemned to freely glow.

School Street

My house is so small
I bang my head
just thinking about it.

The house is old,
and "structurally unsound."
If you smoke inside

all the paint peels off
and the walls
fall down.

I sleep
in the refrigerator
with my feet sticking out,

I'm not sure why.
Somehow
the entire house

manages to face north.
A mad dog paces the attic
and howls

until I give him my dinner.
The backyard
is full of vipers.

The front yard
is an interstate.
To walk out that door

is suicide.
I'm plagued
by the demons of loneliness.

They mix my metaphors,
then brew me
a hellish soup.

The demons of loneliness
sit on my chest
and play with my navel,

leaving me
bruised and out of breath.
They are being punished too.

One of them even said,
"Like you
we are affected

by the cold the noise
and the wretched ceilings,
but the worst

is your endless complaining."
A man came to read the meter,
but he died

of a heart attack.
So they sent another man,
but he died

of one too.
Finally they sent
an archangel.

He lives next door.
All day he practices
sign language

into a mirror,
flexing his wings.
I know

he is there,
staring into his world,
keeping me

awake
with his silent
folktales.

Whoever You Are

As the wayward satellite believes its rescuers
will come with white and weightless hands,
and the rescuers turning and floating believe
in their tethers and all those uninspected latches,
as madness believes in the organizing principle,
and allows it to strap her down on the gurney,
and the tiny island believes the sound
of a harp will arrive on the wings of a gull,
as the olive believes it is filled with light,
and its oil will someday grace a god's tongue,
as my arms flail outward and strike my forehead
in belief of a vestigial prayer process,
and I believe to allow them such historical pleasure
is hardly harmless from time to time,
as the transistor radio hears the woman
muttering and believes she requests
she be buried in the front yard with only her knitting

far from her husband the master of stratagems,
and weeping daughters once believed
their father had coated each grassblade with poison
and woke one morning to some twigs on the lawn
to believe they were dead starlings,
as the mountain believed it could stay hollow
long enough to return the tunnellers home,
and their wives believed in trying to believe
that rumble through clear skies was thunder,
I believe that is not what you wanted,
for you are only a guardian
geared to one particular moment
conjectured in no saintly book of apocrypha
when slowly at last the trucks will pull
into a warehouse shot through with shadows
and wherever I am I will see candles floating
on the ritual arms of two dark canals
and you will allow me to step I believe
into the mechanism
and tear off your wings

Andrew Zawacki

Andrew Zawacki was born in 1972 in Warren, Pennsylvania. He received a BA from the College of William and Mary and, as a Rhodes Scholar, an M.Phil. from Oxford and an M.Litt. from the University of St. Andrews. The recipient of a Fulbright Fellowship at Monash University in Australia, as well as fellowships at the Salzburg Seminar in Austria and the Sorbonne in Paris, Zawacki has published his poetry in *Denver Quarterly*, *New American Writing*, *The New Republic*, *The New Yorker*, *Volt*, and elsewhere in the US, Australia, and Europe. His criticism has appeared in *Boston Review*, *Talisman*, *Times Literary Supplement*, and numerous other books and journals. A former fellow of the Slovenian Writers' Association, Zawacki edited the anthology *Afterwards: Slovenian Writing 1945–1995* (White Pine, 1999) and is translating Slovenian poet Ales Debeljak's latest book. He is also the coeditor of the literary journal *Verse* and *The Verse Book of Interviews* (Verse, 2005). Zawacki is currently a PhD candidate in Social Thought at the University of Chicago, as well as an Assistant Professor of English at the University of Georgia. His chapbook, *Masquerade* (Vagabond, 2001), won the Poetry Society of America's Alice Fay Di Castagnola Award, and his two full-length volumes of poetry are *By Reason of Breakings* (Georgia, 2002) and *Anabranch* (Wesleyan, 2004).

Credo

You say wind is only wind
& carries nothing nervous
in its teeth.
        I do not believe it.

I have seen leaves desist
             from moving
although the branches
            move, & I
believe a cyclone has secrets
the weather is ignorant of.
              I believe
in the violence of not knowing.

I've seen a river lose its course
& join itself again,
            watched it court
a stream & coax the stream
into its current,

                  & I have seen
rivers, not unlike
                  you, that failed to find
their way back.
                 I believe the rapport
between water & sand, the advent
from mirror to face.

                  I believe in rain
to cover what mourns,
                   in hail that revives
& sleet that erodes, believe
whatever falls
              is a figure of rain

& now I believe in torrents that take
everything down with them.

They sky calls it quits,
                 or so I believe,
when air, or earth, or air
has had enough.

                 I believe in disquiet,
the pressure it plies, believe a cloud
to govern the limits of night.

                 I say I,
but little is left to say it, much less
mean it—
            & yet I do.

                 Let there be
no mistake:
            I do not believe
things are reborn in fire.
They're consumed by fire

& the fire has a life of its own.

Velocity Among the Ruins
of Angel Republic

I

In that gesture toward signing the stages to fullness,
even if nothing went without saying, or everything stayed
despite what's been said, distance would have to be structured with all the rest.

Turning around would be figured in too, since what was back there
could only distract, or weaken the will to keep rowing away
from rooftops and towers with ladders propped up,

the customs house and its officer, blind, standing in sunlight
waving good-bye, as if another had already paid for my ticket.
A school had been built on the island from hammered-out hulls,

fallout shelters lit by old lanterns, a hospital covered in palm fronds and snow,
a bunkhouse where boys dreamed of walking on tightrope to morning.
There were uniforms folded on fishline with no one to fill them

and statues too far from the shore for their shadows to reach.
It meant taking whatever heals, or offers a lesser regret for a greater
after loss, being lost, or finding oneself alone and still in love,

framed by a picture that never got painted of parting the water
to measure both sides, here where the trees and the hanged men below
are waiting with me for the branches to break.

II

The weather bureau, he told me, has just announced calm on the coastlines
under a constant assembly of clouds, and whether sirocco evasions
have been handed down or sent up from the colonies,

they're certain to pass one another in transit, since tariffs are higher
after the war, and people ignoring the news from that country have never
exercised themselves with death or prayer. But at the interior

a city resists the dueling hydraulics of maskchange and moonshine frequencies
and the stars in that town flicker like a pierrot drinking honeybees
from a teacup, while leaves keep brimming silver along the sand. It's years,

he said, since the acrobats left, and sundials relinquished ownership of air
to a murder of crows, but the monument shading the courtyard is there,
near sulfur lamps staining pink the settings of cirrus. And whenever

the prologues to night are enacted, the dimming sun and its grace note gloss
on the bay—listen, you'll hear your self-portrait unveiling, an angelus
rising out of indifference, to haunt you with a blueprint of such vacancies

by which we visit ourselves. Those who live here say little of being forgiven
while sculling the waves, but passing into where sirens don't answer,
no longer remember which came before, the punishment or the pain.

III
So that, in a further vicinity, under another arcature, I might be counted
among them, the sceneries sculpted their marble seductions in luminous balance,
piano-wire drizzle, a filigree archive to puzzle whomever would watch it

from a balcony, or the gardener's doorstep, sampan docks where conclusions
awaited departure, and motioned for clearance. Matchflare and torpor, without
interruption, were part of the furniture, nuanced in polish, and instruments

glinting long after the surgeons had gone. Almanacs and atlases made no mention
of lesser solitudes, the survey outlining airdrome and hangar, acres once flushed
by acetylene flares, but what I pulled up there, in galvanized strips, kept leading

toward an accumulation of dusk, a gutted lighthouse from which I could see
prerogatives placed in an order no breath could disturb. The gulf's exertions
gave way to a silence, and raindrops, like questions, beaded the huts to conduct

a woman arranged on a parasol bridge, an aspect of twilight, a choir in herself,
tapping frozen glasses with a spoon, as embers, a chromatic scale,
processions of cartwheeling lights and what else could be staged: tinted water

poised in mid-falling on landscapes still steaming in darkness, a study in form,
geographies pitched at the vanishing point of appearance concealing desire:
space for a leaning, a pivot of air, for where we would stand in that storm.

Vertigo

If wind that wastes its time among the trees
escapes itself, only to end up quarantined
by a derelict squall from the north,

and if the air turns somersaults, miming
the outtakes of dusk, scandaled by an early frost
and punished for its coldness by the cold—

then, like a bullet that lodges in bone,
becoming a piece of the body,
you will not awake apart from your name.

And I will not be not a part of you.

*

There are things I would settle
with myself. Why, for instance,
as autumn unravels, I cannot mortar

myself to myself, nothing but sunlight
littered from here to the sun. By I
I mean a window, redness grazing the lake

at dawn, or an echo winnowing out
along a wall, hard pressed to hide itself
and straining for the voice it vanished from.

I mean so many windows. So much red.

*

Please do not misunderstand.
That woman who carries winter
inside her, dizzied by snowfall

that won't level off—I would say
I love her, but I is too strong a word
and love not strong enough.

[from] Viatica

one of me stuttered and one
of me broke, and one of me tried

to fasten a line to one of
me untying it from me:

one of me watched a fisherman haul
a sand shark from the breaker,

while another was already years later,
returned to where a local man

baited for striper but landed a shark:
one of me sat under olivine clouds,

clouds of cerise, a courtesan sky,
and one of me sunned himself

as a child, imagining a fish rod
turned fermata: one waved a sash

of cornflower blue, one heard
a windmill, one heard the wind,

one waved goodbye to an imminent,
leftover love: and one strolled

barefoot and sunburnt across
the nickel inhibitions of afternoon,

tossing amber bottles at a smoke tree,
the gun lake, swimming toward

his family on the dock as twilight fell,
as the same boy stayed behind

to look at him swim: one believed
a father could be killed by falling rock,

and one woke up to find he'd only
dreamt, although his father was dead,

and one believed in a beautiful house
not built by any hand: one promised

nothing would break, and nothing did,
and one saw breaking everywhere

and could not say what he saw

Rachel Zucker

Rachel Zucker was born in 1971 in New York City. She studied psychology at Yale University and received her MFA from the University of Iowa Writers' Workshop. Since then, she has worked as a photographer, a gem dealer, a certified labor doula, and an Adjunct Professor at Yale and NYU. Zucker is the author of *Eating in the Underworld* (Wesleyan, 2003), *The Last Clear Narrative* (Wesleyan, 2004), and the forthcoming collection *The Bad Wife Handbook*. Winner of the Strousse Award, the Barrow Street Prize, and the Center for Book Arts Award, she has published poems in such journals as *American Poetry Review*, *Barrow Street*, *Fence*, *Pleiades*, and *Prairie Schooner*, and had her work included in *The Best American Poetry 2001*. Currently, Zucker is coediting, with poet Arielle Greenberg, an anthology of essays by women poets on mentorship, while also working on a novel and a book of nonfiction. She lives in New York City with her husband and two sons.

Diary (Underworld)

Only a mother could manufacture such a story:
the earth opened and pulled her down.

She shows my picture all over town
and worries the details of my molestation.

Terrified she screamed for mother...
but I did not scream.

She says it is like having an arm ripped
from her body. But think, Mother,

what it is to be an arm ripped from a body.
Bloody shoulder bulb, fingers twitching, useless.

Did she expect me to starve?
To wither away, mourning the tulip, primrose, crocus?

And if I have changed, so be it.
He did not choose me for my slim ankles or silken tresses.

She moans and tears her hair   *Unfair!*
There was so much I longed to teach her.

Sad Mother, who thinks she knows so much—
teach the farmer to grow seed.

The fields await instruction.

Not Knowing Nijinsky or Diaghilev

A certain kind of man asks the same question
again, again until it isn't a question but
   a threat, shove, spit in the eye.
Phyllis says *you're sitting on your power* but
I know what I'm sitting on: my ass. Obviously,
running out of language.

My desire is "A pre-electric impulse with a too-small synapse."
What a tired image that is. I sit on my power.

Finally, in the boxed-up city, night comes on
without a sunset; books push out their backs,
turn stiff arms away, press closer together.

   The editor says *we have no patience for metaphor.*

In the dream the baby carrier is crammed with plastic bags.
My ex-lover shoots hockey pucks at my breasts through a metal tube.
I want to hold you once before the world explodes I say to the baby
who is not there. Two women screaming "Filthy Jews!" die too.

   The memo from the editor: *it is even sub-Hollywood.*

I sit on my power and try to describe anything.

"My mother inside me": air in a well; a heavy, starless chill.
Her love the texture of canned lotus root, the color
a cross-section of diseased lung; slight smell of vinegar.

   The editor jots: *no patience for description.*

So I am back where I started; another old man and his helpful invective.

He suspects me. Uses the words "musicality," "mimesis";
  what do you know, if anything?

I think: I know what it is to have a child…but (truth is) not now, I only know
                what it is like.

Here: here is a picture of me in labor:

    …hand around the metal bar the body
    crushing in and in the room white-hot,
                exploding

The reason I even mention   [it]   is that I don't know anything
but memory which is nothing except—child, sleeping in my elbow—
marks and tracings, a neural map, my thoughts are like piranha,
transparent and vicious, but no one gets away with similes like that.
Where is the pool of diction the myth described? The old man
spits in my eye, says *a child is no excuse* and points, pushing me
toward the shallow pond.

In Your Version of Heaven I Am Younger

In your version of heaven I am blond, thinner,
but not so witty. In the movie version of your version
of heaven you fight God to come back to me.
It is a box office hit because you are an unbelievable character.
Nothing is real except the well-timed traffic accident
which costs 226 thousand dollars.

In real life, I am on a small bridge over a small creek.
Then it isn't a bridge but a stadium. Then a low table.
A sense of knowing the future.
There is no clear location of fear.
I want you to say you will abandon your dissertation.
I want you to ask the man in the green scrubs if I was pregnant.

Put on the preservers! they announce. *They are under your seats!*
Time to tell your wife a few last things. People are puking
in the rows around us. The jackets sweaty and too big.
We are, in this version, an image of hope.

The broadcasters are just now sniffing us out.
I am pregnant but don't know it and can't know
the fetus would have been, in any event, not viable.
No one survives. No one comes down with cancer.
The fade-out leaves a black screen over the sound of water.

The review says it is a *film noir*. The letter to the editor
says the reviewer should go back to college. The reviewer
is in graduate school writing a thesis about movies
that were never made. If they are made he will not get tenure.
If we die he has a small chance at success. A young woman
writes in: *it should, more properly, have been called an embryo.*

Photo Credits

Rick Barot / *Karim Logue*

Dan Beachy-Quick / *Sergio Vucci*

Josh Bell / *John Branseum*

David Berman / *Bernd Bodtänder*

Erica Bernheim / *Nadya Pittendrigh*

Richard Blanco / *Carlos Betancourt*

Joel Brouwer / *elin o'Hara slavick*

Oni Buchanan / *Ryan Spoering*

Stephen Burt / *Scott Streble*

Dan Chiasson / *Annie Adams*

Carrie Comer / *Benjamin Alsup*

Monica de la Torre / *Nina Subin*

Ben Doyle / *Sandra Miller*

Thomas Sayers Ellis / *John Davison*

Andrew Feld / *Pimone Triplett*

Monica Ferrell / *joanna eldredge morrissey*

Katie Ford / *Harold Baquet*

Arielle Greenberg / *Rachel Zucker*

Jennifer Grotz / *Michael P. Doyle*

Matthea Harvey / *M.P. Osie*

Terrance Hayes / *W. T. Pfefferle*

Steve Healey / *Mark Wojahn*

Thomas Heise / *Kathryn Minas*

Major Jackson / *Marion Ettlinger*

A. Van Jordan / *Carla Fielder*

Ilya Kaminsky / *Katie Farris*

Sally Keith / *Bill Dowling*

Suji Kwock Kim / *RayShortPhotos@aol.com*

James Kimbrell / *Jennifer Westfield*

Joanna Klink / *Mia Zuidaric*

Noelle Kocot / *Damon Tomblin*

Katy Lederer / *Anna Moschovakis*

Dana Levin / *Scott Caraway*

Maurice Manning / *Steve Cody*

Sabrina Orah Mark / *John Dermot Woods*

Jeffrey McDaniel / *Peter King Robbins*

Joyelle McSweeney / *Shannon Welch*

Sarah Messer / *Joel Brouwer*

Alan Michael Parker / *Felicia von Bork*

D.A. Powell / *Shawn G. Henry*

Kevin Prufer / *Eric Miles Williamson*

Srikanth Reddy / *Suzanne Buffam*

Spencer Reece / *Carol Watson*

Matthew Rohrer / *Susan McCullough*

Tessa Rumsey / *Saren Sakuri*

Patty Seyburn / *Kelly Evans*

Robyn Schiff / *Rachel Zucker*

Brenda Shaughnessy / *Heather Caldwell*

Richard Siken / *Mitoki Katsukai*

Tracy K. Smith / *Igor Solis*

Juliana Spahr / *Karen AhNee*

Larissa Szporluk / *Bowling Green University*

Brian Teare / *Cynthia Grace-Lang*

Ann Townsend / *David Baker*

Pimone Triplett / *Nick Twemlow*

Joe Wenderoth / *Tim Boehme*

Emily Wilson / *Kate Gadbow*

Suzanne Wise / *Walter Smith*

Rebecca Wolf / *Natasha Babaian*

Mark Wunderlich / *Mary Jane Dean*

Monica Youn / *Andrew Ranaudo*

C. Dale Young / *Marion Ettlinger*

Kevin Young / *Tod Martens*

Matthew Zapruder / *Primoz Cucnik*

Andrew Zawacki / *Sandrine Garet*

Rachel Zucker / *Arielle Greenberg*

Further Reading

Recommended collections published in 1995 or later by American authors born after 1960 with no more than three books:

Arnold, Craig. *Shells*. New Haven, CT: Yale University Press, 1997.

Barnett, Catherine. *Into Perfect Spheres Such Holes Are Pierced*. Farmington, ME: Alice James Books, 2004.

Barry, Quan. *Controvertibles*. Pittsburgh, PA: University of Pittsburgh Press, 2004.
—*Asylum*. Pittsburgh, PA: University of Pittsburgh Press, 2001.

Belieu, Erin. *One Above & One Below: Poems*. Port Townsend, WA: Copper Canyon, 2000.
—*Infanta*. Port Townsend, WA: Copper Canyon, 1995.

Berrigan, Anselm. *Zero Star Hotel*. Washington, D.C.: Edge Books, 2002.
—*Integrity and Dramatic Life*. Washington, D.C.: Edge Books, 1999.

Blanchfield, Brian. *Not Even Then*. Berkeley, CA: University of California Press, 2004.

Brown, Lee Ann. *The Sleep That Changed Everything*. Middletown, CT: Wesleyan University Press, 2003.
—*Polyverse*. Los Angeles, CA: Sun & Moon, 1999.

Brown, Stephanie. *Allegory of the Supermarket*. Athens, GA: University of Georgia Press, 1998.

Carbó, Nick. *Andalusian Down*. Cincinnati, OH: Cherry Grove, 2004.
—*Secret Asian Man*. Chicago: Tia Chucha Press, 2000.
—*El Grupo McDonald's*. Chicago: Tia Chucha Press, 1995.

Carr, Julie. *Mead: An Epithalamion*. Athens, GA: University of Georgia Press, 2004.

Clark, Jeff. *Music and Suicide*. New York: Farrar, Straus & Giroux, 2004.
—*The Little Door Slides Back*. Los Angeles: Sun & Moon, 1997.

Clover, Joshua. *Madonna Anno Domini*. Baton Rogue, LA: Louisiana State University Press, 1997.

Cooley, Nicole. *The Afflicted Girls*. Baton Rogue, LA: Louisiana State University Press, 2004.
—*Resurrection*. Baton Rogue, LA: Louisiana State University Press, 1996.

Corey, Joshua. *Selah*. New York: Barrow Street Press, 2003.

Corless-Smith, Martin. *Nota*. New York: Fence Books, 2003.
—*Of Piscator*. Athens, GA: University of Georgia Press, 1997.

Day, Cort. *The Chime*. Farmington, ME: Alice James Books, 2001.

de la Paz, Oliver. *Names Above Houses*. Carbondale, IL: Southern Illinois University Press, 2001.

Dhompa, Tsering Wangmo. *In the Absent Everyday*. Berkeley, CA: Apogee, 2005.
—*Rules of the House*. Berkeley, CA: Apogee, 2002.

Field, Thalia. *Point and Line*. New York: New Directions, 2000.
—*Incarnate: Story Material*. New York. New Directions, 2004.

Foust, Graham. *Leave the Room to Itself: Poems*. Boise, ID: Ahsahta Press, 2003.
—*As in Every Deafness*. Chicago, IL: Flood Editions, 2003.

Gallaher, John. *Gentlemen in Turbans, Ladies in Cauls*. Brooklyn, NY: Spuyten Duyvil, 2001.

Genoways, Ted. *Bullroarer: A Sequence*. Boston, MA: Northeastern University Press, 2001.

Gonzalez, Rigoberto. *Other Fugitives and Other Strangers*. Dorset, VT: Tupelo Press, 2006.
—*So Often the Pitcher Goes to Water Before It Breaks*. Champaign, IL: University of Illinois Press, 1999.

Goodman, Joanna. *Trace of One*. Iowa City, IA: University of Iowa Press, 2002.

Gordon, Noah Eli. *The Area of Sound Called the Subtone*. Boise, ID: Ahsahta Press, 2004.
—*The Frequencies*. Oakland, CA: Tougher Disguises, 2003.

Gridley, Sarah. *Weather Eye Open*. Berkeley, CA: University of California Press, 2005.

Gudding, Gabriel. *A Defense of Poetry*. Pittsburgh, PA: University of Pittsburgh Press, 2002.

Hamilton, Saskia. *Divide These*. St. Paul, MN: Graywolf, 2005.
—*As For Dream*. St. Paul, MN: Graywolf, 2001.

Hawkey, Christian. *The Book of Funnels*. Florence, MA: Verse Press, 2004.

Hoch, James. *A Parade of Hands*. Eugene, OR: Silverfish Review Press, 2003.

Hong, Cathy Park. *Translating Mo'um*. Brooklyn, NY: Hanging Loose, 2002.

Hummell, Austin. *Poppy*. Washington, D.C.: Del Sol Press, 2004.
—*The Fugitive Kind*. Athens, GA: University of Georgia Press, 1996.

Israeli, Henry. *New Messiahs*. New York: Four Way Books, 2002.

Jeffers, Honorée Fanonne. *Outlandish Blues*. Middletown, CT: Wesleyan University Press, 2003.
—*The Gospel of Barbecue*. Kent, OH: Kent State University Press, 2000.

Jess, Tyehimba. *leadbelly*. Florence, MA: Verse Press, 2005.

Johnston, Devin. *Aversions*. Richmond, CA: Omnidawn, 2004.
—*Telepathy*. Sydney, Australia: Paper Bark Press, 2002.

Jordan, Judy. *Sixty-cent Coffee and a Quarter to Dance*. Baton Rouge, LA: Louisiana State University Press, 2005.
—*Carolina Ghost Woods*. Baton Rouge, LA: Louisiana State University Press, 2000.

Katz, Joy. *Fabulae*. Carbondale, IL: Southern Illinois University Press, 2002.

Landau, Deborah. *Orchidelirium*. Tallahassee, FL: Anhinga Press, 2004.

Lerner, Ben. *The Lichtenberg Figures*. Port Townsend, WA: Copper Canyon, 2004.

Lubasch, Lisa. *To Tell the Lamp*. Penngrove, CA: Avec Books, 2004.
—*Vicinities*. Penngrove, CA: Avec Books, 2001.
—*How Many More of Them Are You?* Penngrove, CA: Avec Books, 1999.

Mackowski, Joanie. *The Zoo*. Pittsburgh, PA: University of Pittsburgh Press, 2002.

Manguso, Sarah. *Siste Viator*. New York: Four Way Books, 2006.
—*The Captain Lands in Paradise*. Farmington, ME: Alice James Books, 2002.

Mann, Randall. *Complaint in the Garden*. Omaha, NE: Zoo Press, 2004.

Mathys, Ted. *Forge*. Minneapolis, MN: Coffee House Press, 2005.

McCallum, Shara. *Song of Thieves*. Pittsburgh, PA: University of Pittsburgh Press, 2003.
—*The Water Between Us*. Pittsburgh, PA: University of Pittsburgh Press, 1999.

McCann, Anthony. *Father of Noise*. New York: Fence Books, 2003.

McCombs, Davis. *Ultima Thule*. New Haven, CT: 2000.

McDaniel, Raymond. *Murder (a violet)*. Minneapolis, MN: Coffee House Press, 2004.

Meier, Richard. *Terrain Vague*. Florence, MA: Verse Press, 2000.

Meitner, Erika. *Inventory at the All-Night Drugstore*. Tallahassee, FL: Anhinga Press, 2003.

Minnis, Chelsey. *Zirconia*. New York: Fence Books, 2001.

Moxley, Jennifer. *Often Capital*. Chicago: Flood Editions, 2005.
—*The Sense Record and Other Poems*. Washington, D.C.: Edge Books, 2002.
—*Imagination Verses*. New York: Tender Buttons, 1996.

Nelson, Maggie. *Jane: A Murder*. Brooklyn, NY: Soft Skull Press, 2005.
—*The Latest Winter*. Brooklyn, NY: Hanging Loose, 2003.
—*Shiner*. Brooklyn, NY: Hanging Loose, 2001.

Nezhukumatathil, Aimee. *Miracle Fruit*. Dorset, VT: Tupelo Press, 2003.

Northrop, Kate. *Back Through Interruption*. Kent, OH: Kent State University Press, 2002.

Nutter, Geoffrey. *Water's Leaves and Other Poems*. Florence, MA: Verse Press, 2005.
—*A Summer Evening*. Fort Collins, CO: Center for Literary Publishing, 2001.

O'Brien, Geoffrey G. *The Guns and Flags Project*. Berkeley, CA: University of California Press, 2002.

Ossip, Kathleen. *The Search Engine*. Philadelphia, PA: American Poetry Review, 2002.

Pafunda, Danielle. *Pretty Young Thing*. Brooklyn, NY: Soft Skull Press, 2005.

Patterson, G.E. *Tug*. St. Paul, MN: Graywolf, 1999.

Pelizzon, V. Penelope. *Nostos*. Athens, OH: Ohio University Press, 2000.

Philpot, Tracy. *Distance from Birth*. Minneapolis, MN: Elixir Press, 2001.
—*Incorrect Distances*. Athens, GA: University of Georgia Press, 1997.

Richards, Deborah. *Last One Out*. Honolulu, HI: Subpress, 2003.

Richards, Peter. *Nude Siren*. Florence, MA: Verse Press, 2003.
—*Oubliette*. Florence, MA: Verse Press, 2001.

Roberts, Katrina. *The Quick*. Seattle, WA: University of Washington Press, 2005.
—*How Late Desire Looks*. Layton, UT: Gibbs Smith, 1997.

Rosemurgy, Catie. *My Favorite Apocalypse*. St. Paul, MN: Graywolf, 2001.

Samyn, Mary Ann. *Purr*. Kalamazoo, MI: New Issues, 2005.
—*Inside the Yellow Dress*. Kalamazoo, MI: New Issues, 2001.
—*Captivity Narrative*. Columbus, OH: Ohio State University Press, 1999.

Schilpp, Margot. *Laws of My Nature*. Pittsburgh, PA: Carnegie Mellon University Press, 2005.
—*The World's Last Night*. Pittsburgh, PA: Carnegie Mellon University Press, 1999.

Sharma, Prageeta. *The Opening Question*. New York: Fence Books, 2004.
—*Bliss to Fill*. Honolulu, HI: Subpress, 2000.

Singer, Sean. *Discography*. New Haven, CT: Yale University Press, 2002.

Su, Adrienne. *Middle Kingdom*. Farmington, ME: Alice James Books, 1997.

Szybist, Mary. *Granted*. Farmington, ME: Alice James Books, 2003.

Teig, Michael. *Big Back Yard*. Rochester, NY: BOA Editions, 2003.

Thompson, Tom. *Live Feed*. Farmington, ME: Alice James Books, 2003.

Thorburn, Matthew. *Subject to Change*. Kalamazoo, MI: New Issues, 2004.

Wagner, Catherine. *Macular Hole*. New York: Fence Books, 2004.
—*Miss America*. New York: Fence Books, 2001.

Waltz, William. *Zoo Music*. Raymond, NH: Slope Editions, 2004.

Whitcomb, Katharine. *Saints of South Dakota and Other Poems*. Emporia, KS: Bluestem Press, 2001.

White, Sam. *The Goddess of the Hunt is Not Herself*. Raymond, NH: Slope Editions, 2005.

Wiman, Christian. *Hard Night*. Port Townsend, WA: Copper Canyon, 2005.
—*The Long Home*. Ashland, OR: Story Line Press, 1998.

Winter, Jonah. *Amnesia*. Oberlin, OH: Oberlin College Press, 2004.
—*Maine*. Raymond, NH: Slope Editions, 2002.

Witt, Sam. *Everlasting Quail*. Hanover, NH: University Press of New England, 2001.

Woodward, Jon. *Mister Goodbye Easter Island*. Farmington, ME: Alice James Books, 2003.

Yakich, Mark. *Unrelated Individuals Forming a Group Waiting to Cross*. New York: Penguin, 2004.

Recommended additional anthologies of contemporary American poetry:

Aizenberg, Susan and Erin Belieu, eds. *The Extraordinary Tide: New Poetry by American Women*. New York, Columbia University Press, 2001.
Collier, Michael, ed. *The New American Poets: A Bread Loaf Anthology*. Hanover, NH: University Press of New England, 2000.
Costanzo, Gerald and Jim Daniels, eds. *American Poetry: The Next Generation*. Pittsburgh, PA: Carnegie Mellon University Press, 2000.
Davis, Jordan and Sarah Manguso, eds. *Free Radicals: American Poets Before Their First Books*. Honolulu, HI: Subpress, 2004.
Jarnot, Lisa; Leonard Schwartz and Chris Stroffolino, eds. *An Anthology of New (American) Poets*. Jersey City, NJ: Talisman House, 1998.
LaFemina, Gerry and Daniel Crocker, eds. *Poetry 30: Thirty-Something Thirty-Something American Poets*. DuBois, PA: Mammoth Books, 2005.
Lauer, Brett Fletcher and Aimee Kelly, eds. *Isn't It Romantic: 100 Love Poems by Younger American Poets*. Florence, MA: Verse Press, 2004.
Prufer, Kevin, ed. *The New Young American Poets: An Anthology*. Carbondale, IL: Southern Illinois University Press, 2000.
Shepherd, Reginald, ed. *The Iowa Anthology of New American Poetries*. Iowa City, IA: University of Iowa Press, 2004.

Acknowledgments

"Many Are Called" by Rick Barot appears here for the first time. Used by permission of the author. "Eight Elegies" and "Reading Plato" are from *The Darker Fall* by Rick Barot, published by Sarabande Books, Inc. © 2002 by Rick Barot. Reprinted by permission of Sarabande Books and the author.

"Prologue" and "Afterword" are from *Spell* by Dan Beachy-Quick. © 2004 by Dan Beachy-Quick. Reprinted by permission of Ahsahta Press. "Psalm (Traherne)" and "Unworn" from *North True South Bright*. © 2003 by Dan Beachy-Quick. Reprinted with the permission of Alice James Books.

"[Final poem for the gently sifting public begins on the streets…]" by Joshua Beckman first appeared in *Fence*. Reprinted by permission of the author. "[I like your handsome drugs. Your pleasant…]" and "[The canals. The liquor coming through…]" by Joshua Beckman appear here for the first time. Used by permission of the author. "[The thirst of the crowd. We laid the surfer down…]" by Joshua Beckman first appeared in *Conduit*. Reprinted by permission of the author. "Ode to the Air Traffic Controller" is from *Something I Expected to Be Different* by Joshua Beckman, published by Verse Press. © 2001 by Joshua Beckman. Used by permission of Verse Press.

Josh Bell. "Poem to Line My Casket with, Ramona," "Zombie Sunday (Had We but World Enough and Time)," and "Sleeping with Artemis" are reprinted from *No Planets Strike* by Josh Bell, published by Zoo Press. © Josh Bell and reprinted with permission of Zoo Press, all rights reserved. "Meditation on *The Consolation of Philosophy*" first appeared online on *Exquisite Corpse*. Reprinted by permission of the author.

"Democratic Vistas," "April 13, 1865," "Community College in the Rain," and "From His Bed in the Capital City" are reprinted from *Actual Air* by David Berman, published by Open City Books. © 1999 by David Berman. Reprinted by permission of Open City Books.

"I Love How Your Eyes Close Every Time You Kiss Me" by Erica Bernheim first appeared in *Bridge*. Reprinted by permission of the author. "Like a Face" by Erica Bernheim first appeared on *canwehaveourballback.com*. Reprinted by permission of the author. "Anne Boleyn" by Erica Bernheim first appeared in *Gulf Coast*. Reprinted by permission of the author. "Pavese Said Death Will Come Bearing Your Eyes" by Erica Bernheim first appeared in *26*. Reprinted by permission of the author.

"Just Yesterday," "All but Lost," "Groupie," and "Slutty" are from *Sky Lounge* by Mark Bibbins, published by Graywolf Press. © 2003 by Mark Bibbins. Reprinted with the permission of Graywolf Press, Saint Paul, Minnesota.

"The Northern Sun," "Apparition," and "Chrysalis" are from *Shapeshift* by Sherwin Bitsui. © 2003 by Sherwin Bitsui. Reprinted by permission of the University of Arizona Press.

"Elegant Endings," "*We're Not Going to Malta...*," "Perfect City Code," and "How It Begins/How It Ends" are reprinted from *Directions to the Beach of the Dead*. © 2006 by Richard Blanco, published by University of Arizona Press. Reprinted by permission of University of Arizona Press.

"Aesthetics" and "Divorce" © Joel Brouwer from *Centuries*. Reprinted with permission of Four Way Books. All rights reserved. "Hamartia Symbolized by the Stray" and "The Spots" first appeared in *Poetry*. Reprinted with permission of the author. "Kelly, Ringling Bros. Oldest Elephant, Goes on Rampage" is from *Exactly What Happened*. © 1999 Joel Brouwer. Reprinted by permission of Purdue University Press. Unauthorized duplication prohibited.

"The Only Yak in Batesville, Virginia," "The Girls," "The Term," "Room 40," and "Transporter" are from *What Animal* by Oni Buchanan. © 2003 by Oni Buchanan. Reprinted by permission of the University of Georgia Press.

"Thrillsville," "The Power Plant," "In Squire Park with M., Esquire," and "Phantoms of Utopia" are reprinted from *A Little Night Comes*. © 2005 by Julianne Buchsbaum. Reprinted by permission of Del Sol Press. "Slowly, Slowly, Horses" is reprinted from *Slowly, Slowly, Horses*. © 2001 by Julianne Buchsbaum. Reprinted by permission of the author.

"Ocean State" and "Persephone (Unplugged)" are from *Popular Music*. © 1999 by Stephen Burt. Reprinted with the permission of the Center for Literary Publishing. "Paysage Moralisé" and "Morningside Park" © 2006 by Stephen Burt. Reprinted from *Parallel Play* with the permission of Graywolf Press, Saint Paul, Minnesota.

"My Ravine," "Vermont," and "Song for a Play" are reprinted from *The Afterlife of Objects*. © 2002 by Dan Chiasson. Reprinted by permission of the author. "The Elephant" is reprinted from *Natural History*. © 2005 by Dan Chiasson. Reprinted by permission of Alfred A. Knopf.

"The Long Goodbye," "Shelbourne Falls," and "Arbor" are reprinted from *The Unrequited* by Carrie St. George Comer, published by Sarabande Books, Inc. © 2003 by Carrie St. George Comer. Reprinted by permission of Sarabande Books.

"Thirty Years Rising" and "All the Natural Movements of the Soul" are from *And Her Soul Out of Nothing* by Olena Kalytiak Davis, published by University of Wisconsin Press. © 1997 by Olena Kalytiak Davis. Reprinted by permission of the author. "Sweet Reader, Flanneled and Tulled," "The Unbosoming," and "If You Are Asked" are from *shattered sonnets love cards and other off and back handed importunities* by Olena Kalytiak Davis, published by Tin House/ Bloomsbury. © 2003 by Olena Kalytiak Davis. Reprinted by permission of the author.

"How to Look at Mexican Highways" by Mónica de la Torre first appeared in *Circuito Interior: Silvia Gruner*. Reprinted by permission of the author. "Driven by a Strange Desire" by Monica de la Torre first appeared in *Fence*. Reprinted by permission of the author. "Golfers in the Family" by Mónica de la Torre first appeared in *The Germ*. Reprinted by permission of the author.

"Twenty-Seven Props for a Production of *Eine Lebenszeit*," "Three Panels Depending on the Heart," and "Birdsong from Inside the Egg" are reprinted from *Twenty-Seven Props for a Production of Eine Lebenszeit* by Timothy Donnelly. © 2003 by Timothy Donnelly. Reprinted by permission of Grove/Atlantic, Inc. "The New Intelligence" first appeared in *Crowd* vol. 4, issue 2. © 2004 by Timothy Donnelly. Reprinted by permission of the author.

"The War Is Over," "Our Man," and "Forensics" are reprinted from *Radio, Radio: Poems* © 2001 by Ben Doyle. Reprinted by permission of Louisiana State University Press.

"Sticks," "Atomic Bride," "Slow Fade to Black," and "Zapruder" © 2005 by Thomas Sayers Ellis. Reprinted from *The Maverick Room* with the permission of Graywolf Press, Saint Paul, Minnesota.

"On Fire," "Intermission," and "The Boxers" are reprinted from *Citizen* by Andrew Feld. © 2004 by Andrew Feld. Reprinted by permission of HarperCollins Publishers Inc.

"Myths of the Disappearance" first appeared in *Gulf Coast*; "Gerburt des Monicakinds" first appeared in *Southwest Review*; "Stories from the Tower" first appeared in *The Paris Review* as "Dolorous Garde," "Women Singing," "Sleeping Beauty," and "Prisoner of the Golden Cage." All poems © Monica Ferrell. Reprinted by permission of the author.

"Childhood's House," "Miraculous Image," "Subway," "and "Housefire" from *Swallow* by Miranda Field. © 2002 by Miranda Field. Reprinted by permission of Houghton Mifflin Company. All rights reserved. "Scold's Mask" by Miranda Field first appeared in *TriQuarterly*. Reprinted by permission of the author.

"Swarm" and "Hive" are from *Blind Huber* by Nick Flynn, published by Graywolf Press. © 2002 by Nick Flynn. Reprinted from *Blind Huber* with the permission of Graywolf Press, Saint Paul, Minnesota. "Emptying Town," "Cartoon Physics, part 1" and "Cartoon Physics, part 2" © 2000 by Nick Flynn. Reprinted from *Some Ether* with the permission of Graywolf Press, Saint Paul, Minnesota.

"Flesh," "Nocturne," and "The Hands of the Body Without the Body, and Nothing to Hold" © 2002 by Katie Ford. Reprinted from *Deposition* with the permission of Graywolf Press, Saint Paul, Minnesota. "Colosseum" by Katie Ford first appeared in *The American Poetry Review*. Reprinted by permission of the author.

"Afterward, There Will Be a Hallway," "Berlin Series," and "Nostalgia, Cheryl, Is the Best Heroin" are from *Given* by Arielle Greenberg. © 2002 by Arielle Greenberg. Used by permission of Verse Press. "Saints" and "Analogies" reprinted from *My Kafka Century*. © 2005 by Arielle Greenberg, by permission of Action Books.

"The Last Living Castrato," "The Wolf," and "Kiss of Judas" from *Cusp: Poems* by Jennifer Grotz. © 2003 by Jennifer Grotz. Reprinted by permission of Houghton Mifflin Company. All rights reserved. "Not Body" is reprinted from *Not Body* (Urban Editions). © 2001 by Jennifer Grotz. Reprinted by permission of the author.

"Abandoned Conversation with the Senses," Our Square of Lawn," "Ideas Go Only So Far," and "Definition of Weather" © 2004 by Matthea Harvey. Reprinted from *Sad Little Breathing Machine* with the permission of Graywolf Press, Saint Paul, Minnesota. "Pity the Bathtub Its Forced Embrace of the Human Form" from *Pity the Bathtub Its Forced Embrace of the Human Form*, published by Alice James Books. © 2000 by Matthea Harvey. Reprinted with the permission of Alice James Books.

"Wind in a Box" by Terrance Hayes first appeared in *Hunger Mountain*. Reprinted by permission of the author. "The Blue Terrance" by Terrance Hayes first appeared in *Failbetter*. Reprinted by permission of the author. "A Postcard from Okemah" by Terrance Hayes first appeared in *Ploughshares*. Reprinted by permission of the author. "Talk" by Terrance Hayes first appeared in *Gulf Coast*. Reprinted by permission of the author.

"As Western Culture Declined Without Its Knowing," "My Wrist Split Open," and "Where Spring Is" are from *Earthling* by Steve Healey, published by Coffee House Press. © 2004 by Steve Healey. Reprinted with the permission of Coffee House Press, Minneapolis, Minnesota.

"Corrections," "My Pietà," and "Zombie" are from *Horror Vacui* by Thomas Heise, published by Sarabande Books. © 2006 by Thomas Heise. Reprinted by permission of Sarabande Books and the author.

"The Pyramid" by Brian Henry is reprinted from *American Incident*. © 2002 by Brian Henry. Reprinted by permission of Salt Publishing. "Skin" is reprinted from *Astronaut* by Brian Henry, published by Carnegie Mellon Press. © 2002 by Brian Henry. Reprinted by permission of Carnegie Mellon Press. "Submarine" by Brian Henry first appeared in *Gulf Coast*. Reprinted by permission of the author. "Rooms" by Brian Henry first appeared in *Metre*. Reprinted by permission of the author.

"Explanation," "Hume's Suicide of the External World," "Sampler City," and "Comprehension Questions" are reprinted with the permission of New Issues Press.

From *Alaskaphrenia* by Christine Hume. © 2004 by Christine Hume. The author wishes to note that the version of "Explanation" presented here is revised from the version in *Alaskaphrenia*, and appeared in *American Letters and Commentary*.

"Blunts," "Euphoria," "Pest," and "Don Pullen at the Zanzibar Blue Jazz Café" are from *Leaving Saturn* by Major Jackson. © 2002 by Major Jackson. Reprinted by permission of the University of Georgia Press.

"The United States of America" is from *Black Dog Songs* by Lisa Jarnot, published by Flood Editions. © 2003 by Lisa Jarnot. Reprinted with the permission of Flood Editions. "The Girl Who Couldn't Be Loved" by Lisa Jarnot first appeared in *Five Fingers Review*. Reprinted by permission of the author.

"Beggar's Song," "Kind of Blue," and "Public Radio Plays Eddie Harris" are reprinted from *Rise* by A. Van Jordan, published by Tia Chucha Press. © 2001 by A. Van Jordan. Reprinted by permission of Tia Chucha Press and the author.

"Author's Prayer," "Dancing in Odessa," and "Maestro" are from *Dancing in Odessa* by Ilya Kaminsky, published by Tupelo Press. Copyright © 2004 by Ilya Kaminsky. All rights reserved. Reproduced by permission of Tupelo Press.

"Orphean Song," "The Gallery," and "Subtraction Song" are from *Dwelling Song* by Sally Keith. © 2004 by Sally Keith. Reprinted by permission of the University of Georgia Press. "Mechanics" is reprinted from *Design*. © 2000 by Sally Keith. Reprinted with the permission of the Center for Literary Publishing.

"Occupation," "Monologue for an Onion," and "On Sparrows" are reprinted from *Notes from the Divided Country: Poems* by Suji Kwock Kim. © 2003 by Suji Kwock Kim. Reprinted by permission of Louisiana State University Press.

"Empty House," "Letters to a Vanishing Fiancée," and "Salvation" are reprinted from *The Gatehouse Heaven* by James Kimbrell, published by Sarabande Books. © 1998 by James Kimbrell. Reprinted by permission of Sarabande Books, Inc. and the author. "My Psychic" is reprinted from *My Psychic* © 2006 by James Kimbrell. Reprinted by permission of Sarabande Books and the author.

"And Having Lost Track" by Joanna Klink first appeared in *The Kenyon Review*. Reprinted by permission of the author. "Porch in Snow" by Joanna Klink first appeared in *Smartish Pace*. Reprinted by permission of the author. "Mariana Trench" by Joanna Klink first appeared in *Gulf Coast*. Reprinted by permission of the author. "Orpheus. Eurydice. Hermes." is from *They Are Sleeping* by Joanna Klink. © 2000 by Joanna Klink. Reprinted by permission of the University of Georgia Press.

"An Ordinary Evening" and "Bad Aliens" are from *4* by Noelle Kocot, published by Four Way Books. © 2001 by Noelle Kocot. Reprinted with permission of Four Way Books. All rights reserved. "Civilization Day" is from *The Raving Fortune* by Noelle Kocot. © 2004 by Noelle Kocot. Reprinted with permission from Four Way Books. All rights reserved. "Gypsy Summer" first appeared in *Shade*. Reprinted by permission of the author. "I Am Like a Desert Owl, an Owl Among the Ruins" by Noelle Kocot first appeared in *LUNGFULL! Magazine*. Reprinted by permission of the author.

"Sympathy and Envy," "A Dream of Mimesis," and "In Las Vegas" are from *Winter Sex* by Katy Lederer, published by Verse Press. © 2002 by Katy Lederer. Used by permission of Verse Press.

"Ars Poetica (the idea)," "Glass Heart," and "Cinema Verité" are from *Wedding Day*. © 2005 by Dana Levin. Reprinted with the permission of Copper Canyon Press, P.O. Box 271, Port Townsend, WA 98368-0271. "Chill Core" is from *In the Surgical Theatre* by Dana Levin. Published by Copper Canyon Press. © 1999 by Dana Levin. Reprinted by permission of the author.

"First," "On Death," and "On God" are from *A Companion for Owls* by Maurice Manning, published by Harcourt, Inc. © 2004 by Maurice Manning. Reprinted by permission of Harcourt, Inc. "A Condensed History of Beauty" is reprinted from *Lawrence Booth's Book of Visions*. © 2001 by Maurice Manning. Reprinted by permission of Yale University Press. "[O boss of ashes boss of dust…]" by Maurice Manning first appeared in *The Virginia Quarterly Review*. Reprinted by permission of the author.

"Hello," "The Babies," "The Mustache," "Transylvania, 1919," and "The Experiments Lasted Through the Winter" are reprinted from *The Babies* by Sabrina Orah Mark, published by Saturnalia Books. © 2004 Saturnalia Books.

"Portrait of a Child" is from *Renunciation* by Corey Marks. © 2000 by Corey Marks. Reprinted by permission of University of Illinois Press. "Three Bridges" by Corey Marks originally appeared in *New England Review*. "After the Shipwreck" appears here for the first time.

"Logic in the House of Sawed-Off Telescopes," "Opposites Attack," and "Lineage" are from *The Forgiveness Parade* by Jeffrey McDaniel, published by Manic D Press. © 1998 by Jeffrey McDaniel. Reprinted by permission of Manic D Press and the author. "Dear America" and "The Archipelago of Kisses" are from *The Splinter Factory* by Jeffrey McDaniel, published by Manic D Press. © 2002 by Jeffrey McDaniel. Reprinted by permission of Manic D Press and the author.

"Still Life w/Influences" and "Persuasion" are from *The Red Bird* by Joyelle McSweeney, published by Fence Books. © 2002 by Joyelle McSweeney. Reprinted by permission of Fence Books and the author. "The Wind Domes" is from *The Commandrine and Other Poems* by Joyelle McSweeney, published by Fence Books. © 2004 by Joyelle McSweeney. Reprinted by permission of Fence Books and the author.

"Look," "With This Change to Indoor Lighting," and "Rendered Dog" are from *Bandit Letters* by Sarah Messer, published by New Issues Press. © 2001 by Sarah Messer. Reprinted by permission of New Issues Press and the author. "Marriage Proposal" first appeared in *Gulf Coast*. Reprinted by permission of the author.

"Hearing Music Through Dark Trees," "Capstone," "Where Were You" are reprinted from *Accumulus* © 2003 by Ethan Paquin. Reprinted by permission of Salt Publishing.

"Driving Past My Exit" is from *Love Song with Motor Vehicles* by Alan Michael Parker, published by BOA Editions. © 2003 by Alan Michael Parker. Reprinted by permission of BOA Editions and the author. "The Vandals," "The Vandals Dying," and "Practicing Their Diffidence, The Vandals" are from *The Vandals* by Alan Michael Parker, published by BOA Editions. © 1999 by Alan Michael Parker. Reprinted by permission of BOA Editions and the author.

"[sleek mechanical dart: the syringe noses into the blue vein marking the target of me]" and "[*tall and* thin *and young and lovely the* michael with kaposi's sarcoma *goes walking*]" by D. A. Powell, from *Tea* (Wesleyan University Press, 1998). © 1998 by D. A. Powell. Reprinted by permission of Wesleyan University Press. "[when you touch down on this earth.little reindeers]," "[writing for a young man on the redline train: 'to his boy mistress']" and "[coda & discography]" © 2004 by D. A. Powell. Reprinted from *Cocktails* with the permission of Graywolf Press, Saint Paul, Minnesota.

"For the Unfortunates" and "The End of the City" are from *The Finger Bone* by Kevin Prufer, reprinted by permission of Carnegie Mellon Press. © 2002 by Kevin Prufer. "A Car Has Fallen from the Bridge" and "The Rise of Rome" are from *Fallen from a Chariot* by Kevin Prufer, reprinted by permission of Carnegie Mellon Press. © 2005 by Kevin Prufer. "On Finding a Swastika on a Tree in the Hills Above Heidelberg" is reprinted from *Strange Wood* by Kevin Prufer, published by Winthrop University Press. © 1998 by Kevin Prufer. Reprinted by permission of the author.

"Corruption," "Scarecrow Eclogue," "Second Circle," "Evening with Stars," and "Burial Practice" are from *Facts for Visitors* by Srikanth Reddy, published by University of California Press. © 2004 by Srikanth Reddy. Reprinted by permission of University of California Press and the author.

"Portofino," "Autumn Song," and "The Clerk's Tale" are from *The Clerk's Tale: Poems* by Spencer Reece. Copyright © 2004 by Spencer Reece. Reprinted by permission of Houghton Mifflin Company. All rights reserved.

"Strawberry" by Paisley Rekdal first appeared in *Bellingham Review*. Reprinted by permission of the author. "Stupid" and "What Was There to Bring Me to Delight But to Love and Be Loved?" appeared in *Six Girls Without Pants* by Paisley Rekdal, published by Eastern Washington University Press. © 2002 by

Paisley Rekdal. Reprinted by permission of the author. "A Crash of Rhinos" is from *A Crash of Rhinos* by Paisley Rekdal. © 2000 by Paisley Rekdal. Reprinted by permission of the Univeristy of Georgia Press and the author.

"Childhood Stories," "from *The World at Night*," and "My Government," are from *Satellite* by Matthew Rohrer. © 2001 by Matthew Rohrer. "We Never Should Have Stopped at Pussy Island," from *A Green Light*. © 2004 by Matthew Rohrer. All used by permission of Verse Press and the author.

"More Important Than The Design Of Cities" is from *The Return Message* by Tessa Rumsey. © 2005 by Tessa Rumsey. Used by permission of W.W. Norton & Company, Inc. "Man-Torpedo-Boat," "Assembling My Shepherd," "Never Morroco," and "Big Rig the Baroque Sky" are from *Assembling the Shepherd* by Tessa Rumsey. © 1999 by Tessa Rumsey. Reprinted by permission of the University of Georgia Press.

"At Shedd Aquarium," "Chanel Nº 5," "Vampire Finch," "Woodpecker Finch," and "House of Dior" are from *Worth* by Robyn Schiff, published by the University of Iowa Press. © 2002 by Robyn Schiff. Reprinted by permission of the University of Iowa Press and the author.

"The Alphabetizer Speaks" by Patty Seyburn originally appeared in *The Paris Review*, Number 172, Winter 2005. © 2005 by Patty Seyburn. Reprinted by permission of the author. "What I Liked About the Pleistocene Era" and "First Bookshelf" appear here for the first time.

"Your Name on It," "Epithalament," "Postfeminism," "You Love, You Wonder," and "Panopticon" are from *Interior with Sudden Joy* by Brenda Shaughnessy. © 1999 by Brenda Shaughnessy. Reprinted by permission of Farrar, Strauss and Giroux, LLC.

"Boot Theory," "A Primer for the Small Weird Loves," and "Saying Your Names" are reprinted from *Crush*. © 2005 by Richard Siken. Reprinted by permission of Yale University Press.

"Self-Portrait as the Letter Y" © 2004 by Tracy K. Smith. Reprinted from *The Body's Question* with the permission of Graywolf Press, Saint Paul, Minnesota. "History" first appeared in *Callaloo*. Reprinted by permission of the author. "Duende" first appeared in *Gulf Coast*. Reprinted by permission of the author.

"localism or t/here" by Juliana Spahr, from *Fuck You—Aloha—I Love You* (Wesleyan Univeristy Press, 2001). © 2001 by Juliana Spahr. Reprinted by permission of Wesleyan University Press. "December 1, 2002," "December 4, 2002," and "January 28, 2003" are reprinted from *This Connection of Everyone With Lungs* by Juliana Spahr. © 2005 The Regents of the University of California.

"One Thousand Bullfrogs Rejoice," "Meteor," "Eohippus," and "Elsewhere" are reprinted from *Isolato* by Larissa Szporluk, published by the University of Iowa

Press. © 2000 by Larissa Szporluk. "Holy Ghost" is reprinted from *Dark Sky Question* by Larissa Szporluk. © 1998 by Larissa Szporluk. Reprinted by permission of Beacon Press, Boston.

"First person plural is a house," "Set for a Southern Gothic," "Detail from 'Set For a Southern Gothic,'" and "Trick Noir" are reprinted from *The Room Where I Was Born* by Brian Teare, published by the University of Wisconsin Press. © 2003 by Brian Teare. Reprinted by permission of The University of Wisconsin Press. "Dead House Sonnet" by Brian Teare first appeared in *Verse*. Reprinted by permission of the author.

"They Call You Moody" and "Touch Me Not" are from *The Coronary Garden* by Ann Townsend, published by Sarabande Books, Inc. © 2004 by Ann Townsend. Reprinted by permission of Sarabande Books and the author. "Modern Love" is reprinted from *Dime Store Erotics* by Ann Townsend, published by Silverfish Review Press. Reprinted by permission of Silverfish Review Press. © 1998 by Ann Townsend.

Natasha Trethewey. "Countess P—'s Advice for New Girls" © 2002 by Natasha Trethewey. Reprinted from *Bellocq's Ophelia* with the permission of Graywolf Press, Saint Paul, Minnesota. "Native Guard" first appeared in *Callaloo*.

"Story for the Mother Tongue" is from *The Price of Light* by Pimone Triplett, published by Four Way Books. © 2005 by Pimone Triplett. Reprinted with permission of Four Way Books. All rights reserved. "Next to Last Prayer" and "Portraits at the Epicenter" are reprinted from *Running the Picture* by Pimone Triplett. Evanston: TriQuarterly Books/Northwestern University Press, 1998, pp. 9–12, 54–58.

"[Now I promise…]," "If it be event…]," "May," and "Kiss Me Deadly" are reprinted from *Spar* by Karen Volkman, published by the University of Iowa Press. "The Case" is from *Crash's Law* by Karen Volkman. © 1996 by Karen Volkman. Used by permission of W. W. Norton & Company, Inc.

"The Miracles of St. Sebastian" and "What Begins Bitterly Becomes Another Love Poem" are reprinted from *Goldbeater's Skin*. © 2003 by G. C. Waldrep. "Hotel d'Avignon" by G. C. Waldrep first appeared in *Ninth Letter*. Reprinted by permission of the author. "O Canada!" by G. C. Waldrep first appeared in *Black Warrior Review*. Reprinted by permission of the author.

"As Hour and Year Collapsed" and "Send New Beasts" are from *It Is If I Speak* by Joe Wenderoth, published by Wesleyan University Press. © 2000 by Joe Wenderoth. Reprinted by permission of Wesleyan University Press and the author.

"*Italics, Mine*" and "Junkyard" are from *The Silent Partner* by Greg Williamson, published by Story Line Press. © 1995 by Greg Williamson. Reprinted by permission of the author. "Nervous Systems" is from *Errors in the Script* by Greg

Williamson, published by Overlook Press. © 2001 by Greg Williamson. Reprinted by permission of Overlook Press and the author.

"[Wind in bare vines…]," "Relict," and "The Fossil Garden" are reprinted from *The Keep* by Emily Wilson, published by the University of Iowa Press. © 2001 by Emily Wilson. Reprinted with permission of the University of Iowa Press and the author. "Coal Age" by Emily Wilson first appeared as a broadside in the Underwood Poetry Series. Reprinted by permission of the author.

"Testimony," "Confession, "50 Years in the Career of an Aspiring Thug," and "Advice" from *The Kingdom of the Subjunctive* by Suzanne Wise. © 2000 by Suzanne Wise. Reprinted with the permission of Alice James Books.

"Press Play" is from *Manderlay: Poems* by Rebecca Wolff, published by University of Illinois Press. © 2001 by Rebecca Wolff. Reprinted by permission of the author and the University of Illinois Press. "Sybil" and "Lamb, Willow: An Arch Dolefulness Has Taken Me This Far" are from *Figment: Poems* by Rebecca Wolff. © 2004 by Rebecca Wolff. Used by permission of W.W. Norton & Company, Inc.

"Amaryllis" and "Voluntary Servitude" © 2004 by Mark Wunderlich. Reprinted from *Voluntary Servitude* with the permission of Graywolf Press, Saint Paul, Minnesota. "Fourteen Things We're Allowed to Bring to the Underworld" and "Predictions About a Black Car" are reprinted from *The Anchorage* © 1999 by Mark Wunderlich. Reprinted by permission of the University of Massachusetts Press.

"Naglfar," "Night Ferry to Naxos 1," "Night Ferry to Naxos 2," and "Flatlanders" are from *Barter* by Monica Youn, published by Graywolf Press. ©2003 by Monica Youn. Reprinted with the permission of Graywolf Press, Saint Paul, Minnesota.

"Proximity" by C. Dale Young first appeared in *The Southern Review*. Reprinted by permission of the author. "Torn" by C. Dale Young first appeared in *Virginia Quarterly Review*. Reprinted by permission of the author. "Infidelity" by C. Dale Young first appeared in *The Kenyon Review*. Reprinted by permission of the author.

"Soundtrack" and "The Rushes" are from *Black Maria* by Kevin Young. © 2005 by Kevin Young. Used by permission of Alfred A. Knopf, a division of Random House, Inc. "Errata" and " Song of Smoke" are from *Jelly Roll* by Kevin Young. © 2005 by Kevin Young. Used by permission of Alfred A. Knopf, a division of Random House, Inc.

"School Street" and "Whoever You Are" are from *American Linden* by Matthew Zapruder, published by Tupelo Press. © 2002 by Matthew Zapruder. All rights reserved. Reproduced by permission of Tupelo Press.

"Credo," "Vertigo," and "[from] Viatica" by Andrew Zawacki, from *Anabranch* (Wesleyan University Press, 2004). © 2004 by Andrew Zawacki. Reprinted by permission of Wesleyan University Press. "Velocity Among the Ruins of Angel

Republic" is from *By Reason of Breakings* by Andrew Zawacki. © 2002 by Andrew Zawacki. Reprinted by permission of the University of Georgia Press.

"Diary: (Underworld)" is from *Eating the Underworld* (Wesleyan University Press, 2003). © 2003 by Rachel Zucker. Reprinted by permission of Wesleyan University Press. "Not Knowing Nijinsky or Diaghilev," and "In Your Version of Heaven I Am Younger" are from *The Last Clear Narrative* (Wesleyan University Press, 2004). © 2004 by Rachel Zucker. Reprinted by permission of Wesleyan University Press.

Editors' Acknowledgments

For their assistance, we wish to thank Rick Barot, Joshua Beckman, Jericho Brown, Oni Buchanan, Michael Collier, Amber Dermont, Mark Doty, Josh Edwards, Monica Ferrell, Nick Flynn, James Allen Hall, Rodney Jones, Karl Kilian, Brett Fletcher Lauer, Don Lee, Tim Liu, Sabrina Mark, Lee Papa, Pablo Peschiera, Kevin Prufer, Claudia Rankine, Salvatore Scibona, Addie Tsai, Rebecca Wolff, Joanna Yas, and Matthew Zapruder. Our gratitude to everyone at Sarabande: Sarah Gorham, Jeffrey Skinner, Nickole Brown, Charles Casey Martin, and Kristina McGrath, with a special thanks for Kirby Gann.

We also wish to thank our intern, Peter Marsh; Janet Sadowski and Sue Chapman in the English Department at the College of Staten Island; the Marvins and Dumanises; all of the presses who generously assisted us in acquiring permissions; The Corporation of Yaddo; and, finally, our colleagues and students at the University of Houston, Nebraska Wesleyan University, and the College of Staten Island, City University of New York.

The Editors

John Lucas

Michael Dumanis was born in 1976 in Moscow, in the former Soviet Union, and grew up in Buffalo and Rochester, New York. He holds a BA from Johns Hopkins University, an MFA from the University of Iowa Writers' Workshop, and a PhD from the University of Houston. His poems have appeared in *American Letters & Commentary, Black Warrior Review, Denver Quarterly, New England Review, Verse*, and many other journals. The recipient of fellowships from the Fulbright Commission, the James Michener Foundation, and Yaddo, he has previously served as Poetry Editor of *Gulf Coast* and the Poetry Curator at Brazos Bookstore. He now lives in Lincoln, Nebraska, and is an Assistant Professor of English at Nebraska Wesleyan University.

Cate Marvin was born in 1969 in Washington, D.C. She holds a BA from Marlboro College, an MFA in Poetry from the University of Houston, an MFA in Fiction from the University of Iowa Writers' Workshop, and a PhD from the University of Cincinnati. Her poems have appeared in *Boston Review, The Kenyon Review, The Paris Review, Ploughshares,* and elsewhere. Her first book, *World's Tallest Disaster* (Sarabande, 2001), was awarded the 2000 Kathryn A. Morton Prize by Robert Pinsky and the 2002 Kate Tufts Discovery Award from Claremont Graduate University. Her second book of poems, *Fragment of the Head of a Queen,* is forthcoming from Sarabande Books. She is an Assistant Professor of English at College of Staten Island, City University of New York.

The Corporation of Yaddo/Rick Gargiulo